DATE DUE

THE METHUENS
AND PORTUGAL
1691–1708

John Methuen as a young man, from an engraving by W. Humphrey

THE METHUENS
AND PORTUGAL
1691-1708

BY

A. D. FRANCIS

CAMBRIDGE
AT THE UNIVERSITY PRESS
1966

Published by the Syndics of the Cambridge University Press
Bentley House, 200 Euston Road, London N.W. 1
American Branch: 32 East 57th Street, New York, N.Y. 10022
West African Office: P.M.B. 5181, Ibadan, Nigeria

Library of Congress Catalogue Card Number: 66-14188

Printed in Great Britain
at the University Printing House, Cambridge
(Brooke Crutchley, University Printer)

TO
MY WIFE

CONTENTS

CONTENTS

BIBLIOGRAPHY

LIST OF PLATES

MAP

PREFACE

THIS book has evolved gradually. I soon found that surprisingly little had been published on this important period of Anglo-Portuguese history, and that I must rely largely for my information on unpublished manuscript sources. There seemed to be need for a work of a general character, which would set down the whole story in some detail.

All the Allies tended to regard the Peninsular War of 1704–13 as an unsatisfactory episode. The maritime powers had no real reason to complain. The Peninsular diversion had contributed to their victory elsewhere and their defeat in Spain was largely due to their own ambivalent attitude, particularly in the early stages of the war, before Spanish or rather Castilian patriotism had been aroused and the Bourbon sovereign had established himself as a true king of Spain rather than a French minion. The maritime powers were constantly diverting their resources from the war in Portugal, and Portugal felt she was being deserted. They were obliged to do this by pressure from the emperor. Although the war in Spain was ostensibly being fought primarily in the emperor's cause, he was much more interested in Italy. He was unable from the first to give any positive help in Spain, and was soon compelled by the dangers which threatened him in Hungary and Bavaria, and by the need to bolster up the doubtful adherence of the duke of Savoy, to demand peremptorily that the maritime powers help him in the Mediterranean. Nevertheless, there were many recriminations among the Allies about the failure in the Peninsula, and these were directed largely against Portugal. The Portuguese military effort had been disappointing, but Portugal had been conscious of her military weakness from the outset and had only reluctantly been drawn into the war. Portugal indeed had reason to complain. The promises made to her, when she entered the Grand Alliance were not fulfilled, and at the very outset of the war her allies failed to prevent an enemy invasion, and withdrew their fleet from the Portuguese coast to the Mediterranean. Nevertheless, in spite of the shabby treatment Portugal received at the Treaty of Utrecht, she retained the guarantee of her territorial integrity by the maritime powers, which in fact was much more essential to her than the few Spanish forts she stood to gain under the terms of the Grand Alliance.

This work tries to give a general account of Anglo-Portuguese relations before, during, and after the Methuen Treaties, and to integrate the Peninsular story in the very complicated general history of the time. Portugal was distant from the Allied capitals which were trying to co-ordinate the course of the war. Events in Portugal tended to get out of hand and to have a volition of their own; nevertheless the Peninsular part of the War of the Spanish Succession cannot be treated as a separate matter. Everything which happened in Spain and Portugal was dependent upon decisions made elsewhere. Often the Allied representatives in Lisbon were in the dark regarding higher Allied plans and this added to the growth of a feeling of frustration. I have tried to describe the situation objectively and to show that the many difficulties and failures arose from many causes and were not the fault of Portugal alone or of any particular nation.

In trying to produce a coherent and consecutive account of events in Portugal the continued presence of the Methuens has served as a valuable link. Methuen's own role makes an interesting story. He first went to Portugal to look for repose in a pleasant climate and was quite inadvertently drawn into the vortex of European politics. In some ways he was not too well equipped to play a leading part in international diplomacy, but he had several good qualities, and his experience of Portugal was greater than that of any other man available. With the help of this and the constant co-operation of his able son Paul, he succeeded in the mission entrusted to him to detach Portugal from her new

alliance with the enemy and to persuade her to join the Grand
Alliance. King Pedro insisted that he should remain to implement
the execution of his treaties and as far as was practicable he did so,
performing yeoman service in activating the Portuguese war effort.
In 1706, when the allied army entered Madrid, it seemed that he
had also succeeded in this second task. It was perhaps lucky for
him that death intervened, before the disasters came, which so
very speedily ensued.

There followed a time of disillusion, during which the advantages of the Portuguese alliance were little appreciated. During his
lifetime John Methuen was principally known for the part he had
played in promoting the Grand Alliance, and if his reputation had
been based solely on this, he might soon have been forgotten.
However, a few years after his death his commercial treaty came
into the limelight, and under the aegis of the Whigs became a
pillar of English policy. The Methuens owed their enduring fame
to this; and this was appropriate, for John Methuen was more at
home in trade and commerce than in pure diplomacy. Nevertheless, though many hard words were said about him by his diplomatic colleagues and he was often accused of making a bad
bargain, he excelled them all in his understanding of Portugal,
and it is very doubtful whether any other and more orthodox
ambassador could have achieved a better result.

As a mere amateur, starting from scratch after my retirement to
write a history, I am most grateful for the kindness and forbear-
ance I have received from the academic world. I have first to thank
Patrick Bury of Corpus Christi, Cambridge, and Professor Charles
Boxer, of King's College, London, who guided my first faltering
steps. Above all, Dr Ragnhild Hatton has been an infallible guide
and mentor. Graham Gibbs of Birkbeck College read one of my
drafts and many historians have helped me with inquiries on particular points. I am much indebted to the Public Record Office and
to the British Museum, where I found much of my manuscript
material and most of my illustrations. Lord Methuen kindly

allowed me to see his personal archives of the Methuen family. I was able to see the Methuen/Halifax letters at Althorp through the courtesy of Earl Spencer, and the correspondence with Lord Somers through the good offices of the Borough of Reigate. The University Library at Coimbra allowed me to see their Da Cunha Brochado letters, and Dr Japikse of the Dutch National Archives supplied me with a microfilm of the dispatches from Lisbon of the Dutch minister, Francis Schonenberg. I could not have done without the help of the London Library and the Institute of Historical Research. I apologise for any omission to thank specifically others who have helped me, and of course I continue to be responsible for the many blemishes and foibles which, no doubt, I have not succeeded in remedying.

A.D.F.

London
November 1965

ACKNOWLEDGEMENTS

Grateful acknowledgement is due to the following for permission to reproduce photographs: to the Trustees of the British Museum for the Frontispiece and Plates 1, 3, 5, 7 and 8 (a); to the Ashmolean Museum, Oxford (Sutherland Collection), for Plate 2; to the National Maritime Museum, Greenwich, for Plate 4; to the Keeper of Public Records for Plate 6; and to Lord Methuen and the Courtauld Institute of Art for Plate 8 (b).

CHAPTER I

JOHN METHUEN AND HIS ANTECEDENTS

JOHN METHUEN was born in 1650 at Bradford-on-Avon in Wiltshire, the eldest son of Paul Methuen, a clothier. It was natural that the future author of a treaty regarding wine and wool should be brought up in the heart of the woollen industry, but two coincidences also pointed to his destiny. He had, as far as is known, no foreign blood, but in later years he was described by Macky as a dark man, who had much of the Spaniard in his manners. Certainly he had an affinity with the Peninsula for, although he was over forty years of age when he first went to Lisbon, he settled there very happily, and made himself much at home in Portugal and among the Portuguese. It also happened that the house in which he was born stood on a steep hillside facing the south, which John Aubrey described as surrounded by elder bushes, which might well be turned to better profit, 'for it is situated on rocky gravelly ground, which is as well for a vineyard as any place can be'.[1]

The name Methuen, Methwen or Methwin, to give three of the forms used, was of Scottish origin; John Methuen himself signed his name Methwen until 1693, when he adopted the form Methuen, which has been used ever since. Most of the Methuens since their arrival in England in the time of Queen Elizabeth had been clergymen of the Church of England, but Paul Methuen, John Methuen's father, instead of studying at Oxford and taking Holy orders, apprenticed himself to John Ashe, a clothier of Freshford in Somerset. In due course he married his master's

---

[1] John Macky, *Memoirs of the Secret Service* (1733), p. 143; John Aubrey, *Natural History of Wilts.*, ed. J. Britten (1847), p. 56.

daughter Grace, and was given a mill and a property at Bradford-on-Avon, where he so prospered that at the time of his death in 1667 he was described as the greatest clothier of his time.[1]

Throughout the seventeenth century the cloth industry was undergoing great changes. The old staple industry in broadcloth had long been decaying and markets were altering. The old market in Germany and Central Europe was disrupted by the Thirty Years' War, and in the second half of the century the market in France was closed by the protectionist measures of Colbert. This was only gradually offset by the rise in home consumption and by the growth of sales in Spain and Portugal and overseas. However, if the old-fashioned clothiers languished, those who moved with the times were able to make fortunes. There was a ready sale for the new coloured cloths, for the medleys containing fine wool imported from Spain, and for the light worsteds known as the 'new draperies'.[2] John Ashe, Paul Methuen's father-in-law, was one of the go-ahead clothiers who prospered. Paul Methuen followed in his footsteps, developing new processes and bringing Dutch or Flemish artisans to Bradford to teach new skills. Although many clothiers became rich, few of them were classed among the gentry, but the Ashes were among those who crossed the border-line. The Methuens followed them, and in any case as clergymen they had long been respectable. Paul Methuen at his death left legacies in cash of some £10,000, with mills and landed property in Bradford, and a sizable estate he had lately leased at Bishops Cannings near Devizes. This was a substantial fortune for the time, but he divided it equally between his wife and seven children, making no distinction of age or sex, except that John, in return for the responsibilities he undertook, received a double portion. John Methuen therefore inherited a competence but not much more. He was seventeen years of age when his father died, and appears to have left Oxford without taking a degree and to

---

[1] *Victoria County History of Wiltshire*, IV, 156.
[2] Charles Wilson, *Economic History Review* (Dec. 1960).

have gone to London, where he was entered as a member of the Inner Temple. In 1672 he married Mary Chivers, the daughter of a rich Wiltshire clothier, and in 1674 he was called to the Bar. In 1685 he was appointed a Master of Chancery.

Little is known of Methuen's early life, except that he had three sons and two daughters, four of whom were baptised at Bradford. His mother was still comparatively young in spite of her seven children, and lived to survive two more husbands, and as the widowed Mrs Andrews to spend her last years at Leytonstone in Essex near London. This village was a favourite residence of wealthy Whig merchants and bankers, and it was there perhaps that Methuen became friendly with families such as the Childs and the Houblons, who were to figure in his Lisbon career. Methuen made no special mark as a Master in Chancery, save his signature at the foot of his rota of cases. There were twelve Masters in Chancery; it was an ancient office and the Masters had originally formed the personal suite of the lord chancellor. In Methuen's day their principal work was to prepare cases for the Chancery courts. The salary of a Master was only £100, but there were good perquisites, and the Masters enjoyed the free use of the sums of money, often large, which were deposited with the courts during suits about the succession of estates. These cases often lasted for years. The value of the office was growing; in 1621 a Mastery could be bought for £150; Methuen probably had to pay £1,000 and in the eighteenth century as much as £5,000 was asked.[1]

Chancery cases were complicated and protracted and involved reducing all the facts of the case to writing in order to cover every aspect. Whereas the courts of Common Law tried to narrow cases down to a single issue, the Chancery courts, administering Equity Law, followed the opposite course of taking as broad a view as possible. This procedure was cumbrous and from the earliest days Chancery cases had a reputation for length and expense, but

---

[1] Sir W. Holdsworth, *History of English Law* (1956), I, 417, 439.

I-2

Equity Law did aim to achieve a certain fairness and common sense. Methuen's Chancery training probably had some influence in developing the virtues and failings which marked his diplomatic career. He was prone to give too much detail in his reports at the expense of clarity and he was incapable of taking a departmental point of view. He worked like a mole, taking nobody into his confidence, and assumed responsibilities which were outside his province; these proclivities landed him in constant trouble, but he did take a broad and long-term view, and worked towards an eventual solution which was lengthy and expensive, but often produced finally a result which would not have been attained by a more adroit and stereotyped diplomat.

Methuen left no known mark on his profession, but as a barrister and as a Master of Chancery he led no doubt the busy unhealthy life of his kind, spending long hours attending the courts or their purlieus, and eating and drinking enough to lay a firm foundation for the gout which martyred his later years. At some time after the birth of his children, and before his departure abroad, he separated from his wife, and there is no mention of her in the whole of his surviving correspondence, but the earliest letter known in his hand dates only from 1690. It is not known whether he ever travelled abroad in his younger years, but it is likely that he did so, for he had a good knowledge of French and Spanish. Moreover, he admitted in the House of Commons in 1700 that his son Paul had attended a Jesuit school in Paris between the years 1681 and 1684, when he was eight to ten years old. Charles Montagu taunted him with this but Methuen replied that he was a good Protestant for all that.[1]

The circumstances in which Methuen came to be appointed as minister to Lisbon are not known. In 1696 it seems to have become a coveted post and there were several candidates to succeed Methuen, but in 1690 the post had been left vacant for a time and

---

[1] S.P. 89/17, Methuen to Nottingham, 28 June 1692; 'Letters illustrative of the reign of William III', *Vernon Letters*, ed. G. P. R. James (1841), II, 429.

4

there does not seem to have been much competition. Methuen himself seems to have aspired to go to Lisbon, because he believed it would be a pleasant and not too onerous post in an agreeable climate. The rents from his estate at Bishops Cannings were earmarked to pay his wife's jointure, but he had probably saved money during his time as a Master of Chancery, and must have been a man of some substance and influence in his own county, for he had just been elected a member of Parliament for Devizes, and he retained this seat except for one short interval in 1701, when he failed to be elected, until his death in 1706. These qualifications would scarcely have been enough to secure an appointment to represent his country abroad if he had not been well recommended and known to be acceptable in his politics. His brother-in-law Colonel Henry Chivers was a deputy-lieutenant of Wiltshire and a member of the Convention Parliament, but he had voted for Queen Mary and against the prince and princess of Orange being made king and queen, so the connection would scarcely have helped Methuen to the favour of King William. From Lisbon Methuen corresponded on friendly terms with the marquis of Halifax and, in later years, the Methuens were protégés of the elder and then of the younger Sunderland. It is not known who was his particular patron at this time, but he was probably recommended by the Portugal merchants, and his affiliations were definitely Whiggish. He was friendly with Gilbert Burnet, who as bishop of Salisbury was his landlord at Bishops Cannings, and this may have been of help to him, but it is very possible that he had rendered some political service to King William before or soon after his coming to England, for the king seems to have taken a personal interest in him and to have stood up for him in later years.

CHAPTER 2

PORTUGAL AT THE TURN OF THE SEVENTEENTH AND EIGHTEENTH CENTURIES

WHEN John Methuen was appointed minister to Lisbon in 1691, Portugal had declined from her great colonial days. The English and the Dutch had ousted her from the leading place in the Far East, and in Morocco she only retained one small fort at Mazagan on the Barbary coast. But she still had a string of forts along the coasts of Africa guarding her route to her remaining colony of Goa in India, and also her important colonies in Brazil between the Spanish settlements in the Argentine, and the Amazon, where the French were staking their claims. Her trade with the east was reduced to one or two large ships a year, but she sent a numerous fleet annually to Rio de Janeiro, Bahia, and Pernambuco, and the products of Brazil were an essential feature of her economy.

Continental Portugal was and still is a small but united territory. Portugal had indeed been a nation with the same boundaries for a longer time than any country in Europe, not excluding the United Kingdom. She emerged with her territory intact in 1640 after sixty years' domination by Spain, and except for the discovery and incorporation of the Azores and Madeira has not changed her frontiers since the expulsion of the Moors.

The Atlantic coast of Portugal is a little longer from north to south than the east coast of England, but the distance from the sea to the Spanish frontier averages only a hundred miles. Nevertheless, there is a great variety of landscape and climate. The northeastern province of Tras os Montes (beyond the mountains) resembles Spain and is a continuation of the Spanish plateau. Its capital, Bragança, gave its name to the royal house and it was as a fief of the Spanish kingdom of León that modern Portugal began. The provinces of Minho and Beira, which make up most of the rest of the north part of Portugal, are mountainous except for a coastal strip, but have a number of fertile valleys; the Minho in particular has always been noted for its green and luxurious vegetation, for the vines growing up its trees, and for the beauty of its scenery. The climate is damp and foggy near the coast, but changes rapidly inland to a drier climate of hotter summers and colder winters, and it is there that the famous port-wine district is situated. The principal rivers rise in Spain, but though some of them have valleys running inland, they all lose themselves in the mountains before the frontier, and the Douro plunges directly into the hills at Oporto. So communications with the frontier are difficult as several ranges of hills have to be crossed. The most fertile land lies among the hills, where the rugged country is unsuitable for large estates. It is a land therefore of peasant holdings, which extend far into the mountains, and already in 1655 a dense population had grown up, so that a Portuguese writer could say there was no room for more towns in the Minho.[1]

The country opens up towards the south, particularly in the area south or east of the Tagus, where the mountains recede and there are rolling plains extending towards Spain, and towards the Algarve, a small, almost sub-tropical province which is separated by a range of hills from the rest of Portugal. In Methuen's day Lisbon had drawn off the rural population from the provinces of Estremadura and Alemtejo, and particularly from the Alemtejo, south of the Tagus, the province with the largest estates and the best corn-growing land in Portugal.[2]

On the map Portugal looks like an integral part of Spain and there are few apparent natural frontiers. In the south the Spanish highlands merge gradually in the plains, but north of the Tagus a broad area of mountainous country for long formed a no-man's-

---

[1] M. Severim de Faria, printed in *Antologia dos Economistas Portuguesas*, ed. António Sergio (Lisboa, 1924), p. 191.
[2] Damião de Peres, *História de Portugal* (Barcelos, 1934), VI, 400.

land, which separated the Spanish frontier from the densely populated coast. For this reason Portugal developed from the coast inland and not continuously with Spain. The difference between the two countries north of the Tagus is very noticeable. In Spain there are wide plains between the mountains, over which communication is possible in any direction. In Portugal the valleys are narrow and until lately mountain paths were the only links between one village and the next. Even from the air Portugal in the spring looks green and well watered, but once the Spanish border is passed, the prevailing colour is red and there are few signs of woods or green things until Catalonia is reached. By road or rail the change is striking. In Spain the country is vast and rolling; there are immense corn fields naked for most of the year but golden in autumn, or miles of bushes and low scrub. Trees and isolated farmhouses are rare and the villages are gaunt. Here and there a mountain top appears in the distance but the feeling is one of uninterrupted space. As soon as the Portuguese frontier is crossed the scene changes rapidly and the traveller plunges into an enclosed landscape surrounded by mountains. At first there is rough country strewn with enormous rocks, but gradually villages appear and multiply. With their painted houses surrounded by trees and flowers they look gayer than their Spanish counterparts and the countryside is dotted with homesteads and farms. A varied cultivation of vines, maize, olives, tobacco and the lanky ubiquitous cabbage reaches far into the hills, and everywhere there are trees and woods. Maize, though a newcomer, was already a basic food in Methuen's day, and the look of much of the country has probably not changed, except that in the interior many woods of oak and chestnut have disappeared or been replaced by pine and eucalyptus.

The mists and rain from the sea and the diversity of country and climate have done much to differentiate the Portuguese from the Spanish character. The oceanic climate has a mellowing influence and the sea has given the people of the coast their living. It has also

N

Pontevedra
Vigo
Bayona
R. Minho
Viana
R. Lima
Braga
Guimaraẽs
Minho
Bragança
Tras os Montes
Oporto
R. Douro
Lamego
Salamanca
R. Vouga
Almeida
Aveiro
R. Mondego
Guarda
Ciudad Rodrigo
Coimbra
Beira
Covilhão
Figuera da Foz
Penamacor
Monsanto
Castelo Branco
Salvaterra
Almaraz
Berlengas Isles
Tomar
Vila Velha
Alcántara
R. Tagus
Abrantes
Castelo de Vide
Valencia de Alcantara
Santarem
Porto Alegre
Albuquerque
Rock of Lisbon
Estremadura
Salvatierra
Estremoz
Elvas
Badajoz
R. Guadiana
Fort St Julian
Cascais
Lisbon
Belem
Setubal
PORTUGAL
Evora
Cape Espichel
R. Guadiana
SPAIN
R. Guadalquivir
Alemtejo
Algarve
Seville
Lagos
Faro
Cape St Vincent
Rota
Cadiz
Port St Mary
Gibraltar

0   25   50 miles

brought many new settlers, and the culture of the vine and the olive, which came from the Mediterranean round the coast rather than overland. On the other hand the mountains both screened the north of Portugal from Spain and separated the regions and even villages and towns from one another, encouraging the devotion to tradition characteristic of Portugal.

By the time the barbarians reached Portugal many of them had become romanised or even Christian. Consequently Portugal was less affected, and in the north has preserved like Wales or Brittany a Celtic flavour. The Moors remained three centuries even in the north but they did not settle in great numbers beyond the Vouga river, forty miles south of Oporto. However, many New Christians from the south were settled in central Portugal after the expulsion of the Moors, and Lisbon in its great colonial days drew to it fresh exotic elements from Africa and the East. William Bromley, who visited Lisbon in 1693, said that in spite of the persecution of Jews and New Christians, these people still formed a third of the population and many of them looked as swarthy as Moors. This was probably more noticeable in Lisbon than elsewhere, but a Moorish flavour had filtered back into the upper classes and even into the royal family in spite of their Burgundian origin. King Pedro behaved like a pacha to women and preferred to eat his meals alone off a cork mat, seated on the floor. Such habits were usual; some of the wives of noblemen adopted western liberties, but the custom was to receive visitors sitting cross-legged on a dais spread with a mat or Turkey carpet, and middle-class wives lived in oriental seclusion, only emerging on Sundays and holidays to go to mass.[1]

It was perverse that the Portuguese clung to or rather reintroduced these oriental customs, which were unsuitable in a western country, while they rejected what was most valuable in their Moorish

[1] J. B. Trend, *Portugal* (1957), pp. 42–57; Rev. John Colbatch, *Account of the Court of Portugal* (1700); William Bromley, *Travels through Portugal* (1702), p. 6; Add. MSS 23726, fo. 30, etc., *Diary of Thomas Cox*; Sloane MS 2294, fo. 7: *Mémoire touchant le Portugal*.

heritage. The Jews and New Christians had been skilled farmers, craftsmen and traders. The descendants of Moorish water-wheels and works of irrigation can still be seen around the countryside, but every effort was made to destroy Portugal's only commercial class. The growth of native industries and trade was thwarted and a gap was left, which was filled in the seventeenth and eighteenth century by the English, Dutch and other foreign communities or Factories. Although Portugal remained mistress of an empire, she was content to allow her trade to be carried by aliens, who prospered in her cities, but had little intercourse with her people.

To the Portuguese it sometimes seemed that all the profits stayed in the pockets of the foreign merchants. Undoubtedly the foreigners lived better than the Portuguese and kept for themselves a good share of the wealth they produced, but they were performing a vital service in bringing trade to Portugal and in preserving what remained of her colonial empire. Without the interest which the maritime powers took in Portugal on account of her position on the Atlantic, she would have continued to run the risk of being absorbed by Spain. This was the fate of Catalonia, which occupied an analogous situation, but was no longer on the way to the riches of the East, and was debarred by the monopoly of Seville from trading with America.

Portugal owed her liberty partly to the value that the maritime powers attributed to the free use of Portuguese ports and the maintenance of their trade and of their Factories there. But it would be wrong to conclude that she owed her freedom and the integrity of Brazil entirely to the self-interest of her allies. Portugal had a long tradition as an independent nation and, though she was weak in the military sense, she was capable of selling her liberty dearly. Louis XIV appreciated this and did not consider the union of Portugal with Spain was practicable even under a Portuguese king and French auspices.[1] The government of Portugal was

[1] A. Legrelle, *La Diplomatie Française et la Succession d'Espagne* (4 vols. Gand, 1888–92), III, 25.

centralised in the overgrown capital of Lisbon, and the stream of merchants was equalled by the number of soldiers, from the time of the crusades onwards, who came to take the lead in her wars. Many of both settled, and a visitor to Lisbon might form the impression that the life of Portugal was conducted by foreigners. But although the foreigners were treated with courtesy and kindness they lived in their own world. Even in Lisbon the Portuguese kept apart and in the provinces each town pursued its immemorial life and was little influenced by the cosmopolitan life of the ports.

In spite of the small size of Portugal, towns and villages were distant from each other in point of time. There were no roads for wheeled traffic outside Lisbon and even there the streets were too steep and narrow for any vehicle except a litter or a chair. It took a week to travel to Oporto, and Queen Catherine of Bragança on her homeward journey with her retinue took ten days to cover the 130 miles between Coimbra and Lisbon.[1] A strong regionalism reigned in Portugal, and the Portuguese character was very steadfast and enduring in its resistance to change.

Various estimates have been made of the population of Portugal in Methuen's time. Thomas Cox, a young English merchant residing in Lisbon in 1700, estimated the total population at 2,125,000 and quoted Portuguese statistics of those attending confession in Lisbon in 1689 as 187,000. He thought the number might have risen to a quarter of a million by 1700, to which 20 per cent would need to be added for the children under seven, who were too young to go to confession. In the sixteenth century the population had shared to some extent the decline which had also occurred in Spain, and was estimated by one source to have fallen to one million in 1600, but in the seventeenth century it had grown again. Lisbon was far larger than any other city. Bromley estimated Oporto had 50,000 inhabitants, Viana de Castelo 7,000, and that Coimbra was a sizable town with 5,000 students. On

[1] Add. MSS 23726, fos. 29, 34; S.P. 89/17, fo. 82.

the other hand an eighteenth-century traveller estimated the population of Oporto as no more than 24,000 in 1732.[1]

Lisbon had a magnificent situation above the Tagus, but the people were very crowded together, and all visitors decried its stench, filth and poverty. Some of the noblemen's houses looked magnificent and had fine façades and staircases, and doors big enough to take a coach, but they had no glass in their windows and even the king's palace had whitewashed walls and little furniture. There were few gardens of any merit and such splendour of architecture as existed was found in the churches. In spite of a thriving trade Lisbon had no brisk air like London or Amsterdam, and the streets were empty, save when the crowds were tempted out by a bullfight, a church procession or a festival. On account of the sumptuary laws forbidding coloured cloth the men wore sombre clothes and everyone, whether king or cobbler, wore Colchester 'bays' or cloth of that quality. Until 1693, when the decree prohibiting black cloth was revoked, even this colour had been a luxury and suits were turned inside out for mourning. The king himself wore a plain coat and lace band. Gold and silver lace, to which the Portuguese were naturally inclined, were forbidden though an exception was made for foreign visitors. For nether garments the men wore baggy woollen drawers in winter and linen ones, perhaps of Portuguese manufacture, in summer. In this uniform dress with unlined cloaks they could only show their rank by constantly carrying long swords, which were worn by all classes save the lowest and by the use of spectacles, to which they were much addicted. So they stalked along, very slowly and stiffly, counting every step. However, in spite of their pride they were affable and polite even to their inferiors. This may have been prudence, for they were sticklers for the respect due to their rank, but, when all were dressed alike, this was hard to tell. However,

[1] Damião Peres, op. cit. VI, 363, gives a lower figure; W. Bromley, op. cit. pp. 7, 18. See also W. H. Morland, Akbar to Aurangzebe, p. 923; G. N. Clark, The Seventeenth Century (1960), p. 10; and C. F. Dumouriez, Etat présent de Portugal (Hamburg, 1797); J. Elliott, Imperial Spain (1963), pp. 13, 264.

politeness was always a Portuguese virtue and they were naturally better spoken than Englishmen. They were abstemious, eating little and drinking less, so that a man would often go for a month without drinking wine, and they despised the northern races for their fondness for liquor. No insult could be worse than to call a man 'an English sot'. They had many servants, who were as proud as their masters and would answer back in a way no English servant would do, but they were often beaten and ill treated. A footman would never demean himself to carry a parcel, and a lousy boy with no shirt to his back would not carry pots from the market for fear of being taken for a porter. All this pride and laziness gave Lisbon a derelict air but had its better side in an atmosphere of live and let live. The laws were severe but seldom observed. There was freedom of speech, for words were no treason, and a man could say 'Devil take the king' without fear of ill consequences. The king himself was very civil and his laws gave a good deal of grace, allowing for instance a long credit before the customs dues had to be paid. Protestants used to poke fun at the easy-going ways of the Portuguese, and the Reverend John Colbatch had much to say about the indulgence of confessors, which enabled the most solemn vow or penance to be compounded for a sum nicely calculated to suit the finances of the sinner. The cathedral clocks kept an inverted summer time, supposedly to allow the sluggish canons to say six o'clock mass at seven. Foreigners laughed at these loopholes, but they were the first to benefit, for they were allowed to follow their own bent without molestation, except occasionally, when their industry and success, or sometimes their arrogance, provoked jealousy and resentment.[1]

The Portuguese gentlemen, though they did not find their lives as dull as Englishmen supposed, did not have much occupation except gambling and intrigue. There was little entertaining or society, and plays were frowned on. Few of them loved sport or shared their king's enthusiasm for hunting. The ladies kept to

[1] Cox, Add. MSS 23726, fos. 29, 34, 64; Colbatch, *op. cit.* part I, pp. 24–39.

their houses and saw no men except their husbands and priests and friars. No law could entirely cut out fashion and they wore enormous 'guardainfantas', skirts like crinolines, and décolleté dresses, though no sign of their feet could appear, for this would have been the height of immodesty. Even Catherine of Bragança, who was proud of her small feet, and tried hard to shorten the skirts in England, could not change this. All classes loved lace, and the ladies liked to put flowers in their hair, which hung down their backs in two long pigtails, and to wear shoes with heels eight inches high. The men too were particular about their shoes, as they still are, and used to carry with them a piece of 'bays' to wipe off the dirt. Those girls, and they were many, whose dowries or whose charms were too little to get them a husband, entered a convent. Formerly the fashionable convents had allowed visiting and some of the finest ladies had preferred convent life to marriage, because they could live as nuns with more freedom and gaiety. In 1687, when the duke of Grafton with an English squadron escorted the new queen of Portugal to Lisbon, he and his suite took full advantage of this custom to enjoy some female society. However, King Pedro put a stop to it soon afterwards and ordered that the grilles should have a finer mesh, and there should be two screens at least six feet apart to prevent all possibility of any dangerous approximation of the sexes. According to John Methuen the nuns did not give in without a struggle and a few broke out of their convents. Queen Catherine of Bragança, pious as she was, had grown used to freer English ways, and was shocked on return to Lisbon to find this liberty abolished. However, the laws of Portugal allowed some rights to women: a girl could obtain a licence from a magistrate to marry her lover and she could also obtain the grant of her dowry, even if her father did not wish it; she could sue for breach of promise, though she could not be sued. Also the laws about dress were slowly eased. In 1700 new French modes competed with Colchester bays, and crapes and callimachos were being introduced. The latter were a light worsted, for which Lavenham was famous, often striped and used for scarves.[1]

Every Easter there were bull-fights organised by the city of Lisbon and these were almost the sole secular distraction. King Pedro had a passion for riding spirited horses and for fighting bulls, and sometimes appropriated the fiercest bulls for his own pleasure. The only other pleasure of the people, and particularly of the ladies, was the cult of their favourite saints, and participation in the festivals and processions of the Church. The use of sumptuous robes and of precious stones was practically restricted to the Church. Led by their king the Portuguese atoned for their faults and frustrations by their meticulous devotion. There was a craze for flagellations and fasts and for ostentatious acts of penitence. The inquisition was milder than in Spain but it provided nevertheless the occasional spectacle of an *auto-da-fé*. The devotion of the Portuguese did not stop them falling out with the Pope over money. When the coinage was debased papal dues were paid at the same rate in Portuguese currency in spite of his protests. But the amount of money which passed to Rome every year was great. The fee due, for instance, by a new bishop of Evora was 90,000 cruzados.[2] The secular and regular clergy owned large properties in Portugal. The nobles often ran through their estates, but the Church was the great accumulator of wealth and sometimes, as in the case of the famous monastery at Alcobaça, church landlords were good and progressive farmers. The Jesuits, who were the most influential of the regular clergy, had in 1702 twenty-three colleges in Portugal and 17,655 members.[3] Some of the earliest port-wine to reach England was believed to have come from their farms and they were good men of business, managing the remains of Portuguese trade with the Far East and holding a large

---

[1] Add. MSS 23726, fos. 9, 19, 55, 59; Sloane MS 2294, fo. 26; MS at Althorp, Methuen to Halifax, 2 May 1693.

[2] Colbatch, *op. cit.* part II, p. 4. The nominal value of the Portuguese coinage was increased by 20 per cent in 1688 and by 10 per cent in 1694.

[3] *Corpus Institutionum Soc. Jesus*, Antwerp, 1702; Add. MSS 23726, fo. 95; Antonio Sergio, *op. cit.* p. 272.

stake in the trade with Brazil. Other orders too were rich and there were estimated to be five or six thousand friars in Lisbon alone. The clergy would have been even more important as accumulators of capital if so large a contribution had not gone to Rome, but they were not altogether a 'dead hand', for by an agreement with the Pope they were allowed to be taxed. As a body they were also great consumers; the Portuguese economist Ribeiro de Macedo remarked that all the friars and nuns in Portugal were clad in English serges. Their use of luxury materials for their robes and church ornaments was a factor in the economy of the country, and in the case of the Church the sumptuary laws were applied lightly or not at all.[1]

Portugal's trade with the Far East no doubt still provided precious stuffs for church use, though it had greatly shrunk. Three ships were now the maximum sent to the Orient in any one year. These were of 800 tons, the biggest ships of their day, but they were so packed with troops and with supplies for the hazardous eighteen months' voyage that their cargo space was limited. However, their profit was estimated to be as high as 35 per cent and they brought back diamonds, carpets, silks, cotton, pepper, indigo, gold and silver stuffs, and saltpetre. The trade with Brazil was extensive and the annual fleet consisted of thirty ships for Bahia, thirty for Pernambuco, eight for Paraiba and twenty for Rio de Janeiro, all of 250 tons except the Rio ships, which were of 500 tons. The Brazil voyage was long, but it was easy and safe except for the danger from privateers, and the fleet was usually convoyed by six Portuguese men-of-war. The export of gold only began to be important from 1700 and the principal products were sugar, tobacco, hides, and valuable woods which yielded dyestuffs for the cloth industry. For some time the Brazil sugar and tobacco had suffered from the competition of the English and French West Indies, but the sugar was of the best quality and still found a

[1] Add. MSS Sloane 2294, fos. 44–5; Add. MSS 23726, fo. 23; *Somers Tracts* (1748), XIII, 297.

market in the Mediterranean. At some stage before the conclusion of the Methuen commercial treaty the French offered to buy the tobacco and fine sugar, but the Portuguese decided that the offer was not worth the sacrifice of their new market in England for their wines. The profit from the Brazil trade was only 10 per cent in the 1690s, and would have been still less if the wages of the seamen had not been very low, only forty crowns for the voyage. Nevertheless, the Brazil fleets were the mainstay of Portuguese economy; they were of particular interest to the king, who had a monopoly of Brazil woods, which he exported to the value of 300,000 reis, and of tobacco and snuff. Under the 1654 treaty the English merchants were allowed to establish four of their number in each of the main ports of Brazil and to send ships with the Brazil fleet. They had the greatest difficulty in exercising these privileges, but they participated through intermediaries in the trade, owning as much as 50 per cent of it, and they were dependent on the safe arrival of the Fleet every year to obtain payment from the Portuguese for their sales of cloth and of other English goods.[1]

Portugal also took part in the profitable Asiento trade in negro slaves to America. In 1696 the Royal Guinea or Cacheo Company signed a new agreement with the Spanish Supreme Council of the Indies to carry negroes to the Spanish dominions. They obtained a contract for six years and eight months to carry 30,000 negroes, that is, '10,000 tons of pieces of the Indies at three to the ton', who were to be neither old nor decrepit. The Portuguese were to take the slaves in their own or allied ships, and to receive an advance payment of 100,000 pieces of eight, followed by two more payments to be made monthly at the rate of $112\frac{1}{2}$ pieces of eight for each ton. They were to bring back the produce of the blacks in merchandise. In practice the Portuguese had not enough ships of their own and chartered English and other ships for the trade.[2]

[1] Add. MSS 23726, fo. 23.
[2] There is a copy of the agreement in S.P. 103/66 Treaty Papers. S.P. 89/17, 26 May 1699. See Appendix B for an explanation of Portuguese money.

Portugal traded on her own with the Azores in corn and wine and had many small ships going to the Mediterranean. Most of the Madeira trade, which was considerable, was carried in foreign vessels and much of it was direct with America. The trade with England, Holland and Scandinavia was almost all in foreign hands except for a short time in 1693-4, when the Portuguese entered the English trade. Portugal was dependent on Sweden for timber, tar and naval stores, and exported salt in return to Scandinavia and to Holland. The Setubal salt was of a special rough quality for use in curing cod fish, and salt was also exported from Aveiro in the north.[1] All the Portuguese salt came from saltpans on the coast and none of it was mined. The principal import from England was cloth and in return Portugal exported southern fruits, oil, argol, Brazil woods for dyestuffs, sumach from Oporto for tanning, paper and wine. The olive oil was used for making up cloth, and the argol and the dyestuffs, including indigo from the Orient, were also used by the all important cloth trade. The trade in wine had begun in 1678, when French wine was prohibited in England, and after an interruption from 1685 to 1690 was resumed on a steadier basis, first from Oporto and then from Oporto, Lisbon and Viana. Some wine went to Newfoundland, with which there was a flourishing trade in English ships in fish and salt and other commodities. Lisbon consumed in 1700 as much as 20,000 quintals of fish, and English fishing vessels made the triangular voyage between England and Portugal via Madeira and America, but sometimes made as many as four direct voyages in a year between Portugal and America without returning home. From Holland Portugal imported sheets, butter, cheese, rope, iron and some cloth, and from France silks, ribands, lace and finished cloth as far as the sumptuary laws permitted.[2]

The foreign merchants, English, Dutch, French, Italian, Hamburgers and Scandinavians, formed communities in Lisbon and

[1] Virginia Rau, *A Exploração e o comercio de sal de Setubal* (Lisboa, 1951).
[2] Add. MSS 23726, fo. 19. Bromley, *op. cit.* p. 6.

2-2

Oporto, and were represented in the smaller ports elsewhere. The English fared best, as under the 1654 treaty they enjoyed many privileges including the restriction of customs dues to a maximum of 23 per cent *ad valorem*, the right to practise their religion and to have lawsuits tried by their own judge conservator. The Dutch and to some extent the French claimed the same treatment; they did not always receive it but they had their own judge conservators. This official was appointed by the king but the candidate chosen was usually approved by the merchants. There were often complaints, and once or twice a conservator was eventually replaced, but the older and better established firms usually found means to enjoy friendly relations with the conservator, so that the dissatisfaction often arose from the new firms, who had not the same contacts, and represented jealousy between different cliques of merchants, as much as friction between English and Portuguese.[1]

The community of merchants or factors was known as a Factory and such bodies with varying degrees of organisation existed in every port used by English trade from Canton to Danzig. In Lisbon in the 1690s the Factory consisted of eleven or twelve principal firms and a petition addressed to Paul Methuen had twenty-four signatures. This was a decline from the prosperous days that followed the treaty of 1654 and the renewal of the alliance with the marriage of Catherine of Bragança, but English goods imported to Lisbon were estimated to be worth £200,000 annually, and the emoluments of the consul's post, which were mainly derived from a 3 per cent tax levied on imports, to be £1,000. There was little to attract the foreigner in the life of the Portuguese upper classes, as they did not engage in trade and had little in common with the merchants, so the Factory formed a closed circle of its own. It had a chaplain and on Sundays divine service was held at the Legation. A description of this survives.[2] The envoy, in this case Paul Methuen, sat on the left side of the

---

[1] For a description of a dispute about an unsatisfactory conservator see S.P. 89/17, Paul Methuen to James Vernon, 9 June, 1 Aug. 1699.

[2] Add. MSS 23726, fo. 25.

pulpit with a table before him, while John Earle, the consul general, had a seat nearby facing the congregation, who sat on chairs and benches facing the preacher. Regular services were held in the Legation but the Portuguese forbade any sign of heretical worship elsewhere. Funerals had to be conducted unobtrusively. When an Englishman died, he was put in a coffin, and the coffin in a sugar chest, which was carried on board an English ship late in the evening, and taken by boat next day across the Tagus to be buried between the tide marks on the beach. The same practice obtained in Oporto, where the burial took place on the further side of the Douro, and one doubts whether the body's last rest was undisturbed for long by the strong scour of the tide. Although freedom of worship and the use of a burial place were guaranteed by treaty, the privileges were grudged, and in Oporto, where there was no diplomatic protection, the chaplain performed his duties with difficulty, and was at one time expelled, and only allowed to be replaced after long and vigorous diplomatic protests.[1]

There were also a number of English and Irish Catholics in Lisbon, often of Jacobite sympathies, who were not members of the Factory, but found friends in the English and Irish colleges training for the priesthood and in the suite of Queen Catherine. Relations with the Protestant English were usually strained. A chronic source of complaint was the kidnapping of Protestant children to be brought up in the Catholic faith. On one occasion John Methuen took into his house a twelve-year-old boy named William Brereton, the son of a London clothworker, who had been kidnapped in Madeira and brought to the Irish Jesuit college; Methuen hid him until he could unobtrusively be put on board a ship sailing for England.[2]

The merchants were prone to grumble about their occasional troubles with the Portuguese but on the whole they led privileged

---

[1] S.P. 104/198, Jersey to Paul Methuen, 23 Jan., 23 Apr. 1700.
[2] S.P. 89/17, Methuen to Trenchard, 15 July 1693; S.P. 104/196, Nottingham to Methuen.

lives. They imported furniture and the comforts to which they were used, and lived very pleasantly. Their quintas or country villas were very agreeable and it was not necessary to go more than a couple of miles from Lisbon to find the countryside. Methuen took a quinta not long after his first coming to Lisbon and plunged with somewhat indiscriminating ardour into ordering a long list of plants from England and a gardener to tend them. He ordered all kinds of vegetables, currants, gooseberries, raspberries, apples, pears, peaches, tulips, flower-seeds, turnips, and also a fishing-rod and garden tools. It is doubtful how many of these plants were suitable for the Lisbon climate, but the length of the list shows how neglectful the Portuguese were of growing such things for themselves. They seldom had gardens and Queen Catherine searched in vain for an unpretentious house with a garden to walk in, such as she remembered enjoying in Hampstead. They did have vineyards and well understood the growth of the vine, but they took no care of the cultivation of the grapes, picking them all at once, regardless of their sort or whether they were green or overripe, and throwing them all into the vat. So in 1672 it was an Englishman who was reputed to produce the best wine in Lisbon.[1]

There were English Factories at Oporto, Viana de Castelo, Coimbra and Faro, as well as at Lisbon. The Oporto Factory was the only one to rival Lisbon in importance; like Lisbon it declined after 1670 but from 1690 the growth of the wine trade gave it new life. The Lisbon merchants were mostly importers or engaged in general trade; the Oporto merchants were also exporters of Portuguese products. Lisbon also exported wine, principally after the Methuen treaty, but always imported more goods from England than it exported. The wine and fruit trade should have brought the Oporto factors into closer touch with the interior of Portugal and in spite of their difficulties they exercised a powerful influence

[1] MS at Althorp, Methuen to Halifax, 4 Sept. 1694; *HMC Dartmouth*, III, 23; Add. MSS 23726, fos. 16 ff.

in their comparatively small provincial town. But they were an even more closed community than the Lisbon Factory and in 1704 most of their servants were English-speaking negroes, so that they had no need in their homes to speak a word of Portuguese. Viana indeed was the only place where there was evidence of co-operation between the Factory and the local Portuguese, in the form of a petition to the king of Portugal signed by English, Portuguese and Dutch residents, asking for an engineer to be sent to open the entrance to the river, which was silting up.[1]

All the Portuguese ports were upon rivers, which had bars at their entrance; Lisbon was no exception but the way in was comparatively wide. Access to Oporto was only possible for small ships and was often barred for weeks together in the winter by storms at sea or floods coming down the Douro. In time of war enemy privateers were very active and merchant ships had to be convoyed at the cost of great delay. Methuen urged, though usually in vain, that a regular convoy should come out in November, and perhaps another in the spring; an autumn convoy was particularly useful in Oporto, as upon return it could carry the new vintage, which served to pay for the cloth imported, but it was welcome also in Lisbon, where it could follow the arrival of the Brazil fleet. A further advantage was that in England crews were discharged from the navy in the autumn and could be engaged for the round voyage, before joining the navy again in the spring. But convoys seldom came at the best moment and although ships were escorted whenever possible from the bar at Oporto, they often had to find their own way to join a convoy. After suffering heavy losses some merchants began to build galleys to be used for perishable goods and for the Mediterranean trade. These galleys or runners were built for sailing but also had sweeps, which could be used in calm weather or for manoeuvring. They were lightly built fast ships and were alleged to be able to make three voyages in the same time as it took for an ordinary

[1] Charles Sellars, *Oporto Old and New* (1899), pp. 21–3; Add. MSS 38153, fo. 194.

sailing ship to make one, but they required a large crew and could not take much cargo if they were to sail well. The navy disliked them, because they were independent, and it was not practicable to escort them, but outside the Channel they could dispense with a convoy, and in 1703 as many as 91 arrived safely home from Leghorn without a convoy.[1]

From 1690 and until 1702 the Lisbon mail was carried overland to Corunna and thence by packet boat to Falmouth. Cox in 1700 said the post left Lisbon every Tuesday and the merchants could get a reply from England in six weeks. This may have been so in summer but dispatches from the Methuens usually took a month and during spells of bad weather, especially in winter, three or four mails often arrived together and letters could take two months either going or coming. With a fair wind the voyage between Falmouth and Lisbon took only four days, and after the introduction of the Falmouth–Lisbon packet in 1702 communications were better, but the time taken was always variable. South-west winds prevailed in the Channel, but the north wind blew down the coast of Portugal for weeks on end in summer, so at times only one-way traffic was possible. The overland route by France, which could not be used by the allies in time of war, was sometimes quicker, for an express courier could travel from Versailles to Lisbon in eleven days. Sometimes the French ambassador had the advantage over his English colleague, but often the mail by the packet boat came first.[2] Even between England and Holland the mail was sometimes delayed for weeks, so official mail was often relayed or supplemented by the Dutch representatives in London. King William's habit of spending the summer in Holland or on campaign caused further delays; for though the king made foreign policy decisions, the queen, as regent (and after her death the lord justices), had to see the official

---

[1] S.P. 89/17, Methuen to Trenchard, 12 Dec. 1693, 20 Feb. 1694; *HMC H. of Lords*, VII, NS, 182.

[2] S.P. 89/18, fo. 72; Add. MSS 20317, fos. 313–14.

correspondence. The king was accompanied abroad by William Blathwayt, who acted as his secretary and corresponded directly with envoys.[1] Difficulties of communication were important and the rapid arrival of a mail or the delay of a dispatch often had a decisive influence. Ambassadors themselves were valued purveyors of news; the sick king of Spain sometimes could not contain his curiosity, when he saw a courier pass the palace window, and sent an intermediary to ask for the news; King Pedro was equally anxious to know what passed, and ambassadors who were well posted, as the Methuens tried to be, and could bring the latest international gossip, had an advantage at an audience.

King Pedro was not fond of receiving ambassadors and his usual audiences were formal and semi-public affairs. John Methuen managed to establish personal relations with the temperamental king, which enabled him to obtain private audiences. The chance to see the King often was first given him after the return of Catherine of Bragança to Portugal. Methuen had an introduction to her from the marquis of Halifax, and the dowager queen was grateful for his help in obtaining payment of the money due from her English estates. She had for her jointure a considerable fortune, in which King Pedro as heir was interested, but the drawing of income from it was hampered by formalities and dependent on her retaining English good will. Methuen busied himself on her behalf and the queen, who had grown fond of England, and at first felt homesick for much that she missed in Portugal, was glad to see him and to hear the news he brought her.

King Pedro was a man who found it hard to make up his mind and was always taking advice, but he was an autocrat and the central figure in Portugal. Born in 1648 he had become regent in 1667, and king on the death of his brother King Afonso VI in 1683. Afonso, who came to the throne at the age of fourteen,

---

[1] Blathwayt was secretary at war (nominally the C. in C.'s secretary) but at this time (1694) there was no rigid distinction between foreign and military affairs. The post of Secretary of State for War was not created until 1704.

suffered the effects of paralytic seizure in his infancy, and was only intermittently in possession of his faculties, being afflicted by alternate moods of neurotic excitement and depression. He was forcibly suspended from the throne in November 1667 by a Council of Nobles with the support of the people of Lisbon, and was kept in confinement in the Azores, and later in Cintra, until his death. His queen, a French princess named Marie-Françoise de Savoie, had accused Afonso of impotence, and a dispensation was obtained for her to marry her brother-in-law Pedro. She was a lady of beauty and talent, and Don Pedro was much taken with her. He was also urged to marry her by his Council, as the queen's return to France and the repayment of her dowry would have been a grave problem. Until her death in 1683 she exercised a strong influence and Pedro constantly consulted her.

King Pedro shared to some degree the moods of his brother and this and the circumstances of his accession made him temperamental and irresolute. His personality was vividly described in a contemporary manuscript written in French, of which the authorship is variously ascribed to an Italian, a German and a Frenchman.[1] It purported to be a guide to Portugal for the use of a great lady unnamed and also of the newly appointed nuncio, and was headed 'Mémoire touchant le Portugal'. The writer had been in Portugal some time and clearly knew his subject; his description is lurid, but it is perceptive and worth quoting, and its very exaggerations won for it a wide private circulation at the time. It reads:

King Pedro is very tall and has a very dark complexion but is good looking. He is an excellent horseman; nobody is as strong as he is; he has broken with his two hands a horseshoe and stopped a bull, holding it by its horns. He is very sober and never drinks wine; one cannot upset him more, than by coming near him, when one has taken something

[1] MS Sloane 2294 at British Museum. There are long quotations from it in Stowe MS 467 and also printed in *Memorias sobre Portugal no reinado do D. Pedro II (Arquivo Histórico de Portugal*, Lisboa, 1935), by Edgar Prestage, who assesses their value. See also F. D. de Figanière, *Catálogo dos MS Portugueses no Museo Británico* (Lisboa, 1853).

to drink; he has always taken a great deal of exercise, especially hunting; at present he takes less, because he is getting stout; he dislikes showing himself in public and has no regular court; he has no levée to see him dress and he eats in private; some days however he gives an audience, on special days to persons of quality and on other days to everybody; he then receives memorials. The Envoys only see him on ceremonial occasions and otherwise have to ask for a special audience, which is not private, although the King speaks to them at some distance from others present, so conversations are not overheard.

The King does not like persons of quality, and does not hide his pleasure when he has got rid of them. For this reason they are not attached to him and are very independent. He passes his time with junior officers of his household, who bring him all the gossip. He likes to hear all that goes on. He likes to have a few mulattoes about him, as they have more spirit than the Portuguese; he has several, who act incognito for him in the town. He likes to make them fight and often takes part himself. He is very fond of women and he is not particular; he has never been attached to any woman of standing but very few in the service of the palace, even the lowest, escape his attentions. He likes to hear of all the gay girls in the town and to have a look at them; he has them brought to his public audiences; he goes to them at night, escorted by a single mulatto, visiting two or three houses in a night. As this sort of adventure is common in Lisbon, he has several times been attacked and even robbed, being not the strongest, though he is well armed. He likes black girls, and has had several black babies, whom he sends off to the Indies. He shows so little affection and pays so little that most women beware of him, but during the moment that he loves them, he is more jealous than anybody. He killed with his own hand the Count of Antioguia, who had always been on good terms with him, in the room of a maid of the Infanta, whom he loved; it is said that the Count was in the room quite by chance, but knowing the suspicious nature of the Prince, he threw himself at his feet, but was stabbed to death and thrown into the street, so it should be thought he had been casually murdered in a brawl. Naturally the King caught the sickness, but he has never done a thing to cure it, and owing to his strength has suffered less from it than most.

In spite of his debauched life he is very pious and charitable and an easy victim of hard luck stories. He hates the bad in others and does what he can to correct it. He fasts on bread and water on Saturdays. He is scrupulous about rendering justice and always consults his Jesuit confessor. He has reformed the grilles of the convents and is always very pleased, if one attaches oneself to a nun. He is very serious and rarely laughs, but every month is in ill humour for some days, during which he is apt to strike his servants, although at other times he treats them well. During these fits his servants try to keep out of sight; if he is several months without an attack, he feels some very bad effects and makes some excuse not to show himself.[1]

This picture of the king is dark, but not more so than of some other monarchs of the time. In its main lines it is credible in view of the inner stresses to which he was subject. Colbatch in 1700 glossed over the king's worst vices, though he did not deny them; he probably got much of his information from Methuen, in whose household he lived until they quarrelled. Methuen did not give many personal details of the king, and was inclined to be naïve in accepting all he said at face value, but there is no reason to doubt that Pedro had a sense of duty, and applied himself sincerely to the duties of his office when his moods did not distract him. The French ambassador Saint-Romain thought he resembled King Afonso and would have been content to abdicate his throne, on condition that he was allowed to keep his mulattoes, his women, and his worthless companions. This was written in 1683 when French influence suffered a blow from the illness and death of the French queen and King Pedro was in low spirits. In the time of the Methuens he was often ill but he showed a desire to do well. During the life of his second queen he was relatively domesticated and age no doubt moderated his passions though it did not help his melancholy. Prowess in sport and love of women have always been popular qualities and can have done him little harm with the common people. The tackling of a bull by a group of unarmed men called 'forçados' is still a feature of any Portuguese bullfight, but it usually takes half a dozen men to bring

[1] MS Sloane 2294, fos. 14–16.

down the bull and King Pedro's feat in doing so single-handed must have been generally admired.[1]

After his first queen died King Pedro was much shaken, a lonely and violent man with an obsessive conscience. He only had one daughter, who was to die young and unmarried. For the sake of the succession he had to marry again and he agreed to take as his new queen Princess Maria Sophia Elizabeth, daughter of the Elector Palatine of Neuburg. Unlike her predecessor she took little interest in politics, but she disliked the French, who had ravaged her father's palatinate, and she naturally sympathised with her sisters the queen of Spain and the empress. Family affairs included plans to link her children by marriage with the Habsburgs; King Pedro in any case feared a French hegemony in Spain and was inclined to cultivate the Imperialist or, if necessary, the Bavarian party, in the hope that he would have friends at court when one or other claimant succeeded. His first child by his second wife died and there were many rumours about his state of health. But the queen succeeded in bringing up a sizable family to survive their infancy, including the future King John V. King Pedro appreciated this and in his own way became a fond though despotic husband, even deferring to his wife's request to give up fighting bulls. But he frowned on any attempt of the queen to lead a life of her own; at first she had a taste for wine and card parties, but the king stopped such levity, and she soon left her pleasures to devote herself to religious duties and the provision of heirs to the throne.[2]

From 1693 the royal circle included Catherine of Bragança, who after long hesitation returned to Portugal. She lingered some months in France, perhaps in hopes of a Jacobite restoration, and visited King James. In view of her devout catholicism and known

---

[1] Prestage, *Memorias sobre Portugal no reinado do D. Pedro II* (*Arquivo Histórico de Portugal*, Lisboa, 1935). For the king's near breakdown in 1683, see also Lansdowne MS, Brit. Mus. 1152 A. fo. 135.

[2] SP. 89/16, Scarborough to S. of S. 20 Sept. 1688. According to Pedro d'Azevedo, *Doença e Morte de Dom Pedro II* (Porto, 1911), King Pedro caught venereal disease as early as 1670.

dislike for King William and Queen Mary, she was expected to be sympathetic to the Stuart cause, but in Portugal she was not pro-French. She lived quietly and drew the income from her jointure, which in 1694-5 brought in £14,000. Methuen was in doubt what attitude to take up, but he decided to pay the queen dowager every consideration, and he met her at Coimbra and escorted her to Lisbon. He persuaded her to write politely to William and Mary, and helped her to meet Treasury requirements without having to sign a life certificate before a notary in order to draw her money. He wrote regularly about her to the marquess of Halifax and also to Lord Nottingham.[1] During her thirty years in England Queen Catherine had forgotten the stiff ways of the Portuguese court and at first she found the seclusion and the limited conversation of the Portuguese ladies tedious. King Pedro asked what she supposed the ladies could find to talk about, and was horrified to be told that in England ladies discussed politics and current events, and indeed all that interested their husbands. As dowager queen of England Catherine refused to give precedence to the queen of Portugal and supported her lady-in-waiting Lady Fingal when in consequence she refused to kiss the king's hand. King Pedro was unused to the authority of an elder sister and for once was nonplussed by a woman; he told them they must settle the question among themselves.[2]

The Portuguese, who perhaps remembered the rigour with which Queen Catherine's suite had been cut down when she arrived in England, did her best to wean her from her English retainers and her English ways. Many returned home, including, to the regret of John Methuen, Lady Fingal and her lovely daughter Lady Emily. Methuen complained that the queen attracted a crowd of hangers-on, who were mostly Jacobites. Perhaps he exaggerated, for one lady-in-waiting at least, the widowed countess of Ericeira, was a woman of talent and education. The queen did

---

[1] S.P. 89/17, Methuen to Nottingham, 15 Jan. 1693; *HMC H. of Lords*, II, 18, mentions £13,709 15s. 3d. paid to Queen Catherine from Oct. 1694 to Oct. 1695.
[2] *Visconde de Santarem, Quadro Elementar*, ed. L. A. R. de Silva (Lisboa, 1860), IV, ii, 151.

not encourage the Jacobites among her suite. More and more she devoted herself to her great interest in religion and began to regard all worldly matters as tiresome interruptions of her prayers. But her interest in England continued to be keen and Methuen said her greatest entertainment was to get the English news, and she was always vexed when the packet boat was delayed. She had chosen a house in order to be near to a convent and chapel, but it proved inconvenient, and Methuen tried hard to find a place which would house all her suite, and at the same time be comfortable and small, and handy for the queen's devotions. This was difficult in Portugal, where a taste for the simple life was not understood. However, Queen Catherine sometimes managed to cut out protocol. When Queen Maria Sophia had her fourth miscarriage she hastened to her bedside to recommend 'the English management of ladies on these occasions', and when the queen died she went over at once, attended by only one footman, to console King Pedro and care for his young children. As time passed her English memories faded, but when she was obliged to act as regent in 1704–5 her friendship was invaluable to Methuen, though her patriotism and zeal for Portugal sometimes imposed a severe strain on the cordiality of their relations.[1]

Although King Pedro kept the diplomatic corps at a distance, and the normal contacts of diplomatic society in Lisbon were much restricted, Methuen by the close relationship which he established with the king and the care he took to cultivate the Portuguese was able to avoid these difficulties. Paul also was an attractive and gay young man and made friends among the younger Portuguese nobility. King Pedro himself was well informed. He did not confine himself to the advice of his councillors and official entourage, and the reports from the ambassadors. He gave public audiences to all his subjects twice a week and to officials and nobles on Saturdays, and heard all the gossip of

[1] S.P. 89/17, Methuen to Nottingham, 11 Jan., 17 March, 30 Oct. 1693, and to Vernon, 17 March 1696. Also Paul Methuen to Vernon, 11 Aug. 1698, and Methuen's correspondence with Halifax, MS at Althorp.

Lisbon through his friends and employees in the underworld. Foreigners were apt to find themselves isolated and there was little general society in Lisbon at that time. Apart from the clergy few people circulated among all classes or ever associated with ladies outside their own immediate family. However, the Portuguese were great talkers, and spoke freely before their servants. So Lisbon was a hive of gossip, in which even some foreigners took part, though the situation changed in the next reign. In John Methuen's day political secrets usually filtered out. At the time of the Partition Treaty Paul Methuen scoffed at the belief of the French ambassador that any diplomatic conversation could remain secret in Lisbon for long.[1] The Methuens themselves were usually well informed, and although John Methuen prided himself on the secrecy of his discussions with the king, the gist of them often leaked out.

When the king was faced with demands from ambassadors, he invariably told them that he must consult his Council of State. This, the major instrument of his policy, was a small body of six noblemen, who often disagreed, but were closely related and constantly meeting in other capacities. The two leading figures were the duke of Cadaval and the marquis of Alegrete. Cadaval was the premier nobleman of Portugal. He had himself some royal blood and one of his sons married King Pedro's only recognised illegitimate daughter.[2] King Pedro owed gratitude to the duke for being the first to support his accession to the regency thirty years before. As a man of great wealth and estates he could afford to be independent, but he set great store on standing well with the king. He was commander in chief of the army and not uninterested in trade, for he showed practical capacity in reorganising the tobacco monopoly, which he framed. He married twice, both times a French lady, and was the leader of the Francophil party. But he was not always considered reliable by the French, and he put his

---

[1] Colbatch, *op. cit.* I, 12–13; Add. MSS 9744, fo. 64, Paul Methuen to Blathwayt.

[2] The king's daughter married another son of Cadaval when her first husband died.

own interests, and those he believed to serve Portugal, first. He had a special interest in the independence of Portugal, for some of his estates were subject to old Spanish claims, and he kept up his contacts with Spain, particularly with the count of Oropesa. In himself he was a pleasant man, so jolly that he was nicknamed the duke of Carnival. He had a deep pride, but his unassailable rank allowed him to dispense with ceremony. The marquis of Alegrete had begun by being his protégé. He served as a young colonel in the war against Spain and took part in the events leading to the regency. His successful embassy to ask for the hand of Princess Maria Sophia of Neuburg for King Pedro established his position, and he came to be regarded as the premier statesman of Portugal. In addition to foreign affairs he was concerned with finance and he took an interest in military matters. His son married a daughter of Cadaval, and he was related by marriage to two Portuguese generals, the marquis of Minas and the count of Atalaya. He was a man of piety and some literary attainment, being the author of a history in Latin of King John II of Portugal.

Another councillor, the marquis of Arronches, had been ambassador in London. He was not personally eminent but until his death in 1702 he was the mouthpiece of his brother Cardinal Sousa, archbishop of Lisbon. The foreign secretary, Mendo de Foios, had been a protégé of Arronches. The three other councillors were the counts of Alvor, Ericeira and Galveas. Ericeira, a surviving brother of the Colbertist minister of that name, was an old man and died in 1699. Alvor, a comparatively young man, had won fame for his defence of Goa against the Mahrattas during his viceroyalty. His son married a daughter of Cadaval and he was military governor of Tras os Montes, but he exercised no special influence. Galveias was also a soldier and became principally known as the octogenarian governor of the Alemtejo in the War of the Spanish Succession.[1]

---

[1] J. Lúcio de Azevedo, *Épocas de Portugal Económico* (1947), p. 281; Add. MSS 23726, fo. 51; *Recueil des instructions aux ambassadeurs de France*, ed. Vicompte de Caix de St-Aymour (1885), III.

33

King John IV, Pedro's father, had been used to work long hours with his Council. King John V, Pedro's son, made little use of the Council. King Pedro used it but did not normally attend personally, though during his last illness it sometimes met at his bedside. According to contemporary accounts discussions in the Council were always lengthy and often inconclusive. Questions were threshed out there, and the minutes of the Council were the formal basis for government policy, but the actual decisions were taken elsewhere. In Portugal, as in most of the smaller courts of Europe, the example of Versailles was much admired and there was a strong trend to centre all power in the king. This process matured in the following reign but already in King Pedro's time the private meetings which he held with his Councillors in the evenings tended to be more important than those of the Council itself. Final decisions were subject to the approval of a secret commission of three, which met later still.[1]

Even an absolute king has to delegate his authority and to pay some attention to public opinion. Inevitably the advisers, often somewhat shadowy, in his immediate entourage exercise an influence which is enlarged if the monarch is weak. King Pedro's advisers suffered much from his moods, and ambassadors when they failed to make headway with him reported that he was irresolute and weak. Undoubtedly he found it hard to make up his mind, but possibly he was not personally so weak. As the head of a small power under constant pressure from greater powers his situation was often puzzling. There was much to be said for a policy of procrastination and sitting on the fence. Except for the last two years of his life, when he was incapacitated by illness, he was active and even conscientious in pursuing the interests of his country and of his dynasty. He sought advice in every quarter, but principally that of Cadaval, Alegrete, his confessor, and his secretaries. He was also influenced by Methuen, and, as on the whole he favoured the allies more than France,

---

[1] Sloane MS 2294. Damião Peres, *op. cit.* VI, 2.

Methuen's opinion of him was correspondingly good. In spite of his violent nature King Pedro was a prudent man, and the drift towards absolutism, which was in keeping with the spirit of the times, was perhaps slowed down by his scruples. He was not blind to the fact that parliamentary government had some advantages for a king and perhaps thought seriously of trying it out, in order to raise money and to keep the nobles in check. King Pedro had no reason to fear any individual nobleman, and to some extent he owed his throne to them as a class, but he was a little jealous of them corporately, and in the following reign John V found them troublesome.

The king's confessor, Father Sebastião de Magalhães, was probably the principal power behind the throne. He attended the meetings of the secret commission of three, and even matters which were secret from ministers were revealed to him. He was gaining influence during Methuen's first mission and took the initiative in confiding to him his fears of the growing power of France. This did not prevent him supporting the alliance with France in 1701, but he soon regretted this, and Methuen always found him helpful. In 1697 the instructions to the French ambassador spoke of his value as a contact and of his intimacy with Methuen. Little is known of him personally, save that he was born in Tangier, and edited a book about China. His two nieces were rumoured to have received handsome dowries from John Methuen at the time of his treaties; this was probably gossip, but no doubt he gave them good wedding presents.[1]

Magalhães was a Jesuit and the Jesuits were the leading order in Portugal at the time. There was great rivalry between the various orders, but they usually took sides with the nuncio against the national church of Portugal led by the archbishop of Lisbon. An exception occurred to this in 1706, when the Jesuits fell out with the nuncio over a question of payment of taxes by their seminaries.

[1] S.P. 89/17, Methuen to Nottingham, 28 Nov. 1693; Add. MSS 29590, fo. 28; *Recueil*, III, 239.

Queen Catherine asked King Pedro to expel the nuncio and her chagrin at his refusal was said to have been one of the reasons for her giving up the regency. In the Council of State and among the king's advisers the archbishop was represented by Arronches, the Jesuits by Magalhães and Queen Catherine, the Augustinians perhaps by Mendo de Foios, who had a brother in the order. The dissensions and shades of opinion within the Church had some effect on general policy. In 1703, for instance, the Pope was suspicious of the Archduke Joseph's claims to certain Italian fiefs, and Archduke Joseph hated the Jesuits, who consequently favoured the cause of the Archduke Charles.[1]

Mendo de Foios Pereira, mentioned above, was foreign secretary and also secretary of the Council of State. He had no say in their proceedings but he kept the minutes and prepared their agenda. In his youth he was the author of several poems. He had served on a mission to Spain and could qualify as a Spanish expert. He was not of high birth and was sometimes spoken of slightingly, but his good qualities were widely admitted, and Methuen regarded him as a friend. He was obliged by ill health to resign his office in 1702, just as the negotiation of the treaties began, and for some time before this had often been absent on account of sickness, but until his death in September 1703 he was helpful, when possible. The acting secretary José de Faria succeeded Mendo de Foios; he was often spoken of as pro-French, but he appears to have been mainly an office man, who disliked taking responsibilities. He had diplomatic experience as minister in London and Madrid, but was principally known as a genealogist and historian, in which capacity he was custodian of the archives at Torre del Tumbo. Faria also died in 1703, and the office of foreign secretary declined in importance until the appointment in 1706 or 1707 of Diogo Mendonça de Corte Real. The king took a special interest in foreign affairs and the tendency to deal with them through his

---

[1] Rijksarchief 7370, 9 Sept. 1705; Coimbra MS 3008, fo. 129; S.P. 80/20, Stepney to Hedges, 23 May 1703.

private secretary had been encouraged by the fact that Roque Monteiro Paim, in his capacity of commissioner for the treaty negotiations together with the marquis of Alegrete, had handled so much in the years 1702–4.[1]

Roque Monteiro was a confidant of the king and a somewhat enigmatic character. He held various offices and after the death of Faria became known as the first secretary of state, while the foreign secretary was called the second secretary. He was better known as the king's private secretary, and as head of the secret service or 'inconfidencia'. In this he followed his father, who had been judge of the secret court. Born in 1643 he was educated as a lawyer, and as a young man wrote a book entitled *Perfidia Judaica* which violently attacked the Jews. He came into conflict with the Methuens over cases regarding New Christians, whose surveillance was part of his work, but in later years he perhaps modified his opinion. As the commissary attached to the imperial ambassador he was no friend of England during the treaty negotiations, but afterwards Methuen was on good terms with him and he became a particular good friend of the Dutch minister Schonenberg, in spite of the fact that he was a Jew. His importance was noted in a French report as early as 1692 and he remained a key man until his death in 1706, or nearly so, for in his last days there were rumours that he had fallen out of favour with the king. His qualifications were generally recognised and he had the reputation of being a good patriot.[2]

Besides the Council of State the highest legal organ was the Desembargo de Paço, which was a kind of Judicial Privy Council and consisted of six members appointed by the king. Finances were handled by the Fazenda or Treasury Office, which had two principals, one of them Alegrete, the other for a time Roque Monteiro. There was also an advisory council on financial affairs

---

[1] Luiz Teixeira de Sampayo, *O Arquivo Histórico do Ministerio dos Negocios Estrangeiros* (Coimbra, 1926), pp. 11–12 ff.

[2] Coimbra MS 3008, fos. 120, 125, 173, José da Cunha Brochado to Luis da Cunha.

called the Council of the Three Estates. This consisted of seven members, one named by the king, one by the nobles, two by the Church, and two by the Third Estate. The latter had formerly been citizens, but the nobles objected, and the Cortes then named two gentlemen. In King Pedro's day the only body of importance which still included ordinary citizens was the Lisbon Senate; the Senate administered the city and collected local taxes, and in view of the importance and relative wealth of Lisbon retained some influence. The Council of Three Estates fell into desuetude with the disuse of the Cortes.

During the regency King Pedro had reason to be grateful to the Cortes. They had helped his accession and the quashing of a plot to reinstate King Afonso his brother. He was obliged to summon them in accordance with the constitution, in order to prove the right to the succession of his daughter, and then to approve her betrothal. He had used them in 1674 to vote new taxes, though after the six years for which they had been voted elapsed he continued to levy them. In December 1697 the Cortes met to approve the succession of the new heir-apparent Prince John and prolonged their session until April 1698. They voted a subsidy and new taxes for defence, and King Pedro seriously contemplated summoning the Cortes regularly. He did not do so, but tried to meet his expenses from existing taxes and his own resources. The royal patrimony had been depleted by the wars with Spain, but King Pedro's father had been a wealthy man and as duke of Bragança had retained the valuable pepper monopoly and estates such as those at Moncorvo, where he owned a soap works and a factory for making rope from hemp. King Pedro drew 300,000 milreis a year from his monopoly of Brazil woods and a million crowns a year from the taxes on meat and wine. He made considerable improvements in the customs service, which collected 20 per cent on all imports, and in the tobacco monopoly. In 1700 his revenue was reckoned to be 10 million milreis, but half of this was earmarked for pensions and other obligations, and the king would have been hard put to it if from 1700 onwards his revenues had not received a substantial increment from the opening of the gold mines in Brazil. The royal resources were exhausted almost at once by the cost of a major war, but in the succeeding reign in time of peace they were sufficient to keep an absolute monarch in considerable splendour though they did little to relieve the poverty of the Portuguese people.[1]

While financial matters became a personal affair of the king and policy decisions tended to be taken behind the scenes rather than in formal council, military matters in time of war still had to be settled in the Council of War. Sometimes its members were co-opted to sit together with the Council of State. The Council of War of five members tried to exercise a close control over the generals in the field, who found they were sorely hampered by the constant requirement to refer back to Lisbon. During the War of the Spanish Succession it was the aim of the allies to loosen this stranglehold and to associate themselves and the allied generals with the deliberations of the Council. Some progress was made but it was uphill work and in the last campaign, which culminated in the march to Madrid in 1706, Methuen had to insist on seeing a copy of the orders, in order to assure himself that the army had been ordered to advance.[2]

Such in brief were the organs of government in the later years of King Pedro, and the principal persons in the royal circle. The minutes of the Council of State and most of the archives were destroyed in the Lisbon earthquake, so information on the period must be gleaned from stray papers and surviving correspondence, mostly that of diplomatic ministers. However, so much went on behind the scenes that even the official papers, if they survived, would not give a complete picture. On the other hand, the circle of persons in the confidence of King Pedro was small and remained very much the same from the beginning of Methuen's first

[1] For Portuguese money see Appendix 2.
[2] Add. MSS 28057, fo. 109.

mission until the death of both men in 1706. In spite of differences these advisers derived a common outlook from belonging to the same generation. The Portuguese statesmen were for the most part men of literary and academic attainments, but they were elderly; several of them were old beyond their years and died before 1706. One would expect such men to be sagacious, but not to excel in dynamic executive capacity. In any case the situation of Portugal did not invite any spirited and positive policy; it is not surprising that the story which follows, of the years of the Methuen diplomatic missions, contains many hesitations, disappointments and tergiversations.

CHAPTER 3

JOHN METHUEN'S FIRST MISSION
TO LISBON, 1691–6

METHUEN was appointed as minister to Lisbon on 13 May 1691, but he had to wait to see the king on his return from Holland, and did not reach Lisbon until the spring of 1692. Diplomatic service abroad still often tended to be a string of individual missions and Methuen's predecessor Lord Scarborough had left in 1690. Normally some continuity was preserved by the consul general, who was an official of standing in Lisbon owing to the importance of English trade and of the community or 'Factory'. Thomas Maynard had held the post with distinction since Cromwell's day, but he had been superseded in 1690; his successor was soon removed, and John Earle, a Lisbon merchant of long standing, was appointed. Little is known of him except for a few routine letters in a neat handwriting, but Methuen stayed with him on his first arrival and found him useful. The two men were probably acquaintances, as Earle came from the neighbourhood of Bradford-on-Avon.[1]

Methuen had to delay the presentation of his credentials until he could provide himself with a litter and mules. He did not in the end need these, as he was fetched by two royal coaches and attended with some ceremony by all the merchants of the Factory. But this was some weeks later. His audience was again delayed by the king's absence on his annual hunting holiday at Salvatierra. The king used to go there every year and on return often suffered a reaction after his long days in the sun and wind and went sick. Yet another postponement was caused by the rumour of a

---

[1] *Calendar of State Papers*, 13 May 1691. Luttrell, *Brief Relation of State Affairs* (1857), II, 363.

Jacobite invasion of England. After the news came that William and Mary were safe on their thrones, and Methuen had protested at the delay, he was received on 25 June. This public audience was confined to an exchange of compliments, and to avoid using an Irish friar as his interpreter Methuen spoke in Spanish, the king replying in the same tongue. At his following audience with the queen Methuen spoke in French, a language in which he felt more at ease.[1]

Methuen had little to do at first. He told Nottingham that he found Portugal more pleasant than he could believe and was enjoying better health than he had done for the past ten years, finding that 'the strict temperance of a retired life agreed very well with his inclination and made him master of a great part of his time'. By 1694 his work was heavier, and he told Halifax that affairs looked 'as to keep him continually solicitous, so that he thought and dreamed all day, and started in his sleep at night'. But he was not yet tormented by gout and he still regarded Lisbon as an easy post. He devoted himself enthusiastically to his house and garden, and his vines, and wrote that he preferred being an envoy to employment at home, and spent his leisure in reading history and studies of a like nature.[2] Actually he had other interests. We would scarcely know of them, if it were not for the quarrel he had with John Colbatch, chaplain to the Legation and to the Factory. Colbatch was a scholar and wrote a book of merit about Portugal. He was also a man of sincere piety, but he was frustrated by the worldly ways and unending gossip of the Factory, and was accused of saying 'the Factory was such a horrid crew, that he fancied himself in hell, while he was among them'. He was a man of strong prejudices, and had a cantankerous side, which was to be shown in the violent feud which he had with the

[1] S.P. 89/17, Methuen to Nottingham, 14 June, 16 July 1692. Dates in England are Old Style, dates abroad New Style. [A few of Methuen's dispatches inadvertently dated O.S. have been altered to N.S; so have replies to dispatches and letters to him from ships.]
[2] S.P. 89/17, Methuen to Nottingham, 21 July 1692; MS at Althorp, Methuen to Halifax, 12 March, 28 Oct. 1694.

famous Dr Bentley, Master of Trinity College. His quarrel with Methuen arose primarily from the fact that Methuen treated him as his personal chaplain, whereas Colbatch regarded himself as an independent minister appointed to be chaplain to the Factory by the bishop of London. The wording of his commission supported this point of view, but as far as the Portuguese were concerned only his Legation chaplaincy allowed him the privilege to function. Friction grew between the two men and Methuen enjoyed teasing Colbatch by quoting Hobbes at him. Finally Colbatch left Methuen's household in high dudgeon, and wrote a long letter to the bishop of Salisbury complaining that Methuen gave him no support, was a Hobbist and was causing scandal by his intimacy with Sarah Earle, the consul-general's young wife. In return for their hospitality Methuen had asked the Earles to stay with him at his quinta or country villa. He became fond of Sarah and began to call her cousin. Soon afterwards she caught smallpox and Methuen said she needed country air and must stay with him at another and larger quinta which he had taken. Colbatch, when he found his remonstrances were unheeded, spared no ink to denounce Methuen, but the bishop of Salisbury was Methuen's patron and friend, and after he had made inquiries and satisfied himself that the Portugal merchants sided with Methuen, he replied that no one doubted Colbatch's piety and faith, but he had perhaps allowed himself to show too much heat, and the whole affair might be given a more innocent interpretation.[1] Methuen went back to England soon afterwards and by the time he returned to Lisbon in 1702 Colbatch had left. Sarah had remained in Lisbon, but from 1702 until Methuen's death she and another 'cousin', Ann Browne, probably a daughter of Methuen's merchant friend William Browne, kept house for him. The arrangement was apparently a happy one save for the unfortunate John Earle, who is not known to have made any protest before

[1] See S.P. 104/196, fos. 251, 258, for a chaplain's and a consul's commission; Add. MSS 22908, Colbatch to bishop of Salisbury, 27 Oct. 1696, and reply, 27 March 1697.

43

the end of 1704. This affair is almost the only light we have on Methuen's private life and the liaison, if such it was, lasted until his death.

The question which first began to draw Methuen into negotiations of importance in Portugal was that of contraband control and trade with the enemy. There were several theories on the subject, none of which had been internationally accepted. The Dutch, who were the greatest carriers, were the most liberal in their ideas, and tended to adopt the principle 'free ships, free goods; unfree ships, unfree goods,' which meant that the flag covered the cargo and a neutral ship could pass without hindrance, unless it were known to be carrying contraband. But there was no internationally accepted definition of contraband. The French, who had least to protect and most to attack, went to the other extreme, and laid down in their Marine Ordinance of 1681 that enemy goods found in enemy ships could be confiscated and the ships taken as prizes. However, in some of their treaties they had allowed concessions from this principle. England was becoming as great a carrier as Holland, but tended to follow a middle course, and to be guided by a principle established in the fifteenth century, and embodied in a doctrine known as the 'Consolato del Mare'. This laid down that enemy merchandise could be seized, but the ships themselves could go free. In her treaties with Portugal, Sweden and Denmark, England had recognised the principle of 'free ships, free goods', but in her 1661 treaty with Sweden, and more explicitly in her 1670 treaty with Denmark, she had qualified this principle by the condition that ships of the powers concerned, trading with the enemy, must carry a passport certifying the neutral ownership of the ship and cargo, and a legally sworn bill of lading. England had disputed the interpretation of the Swedish Treaty in the 1680s, and in 1689 at the outbreak of war had signed a convention with the States General, which aimed at imposing greater restrictions on neutral trade with France. Sweden was already nominally an ally, and constant negotiations were pursued to draw the two northern powers closer to the allied side; Denmark and Sweden were often jealous of each other but they worked together to oppose the restriction of their trade either by the allies or by France. In March 1691 Denmark signed a convention with Sweden and a neutrality pact with France. England and Holland were obliged to fall back on their old treaties; the treaty with Sweden was reaffirmed and a new convention with Denmark was signed in June 1691, which was based on the 1670 treaties but brought several articles up to date. The argument between the allies and the northern powers narrowed down to differences about the articles concerning ships' passports and the certified bills of lading required to ensure a free passage. Some progress was made towards a definition of contraband. Tar was included in the convention with Denmark, and in order to win a decided advantage against France, which had a bad harvest in 1692, the allies included corn. At first they agreed to compensate Sweden and Denmark for any corn confiscated, but in June 1693 Nottingham found that the existing treaties precluded the sending of provisions to France, and decided that provisions included corn.[1]

The neutral trade to Portugal was largely carried by Danes, Swedes and Hamburgers, and was regulated by treaties with those powers. Portugal's position differed from that of the northern powers, in that her trade with France was greater, and she was not in so good a position to take reprisals as was, for instance, Denmark, who had a fleet of 30 ships as well as an army as large as the nominal strength of Portugal. The Portuguese minister had often complained of seizures of Portuguese ships by English men-of-war or privateers. On the other hand Methuen had protested against the liberty allowed to French privateers and the sale to French buyers of lead and other contraband through Portuguese

[1] S.P. Oakley, 'William III and the Northern Crowns' (London thesis, 1961), pp. 122, 136–40, 170, 203. The treaties are printed in Dumont, *Corps universel diplomatique* (La Haye, 1731), 6. ii. 384 and 7. 132; Add. MSS 15572, fos. 67, 70, Hugh Greg, minister at Copenhagen, to Blathwayt.

intermediaries, who acquired it from English merchants. Methuen did his best to stop this trade but the most he could achieve was to ensure that such contraband, if re-exported, paid the full Portuguese customs duties. Heinsius, the Grand Pensionary of Holland, had protested against the importation by Portugal of naval stores from Sweden, but Methuen inspected these personally and certified that they were genuinely for Portuguese use.

Nottingham confessed that he was baffled by the problem of reconciling the control of neutral trade with neutral complaints. King William had ordered that the treaties must be observed, but the 'Heads of Instructions for the Trade of Neuters' finally agreed with the Dutch in August 1692, and published in May 1693, provided that captains should stop ships trading to France. Yet the treaty with Sweden, and even that with Denmark, though the recent convention had tightened the regulations, allowed some liberty to trade with the enemy, and Nottingham feared that Denmark would complain that she was more strictly handled than Sweden. The situation of Portugal was the most difficult of all, for under her treaty she was entitled to 'free ships, free goods', and she had made no agreement about ship's passports. So there was danger of Portugal expanding her trade with France, and usurping English and Dutch trade. Nevertheless, Nottingham had been obliged to give assurance that the principles of the Dutch convention would not be applied rigorously and that the treaty rights of Portugal would be respected.[1]

However, although Nottingham admitted that Portugal was within her rights in complaining of the seizure of her ships, he argued that some control was necessary to prevent the fraud and collusion between merchants to carry contraband for the French. He proposed that Portugal should adopt the system applicable to Sweden, by which Portuguese ships would have to carry an

---

[1] Nottingham's Letter Book at HMC, fos. 104, 140, 147, 172, 194; Add. MSS 15572, Greg to Trenchard, fos. 95, 263–4; S.P. 89/17, list of naval stores and Methuen to Nottingham, 21 Feb. 1693; S.P. 84/22, fo. 304, Dursley to Nottingham; Add. MSS 37991, fos. 22 and 122, Blathwayt to Nottingham; S.P. 104/196, fo. 28.

official Portuguese certificate of the ownership of the crew and cargo and a sworn certificate, legally certified, of the bill of lading. It was true that this would mean a restriction of Portuguese trade with France, but it would be no worse than the restriction applied to Denmark, and France herself now denied the principle of free trade. It would be unjust, therefore, if Portugal could carry French goods but not English goods freely, and in any case Portugal was in the wrong in allowing French privateers to bring their prizes into Portuguese ports.

Nottingham was at first inclined to think Methuen was over-optimistic in hoping that Portugal would be provoked to a breach with France, but Methuen was confident that Portugal would resist French pressure, and was only afraid that France might make some conciliatory gesture before Portugal had reached the point of taking any action. He reported that about forty cases of French seizure of Portuguese ships were outstanding and that ill-feeling against France was growing. The Portuguese ministers were still reluctant to believe that France would not give satisfaction, but if it was denied much longer he was sure that he could persuade the king to break with France and join the Grand Alliance. He was on very good terms with the king, who allowed him to submit memorials to him personally and to discuss affairs very calmly. This was much preferable to making representations through the ministers and he did not think that any other diplomatic minister enjoyed such freedom with the king.[1]

At an audience on 18 April the king admitted that he had received better treatment from the allies than from the French, and Methuen put forward Nottingham's proposals for contraband control. He also suggested that the king should take reprisals against the French for any losses inflicted by them, and if he did this and denied the misuse of Portuguese ports by French privateers

[1] Nottingham's Letter Book at HMC, fos. 171, 190; S.P. 89/17, Methuen to Nottingham, 7 March, 30 May 1693.

he would enjoy an honourable and advantageous neutrality. Acting then on his own initiative Methuen went somewhat further and suggested that if France proved obdurate, the neutrality of Portugal would be humiliating and worse than a war, in which Portugal could count on powerful allies, for he believed that 'the King his Master would be willing to enter into a stricter Alliance with King Pedro to hinder the King of France pretending to give laws to all the Princes'. The king appeared sympathetic and said he would be sure to keep a benevolent neutrality. In May the Portuguese showed signs of stirring and the duke of Cadaval, as commander in chief, began to try to put the defences in order. Methuen wrote enthusiastically about his great designs to his friend the bishop of Salisbury, but he admitted to Nottingham that there was little prospect of Portugal joining the Grand Alliance, and his protest about the French privateers, which he handed to the king personally in May, had no result. However, the king was friendly enough and talked freely about his hopes of bringing France to reason, and of what had passed between him and the Dutch Minister Resident at a recent audience. Methuen suggested that if France proved conciliatory and there was no need for King Pedro to join the allies, he could still propose a Defensive Alliance to Spain, with an offer of 5,000 troops to help her if she was attacked. Methuen hoped that the king would be tempted by the idea of defending a power which had so recently claimed to be his suzerain, but Pedro had already been approached by the Spanish minister and supposed that Methuen was acting on his behalf. Methuen denied this and in fact he did not receive instructions to concert proposals for a Defensive Alliance with his Dutch and Spanish colleagues until the end of May. He then found that the Spanish minister was more optimistic about the possibility of a Portuguese breach with France than he was himself, but was inclined to work for a general alliance rather than a Defensive Alliance, which might carry the implication that Spain was too weak to defend herself. However, Nottingham decided that a

Defensive Alliance would be sufficient and would do very well to draw Portugal into the war. Alexander Stanhope, His Majesty's minister in Madrid, was told to discuss the question on these lines and Methuen's representations were approved, though he was castigated by Nottingham for writing about so confidential a subject to the bishop of Salisbury.[1]

The Portuguese themselves had already taken up the question of Portuguese shipping difficulties and of a possible treaty through their minister at The Hague, Diogo Mendonça de Corte Real. This had led to the Dutch Minister Resident Woolfsen inquiring, at the audience of which King Pedro informed Methuen, the terms on which Portugal would join the allies. The king had replied non-committally, emphasising his desire to be friends with everybody and the advantages of the principle 'free ships, free goods'. The question of an alliance had now been raised independently by all parties from differing points of view, and there was hope that the activities of the three allied Lisbon representatives would be co-ordinated.[2]

King William formed the opinion that the Spanish and Portuguese representations were only concerned to win advantage for their own trade, but he allowed Methuen some discretion. Consequently, when events forced the pace there was a disposition to give him full authority to take advantage of what proved to be a very brief opportunity. This was occasioned by the crisis following the appearance of the French fleet on the coast of Portugal, of which news reached Methuen on 13 June.[3]

Before describing the repercussions of this event and of the destruction in the Straits of the Smyrna fleet, some account should be given of the fortunes of the allied navies, which influenced the

[1] S.P. 89/17, Methuen to Nottingham, 18 Apr., 16, 30 May 1693; S.P. 104/196, fos. 39, 48/9, 51/3, Nottingham to Methuen; Nottingham's Letter Book at HMC, fo. 205; S.P. 84/73, fo. 188, Stanhope to Nottingham.
[2] S.P. Office, British Museum, resolutions and secret resolutions of States General, p. 11; Rijksarchief 7024, Woolfsen to Fagel, 12 May 1693.
[3] MS at HMC, Blathwayt to Nottingham, 4 May 1693; S.P. 89/17, Methuen to Nottingham, 15 June 1693.

attitude of Portugal. In the first years of the reign of William and Mary the major naval engagements had taken place in the English Channel. The French won a notable victory at Beachy Head in 1690, but this was offset by their defeat with the loss of fifteen ships at La Hogue in May 1692. The action proved to be a turning point, for the French preferred afterwards to concentrate on privateer warfare rather than to risk again their capital ships.

King William's Mediterranean policy evolved slowly. In 1691 an Anglo-Dutch agreement with Spain for co-operation in the Mediterranean was signed, but although Admiral Blake had wintered in the Straits in 1656, and there was still little idea of wintering a fleet abroad or of doing more than dispatching an annual convoy through the Straits and supporting Spain with a small squadron. But after the battle of La Hogue King William became interested, and he planned to use sea power for diplomatic objectives as well as for the protection of trade. On 16 June 1692 Blathwayt proposed to Nottingham the dispatch of a strong squadron to the Mediterranean. The Admiralty and Admiral Shovell opposed this, though they admitted the need to help the Levant Company, who were complaining that they had 60,000 cloths and other commodities worth £6,000–7,000 waiting for shipment. However, they promised to provide a convoy of the usual strength to be ready in August or September.[1]

Blathwayt replied that the convoy ought to be strengthened, so that it could help Spain and influence Turkey, as well as protect trade. His argument was reinforced by the representations which the Imperial minister Count Windischgratz had made to the Congress of Allied Ministers at The Hague. Heinsius had criticised the inactive proceedings of the imperial forces on the Rhine. Windischgratz admitted their shortcomings, but retorted that nothing could help the emperor more to act vigorously against the French than a peace with the Turks, and nothing could be

[1] John Ehrman, *The Navy in the War of William III* (Cambridge, 1953), pp. 395–8; G. J. Marcus, *Naval History of England* (1962), p. 49; S.O. 94/73, fo. 86, Stanhope to Nottingham.

better calculated to move the Turks than the arrival of an allied fleet in the Mediterranean, for otherwise they would never believe that the allies had won a great victory and had mastered the French at sea. He won general agreement and the English minister, Lord Dursley, was asked to forward the views of the Congress to London to be laid before Queen Mary.[1]

King William continued to press for the project and the Spanish envoy at The Hague, Francisco Bernardo de Quiros, also made representations. On 31 October a new Anglo-Dutch-Spanish convention was signed with Spain for the two maritime powers to provide eight ships each for joint operations in the Mediterranean. Questions of protocol were carefully defined. The Dutch were to yield precedence, and the choice of an English or Spanish commander in chief was to be settled by agreement, or if necessary by casting lots, but councils of war were to be held on the Dutch flagship. The thorny problem of salutes was solved by a provision that none were to be given. Although Nottingham favoured the scheme the Admiralty still pleaded that they were acutely short of ships, but they consented to raise their quota to eight ships to equal the number promised by the Dutch and achieve the required number of sixteen, and to speed their preparations as much as possible. Nottingham hoped the squadron would be ready by the end of November. The Dutch had six ships ready but the sailing had to be postponed until January 1693, and then to the spring.[2]

In April the Dutch Levant merchants complained that the delay had already cost them 70 per cent of their capital. Complaints were also coming in of the depredations of the Barbary pirates and of the supply by the dey of Algiers of corn to France. Sir George Rooke was appointed to command and ordered to detail three of his ships to visit Algiers, Tunis and Tripoli, but although

---

[1] Nottingham's Letter Book at HMC, fo. 74; Add. MSS 37991, fo. 22, Nottingham to Blathwayt; S.P. 94/22, fo. 290, Dursley to Nottingham.
[2] For the convention see Dumont, *op. cit.* 7. ii. 320; Nottingham's Letter Book at HMC, fos. 104, 126; Add. MSS 37991, fo. 182; S.P. 84/22, Prior to Nottingham, 3 Dec. 1692.

most of the squadron was ready in March, it was still held up by shortages of supplies and by persistent bad weather. Complaints of the delay came from Naples, where it was represented to be a breach of the recent convention, and from the minister of Savoy at The Hague, who said the command of the sea was essential to enable Imperial and Spanish troops to join those of Savoy in the invasion of Provence, which had been agreed. The matter was urgent, as the duke of Savoy was known to be wavering in his loyalty. Blathwayt told Nottingham, 'Your Lordship will see the Tempter is at hand and that more than the strongest appearances are necessary to keep the Duke steady in the Alliance.'[1]

Rooke finally sailed with eleven English and five Dutch ships on 30 May in the company of the Channel fleet and of three hundred merchant ships bound for all destinations. King William was delighted to hear that the fleet had sailed at last, but was dismayed when he heard that Rooke was to proceed alone from a point thirty leagues south of Ushant with the convoy and his squadron. The Admiralty were convinced that Count d'Estrées from Toulon would soon join Admiral Tourville at Brest, and that they must reserve their main force to guard the Channel. The precise sequence of events is hard to determine, but there is evidence that at least one account of the sailing of Tourville from Brest was received before the fleet sailed and that this was corroborated from another source before the fleet was out of reach of a message.[2] However, the joint admirals in command, Shovell, Delaval and Killigrew, only sent three ships under the guidance of a Huguenot, who was familiar with Brest, to make a reconnaissance. These returned without having obtained any definite evidence either way, but no French ships were sighted by the fleet and the admirals concluded that Tourville was still in Brest. They parted from Rooke fifty leagues south of Ushant, and, having missed a rendezvous with their supply ships, were obliged by a

[1] Add. MSS 37992, fos. 3, 8.
[2] *HMC H. of Lords*, MS, i, 109, for 1694, inquiry into these events. MS at HMC, Nottingham to Blathwayt, 25 May 1693.

shortage of beer, butter and cheese to return to Tor Bay at the end of June 1693.[1]

King William believed that D'Estrées would stay in the Mediterranean but that Rooke was strong enough to be a match for him. In mid-June D'Estrées was supposed to be still off Catalonia, where as a result of his support the French had taken Rosas. But on 27 June news reached Nottingham that there was alarm in Madrid and Lisbon about the approach of the French fleet, and on the same day the Paris *Gazette* announced that Tourville had sailed from Brest, and news came that he had joined D'Estrées at Lagos in the Algarve. King William was already expecting this and urging that Rooke should be reinforced, and complaining that no advice boats had been sent to the fleet. He heard the news on 2 July and Blathwayt spoke of his unspeakable concern, saying 'he never saw the King so sensibly afflicted with any accident as this, which had all the worst consequences, which could be agreed'. Nottingham wrote that the importance of the Mediterranean squadron was so vast that it was impossible not to be afraid of it, but that he hoped Rooke would have news of the French fleet from Lisbon and could take steps to avoid meeting it. There was general alarm and Harley wrote: 'I hope God will be gracious to the nation in preserving the rich fleet, but the folly of sending them thus is not to be paralleled with anything that we have seen done before this.'[2]

Methuen heard on 13 June that the two French fleets had joined, and tried at once to hire a boat to take the news, but no boat would venture, so he could only send letters by way of Oporto and Corunna. The Portuguese feared an immediate French invasion and King Pedro issued a decree increasing the army to 20,000 foot and 4,000 horse. Methuen found that he was

---

[1] De Jonge, *Geschiedenis van het Nederlandsche Zeewezen* (Amsterdam, 1841), IV. i. 411–17; *HMC H. of Lords*, I, NS, 199–200, 292–3 and 107–9; Add. MSS 37992, fos. 29 and 33; Dalrymple, *Memoirs of Great Britain* (1790), III, iii, 45.

[2] Add. MSS 37992, fos. 30, 32, 35; Nottingham's Letter Book at HMC, fo. 203; *HMC Portland*, III, 529.

now ready to enter a Defensive Alliance with England, the United Provinces and Spain, provided that Methuen was prepared to treat of the measures required for his protection in the war that would inevitably follow. Methuen assured the king that King William would do all things necessary for the safety of Portugal, and commissioners were appointed to confer with him in secret. News now came by a Hamburg ship that Rooke had parted from the main fleet and was sailing southwards from Finistère. Methuen succeeded in hiring a Portuguese caravel to take a message to Rooke and he reported his audience with the king by every possible route, to Nottingham, and to Portland in Holland. But the caravel failed to meet Rooke and was driven into Viana and all the dispatches were delayed; the letter to Portland did not reach him until August.[1]

Rooke had taken a course far out to sea in order to avoid the French and with a following wind he had sailed too fast to have any chance of sending to Lisbon for news. He sent the *Lark* to Lagos instead, but before she returned he was able to take a French fireship and interrogate the officers. They were loyal and clever, and led Rooke to believe that Tourville was in the neighbourhood, but that he only had fifteen ships with him and had not joined D'Estrées. Later two Portuguese on a small boat selling fruit and vegetables were captured and told the truth about Tourville, but Captain Martin formed the impression that they were lying and had been put up to tell this story by the French. There were few French ships in Lagos itself, when Rooke arrived, but they cut their anchors and fled under the impression that the allied main fleet was approaching. Rooke concluded that he only had to face a small squadron, which he had heard had left Brest under Admiral Gabarat, and it was only after he had put to sea again and sighted the French fleet, that he realised the truth. He was in no position either to engage the enemy or to protect his

[1] Claudio de Chaby, *Synopse dos decretos remitidos ao Extincto Concelho de Guerra* (Lisboa, 1872), III, 250–1; S.P. 89/17, Methuen to Nottingham, 13 June, 24 June, and to Portland, 24 June 1693.

convoy; only two Dutch ships engaged; the remainder scattered towards the Straits or Madeira. Many of the merchants were sunk or driven ashore; others took refuge along the Spanish or Portuguese coasts.[1]

Methuen heard the news on 4 July and took immediate steps to raise money on his own credit, in order to save as many seamen, ships and goods as possible. Forty ships were believed to be lost; later it was found that the French had taken twenty-five ships, including two Dutch men-of-war, while the survivors included forty-eight ships, scattered along the coast from Cadiz to the Algarve. Half of them were English and of the rest fourteen were Dutch, six Hamburgers, three Danish, and one a Swede.

King Pedro gave strict orders to prevent the misappropriation of goods and the plundering of ships cast ashore, authorising search to be made for stolen goods in gentlemen's houses, and even in convents and churches. Methuen saved what he could, and the Portuguese continued the mobilisation of their army and the refitting of their ships. In November King Pedro spoke of calling the Cortes and of requesting them to vote a 10 per cent land tax to raise a million pieces of eight for defence.[2]

Nottingham on hearing the news told King William that he had never written to him before with so sorrowful a heart. The king was equally distressed but hoped that the Channel fleet would pursue the enemy. There was a natural tendency to look for a scapegoat. Methuen's dispatches were delayed and he was blamed for not having done enough to warn Rooke. However, when they finally arrived, it was appreciated that he had taken every possible step and he was given credit for it. Methuen on his side blamed Rooke for remaining so far out at sea that he lost contact and never heard that Tourville had left Brest on 26 May, though the

[1] *HMC H. of Lords*, I, NS, 200–3, 215–16.
[2] S.P. 89/17, Methuen to Nottingham, 15, 26 July 1693; Nottingham's Letter Book at HMC, fo. 213; Add. MSS 37992, fos. 11, 19, 21, 35–7.

news had long been generally known. He remarked, 'This conduct rendered vain all ye diligence both of Dutch and myself could use, which I may say without vanity was very great.'[1]

Rooke had been merely unlucky, but the Admiralty had been negligent and the admirals perhaps something worse. Delaval and Killigrew were suspected of Jacobitism, and Marlborough was believed to have warned the French about the proposed attack on Brest. It was also a victory for the French intelligence, which had persuaded the allies that Tourville would join D'Estrées at Brest and not at Lagos. The opposite might have happened, for Tourville could never be sure that he would not be confronted in the Straits by the combined forces of the allied fleet, but the importance of having reliable information and rapid means to communicate it was made manifest. To prevent such accidents in future Methuen was ordered to station agents in Gibraltar and the Algarve to report on enemy naval movements. He repeatedly asked to be given a yacht at Lisbon to stand by for urgent messages to the fleet, but his request was turned down, apparently by King William himself on grounds of economy.[2]

In due course the full powers for which Methuen had asked were sent to him and to Woolfsen the Dutch Resident, and fresh instructions to Stanhope in Madrid. Nottingham warmly approved Methuen's talks with the king and said he need have no fear of having exceeded his instructions in so good a cause. In The Hague Lord Dursley found de Sousa Pacheco, the Portuguese minister, well disposed, and believed he could be taken seriously, as he was a great friend of Mendo de Foios, the Portuguese secretary of state.[3]

After the disaster to Rooke Methuen did not venture to approach the king again until 3 October, when the subject was

[1] S.P. 89/17, Methuen to Trenchard, 25 July, and to Nottingham, 8 Aug. 1693; S.P. 104/196, fo. 48.
[2] S.P. 104/196, fos. 67, 73.
[3] S.P. 84/222, Dursley to Nottingham, fo. 333; Add. MSS 37922, fos. 21-2, Blathwayt to Nottingham; S.P. 104/196, fos. 41, 55, 56.

referred to the Council of State. Methuen feared that the French would now soon hear of the negotiation and launch a counter-attack. Meanwhile the Portuguese were in a distinctly cooler frame of mind. The French had behaved very correctly while they were in Portuguese waters, and had shown no aggressive intentions. Furthermore, the French ambassador told King Pedro that peace was imminent and was on the point of being concluded with the emperor. Methuen had difficulty in persuading the king that the allies were determined to carry on with the war, and his co-operation with the Spanish envoy was made difficult by the fact that he was instructed to work for an Offensive rather than for a Defensive Alliance. It was becoming clear that not much could be expected until the allies avenged the Smyrna fleet disaster. The Spanish representatives were clamouring for a fleet to be sent to the Mediterranean and so were the English public. King Pedro took Methuen to task for the allied failures and for 'the Fleet, which was promised the Spaniard for Christmas, but did not sail until June, a month after the French were ready'.[1]

Nevertheless, in November the Council of State, including even Cadaval, were inclined to favour an alliance, and the Spanish minister offered to pay for Portuguese help. However, it soon transpired from conversations in London and The Hague that Spain expected the allies to refund the cost. He also embarrassed Methuen by saying that he had asked for authorisation to offer a suitable *douceur* of £2,000 to two of the King's Council, and to two of the king's favourites, and they must act quickly, if they were to anticipate the French. Methuen did not see how such a charge could ever be met in a parliamentary vote, an attitude which is interesting in view of the accusations of bribery which were made against him in later years.[2]

---

[1] S.P. 89/17, Methuen to Nottingham, 3, 21, 31 Oct. 1693; S.P. 84/222/336, Dursley to Trenchard.
[2] S.P. 89/17, Methuen to Nottingham, 13, 28 Nov. 1693.

King William was pressing tirelessly for the whole fleet to be sent to Cadiz and for supplies to be made ready at Lisbon and Cadiz. Methuen was authorised to facilitate the clearance to King Pedro of ships' masts and naval stores from Hamburg and Sweden. But the difficulties were too great. The fleet cruised off Brest in the early autumn in the hope of intercepting Tourville, but the latter remained in the Mediterranean until mid-November, when he returned safely to Brest without incident. The most that could be done was to send the sixteen ships required by the convention with Spain to the Straits in December. This proved disastrous. It was as much as Admiral Wheeler could do to cope with the cruisers and privateers in the Mediterranean, which the French left after their fleets had returned to port. The Spanish treasure fleet returned safely to Cadiz but Admiral Wheeler did not take shelter in a Spanish port, and in February he lost his flagship and his own life in a storm together with two more ships and eleven merchant vessels with 800 lives. The men-of-war returned to England and the surviving merchant ships took refuge in neighbouring ports.[1]

Methuen had only general assurances to offer and it is not surprising that the negotiations now hung fire, in spite of the fact that the Councillors of State were rather more inclined to favour entering the alliance than they were to be in 1702 and 1703. King Pedro insisted that the cost of any Portuguese troops used in Spain should be met by the allies and that in case of war a squadron must be sent to winter in Lisbon. Methuen tried to put a good face on it by pointing out to the king that the House of Commons had passed a large vote of supply for the navy, but he had nothing specific to offer and the Council of State decided that the question of the alliance should be left pending until the reorganisation of the Portuguese defence forces was complete. King Pedro told Methuen that he did not believe Spain was interested any longer

[1] Add. MSS 37992, fos. 39/44, Blathwayt to Trenchard; Ehrman, *op. cit.* p. 510; S.P. 89/17, Methuen to Trenchard, 21 March 1694.

in an alliance and he thought there would soon be peace. By February he was again convinced that the war would continue and was talking of intervening in Catalonia, but his Council of State pointed out the expense would be beyond his means. Methuen still felt that the deadlock was due more to 'the natural creeping pace of the government' than to any lack of good will, and he made some progress in minor matters. He obtained an assurance that French privateers would not be allowed to sail from Lisbon without giving due notice and he stopped to some extent the French trade in corn. But he could do nothing towards the alliance or the settlement of the question of ships' passports. Meanwhile no convoy came from England to bring the cloth and take the wine, with the result that much of the vintage was shipped in foreign or Portuguese vessels at excessive freights.[1]

King William was eager to instigate an attack on Brest, before Tourville sailed in the spring, but he failed to do so. A reconnaissance in May proved futile and on 1 June a serious attack on Brest with a landing force of 7,000 men was repulsed. The only good news was that the remainder of the Smyrna fleet sheltering in the Straits was given protection by the arrival of a squadron under Admiral Neville on its way to the West Indies, and succeeded in making its way home safely.

The French were now advancing in Catalonia and threatening to attack Barcelona. Methuen took the opportunity to parry King Pedro's criticisms by pointing out that he was now in a position to send more troops to Catalonia than even France could spare, but the king refused to be drawn. However, he assured Methuen that when the allied fleet did come, it could be sure of a welcome in Lisbon. Methuen continued to be optimistic, but he confessed that the Portuguese were most irresolute and he could not understand the failure of the allies to send their fleet to relieve Spain. He was also obliged to admit that the vaunted Portuguese

[1] S.P. 89/17, Methuen to Trenchard, 26 Dec. 1693, 20 Feb. 1694; S.P. 100/37, fo. 31, Hedges to Portuguese minister.

mobilisation was largely show. Funds were running low and a shortage of corn had slowed down the programme and stopped the raising of a cavalry regiment in the Algarve. So there would be no Portuguese supplies available if the fleet came to Lisbon.[1]

In England the power of the extreme Tories to obstruct was being overcome. Sir John Houblon, the banker and city merchant, was made a commissioner of Admiralty, and the duke of Shrewsbury became secretary of state. The long-promised fleet at last set sail under the command of Admiral Russell and Admiral Rooke and on 1 July passed the Straits. Methuen's friend William Browne made 'a noble treat in honour of the news, at which the company drank plentifully', and there was joy in the Factory. But Methuen's youngest son Henry, and a son of Sir John Houblon, were tempted by the cool of the evening to explore the streets of Lisbon, and became involved in a brawl with the servants of a Portuguese nobleman and were killed.[2]

Russell was held up by a 'Levante' wind and could not reach Barcelona until August. The French had taken Gerona, but Russell's approach was enough to stop their advance and to make D'Estrées withdraw his squadron towards Toulon. Russell was unable to do more than make a demonstration. He was already short of provisions and autumn was approaching. He had therefore to make up his mind to return at once, before the autumn gales made it difficult, or to winter in the south. King William pressed hard for the latter, and although the Admiralty were very reluctant, they agreed to send out the necessary stores and to order Russell, though not so explicitly as the king desired, to winter abroad.[3]

The Spaniards did not relish the idea of a foreign force at Cadiz,

[1] S.P. 89/17, Methuen to Trenchard, 29 May, 10, 26 June 1694; Chaby, *op. cit.*, III, 260.
[2] Luttrell, *Brief Encounter*, III, 362; MS at Althorp, Methuen to Halifax, 7 Aug. 1694; S.P. 94/73, Stanhope to Trenchard, fo. 289.
[3] Ehrman, *op. cit.* pp. 522, 577; Add. MSS 37992, fos. 58–62, Blathwayt to Trenchard and Russell.

and recommended the use of Port Mahon, which was a better base for the defence of Catalonia. They promised to send supplies from Majorca and carpenters and workmen from Barcelona. Port Mahon had a much better harbour than Cadiz, which only had a roadstead exposed to the Atlantic and a small inner harbour. William Aglionby had inspected Port Mahon in the previous August, and Stanhope reported that it was preferable and that Cadiz did not have the facilities attributed to it by his Dutch colleague Schonenberg. However, Cadiz commanded the Straits and was the base of Spanish overseas trade. From the Admiralty point of view it was nearer and easier to supply. Cadiz was chosen. Although the Admiralty hated to keep their large ships abroad in winter and found it hard to supply them throughout the year even in home ports, they rose to the occasion. By the spring the Mediterranean worm had damaged many ships, but some had been careened and adequate supplies had been sent with a narrow margin. The Spaniards had promised a subvention of 80,000 crowns and to supply stores, but their promises were unkept, and they became increasingly obstructive.[1]

Admiral Russell did not succeed in bringing the French fleet to action, but he halted for the time being the French advance in Catalonia, and dominated the Mediterranean, including the Barbary pirates. The effect of his fleet in Portugal was disappointing. French privateers still infested the coast and in October as many as thirteen were reported in the Tagus. The English navy had no ships to spare to protect Portugal, or at times even the Channel and the Isle of Wight, from individual privateers.[2] Now that the immediate threat of war was removed King Pedro reverted to his ambition to be a mediator. In 1692 it had been said that 'the King of Portugal thought himself ye only Prince that had been a perfect Neuter in the war, and therefore might with

---

[1] Add. MSS 37992, fos. 60–1, 90; Ehrman, *op. cit.* pp. 826 ff.; *HMC H. of Lords*, I, NS, 109. Besides Port Mahon the Spaniards recommended Cartagena and Porto Longone as bases.

[2] For complaints of privateers in the Channel, see S.P. 32/5, fos. 158–9.

most reason offer his mediation to all ye Parties'. Sweden offered to mediate in 1690 and Denmark made an offer; Venice thought of it and the Pope made a regular habit of peace offers. King William opposed mediation as contrary to his war aims. In the end the good offices of Sweden were accepted but meanwhile some voices had been raised in favour of Portugal. The Abbé d'Estrées had orders not to oppose in Lisbon King Pedro's mediation or the appointment of Portuguese ambassadors in Paris and The Hague for the purpose. In 1695 a correspondent wrote to His Majesty's minister at Vienna: 'The King of Portugal is solicited to take steps to interpose his mediation. This Prince is less distrusted by France than any of those, who would engage in this affair. It is thought that an inclination towards the Allies may be detected in the others or at least, that they may show a dislike to favour the pretension of France.'[1]

D'Estrées had also been empowered to offer King Pedro a treaty for the defence of Spain with guarantees of Portuguese independence and the promise of concessions in Galicia, Estremadura and America. Nothing came of this, but in 1694 new Portuguese ambassadors were appointed to Paris and Vienna to bring up the question of mediation and there was talk of raising the Legations in Paris and London to the rank of Embassy for the same purpose.[2]

Methuen reported that King Pedro had little confidence that his mediation would be accepted and scarcely had the courage to make a formal offer. Nevertheless, in a private letter to Lord Halifax he was more hopeful and said that if King Pedro's mediation was accepted he might hope to take part in some great negotiation. King Pedro may have hoped for support from Vienna. He got none from King William, who in November 1695 finally instructed Methuen to discourage the idea. In April 1694

[1] Methuen to Nottingham and Trenchard, 26 July 1692, 2, 30 Oct. 1694; S.P. 32/5, fos. 148–9 for complaints of French privateers; S. P. Oakley, London thesis 1961, pp. 149–323.
[2] Recueil, III, 202.

Methuen had asked for leave in order to attend to his duties in the House of Commons; this was granted in October and clearly no important diplomatic activity in Portugal was expected.

Methuen sailed in December leaving his twenty-two-year-old son Paul in charge. Portugal relapsed into her usual tranquillity, and as Paul observed it was easier in Lisbon to have news of Brazil and the Indies than of Europe.[1]

No doubt this period of quiet owed much to the presence of Admiral Russell in the Mediterranean. As a Privy Councillor and a lord of the Admiralty he had direct contact with the Cabinet, and his flagship became a sort of senior embassy. His influence was felt as far as Turkey, but his main objectives, to engage the French fleet and to attack Toulon, were not achieved. In 1695 he landed a force in Catalonia in an attempt to help the mixed Spanish-Imperial force fighting under the command of Prince George of Hesse-Darmstadt and to relieve the siege of Palamos. He also reconnoitred Toulon but was driven away by a gale. His ships needed refitting and he was obliged to send home seven of the largest so that he was no longer strong enough to confront the French, even if the opportunity arose. A reinforcement led by Rooke was on its way, but he re-embarked his troops and sailed for England before it arrived. Rooke was strong enough to keep control of the Straits, but not to take the offensive, and in Catalonia Hesse was obliged to retire.[2]

The Portuguese remained friendly but inert. In Spain relations with the allies deteriorated rapidly. In September 1695 the Dutch minister Schonenberg was implicated in customs offences committed by two Dutch merchants named Moll, and was told to leave the Court. Count Auersperg, the Imperial ambassador, tried to mediate in London, but in defending Schonenberg King William broke off relations with the Spanish ambassador, and

[1] S.P. 89/17, Methuen to Trenchard and Paul Methuen to Vernon, 3 Apr., 29 May, 21 Sept., 2, 30 Oct., 24 Nov. 1694 and 14 June 1695; MS at Althorp, Methuen to Halifax, 21 Sept., 2 Oct. 1694.
[2] Ehrman, *op. cit.* pp. 548–51; S.P. 94/74, fos. 4–8.

in Madrid Stanhope was also banned the Court and remained ignored for some months.[1]

After Russell's departure the Spaniards asked the Dutch to leave a squadron in return for a subsidy, but this overture came to nothing. They had resented Russell's high-handed ways and were at first civil to Rooke, but they neglected the terms of the Naval Convention, and Stanhope was not helped to urge its enforcement by the failure of London to provide him with a copy. As soon as he procured one, he conveyed a requisition for stores to the Spanish ministers by backstairs ways, but Rooke made no bones about his dislike of wintering abroad and sailed home in the spring of 1696 with the first favourable wind, narrowly missing an encounter with the French fleet on the way.

Methuen said that the situation of the fleet in the Mediterranean had shown the greatness of England more than any other thing that ever we undertook. Nevertheless, the positive effects in Portugal had been disappointing. King Pedro's own relations with Spain were for a time rather good. He lent 1,000 men to defend Ceuta in Morocco against the Turks and in July 1696 the Portuguese Guinea or Cacheo Company reached an agreement with the Spanish Council of the Indies to share in the *asiento* or slave trade. English merchants under one Jeffreys failed to secure a similar agreement in Madrid, but Portugal could not handle all her African trade, and chartered English ships to carry some of it.[2]

On return to Lisbon in June 1695 Methuen found that the currency crisis in England was causing a serious loss of trade. The value of the milreis rose from about 5s. 10d. to a record figure of 7s. 6d. Rumours encouraged by the French ambassador and by the reports from London of the Portuguese minister, the Visconde de Arcada, spoke of an imminent Jacobite invasion. Methuen pro-

[1] S.P. 94/74, fos. 10, 14, 47, 69. O. Klopp, *Der Fall des Hauses Stuart*, 18 vols., 1875–88, VII, 141. *Lexington Papers*, ed. H. Manners Sutton (1851), pp. 144, 157.

[2] S.P. 94/74, fos. 68, 72, 84, 90, 92, 95; MS at Althorp, Rooke to Halifax, 2 Oct., 30 Dec. 1695; S.P. 89/17, Methuen and Paul Methuen to Vernon, 20 Sept., 5 Nov. 1695, 28 May, 23 Aug. 1696; S.P. 103/66 has a copy of the *asiento* agreement. See also above, ch. 2, p. 18.

tested and was also able to be the first to give the news that a plot to assassinate King William had been foiled. King Pedro remained cordial and was still engaged in a dispute with the French, about the ships they had confiscated.[1]

After the Toulon fleet returned to Brest in the spring there was an unprecedented concentration of naval forces and great expectation of a naval battle. This did not materialise and the only naval event was a successful attack by the privateer *Jean Bart* on the Dutch Baltic fleet. It was announced that Admiral Shovell was preparing a fleet for the Mediterranean and relations with Spain showed a temporary improvement. The duke of Shrewsbury was even able to arrange directly with the governor general of Andalusia the supply of 1,225 tons of wine and 134 tons of oil for Shovell's 6,461 men. Shovell was preparing all the autumn and persuaded the Admiralty to allow him to take as his flagship *The Queen*, a new first-rater which was thought to be too big to hazard so far, but then he was detained to keep a watch over Brest and he never reached the Mediterranean.[2]

In April Methuen heard that he was to come home to take up an appointment as commissioner of trade. This commission was set up to meet the merchants' complaints and its constitution was discussed at length in the House of Commons. The Opposition favoured a Council of Trade to be elected by London and perhaps some provincial merchants, but the Government disliked the idea of an outside body being given power to overrule the executive in such matters as Admiralty decisions about convoys. However, in order to satisfy criticism they agreed to the appointment by Parliament in May 1696 of a Commission of Trade of fourteen members, who were mostly ministers or high officials but included one merchant. The questions with which the Commission

---

[1] S.P. 89/17, Methuen to Vernon, 24, 29 Nov., 27 Dec. 1695, 31 March, 17 Apr., 26 May, 7 July 1696.
[2] Schomberg, *Naval Chronology* (1802), I, 98; Ehrman, *op. cit.* p. 610; S.P. 94/74, fo. 98; S.P. 104/196, fo. 126; *Cal. of S.P.* (1696), p. 360; Burchett, *Naval Transactions* (1720), pp. 550–1.

65

was likely to deal were of interest to Methuen. They concerned obstacles to trade caused by currency problems, failures to provide convoys, commercial policy in general, and the possibility of procuring naval stores from the American dominions rather than from the Baltic. All parties agreed that a solution of these problems was desirable, but each one tried to use them for its own political ends. Methuen therefore was reluctant to commit himself, for he had doubts about the future of the Commission and feared the risks of becoming involved in its politics. Colbatch attributed his unwillingness to leave Lisbon to simple reluctance to part from Sarah Earle but Methuen also gave some good official reasons to Shrewsbury. He said he doubted his qualifications to be a commissioner and the future of the office at the hands of Parliament. He also doubted whether he ought to leave Portugal, for the last two years of negotiation had brought him very near to the king, so that any successor, though personally better qualified, would find it hard to pick up the threads. Upon learning of Methuen's views King William suspended the appointment of a new minister to Lisbon, but ordered Methuen to be back in England for the autumn session of Parliament. Lisbon had now come to be considered a desirable post and there were several aspirants, including a couple of Worcestershire parliament men and Matthew Prior. The latter was much disgusted when Vernon told him that Methuen planned to leave his son as 'curate', and grumbled that 'the Envoyship was entailed for Methwyn to succeed Methwyn, till Shiloath comes'. In fact, in spite of his youth, Paul Methuen was given the post. He had won the liking of King Pedro and of the Portuguese nobles. His credentials described him as having been brought up in the art of negotiation and almost educated in King Pedro's royal court, and therefore deemed a not unworthy successor to his father. This proved to be the case.[1]

[1] For the Council of Trade see R. M. Lees in *English Historical Review*, no. 54 (Jan.–Oct. 1939); *HMC Portland*, III, 576–7, 588 and *Bath*, III, 81, 113; S.P. 89/17, Methuen to

The office of commissioner of trade was to turn, as Methuen suspected, into a backwater, but he did not hold it for long, though he was often to be consulted on trade matters. It happened that a new lord chancellor was required for Ireland, preferably a Whig but a good government man. Soon after his return to England Methuen attracted the favourable attention of James Vernon by his effective speeches on behalf of the government in the debate on the Act of Attainder of Sir John Fenwick. Vernon put up Methuen's name for the post of lord chancellor, and though he was inclined to have second thoughts, when Methuen pressed for the further favour of the Lisbon appointment for his son and Lord Somers had doubts about Methuen's qualifications, the appointment was approved by Lord Sunderland and the duke of Shrewsbury.[1]

Methuen's work in Ireland was important and the more so as the earl of Galway leant heavily upon his help. As lord chancellor he had a number of legal duties, but he was also Speaker of the Irish House of Lords and his main task was to manage the Irish Parliament, and to help the lord justices in the general administration. It might have been expected that the guidance of the Irish Parliament would not have been too difficult, in so much as the government had greater power and patronage than in England, and the parliament consisted of Protestants of English descent to the exclusion of Catholics and Nonconformists. Methuen at first thought it would be easy, but the interests of true Irishmen and English Irishmen had already been blended since 1690 by many transfers of property, so that the distinction between former supporters of King James and of King William was no longer clear. Methuen soon found that the Irish Parliament was tenacious of its rights and of its independence and that in most questions the

---

Shrewsbury, 9 June, 23 July 1696, and to Vernon, 17 Sept., 12 Oct. 1696; MS at Reigate Town Hall, Rushout to Lord Somers, 7 July 1696; Add. MSS 37992, fo. 129; S.P. 104/196, fo. 131.
[1] *Vernon Letters*, 'Letters illustrative of the reign of William III', I, 101, 481; T. B. Howell, *State Trials* (1812), XIII, 711-17.

Anglo-Irish defended Irish interests and resisted the claim of the English Parliament to control their deliberations with as much fervour as if they had been Catholics and Celts.

Methuen had a difficult course to steer, for he had to assist the lord justices to frame a legislative programme which would be acceptable in London and in the Irish Parliament. He could bring considerable pressure to bear, and the Irish were in a better position to obstruct rather than positively to reject, but incessant lobbying was necessary to pilot controversial measures through both houses. Methuen took infinite pains to court both Lords and Commons and to the surprise of James Vernon undertook a strenuous course of entertainment, which was contrary to his careful and homekeeping nature. The result was that he soon became a martyr to disabling fits of gout, which continued to afflict him throughout his remaining years.

On the whole Methuen succeeded in putting through the legislative programme for the session of 1697. He spent some months in England, until the Irish Parliament met again in the autumn of 1698, and was active in the House of Commons. There were rumours that he was being considered for promotion to be secretary of state or lord chancellor, but these soon passed when the political tide set against him. His patron the duke of Shrewsbury, who had been spoken of for lord lieutenant in Ireland, faded out of office, and he incurred the displeasure of Lord Somers. He was even near at one moment to falling out with Lord Sunderland. At the same time his handling of Irish matters failed to please either Whigs or Tories. In his efforts to do what was required of him he was obliged to study the Irish point of view and to some extent to appreciate it. His chancellorship marked a further stage in the subordination of the Irish Parliament, but he did not move fast enough to satisfy the English House of Commons. At the end of 1698 he was in danger of losing office, but King William himself was satisfied with him and continued to support him, though ultimately in deference to the outcry against the employment of aliens he was obliged to remove the earl of Galway from Dublin. When both parties were attacking Methuen and a ribald ballad in the form of *Lillibullero* was being sung against him in the streets, the king particularly assured Galway that Methuen still enjoyed his confidence. He wrote:

I am well satisfied with the Chancellor of Ireland. At his first coming here to the Parliament he committed a great oversight, which got him many enemies, and all the ministry here are much incensed against him, as well as the Whig Party. But in Ireland it is just the contrary; it is the Tories; so he will find it hard to behave in such a manner, as not to be involved in difficulties. If bad success attends you in parliament, it is certain that here blame will be laid upon him. I thought it necessary to inform you of the circumstances, that you may take your measures accordingly.

Again in October the king wrote from Holland that Ireland was too far away for him to give any precise orders and there were many in England who wished for the coming Irish session to be a failure, but it was important that it should be a success, and particularly that provision should be obtained for the upkeep of his troops in Ireland, though he feared the hatred for Methuen would be a great obstacle.[1]

Methuen was unable to prevent the ultimate disbandment of King William's troops or to save the forfeited estates, which the king had given to his friends, from being reclaimed by Parliament, but he succeeded in keeping up the Huguenot regiments in Ireland for a while, and when the Irish Parliament adjourned on 26 January 1699 it had passed the money bills submitted to it, and had provided sufficient funds to enable the Irish government to carry on until the end of the reign without the need for any further parliamentary session. Methuen was not superseded and in spite of the many criticisms of him, the disappearance of Whig friends

---

[1] Rev. D. C. A. Agnew, *Life of Henri Massue de Ruvigny, Earl of Galway* (Edinburgh, 1864), pp. 82 ff. The ballad about Methuen is attached in Appendix 1. Sources for Methuen's lord chancellorship are *Cal. of S.P.* (1697–1701); *HMC. Buccleuch*, II, ii; *Vernon Letters*. See also H. F. Kearney in *Economic History Review*, ser. 2, II, 487–96, and Sir G. N. Clark in *Economic History Review*, ser. 2, IX, 251.

from office, and the loss for one session of his parliamentary seat at Devizes, he emerged comparatively unscathed with a reputation as an expert on foreign affairs and commercial questions, and as a good government rather than a party man.

This interlude in Ireland did not part Methuen altogether from Portuguese affairs. Paul Methuen sent him copies of his dispatches, and in 1700, when Paul was in difficulties, Methuen intervened on his behalf and was given permission to write directly to Mendo de Foios, the Portuguese secretary of state. He seems to have used the opportunity to correspond on other subjects, besides that of Paul, and kept in touch with the Portuguese minister in London, Da Cunha, and early in 1702 discussed with him the possibility of a new treaty of alliance.[1]

Although Ireland was on the periphery of Europe, Irish questions occasionally came up in international affairs. The treatment of Catholics there was of general interest and the French and the Imperial ambassadors sometimes brought up the subject and suggested that guarantees favouring Irish Catholics might be exchanged for concessions to Huguenots and Hungarian Protestants.[2] There were also trade links. Ireland exported corn and butter to Portugal, and Methuen tried to open a market for Irish linen there. This was of some importance to Irish politics, for the English ministers had hoped to conciliate Ireland by giving encouragement to the linen trade in compensation for the restrictions they were imposing on the export of Irish cloth. Unfortunately the Irish Parliament took little interest in the linen trade, which was largely in the hands of Huguenot immigrants or Ulster Protestants, and to the dismay of Whitehall rejected the bill submitted to them. On the other hand they passed the bill to restrict the Irish cloth trade, which was imposed upon them in deference to the clamours of the clothiers of England against foreign and Irish competition.

[1] L. T. de Sampayo, O Instituto, LXXVI (Coimbra, 1928), 6.
[2] Klopp, op. cit. VIII, 93, 121–2, 203.

Methuen's lord chancellorship throws a fuller light on his talents and weaknesses than the documents available about his Portuguese missions and contains one or two common themes. Some of his personal relationships in Ireland influenced his later career. In a humble way he was a rival to the great and wealthy duke of Ormonde, leader of the Opposition. Ormonde did not relish Methuen and his appointment to be commander in chief of the Cadiz expedition was no help to Methuen in Portugal. On the other hand Methuen worked in close and friendly co-operation with the earl of Galway, who was lord justice from 1697 to February 1701, and when Galway was appointed in July 1704 to command the English forces in Portugal, he proved a firm friend and collaborator of Methuen's.

CHAPTER 4

PAUL METHUEN, MINISTER AT
LISBON, 1697–1702

PAUL METHUEN returned from Italy in time to relieve his father, who sailed home in October. His instructions were largely of a general nature, such as were repeated from minister to minister. They were not so explicit, for instance, as those of his new French colleague De Rouillé. He was told to protect trade, 'yett for our honour as your own You must not engage yourself in any complaint, which may raise clamour without justifiable cause or any legal proof, but only such as may deserve the interposition of our name'. He was enjoined to protect 'the privileges of our religion, but these would better be preserved, if those who enjoyed the benefits thereof behaved with modesty and prudence', and to encourage the chaplain and attend divine service. He was particularly to co-operate with his Dutch colleague and to tell the king of Portugal 'how much we are pressed with the continual complaints of our subjects, to whom a great sum of money has long been due from that Crowne by virtue of the Treaty of Peace'.[1]

The duke of Shrewsbury wrote a personal letter saying:

Upon my coming to Town, I took the first opportunity of getting your credentials, and instructions and other despatches signed and have put them in your father's hands to be sent to you. It remains only therefore to acquaint you with the particular satisfaction I have to find your father preferred to a post he so well deserved and that you succeed him at that Court, where I don't doubt, but you will tread in his steps and recommend yourself by it.[2]

Paul's entry into the diplomatic service at the age of 24 with the rank of a head of mission may have caused jealousy, but few

[1] S.P. 104/196, instructions dated 8 March 1697.   [2] S.P. 104/196, 6 March 1697.

newly appointed envoys can have received a kinder introduction from their secretary of state.

The war was now drawing to a close, and apart from the alarms caused by the recurrent crises in the health of the king of Spain, affairs in Portugal were quiet. For some months Paul had little to report except the departure of the king for his annual holiday at Salvatierra and the passing through Lisbon of a Dutch squadron. At the end of the year he celebrated the Peace of Ryswick, entertaining the diplomatic corps including De Rouillé, the French ambassador, the Portuguese ministers and, at two other parties, Queen Catherine's household, and the consul and Factory.[1]

Although there was peace the question of the Spanish Succession created a serious threat of a new war. In Madrid the imperialist party still prevailed and it was believed that the emperor's younger son the Archduke Charles would be declared the king of Spain's heir.[2] De Rouillé was instructed to stress the danger to Portugal of the Habsburg candidature and the advantage to her of friendship with France, but to assume an aloof attitude, as there was little danger of the Portuguese ending the long period of peace they had enjoyed. Back in London Methuen thought otherwise and told James Vernon that the Portuguese would react vigorously and probably intervene in the spring against the French. The Portuguese tried to give that impression and King Pedro had concerted a plan with the count of Oropesa to send Portuguese troops, who would be employed as mercenaries and replace the German troops in Catalonia.[3] After De Rouillé had reported Portuguese military preparations he was told to express surprise and to propose an offensive and defensive alliance, which would give Portugal all the defence she needed. King Pedro informed Paul Methuen that he had refused the French offer

---

[1] *Cal. of S.P.* (1698), p. 234.
[2] Count F. B. von Harrach, 'Tagebuch', *Arch. für Öst. Gesch.* 48, ed. A. Gaedeke (Wien, 1872). A. Legrelle, *La Diplomatie Française et la Succession d'Espagne* (1889–94), II, 425; *Recueil des Instructions aux Ambassadeurs de France*, ed. Vicompte de Caux de St-Aymour (1885), III, 215.   [3] *Vernon Letters*, I, 204; Legrelle, *op. cit.* II, 415.

politely but had insisted that the troops he had raised were necessary for his defence. The Cortes had met recently for the formal purpose of according formal recognition to King Pedro's eldest son Prince John as heir to the throne, but had also discussed questions of supply. This was the result of a message from the king drawing their attention to the fact that the royal revenues, encumbered with pensions as they were, were insufficient to put the country into a proper posture of defence. A sum of 600,000 cruzados was required and they were asked to consider how this sum could be raised with the least grievance to the king's subjects.[1]

King Pedro was probably inspired by the example of England. He followed the proceedings of Parliament with interest and in February 1694 had been amazed at the generosity of the sum of £5,000,000 voted for defence. As Methuen remarked, it sounded even more in cruzados. Latterly James Vernon had taken to sending regular newsletters from London. John Methuen as a member of Parliament was interested to have them, and both he and Paul found these letters useful for giving regular news to the king.[2] The Portuguese minister Luis da Cunha also used to keep King Pedro posted with parliamentary news. He took a cynical view of parliamentary proceedings, but he saw that Parliament could be managed and told the king that the only way in which King William could govern was by playing off the Lords against the Commons.[3] King Pedro saw that Parliament was a good means for raising money and that its good will was necessary for the Crown. He may have thought that he could play off the Portuguese nobles against the Commons and the Church. He owed much to the nobles for the help they had given him in earlier days, but he had curbed their pretensions and he was not popular with them. They were not formidable individually but they could still

---

[1] S.P. 89/17, Paul Methuen to Vernon, 13 May 1698. H. V. Livermore, *History of Portugal* (1947), p. 340, and E. Prestage, *The Royal Power and the Cortes in Portugal* (Watford, 1927), p. 26, ignore this incident.

[2] MS at Althorp, Methuen to Halifax, 6 Feb. 1694; S.P. 89/17, Paul Methuen to Vernon, 7 Jan. 1697.

[3] Add. MSS 20817, fo. 209.

be obstructive. The Commons counted for little in Portugal except for vestiges of medieval liberties in the Senate of Lisbon and the city of Oporto.[1] The Church, on the other hand, which constituted a third estate in the Cortes, was wealthy and powerful. Its members were drawn from all classes and formed a link between nobles and commons. They were more in touch with public opinion than the nobles and sometimes took sides with the Commons.

The experiences of King William with Parliament in the years following the Treaty of Ryswick were not encouraging and may have dissuaded the king from persisting in his efforts with the Cortes, but the experiment was not entirely fruitless and went on for some time. The decree inspired by the war scare of 1693 for the raising of 20,000 foot and 4,000 horse had only partially been carried out. There had been a shortage of corn, and the sense of urgency diminished whenever the king of Spain's health took a better turn. However, a fresh alarm at the end of 1696 provoked another attempt to bring the army up to its full establishment, and although the excitement died down when the king recovered, the Cortes discussed ways and means in the autumn of 1697. They reached no decision but they met again before Easter, and were then galvanised by another relapse of the king into passing a decree to raise new levies. The Church and the Commons favoured a new excise duty on tobacco, but this proposal was blocked by the nobles led by the duke of Cadaval. However, it was agreed that 600,000 cruzados should be raised to provide two regiments of infantry and five troops of cavalry, and ultimately the duty on tobacco was also agreed, but only to begin in 1699. The supply of the money was held up by a dispute regarding the proportion to be paid by each estate, as the nobles protested that they could not afford so much as the Commons or the Church. But finally the nobles consented to pay an equal share with the other two estates and on 7 June an army decree supplemented the measures for

[1] Oporto, for instance, still raised and paid for its own regiment (Chaby, *Synopse dos decretos remetidos ao Extincto Conselho de Guerra*, 1872, III, 277-9).

mobilisation. Allusion was made to the fact that the principal reason for calling the Cortes had been to provide for the defence of the realm, and the regular forces were established at 15,000 infantry and 3,500 cavalry, a rather higher figure than that fixed in the treaties of 1703. Intermittent efforts were made to achieve this programme and as early as 1694 there was a garrison of 1,000 foot and two troops of horse at Viana de Castelo near the Galician frontier and a storehouse alleged to contain arms for 20,000 men and for cavalry. Methuen several times facilitated the delivery of arms and munitions ordered in Holland, but each new effort petered out, so that upon the next alarm all was to begin again. A letter written on 9 September 1701 by the Visconde de Barbacena, military governor of the Beira, showed how difficult it was to implement the army decrees.[1] His report dealt with the militia only but was no doubt typical of the general situation. He found the local formations in Aveiro in such a miserable state that he thought the best course would be to disband them and start afresh. The captains did not know the few soldiers and the soldiers did not know their officers. No captain had a list of his men and the soldiers had not been drilled since their units were raised. Many of the officers had commissions but had not registered them; others resided outside the province or were dead. The commands of other companies were vacant. In 1697 he had given orders for a muster roll to be taken and for those incapable of service to be struck off the list and to be replaced by new enlistments of a hundred men for each unit. Lists had been prepared and submitted, but they were so badly drawn up that they were useless, for they were mere lists of names, and no steps had been taken to verify their availability and fitness. So these formations continued to exist on paper alone; the camp marshals appointed had not presented themselves and the regimental sergeant majors were incapable; one of them lived at the further end of the province at

---

[1] Chaby, op. cit. III, 288, 297, 328; S.P. 89/17, Paul Methuen to Vernon, 13 May 1698; W. Bromley, Travels through Portugal, Spain (1702), p. 21; Legrelle, op. cit. II, 414.

Lamego and was too senile to leave his house, while the other also resided some distance away and was unable to stir a step, having suffered from gout for many years. The sad roll of sergeant majors continued with the officer at Aveiro, who had been a very good man but was now so old that he was scarcely able even to go to mass, and the Coimbra sergeant major was utterly decrepit. Barbacena wished to dismiss those who from age or sickness were incapable of service and to appoint new men and place matters on a proper footing. But these defects persisted in spite of all that better officers could do.

The programme of defence begun in 1693 was never completed and the Portuguese forces were never fully armed, equipped or mustered. They were regarded cynically by the Great Powers, but their existence was noted in the chancelleries of Europe, and they played their part in causing Louis XIV and the allies to bid against each other for Portugal's friendship and to offer substantial aid and subsidies for the privilege.

A naval programme was also planned and Da Cunha said that if King Pedro kept up an efficient force of twenty ships, he would be able to reduce his army and maintain his neutrality. The navy in 1698 consisted nominally of twenty-one ships, but only a quarter of the men were seamen, and the captains, if they were gentlemen, despised their calling and were ignorant of the sea, while those of low birth could obtain little obedience. Even in England the promotion of idle younger sons over the head of the old 'tarpaulins' long hampered the progress of the navy. In Portugal the evil was far worse. In spite of Portugal's great seafaring past naval officers had the same low status as they had in Spain. Some naval construction was planned and two frigates were built in 1697 but the navy was never made strong enough to protect the coast of Portugal effectively, and could scarcely do more than provide the ships required annually to convoy the all important Brazil fleet.[1]

[1] Chaby, op. cit. III, 269, 287.

King Pedro thought of calling the Cortes to vote a new 10 per cent tax in the autumn of 1701, but he was afraid that the opposition would be violent, and he gave up the idea. He was still talking of it in 1705 but he did no more than raise an increased tax from the local Lisbon Senate and after 1698 he summoned the Cortes no more.[1] In this way he parted with the last traces of medieval liberties, but he deprived himself of a means to augment his revenues and henceforward had to make do with the income from his estates and from existing taxes. He was protected from the worst consequences of this by the increase in the revenue from Brazilian gold and the growth of the wine trade, but he could no longer hope to pay for the cost of a war without receiving foreign subsidies, and any slight hope that Portugal might gently evolve towards a more democratic form of government was eliminated.[2]

But in 1698 King Pedro still hoped to bring his army up to establishment and to be able to stand on his own feet. He was in touch with the Imperialists in Spain and planned to support the Habsburg, or possibly the Bavarian, claim to the Succession. He hoped that the French claim could be resisted and that in return for his help to the successful claimant he could obtain the concessions he desired. Nevertheless, he feared the power of France, and in May 1698, when the death of the king of Spain was generally expected, he very cautiously and confidentially suggested to Paul Methuen that the interests of England and Portugal would not be different when the king died, and he might be ready to join in measures against France. He was free from commitments to other princes and, though he could not take the lead, he believed other countries would be glad to follow King William and to take part in negotiations, which he thought could best take place at Lisbon. Then, speaking in a low voice so as not to be

[1] F. M. Mayer, 'Die Allianz Portugal's', *Zeitschrift für die Österreichischen Gymnasien* (35. Jahrgang, Wien, 1884), p. 5; Borges de Castro, *Tratados, Supplemento*, ed. J. Biker (Lisboa, 1873), x, 171.
[2] For the increase in the revenues from Brazil see C. Boxer, *The Golden Age of Brazil 1690–1750* (Cambridge, 1963), appendix II, p. 333.

overheard at this semi-public audience, he admitted that he thought there would soon be another war, an even bloodier one than the last, and one in which he could not stay neutral. He protested that he was as much moved by concern for the interest and safety of Europe as for his own country. Paul replied that he had no special instructions but King William was equally concerned for Europe. He would ask for instructions urgently and was sure that he would be authorised to make proposals agreeable to the king.[1]

King Pedro was justified in his anxiety about developments in Spain, where the French cause, with the help of a new ambassador the marquis of Harcourt, was making rapid progress. The Imperial ambassador Count Harrach was pompous and tactless and had estranged the queen of Spain, who was rumoured to be weakening in her attachment to the Habsburg cause. King Charles was believed to have made in 1696 a will confirming that of his father Philip IV, which preferred the claim of the emperor's heirs to those of the descendants of his first wife, and in November 1698 to have made a new will to the same effect, naming the six-year-old Electoral Prince of Bavaria as heir. But, according to Stanhope, the French party were gaining ground and their Embassy was so full of colonels and brigadiers as to look like an armed camp, and their fleet under Count d'Estrées had gained permission through Harcourt to use Spanish ports and in particular Cadiz. However, Louis XIV did not feel strong enough to back the Dauphin's claim, so he was inclined to support the Bavarian candidate. Nevertheless, it was publicly known that he had withdrawn his renunciation of the rights acquired through his wife Maria Teresa of Spain on the ground that her dowry had never been paid.[2]

King Pedro himself was descended from Maria of Castile, daughter of Ferdinand and Isabella. He did not presume on this, but it gave him standing in the Succession question. His queen

[1] S.P. 89/17, Paul Methuen to Vernon and to Shrewsbury, 13 May, 24 June 1698.
[2] Legrelle, *op. cit.* II, 86–8, 581–2; S.P. 89/17, Stanhope to Yard, 25 and 29 June 1698.

corresponded with her two sisters, and he was in close touch with the count of Oropesa, who just then was also inclining to the Bavarian side. Apart from his ambition to obtain frontier adjustments to help the defence of Portugal King Pedro was principally interested in arranging good marriages for his children. The Habsburgs figured largely in these plans but the Electoral Prince was an equally desirable match for one of his daughters.

As the king of Spain's health deteriorated and the regular rumours of his queen's pregnancy grew more incredible, King Pedro had ever more cause to worry. He appeared delighted when Paul Methuen delivered a friendly message from King William, and said he must consult his Council, though he did not commit himself. Paul did his best to bring Pedro to the point by repeating the alarming accounts he had from Stanhope of the king of Spain's health, and emphasising that if he died the chance of reaching any agreement would be irretrievably lost. King Pedro agreed and the prospects for a negotiation looked bright.[1]

But some vexatious interruptions now occurred. Anti-Catholic opinion in England had been inflamed by a recent plot against King William's life, and the Imperial and French ambassadors were alarmed lest there should be anti-Catholic legislation in Ireland and persecution in England. They proposed an agreement by which England should forgo any such measures in return for concessions to Protestants in Germany, Hungary and France. Little could be done to satisfy the Catholic powers in view of the climate of public opinion. At the same time Catholics everywhere were up in arms and in Lisbon the Jacobites and the Irish friars agitated their utmost.[2]

It happened that Paul Methuen was instructed now to protest against the number of chaplains employed by the Portuguese minister in London. All the Catholic Embassies employed too

[1] S.P. 94/74, fo. 115; S.P. 89/17, Paul Methuen to Vernon, 8 July 1698.
[2] *Lexington Papers*, p. 307; *Recueil*, III, 199; Klopp, *Der Fall des Hauses Stuart*, VIII, 121, describes John Methuen's assurances to the Imperial ambassador about Catholics in Ireland.

many but Portugal was the worst offender. Vernon complained that Da Cunha had ten chaplains, of whom nine were British subjects. The Portuguese were inclined to be reasonable but unfortunately Mendo de Foios, the secretary of state, was ill and his replacement Roque Monteiro was anxious to assert himself. An opportunity for him to take a stiff line was afforded by the case of a naval deserter named Bond. This man was a Catholic and had been living in Lisbon for some time with a Portuguese woman. One day his old ship H.M.S. *Betty* entered the Tagus and some men from on board recognised Bond as a deserter and apprehended him. The *soi-disant* Mrs Bond protested and orders were given to stop the *Betty* when she next entered the Tagus. This was done and Paul Methuen found that King Pedro had been moved by this hard-luck story of the kidnapping of a Catholic, and a hornet's nest had been stirred up. However, he handled the case with patience and firmness, and with the help of Mendo de Foios, as soon as he returned to duty, was eventually able to secure the release of the *Betty* with Bond still on board. He told his father that the Portuguese had expected so young a man as himself to be provoked to hasty action, but that he had made up his mind to be fair to both the English and Portuguese points of view, and to act with such moderation, that even his father, who was the greatest master of his temper he had ever met, could not have done more. Paul succeeded in this and so vindicated his competence as a diplomatist that the Portuguese nobles, among whom he had many friends, began to applaud him, but until 28 September his negotiations, with the king were interrupted.[1]

This audience, which he reported in an urgent dispatch, encyphered and sent overland to Blathwayt in Holland, was of some interest. The king was distressed that King William had said nothing about the Spanish Succession to Parliament. He watched the proceedings of Parliament with constant interest and both he

---

[1] Add. MSS 34335, fos. 8, 18, etc.; *Vernon Letters*, II, 116; S.P. 89/17, Paul Methuen to Vernon, 5 Aug. 1698, and to John Methuen, 2 Sept. 1698.

and his ministers were sometimes inclined to attribute to it more power than it yet possessed. Indeed they were apt to imply that no agreement with English ministers was safe until Parliament had ratified it, and to use this argument as an additional excuse for their habitual procrastination. Paul had to try to explain to the king the niceties of the English constitution and to convince him that King William did not have to account for his foreign policy step by step, but had power to deal with foreign affairs and defence without the necessity to consult parliament on such delicate issues.

At the audience the king said the French had won over the common people in Spain, who had been so much against them before, and the allies might soon be faced by the *fait accompli* of a French succession. He added that little was to be hoped for from the emperor; his minister Pacheco had just been to Vienna and had found very little interest in Spain.

The next day news came of another relapse in the king of Spain's health and Mendo de Foios spoke to Paul of his anxieties and of the need for Portugal to take measures of defence. He gave the impression that Portugal was opposed to France, but afraid of her power. Nevertheless the Count d'Estrées was refused facilities in Portuguese ports, such as had been given him in Spain, and was restricted to the six ships at a time allowed by normal treaty rights.[1]

Paul Methuen had assured the king that although King William had no personal interest in the Spanish Succession, it was his dearest wish to see a settlement and he would be working on the question in Holland. He did indeed do so, but the negotiations for the First Partition Treaty, on which he was engaged, took little account of Portugal. On 14 October, not long after Paul's audience, this treaty was signed, and already on 15 September Louis XIV had informed his ambassador in Madrid that he had decided to agree to a Partition. Negotiations had begun in the spring in London at the instance of King Louis, and on 29 May

[1] Add. MSS 34335, fo. 69, Paul Methuen to Blathwayt.

Count Tallard, the French ambassador, had reported that he had overcome the reluctance of King William to treat of a Partition during the lifetime of the king of Spain.[1]

The treaty provided that the Electoral Prince should reign in Spain and her colonies, and in Luxemburg and the Spanish Netherlands. The Dauphin was to have San Sebastian and Guipuzcoa, Sicily, Naples, and the Tuscan coastal towns with the port of Final. The emperor was to be compensated by the grant of the duchy of Milan to his younger son the Archduke Charles. By a secret article the Elector of Bavaria was to be regent during his son's minority and to succeed him in the event of his death. The Elector was already governor general of Flanders. In due course the Dauphin and King Louis were to renounce their rights in favour of the duke of Anjou, King Louis's grandson.

At the outset King Louis had made alternative proposals. He had suggested giving Spain and the Indies to his grandson, Italy to the archduke, the Spanish Netherlands to the elector, and Port Mahon or some Mediterranean port and concessions in the West Indies to King William. Several other permutations were discussed, including the grant of compensation to the duke of Savoy. King Pedro's claim was not seriously considered, for King Louis decided that the mutual hatred of Portugal and Spain rendered any union between the two countries impossible, while the maritime powers would never tolerate a union between the Spanish and the Portuguese colonies. Nevertheless, he was readier than King William to offer Portugal some compensation. King William was very sensitive on the subject of his legitimacy as a monarch and, perhaps among other more solid motives, felt a little jealous of King Pedro, who was a less important king and had himself had a dubious accession, but could possibly claim to outrank him. It is rather surprising that he never persisted with the question of concessions for the Allies in the West Indies or

---

[1] Legrelle, *op. cit.* II, 564–8; P. Grimblot, *Lettres de Guillaume III et Louis XIV* (1848), II, 7; *Hardwicke Papers*, II, 333–4.

Mediterranean. However, Heinsius had pointed out the danger of mixing up English and Dutch commercial interests with the Partition negotiations. It was agreed that such a complication, perhaps encouraged by France, might involve Sweden and Denmark, and also Portugal, and imperil the chances of a settlement. These interests were not forgotten, least of all by the merchants of London and Amsterdam, but they were omitted from the Partition Treaties.[1]

The Partition Treaty was concluded with the utmost secrecy. If King Louis had not vetoed it, King William would have preferred to consult the emperor, but he was content to keep his negotiations secret in England, and as far as possible in Holland. This secrecy was to cause him serious trouble later, but in view of the obstinacy of the emperor, the touchiness of Spain, and the pretensions of France no question was less amenable to be settled by open diplomacy than the Spanish Succession. King William negotiated exclusively through the French ambassador in London and the earl of Portland. Even Vernon only heard of the negotiations, and informed Somers and other ministers, when their signatures to the treaty became essential. Heinsius kept the matter to himself as long as he could, but he was obliged to consult the States General and soon there were leaks. The Spanish envoy at The Hague, De Quiros, reported on them and by November merchants in Madrid were discussing the probable terms.[2]

The Partition appeared in principle to be a good compromise. At first sight France appeared to be the gainer, but she had been obliged to give up Luxemburg and to accept exclusion from the Spanish Netherlands. The allotment of Naples and Sicily to France aroused the greatest resentment as soon as it became known. British and Dutch merchants thought this concession turned the Mediterranean into a French lake. King William had taken an opposite view. He believed that these kingdoms were hostages to fortune, for they were vulnerable to attack by sea, and

[1] *Rijksgeschiedkundige Publicatien*, ed. N. M. Japikse (Den Haag, 1927), kleine serie, XXIII, p. 475, Heinsius to King William, 29 Apr. 1698; Legrelle, *op. cit.* III, 25.
[2] *Ibid.* II, 578.

their possession would compel King Louis to go carefully in order to avoid war. For the same reason King Louis was not at first eager to have them. The emperor too at this stage would have been willing to give them up, though later their possession became his most ardent ambition. In Spain too the succession of the Bavarian candidate was accepted. There were even proposals to bring him to Madrid and to ask the Cortes to approve his succession. This was a different matter from any kind of Partition being approved in Madrid but it at least meant that there was agreement about Spain itself. It cannot be known whether the First Partition, if it had not been annulled by the death of the Electoral Prince on 6 February 1699, would have held in check the many divergent interests and ambitions more effectively than the Second Partition did, but the prospects were hopeful.[1]

Meanwhile, with the agreement of King William, King Louis lodged a protest in Madrid to reserve his rights, such as were affected by the new will in favour of the Electoral Prince believed to have been made by the king of Spain. King Louis decided that King Pedro could not safely be entrusted with the secret of the Partition Treaty, but he was informed of the Madrid protest, and given an assurance that the Dauphin would renounce his rights in favour of the duke of Anjou in due course. As regards Spain the Portuguese accepted the idea of a Bavarian succession and were correspondingly disappointed at the death of the Electoral Prince, which they regarded as a blow to the prospects of peace. De Rouillé tried to scare King Pedro with a suggestion that war was imminent, but King Pedro took his representations calmly enough and replied that King Charles might yet live and have children, as was much to be desired. Meanwhile, in spite of the progress of his cause in Madrid and the zeal of his ambassador for a French succession, King Louis opted at once for moderation and a new treaty of partition.[2]

[1] S.P. 94/74, fos. 133–4, Stanhope to Yard; Grimblot, *op. cit.* II, 40, 93.
[2] Legrelle, *op. cit.* II, 537–8, 597, 600.

Ignorance of the details of the Partition reflected on no one. Portugal was still to be kept in the dark officially for over a year, and De Quiros alleged that the Elector of Bavaria himself in agreeing to the First Partition had not realised that the Italian possessions had been shorn from his son's heritage.[1] English ministers were no more in the know than Paul Methuen, but his inability to keep King Pedro informed or to help his ambitions naturally reflected on his prestige. It also happened that political changes in England were tending to leave the Methuens in the cold. John Methuen had for a short time been in the running for promotion, but he had mismanaged his relations with the Whigs and at one moment had offended his patron the earl of Sunderland. The duke of Shrewsbury, his other patron, faded out of office and was succeeded by the earl of Jersey in May 1699. Jersey was no friend of Methuen or of Methuen's Irish colleague and friend the earl of Galway, and he appointed Matthew Prior and Robert Yard his assistants in place of James Vernon, who was transferred to the northern department. Prior had his own grouse against Methuen, and soon after his appointment Jersey wrote to him, 'Mr Blathwayt writes me word to put the "Holx" in Ireland.' Holx was a nickname for Methuen and meant Hocus-Pocus, conjurer or mountebank, as Methuen was called in the burlesque of *Lillibullero* current about him at the time. Hocus-pocus was also at one time applied as a nickname to Marlborough.[2]

A proposal was mooted to reduce Lisbon to the status of a Residency and to replace Paul Methuen. Matthew Prior would have liked the Lisbon post and John Methuen suspected him of having somehow instigated a complaint against Paul, signed by one Francisco de Castro, which reached Jersey's desk. Jersey thought the letter came from the Portuguese secretary of state and submitted it to Blathwayt, who ordered Paul's recall. But Vernon

[1] Legrelle, *op. cit.* III, 159; S.P. 89/17, Paul Methuen to Vernon, 17 Feb., 26 March, 1 Apr. 1699.
[2] *HMC Bath*, III, ref. 375; to Marlborough is in *Later Stuart Papers*, ed. E. Arber (1903), p. 285; see Appendix 1.

intervened and Jersey was genuinely abashed to find that there had been a mistake and that nobody knew who de Castro was. Meanwhile Lisbon had assumed importance again with the negotiation of the Second Partition Treaty. King William decided that Paul should remain in Lisbon and must be suitably briefed. John Methuen had explained to Vernon the difficulties Paul was experiencing as a result of his knowing nothing of the king's thoughts, and Vernon, who was now back in the southern department, lent his good offices. Blathwayt wrote to Paul immediately and John Methuen was authorised to clear up any doubts about Paul's standing directly with Mendo de Foios.[1] Blathwayt wrote to Vernon: 'Mr Methuen had some lucky accidents on his side, since notwithstanding the despatches prepared for recalling him, the present conjunction of affairs in Portugal happened to be such by ye late treaty between ye crown of Portugal and France as to make his longer continuance there necessary, so these orders are laid aside.' In September 1700 full powers for Paul to negotiate were prepared, but these became as obsolete as the letter of recall also drafted, because King William decided that King Pedro should not take part in the treaty but only adhere to it.[2]

The subject of the complaint against Paul is unknown, but may have been connected with the question of the Old Merchants' debts. The Portugal merchants were demanding to be allowed to fit out privateers to collect their own recompense. To forestall this Paul was told to take up the matter forcibly, but was inclined to advise against it, though he was eventually instructed to deliver a protest in the form of a personal letter to King Pedro from King William. He had other troubles in 1699 and 1700. He overcame them but they did not help his position in 1701, when he needed all the authority possible to resist the growing power of France.[3]

[1] HMC Bath, III, 414, 420; Cal. of S.P. (7 Jan. 1701); Add. MSS 37992, fo. 248; Cal. of S.P. (10 Jan. 1699).
[2] Add. MSS 34355, fos. 91, 94 and 37992, fo. 249.
[3] S.P. 89/17, Paul Methuen to his father, 2 Sept. 1698; S.P. 104/198, Jersey to Paul Methuen, 13 June, 24 Aug., 12 Sept. 1699; S.P. 104/195, King William to King Pedro, 7 Feb. 1700.

Until June 1700 King Pedro had no official information about the Partition Treaty negotiations. He continued to build up his army and to try to improve his position in Spain, but a shortage of corn in 1699 made it hard for him to feed his troops. He bought 5,000 bushels of corn in Andalusia but the Spanish governor stopped its export on the ground of a local shortage. However, some corn came from Spain, for during the bread riots in Madrid in May a principal grievance against the count of Oropesa was the allegation that he had accentuated the famine by allowing 400,000 fanegas to go to Portugal.[1] Permission was also asked to import corn from England and Ireland and this was given on condition that the state of the market allowed it. England exported wheat and barley to Portugal in 1700 and 1701, and Ireland sent a little corn and an appreciable amount of butter.[2] This trade tended to increase and Methuen well understood its help to the allied cause. The fickle mob in Lisbon was less formidable than that of Paris, but it formed in the crowded capital a force strong enough to influence the government. The heretic English were hated as much as Jews, New Christians or Spaniards, but the people of Lisbon saw the foodships entering the Tagus, and understood well enough that their daily bread could depend on the good will of the maritime powers.

Events in Spain in 1699 had moved against the allies. After the suspension of diplomatic relations in 1695 Stanhope managed to communicate with the government by backstairs ways, and from 1696 the tension was relaxed; but late in 1699 the Spanish ambassador in London was declared *persona ingrata*, as a result of his protests against the Partition negotiations, and Stanhope had to leave Madrid. In August 1700 Schonenberg was permitted to return and for a time represented England.[3]

[1] S.P. 89/17, Paul Methuen to Vernon, 25 Nov. 1698; S.P. 94/74, fos. 146, 159; Stanhope to Yard, 15, 29 Apr. 1699. *Fanega* is a Spanish bushel = 1 or 1½ English.

[2] S.P. 104/198, Jersey to Paul Methuen, 7 Nov. 1699. For corn exports see at the P.R.O. Irish Customs 15/3 and 4 and English Customs 2/8 and 9, also M.A.F. 7/1.

[3] S.P. 94/73, fo. 198; S.P. 94/74, fos. 13, 69, 78; Legrelle, *op. cit.* III, 148–9; Cole, *Memoirs of Affairs of State* (1733), p. 144.

In 1699 the position of King Pedro in Spain also weakened. He had been accustomed to rely upon the count of Oropesa as an influential and friendly contact, but in May Oropesa fell into disgrace. In July the queen of Portugal, Maria of Neuburg, died and, although she had exercised little political influence, the close link with the Austrian and Spanish Courts through her two sisters, the queen of Spain and the empress, disappeared. Her death affected King Pedro, for in his own way he was a fond husband. He was now left alone with only his young children and his elder sister to console him. Catherine of Bragança went over at once to comfort him, accompanied only by one attendant and without ceremony. There was little room for the influence of women in Portugal but as King Pedro's only adult near relative Catherine was treated with respect.[1]

Meanwhile, the Second Partition Treaty was being secretly negotiated. King William had been deeply distressed by the wreck of his plans and King Louis was tempted by the progress of his cause to stiffen his terms. Nevertheless, he began fresh negotiations without hesitation. In the First Partition the Elector of Bavaria had been named heir to his son and King William thought of him as the obvious substitute. But he had no personal hereditary claim and King Louis rejected his candidature out of hand. However, to the surprise and pleasure of King William he proposed the Archduke Charles instead. He was also prepared to consider the duke of Savoy, or even King Pedro, but King William had not forgiven the duke for his treachery in 1696 and would not hear of him, saying that there was some chance of the emperor agreeing to a reduced heritage for his son, but none at all of his accepting the candidature of Savoy. The duke was unlikely to protest, as he had no wish to antagonise the emperor by claiming the succession, and he was eager to claim the duchy of Milan. King Louis was willing to give King Pedro a little encouragement,

[1] S.P. 89/17, Paul Methuen to Vernon, 11 Aug. 1799; S.P. 94/74, fo. 158, Stanhope to Yard.

but King William was not, and received Da Cunha's approaches coldly.[1]

A provisional partition treaty was agreed on 11 June 1699. The Archduke Charles was awarded the heritage of the Electoral Prince. The Dauphin was to have Naples and Sicily, and also Lorraine, provided that the duke of Lorraine agreed to exchange it for Milan; but if the duke refused, Savoy was to be offered Milan in exchange for Savoy and Nice, which were to go to the Dauphin. A period of three and a half months' grace was to be allowed, during which the emperor would be invited to accede to the treaty. King William was sometimes suspected of having failed to keep the secret, but he does not seem to have done more than speak once or twice in a general way to the Imperial envoy, and agree with Heinsius that Jacob Hop, the Dutch envoy in Vienna, should sound the emperor. Louis XIV had no objection to this, though it created difficulties with his own ambassador Villers, who was cut off by a dispute about protocol from communication with the Vienna Court and became very suspicious. Louis was nervous lest rumours should reach Madrid, but the Imperial ministers were equally anxious to prevent this. They were not altogether adamant and in London Count Auersperg hinted privately to King William that concessions might be possible. At this time he was cultivating Whig members of Parliament and was assured in all sincerity by Methuen that there was no truth in the suggestion of any *rapprochement* with France. The very secrecy of the Partition negotiations and the denial of their existence, by persons who might be expected to be well informed, may have helped to stiffen the emperor's attitude. Nevertheless, in Vienna after much haggling the emperor offered to let the Dauphin have the Spanish colonies and even Naples and Sicily. But he would never consider the loss of Milan or of any part of Navarre to France, and these approaches, on which King William built great

[1] Grimblot, *op. cit.* II, 254, 257–70, 283–4, 290; *Hardwicke Papers*, II, 364; Legrelle, *op. cit.* III, 14, 417–18, 678; Add. MSS 20817, fos. 177–8.

hopes, reached a deadlock. The English and Dutch tried to extend the period of grace, but the emperor gave no sign of yielding, and after nine months the Partition Treaty was concluded without him.[1]

The last stages of the negotiation were difficult. King Louis was strong enough to insist on good terms, King William became suspicious, and the United Provinces, especially Amsterdam, were obstructive. From August onwards matters were made worse by a leakage. Da Cunha attributed this to Louis XIV, but it is unlikely. He was not averse to the negotiations being known in a general way but was anxious to keep the details secret. He himself ascribed the leak to the indefatigable De Quiros; French ambassadors blamed King William. The whole matter was so complicated that it is not surprising that in spite of the precautions taken, some part of the truth was deduced, even if it were not directly leaked. In any case the rumours of the Partition infuriated Spain. De Canales, Spanish ambassador in London, appealed to the whole English nation against the division of the Spanish monarchy and threatened to lay his memorial before both Houses of Parliament. As a result he was asked to leave and diplomatic relations were suspended.[2]

It was 25 March 1700 before the last of the United Provinces signed the treaty. The settlement of the Spanish Netherlands provoked anxiety. King Louis favoured the retention of the Elector of Bavaria as governor, but was disturbed by the disclosure of a convention concluded by him with the Dutch on 28 August 1699. Under it the Dutch undertook to defend the Southern Netherlands, and in return received a fort on the Scheldt below Antwerp, and terms which in effect strangled inland navigation between Antwerp and France. There was an outcry in Brussels and in November 1699 the Elector denounced the agreement and a supplementary one made later as forgeries. The States General

---

[1] Grimblot, *op. cit.* II, 104–51, 133–7, 339; Legrelle, *op. cit.* III, 104–5, 126, 131–9.
[2] Legrelle, *op. cit.* III, 147–9; Cole, *op. cit.* p. 144; Grimblot, *op. cit.* III, 128; Add. MSS 20817, fos. 173–4.

confirmed his statement, but there was smoke enough to upset King Louis, even if there had been no fire, and it was a fact that the Dutch troops lent to garrison the Barrier Forts had been reinforced. This incident does much to explain and even to justify the occupation of the forts by King Louis in February 1701.[1]

After the death of the Electoral Prince, de Rouillé thought that King Pedro had neither the resolution nor the resources to take a line of his own. This might be so, but it was not yet proved. He continued to intrigue and to talk of action. The archduke was banned under the Partition Treaty from entering Spain, but there were rumours of his being fetched from Italy and landing by a Spanish fleet in Portugal. It was even said that the new Spanish ambassador the duke of Moles had taken to Vienna a declaration to that effect. However, nothing more positive happened than the appointment at last by the emperor of an ambassador to Portugal.[2]

The treaty was now notified to Vienna and Madrid, and the next step was to invite the other princes of Europe to take part. King Pedro was one of the last to be informed, but once the decision was taken a courier was rushed to Lisbon in eleven days from Versailles. King William had agreed that King Louis should take the initiative and De Rouillé lost no time in seeking an audience. He took a condescending line and emphasised to King Pedro the uncommon kindness of this invitation from his master and the great desire of King Louis for peace. King Pedro temporised as usual, but the duke of Cadaval delivered a reply quite promptly conveying the king's provisional acceptance. Pedro asked to take part in the choice of the alternative candidate, if the emperor rejected the Partition and declined the succession for his son; he also asked for the possession of the Spanish forts of Alcantara and Badajoz to be guaranteed to him in case of war. De Rouillé asked for instructions, and was informed that England

[1] Legrelle, *op. cit.* II, 498 ff.; for copy of Dutch Bavarian treaty see 690/706, and G. de Lamberty, *Mémoires pour servir à l'histoire du XVIII*e *siècle* (1735), I, 115–20.
[2] Legrelle, *op. cit.* III, 338/9, 403, 406.

and the United Provinces objected to the Portuguese terms, but that he could agree to them upon King Louis's personal responsibility, if he found this concession unavoidable.[1]

It was the end of July, that is two months after his first audience, before De Rouillé had orders to confer with Paul Methuen and de Famar, the Dutch Resident, and it was not until 10 August that Paul Methuen had any instructions. De Rouillé told Paul that his full powers were on the way, but in fact his orders consisted only of a short dispatch from Jersey, forwarded by the overland route through Paris, telling him to notify King Pedro of the treaty, and explaining that no earlier intimation had been sent because King Louis had wished to be the first to inform King Pedro.[2]

Paul Methuen refused to be rushed by De Rouillé into moving faster than his instructions warranted. He drew up a long and clear summary of the position, which he sent directly to Blathwayt in Holland. In it he said that De Rouillé had supposed his talks with the king could be kept secret, but this was impossible in Lisbon, and he had learnt the gist of them from Portuguese friends before De Rouillé ever came to see him. He also gave a good account of the part that the Imperial ambassador Count Waldstein had played. He had been long expected but arrived finally on 10 July and was received at once in private by the king. His business was nominally only a visit of condolence for the queen's death and he did not present any credentials. However, the king informed him about the Partition Treaty, whereupon Waldstein replied that the emperor would not recognise it, and desired King Pedro not to enter into it. The king was reluctant to offend the emperor and told the allied envoys that he hoped some means of satisfying him could be found, but he explained the situation firmly to Waldstein. The latter damaged his cause with the Portuguese by his quarrels with them about protocol, and

[1] *Rijksgeschiedkundige Publicatiën*, kleine serie, XXIII, 512. Heinsius recommended that the emperor should be told first and this was done through his envoy in Paris on 18 May.
[2] S.P. 104/108, Jersey to Paul Methuen, 24 June 1700.

annoyed Paul also by refusing to name an hour for his visit, although he offered to make the first call.[1]

Paul Methuen notified the king of the treaty on 13 August, when the French proposals were already being considered by the Council of State. King Pedro replied at length. He gave the impression that he did not much like the treaty, and was worried and anxious, but that he would nevertheless stand by it. He also expressed his apprehensions about the concessions to France, especially in Guipuzcoa, and was very desirous of knowing the name of the alternative candidate to the archduke.

On 15 August De Rouillé told Paul Methuen that he had concluded the treaty with Portugal and in due course Paul was shown a copy. A secret article guaranteed Portuguese possession of Badajoz and Alcantara in the event of war and for four years after the conclusion of peace. King Louis undertook to secure the agreement of the English and the Dutch and, if the emperor rejected Partition, to inform King Pedro of the name of the alternative candidate before he need ratify the treaty. King Pedro then informed Waldstein that the emperor could expect no help from him in the event of war. Owing to the death of the king of Spain Portugal never in fact ratified the treaty.[2]

Sutton had reported that the Vienna Court was absolutely against the treaty, but that if the king of Spain showed signs of complying, the emperor would probably come to terms rather than lose the substance in order to clutch at the shadow. King William reflected this view in his reply to Da Cunha about King Pedro's aspirations, and remained stubborn on the subject of his desire for concessions.[3] He was disappointed that King Louis had not taken a firmer stand in Lisbon, but he decided to offer some

[1] Add. MSS 9744, fos. 63–7, Paul Methuen to Blathwayt; Cole, *op. cit.* p. 144; Paul Methuen to Stanyan, 15 June 1700.

[2] Add. MSS 9744, fos. 75–7; *Quadro Elementar*, IV, ii, CCCLXIV, speaks of ratification, but this is probably a confusion with the Amazon agreement of 4 March 1701. See Damião Peres, *A Diplomacia Portuguesa e a Sucessão de Espanha* (Barcelos, 1931), p. 23, and Borges de Castro, *Tratados*, II, 83.

[3] Cole, *op. cit.* p. 160, Sutton to Manchester.

form of compromise, for he feared that if he offended King Louis, 'the treaty would dissolve like snow'. After consulting Heinsius he resolved not to admit King Pedro formally into the treaty, but to offer to exchange with him an instrument of adhesion for an instrument of acceptance of Portuguese adhesion. The orders to Paul again went by Paris and they did not reach him until 13 October. They laid down that King William was unwilling to sign a treaty, though he had no objection to France having done so, but instead he would be glad to exchange declarations with King Pedro. These documents could be in Latin, if preferred, but there would be no need for Paul to have full powers to conclude this agreement between kings. King Pedro was persuaded to sign the instrument but it was 6 November before it was ready for dispatch, two days after the news of the king of Spain's death. Instructions to meet this contingency had been discussed in London in 1698, but they were never sent, so ministers abroad were left to rely on their own judgement. In Lisbon Paul had had little opportunity latterly to play a positive part, so that his French colleague began the new era with a definite lead.[1]

After many rumours and counter-rumours the king of Spain had signed the will in favour of the duke of Anjou a month before his death. The Council of State had approved his decision, and the Pope, when consulted, had advised the king to follow his Council. The Church had followed the same line and had profited by the opportunity to emphasise that the emperor was the ally of heretics who were plotting to divide the Spanish colonies between them.

No one could be sure of the contents of the will until they were made public, but King Louis had a fair idea of them, and there is no doubt that the Imperialists had an inkling also, and that St-Simon's story of the humiliation and discomfiture of Count

---

[1] Grimblot, op. cit. II, 427, 435–7; Legrelle, op. cit. III, 407, 585; Cole, op. cit. p. 235. For the instrument of adhesion see Borges de Castro, Tratados, II, 91; Add. MSS 40744, Blathwayt to Paul Methuen, 21 Sept. 1700.

Harrach in Madrid, when the news broke, was exaggerated. The will was currently discussed in Madrid and Schonenberg told Manchester on 21 October that it favoured the duke of Anjou, but that as soon as he felt better King Charles had wished to revoke it.[1] In the last days of the king of Spain's life King Louis was still inclined to respect the Partition Treaty, and even after he knew of King Charles's death and of the contents of his will, he drafted but did not send a last-minute offer of compromise to the emperor. King William therefore had reason to count on King Louis keeping his word and was correspondingly shocked by the news of his acceptance of the will.[2] King Louis argued that the maritime powers had failed to make the treaty a true expression of the will of Europe for peace by making serious efforts to persuade other princes to participate, and had not backed his efforts to persuade the duke of Savoy to exchange Savoy and Piedmont for Naples and Sicily. He would have been glad to give up the bastion in the Mediterranean in order to consolidate his position in the north of Italy, but he now felt that if he rejected the will, the emperor would be more uncompromising than ever, and war would be inevitable. These reasons were good in French eyes, though shameful in those of King William, and it would have been very difficult for King Louis to withstand the advice of his councillors and the enthusiasm of Versailles. The heads of the French Court were turned by the glorious news, and the duke of Shrewsbury, who passed through Paris at the time, said they could think of nothing else.[2]

Opinion in England was inclined to favour the will. Parliament had been alienated by the failure of King William to consult them and by the cession of Naples and Sicily to France. King William was obliged to bow to circumstances. He went as far as he could to conciliate the new Spanish régime without specifically recog-

---

[1] Cole, *op. cit.* p. 226; H. Künzel, *Das Leben und der Briefswechsel des Landgraven Georg von Hessen-Darmstadt* (Friedberg and London, 1859), p. 194; *Mémoires du Duc de St-Simon*, ed. Boislisle (Paris, 1890), VII, 291; Grimblot, *op. cit.* II, 451, 472–7.

[2] *HMC Buccleuch*, II, 747; Legrelle, *op. cit.* IV, 821.

nising King Philip. In reply to the Spanish regent's letter notifying him of the death of the king, he wrote a letter of condolence to the dowager queen and to the regents, which made no mention of King Philip. However, he appointed William Aglionby to go to Madrid with the rank of envoy and instructions to appease the new government. His departure was delayed but he reached Madrid by the end of January. The formal recognition of King Philip was only given on 15 April in reply to a letter from King Philip announcing his accession. Paul Methuen was told to explain that this recognition was only a matter of form.[1]

Paul Methuen's uneasy co-operation with De Rouillé was now over. However, he had used it to take his measure, and it was perhaps lucky for him that the ambassador underestimated his capacity and regarded him as no more than a pleasure-loving young man. On the other hand his cheerful ways stood him in good stead with the king, who normally regarded ambassadors as bores, but enjoyed the company of the Methuens. Paul used to catechise him, and even when the French influence was at its peak was still able to have talks with him and use long arguments to persuade him of his errors. An older or more pompous man would have given offence or have worn out the king's patience, which was apt to be short in matters of business, so that, when he was in a bad mood, his councillors found it hard to hold his attention. But Paul's personal qualities were not enough to remedy a worsening political situation.[2]

King Louis still hoped to avoid war and he began by being conciliatory. He was encouraged by Count Torcy's reports from London that English opinion had been outraged by the Partition Treaty and was all for peace. But there were signs that the situation might change and Louis was tempted to use a high hand, while his position was still so advantageous. In February he

[1] Legrelle, *op. cit.* IV, 829, seems to be incorrect in describing this letter of condolence as one of recognition of King Philip; S.P. 104/196, fos. 188, 190, 203–4.
[2] Legrelle, *op. cit.* IV, 207; Cole, *op. cit.* p. 243.

occupied the Barrier Forts and obliged the States General to recognise the new king of Spain.[1]

On the allied side only the emperor was as much concerned with the Spanish Succession as King Louis. He was the first of the allies to take a strong line and began with a diplomatic offensive, announcing that he would appoint a number of new ambassadors. Count Wratislaw, his choice for London, was a fiery and demanding man. When he arrived on 28 December 1700, King William assured him cordially of his friendship, but poured cold water on his projects. He explained that although he was king he was dependent on the support of Parliament. At present the English thought only of the danger of losing their trade and did not realise the danger from France. Public opinion would have to be won over before he could carry out his intention to support the emperor.[2]

For some months King William's diplomatic efforts were directed towards a renewal of some kind of partition negotiation at The Hague. Afterwards it appeared that he had only been temporising, but both he and King Louis were equally sincere in preferring a peaceful settlement, if it could be had on their own terms. His first aim was to reach agreement with King Louis, but he no longer thought of imposing this settlement on the emperor afterwards as at the First Partition, or of offering it to the emperor after a separate negotiation had brought him to agree to the terms, as at the Second Partition. He wished to bring all the parties together at The Hague. Unfortunately King Louis would not agree. He began by trying to separate the English from the Dutch; he then treated with the maritime powers jointly, but still refused to allow the Imperial envoy to join in.[3]

Count de Goes, the Imperial envoy at The Hague, was a more amenable man than Wratislaw, but he did not find the terms offered by the maritime powers acceptable. In 1699 the emperor

[1] Klopp, op. cit. IX, 214–44.   [2] Ibid. IX, 212.
[3] J. B. Wolf, Emergence of the Great Powers (New York, 1951), p. 64.

had indicated that he might be satisfied with the acquisition of Milan and the Spanish Netherlands. Now as a matter of principle he claimed the undivided Spanish heritage and was actively planning an invasion of Italy. It was clear that he would insist on having in addition at least Naples and Sicily.[1]

Waldstein had already been in Lisbon since June 1700, but he had done little since his rebuff over the Partition Treaty. It was not until July 1701 that he presented his credentials and had instructions to make positive representations, but it was already too late for him to have any chance of success. Paul Methuen had offered Portugal a Defensive Alliance in April 1701, but at this time the negotiations with France were well advanced, and Paul had no authority to offer any definite guarantees. Waldstein reported the progress of the Franco-Portuguese negotiations and in Paris Count Torcy boasted that the Portuguese ports would soon be closed to the allies, but the allies were reluctant to face the truth, and were correspondingly shocked, when the news reached them that Portugal had entered an alliance with France and Spain.[2] However, it was admitted that the allies had been remiss and that their failure to act was to blame rather than any lack of good faith on the part of Portugal. The recognition of King Philip had not been easy to explain and King William had appeared to be disarmed and powerless, and the House of Commons to be King Louis's best friend. King William was wise to remain impassive, until the logic of events won people and Parliament to his side, but the immediate cost to his prestige was very heavy.

For a while King Pedro continued to resist the French proposals, but he weakened as soon as he understood that Spain as well as France would guarantee the integrity of Portugal. His councillors were convinced that the allies were powerless to help them, and that the only practicable course was to accept the new alliances. According to Da Cunha King Pedro still hesitated and was only

---

[1] S.P. 105/62, Stepney to Vernon, 25 June 1701; Klopp, *op. cit.* IX, 284, 291, 299, 313, 333, 345, 406.　　　　　[2] S.P. 104/196, fo. 204.

persuaded by the influence of the Pope and the pressure from his advisers. Waldstein went so far as to say that he threw the treaties on the ground and stamped on them, before he could be induced to sign.[1]

The treaties with France and Spain were signed on 18 June and rapidly ratified. Schonenberg and Aglionby made desperate efforts in Madrid to find out the terms, but had to confess failure, and could only hope that Paul Methuen had sent in a full report. Paul badgered the ministers and tried to bribe an employee with £150, but with equal lack of success, and no details were made public except those of the *asiento* agreement. However, within a month he sent home a fairly accurate report. The treaties allowed France and Spain the use of Portuguese ports and denied them to the allies. They included a French guarantee of naval aid, compensation to the Cacheo Company for the loss of the remainder of their contract, and an agreement about the Portuguese settlements on the Amazon and the Rio de la Plata. Paul Methuen was surprised that there was no public reaction against the treaties, and thought the ministers were afraid to publish the terms from fear of provoking riots among the populace.[2]

Spain had been reluctant to join in the guarantees given to Portugal. The old enmity had been dormant for some time, so that in 1700 John Colbatch could believe that it was forgotten, but the Spanish grandees still regarded Portugal as a wayward vassal. Cardinal Portocarrero and Don Manoel Arias both opposed the treaty. Don Manoel is said to have told King Philip that Portugal belonged to Spain as his cap to his head, and to have doffed his cap to show how closely it fitted. Medals had been struck and pamphlets printed in Paris showing King Philip as king of Portugal. King Louis censored them, but the news of them reached Lisbon, and the elderly Portuguese nobles, who had once

---

[1] Mayer, *op. cit.* p. 4.
[2] Add. MSS 21491, fo. 3, Paul Methuen to Manchester, 8 July 1701. For text of the treaties see Borges de Castro, *Tratados*, II, 115, 122, 128 and for the Amazon Treaty of 4 March, p. 83.

fought against Spain, could not fail to recall the days of their youth.

The allies were inclined to accuse the Portuguese ministers of having been bought by the French. It was true that King Louis was more generously inclined than King William and had more command of his funds, even though his treasury was emptier. No doubt some favours oiled the wheels, and the close parliamentary control of money at this time made it hard for English or Dutch ministers to compete. But Paul Methuen's attempt at bribery failed, and it is unlikely that corruption affected the main issue. After the treaties were signed Spain distributed a largesse of 80,000 pieces of eight, but this was customary. The ministers had very good reason to accept the alliance which had so often before been rejected. They were not made for heroism or helped to be firm by the vagaries of the king. Portugal had only ten men-of-war fit for service and her attempts to mobilise an army had been disappointing. The allies were neither able nor willing to help them and the treaties seemed to assure their safety. The nobles were relieved of old worries regarding Spanish claims on their estates dating since the Spanish war and King Pedro was consoled by the promise of 300,000 pieces of eight to be paid to the Cacheo Company, in which he had a personal interest.[1]

The negotiations at The Hague were activated at the beginning of July by the arrival of King William and the appointment of Marlborough as ambassador. It was generally expected that he would be a go-between with the French and his appointment aroused grave suspicions in Vienna. However, these were alleviated by the fact that Marlborough himself sponsored the addition of Naples and Sicily to the emperor's share of the Succession and by the withdrawal from The Hague of Count d'Avaux. King Louis probably only meant this as a diplomatic manoeuvre, but by doing so he opened the way for the Grand Alliance and closed the door for his own negotiations. Meanwhile Waldstein was being

---

[1] Colbatch, *Account of Portugal* (1700), II, 44; Klopp, *op. cit.* IX, 272.

sent instructions to offer an offensive alliance to King Pedro, backed by 5,000 German troops. This force was to be commanded by Prince George of Hesse-Darmstadt, and was to have as its nucleus the remains of the troops which Hesse had commanded in Catalonia against France. However, the instructions reached Lisbon too late to be of any effect, and in any case they depended on the use of an allied fleet to transport the troops, and no fleet was available.[1]

Marlborough now drew up a project for the Grand Alliance. He kept this secret and did not reveal the details even to Blathwayt. However, Stepney succeeded in obtaining a copy in Vienna, which he circulated to Blathwayt and Hedges. He expressed professional dismay at the tactless way in which Marlborough based his proposals on Anglo-Dutch pretensions in the Mediterranean and West Indies rather than on the rights of the House of Austria. The terms empowered the maritime powers to keep any possessions they conquered in the West Indies. They were included in the treaty of Grand Alliance signed in September and were well received in England, when they became known, but Stepney pointed out that they would cause trouble between English and Dutch, and that the Catholic Powers could never agree to Protestants ruling over their co-religionists. Indeed, the Pope expressed his alarm and the emperor soon sought to go back on his agreement. Such a change was difficult to arrange with Parliament, but Marlborough promised that the Faith would be respected and King William assured the Imperial envoy that a party of friars should go with any allied expedition to look after Catholic interests. The idea of conquest, except for the emperor, was given up and claims for trade privileges were substituted. However, practical difficulties arose which prevented any joint expedition to the West Indies materialising. Admiral Benbow took a squadron there in 1701, but it met with disaster. Plans for

[1] S.P. 105/62, Stepney to Hedges, 21 May, 25 June, and to Tucker, 28 May 1701; Coimbra MS 3008, fos. 18–19.

Imperial participation were discussed until at least 1705, but only Anglo-Dutch expeditions proceeded, and plans to rouse the Spanish colonies to declare for the Habsburgs had no success.[1]

King Louis did not learn the details of the Grand Alliance until November after the death of King James II and his recognition of the Pretender. The recognition outraged England, and moved even loyal Tories against France, but did not perhaps make war inevitable, for both kings were willing to play the issue down. Various points in the treaty continued to be argued and there were many ancillary negotiations. Prussia and some German princes joined the allies, and Denmark, though technically neutral, agreed to supply mercenaries. The other northern powers reserved their strength for a war of their own. Bavaria and Savoy were courted by both sides and were won by King Louis.

The treaty had left the question of Spain open. The emperor could not publicly renounce any part of the Spanish heritage and was anxious to find a throne for the Archduke Charles, but in the eyes of his Court the interest of the heir-apparent, the Archduke Joseph, came first. Joseph had no wish to spend Imperial resources on a kingdom for his brother and was personally interested in Italy. He favoured intervention there and supported the appointment of Prince Eugène to lead an expeditionary force. At the same time it was believed in Vienna and by the allies generally that Spain would need no more than a demonstration by the fleet to spark off a revolution, which would place the Archduke Charles on the throne. This complacency was shaken by the defection or Portugal.[2]

The Portuguese denied that their new engagements necessarily meant a break with the allies, and for a time the allies toyed with the idea that if they declared war against French aggression rather than in support of the claims of the House of Austria to the

[1] F. B. Davenport, *European Treaties* (1934), III, 75–6; Stepney's dispatches in S.P. 105/63, fos. 99, 118, 152, 178, and 105/64, fos. 21, 236.
[2] S.P. 105/65, Stepney to Vernon and to duke of Ormonde, 8, 26 Apr. 1702; Gustav Otruba, *Prinz Eugen und Marlborough* (Wien, 1961), preface.

Spanish Succession, Portugal could remain neutral. But this was incompatible with intervention in Spain, and the allies were obliged to conclude that this was essential. Furthermore, the emperor demanded the dispatch of a fleet to Naples, and this was not easy if Portuguese ports were at the disposal of France. In his last days King William agreed to send a fleet to Naples, but revived the emperor's suspicions by deciding that he would have to occupy a Spanish port first, and by giving priority to an attack on Cadiz. In 1702 the Imperial plans to occupy Naples were foiled by King Philip landing there.[1]

Although the recognition of the Pretender had provoked many Tories as well as Whigs to face the necessity for a war with France, the opposite idea of a maritime war, which would help the Habsburgs in Spain but would be principally waged in the West Indies, was also mooted. The arguments were summarised in a pamphlet published in November 1701. It was suggested that the issue of the recognition of the Pretender was after all of no real importance. It would be better to ignore it and to concentrate on a war against Spain, which might pay for itself with the trade of the Indies and the plunder of the Spanish Main. This notion had the merit of appealing alike to Whig merchants, Tory gentlemen and even Jacobites. It was fantastic, but it was good propaganda to unite the nation in favour of war. Some of the merchants, who felt the navy in the last war had pressed their merchant seamen but had still failed to provide the convoys to protect their trade, advocated a privateer war to be financed by themselves. They dreamed of arming fifty privateers to revive the great days of Queen Elizabeth, and to bring back silver from the mines of Peru.[2] The argument that too much was being made of the recognition of the Pretender was not perhaps distasteful to King William. He was more anxious to obtain full recognition of his

[1] Damião Peres, *Sucessão*, pp. 69, 72, 77; S.P. 105/64, fos. 74–5, report from Dutch Resident at Lisbon.
[2] Daniel Defoe, *Reasons against the War with France* (1701); Add. MSS 17677, WWW, 5 Aug., 21 Nov. 1704.

own rights than to impugn the rights of others, and while he was representing that his recognition of King Philip was a formal courtesy, King Louis was using much the same arguments about his recognition of the Pretender. After all, the king of England still included the title of king of France in his description and King Louis had never troubled to take exception to this.[1]

In spite of Portuguese protestations of their desire for peace, Lisbon in the autumn of 1701 began to present a warlike aspect. The army was mobilised and French engineers were working on the forts. The king asked for naval protection in accordance with the new treaty and was promised twenty ships and a convoy for the Brazil fleet. There were frequent rumours that the allied fleet was approaching. Sir George never got beyond Ushant in 1701 but on 6 September there was a general alarm that he was coming; the soldiers were called from their beds to man the banks of the Tagus and the sentries left their posts at the royal palaces. King Pedro rode down to Belem with an escort of his nobles, some of whom had not been on horseback since the war with Spain, and cut an odd figure. Eventually a number of ships were sighted, but they proved to be a convoy of Hamburgers, of which six laden with foodstuffs entered the Tagus and the remainder continued southwards. During the alarm the mob had threatened to sack the houses of allied merchants and particularly the house of Paul Methuen. However, when Paul protested to the king, Pedro received him cordially and expressed indignation at the disorders and at the suggestion that the merchants might have to be evacuated. He promised to punish the rioters, saying that he had a particular affection for the English, and the merchants would find him more than a father and a mother to them.[2]

No doubt the king was sincere and the lesson of the foodships entering the Tagus was not lost on him. This was not the last

[1] Legrelle, op. cit. IV, 251, 831; S.P. 105/64, fo. 69.
[2] Os Manuscritos da Casa de Cadaval respeitantes ao Brasil, ed. V. Rau (Lisboa, 1958), pp. 46 ff.; Mayer, op. cit. p. 6; Soares de Silva, Gaçeta em Forma de Carta (Oeiras, 1931), p. 12; S.P. 89/18, fos. 7–9, Paul Methuen to Blathwayt, and fos. 15–16 to Vernon.

rumour that Rooke was in the offing and a Danish ship even claimed to have seen him sail from Plymouth. Paul Methuen took the opportunity to deliver a last homily to the king but the very next day Château-Renault's squadron of sixteen ships appeared in the Tagus. The Portuguese squadron had sailed to meet him and contrary to French custom on land, which yielded precedence to no one, Château-Renault allowed the Portuguese admiral the flag privilege. There was a strong reaction from the fears that had previously reigned and the Portuguese began to talk over-confidently. But Château-Renault, who was a practical seaman and knew that his sixteen ships were not strong enough to stand up to Rooke's fifty, told the Portuguese frankly that he had been glad to avoid Rooke, for he had no orders about saluting, and if Rooke had chosen to pick a quarrel with him, he could easily have suffered so that not one of his squadrons returned safely to France.

As long as Château-Renault remained, warlike preparations continued to be in evidence. Field guns and cannon arrived from the frontiers; others were landed from the French ships and drawn to the forts by 1,000 oxen brought to Lisbon for the purpose. Seventy gunners had arrived from France to join the Portuguese army, which was said to number 12,000 men under arms, while Château-Renault had a large force on board his squadron. Paul Methuen wrote that he would pay respect to the king, as before, but that he would not make, for the time being, any further representations. He wrote to the Factories at Oporto, Faro and Coimbra to prepare for evacuation and some merchants left at once in an English warship. Many of the Factory wished to address a memorial to ask for the King's protection in case of war and this suggestion was backed by the Portugal merchants in London. But Paul set his face against the proposal, saying that such a memorial would only be a sign of weakness; it would not help, if matters grew worse, and would be unnecessary if they improved. He added that he did not think the Portuguese would change their minds again until they felt the sad effects of the decay of trade and learnt to appreciate that their ruin was unavoidable if they continued in the power of the French. However, Paul did not despair personally, for he wrote to his uncle in London to order new liveries for his servants, unless Vernon intimated that there was any intention to move him from Lisbon.[1]

The sad effects foreseen by Paul soon began to show themselves. Provisions were scarce and dear, and money ran short. The king proposed a new 10 per cent tax, but the rumour of it aroused such violent popular opposition that he never again ventured to impose new taxation or to call the Cortes for the purpose. News arrived from Italy that Prince Eugène had crowned his success in crossing the Alps by a victory at Chiari and on 18 October, after the arrival of couriers from Versailles and Cadiz, Château-Renault began to prepare to depart, loading provisions and some of the munitions he had stored in the king's magazines. It was too dangerous and costly to winter in Lisbon and on 20 October he sailed. The French ambassador arranged for fifty guns, a bombardier and three engineers to be left behind and for a large credit to Portugal to buy 500 guns in Paris, but the Portuguese troops were demobilised and in general the war fever abated. The Court went into mourning for King James II, who had died on 20 September, and so by order from King William did Paul Methuen, but the French ambassador moderated his tone and made no attempt to oblige King Pedro to recognise the Pretender.[2]

It was now that Paul Methuen received an unexpected visit from Count Waldstein. Waldstein's public entry, delayed until July 1701, and his offer of an alliance and a German expeditionary force to invade Spain had coincided with the conclusion of the new Portuguese alliances and had been fruitless. Personally Waldstein was an imposing ambassador. He was a Privy Councillor, the son of the Imperial grand chamberlain, and a man of wit and pleasant conversation; but as Paul Methuen put it 'he had

[1] S.P. 89/18, fos. 4, 15, 16, 18–20, 25, 27, 30, Paul Methuen to Blathwayt and to Vernon.
[2] Mayer, *op. cit.* p. 5.

not the good fortune to be loved in the Court of Portugal, by reason of several Jarrs that had happened between him and the Nobility concerning points of ceremony, at his first reception and public audience, which occasioned his receiving few visits from them, and made his life so dull and contrary to his own natural temper, which was brisk and lively, that he was very desirous of returning to Vienna'. This made him an obstructive and difficult colleague, but he was now affable, as he wished Paul to join him in an attempt to persuade the king to declare his neutrality. Paul told him that he was inclined to accept a policy of neutrality for Portugal, and had written home to that effect, but he could do nothing without fresh instructions. However, he had no objection to Waldstein taking the initiative. He did so and had an audience with the King but failed to make any impression.[1]

Paul also had an audience and told the king that after the recognition of the Pretender the earl of Manchester had quitted his Embassy in Paris without taking leave and war was inevitable. But war would not be declared on account of the Spanish Succession, so King Pedro need not feel himself bound by his recent alliances. The French allegation that the allies would attack Lisbon had been proved false, and the king should now declare plainly, whether he would continue in amity with England and the United Provinces, if war broke out as a result of the recognition of the Pretender. Pedro replied that the recognition of the Pretender had astonished him and he admitted that it would justify a declaration of war by King William; however, he had not yet been officially informed of the recognition and he hoped they might remain friends. He agreed to give a more specific assurance through Mendo de Foios, but the latter was friendly but non-committal. However, the next weeks showed some recession of the French influence; the king refused to receive a party of French grenadiers and let it be known that he had only asked for them out of curiosity. M. de Caisson, a French export on fortifica-

[1] S.P. 89/18, fos. 32–7, Paul Methuen to Vernon.

tions, was dismissed and a complaint of the British merchants about a new and irksome customs regulation was given satisfaction. Finally, when the notification of the accession of King James III arrived, King Pedro did not accept it, though the nuncio asked him to agree. However, though the new Pope Clement XI had himself recognised James III, he was trying to mediate, and his orders to the nuncio had not been very pressing.[1]

Waldstein took his formal leave of the king in February, as soon as he had collected the jewel which it was customary to present to ambassadors on departure, but although he said he was sailing in the next ship, he remained in Lisbon. The Portuguese were again in a confident mood as a result of the safe homecoming of the Brazil fleet, and Waldstein suggested to Paul that an offer to pay 300 or 350 thousand pieces of eight indemnity to the Cacheo Company might still induce them to remain neutral. Paul agreed that this was a practical suggestion but thought it would be unwise to take the initiative. To his cousin Count Wratislaw in London Waldstein wrote that the sending of the allied fleet would win over Portugal. Wratislaw replied that the presence of the fleet would be required to keep Portugal neutral, but that England would be content with this. Paul heard a rumour that the French were agreed on Portuguese neutrality too, and that De Rouillé had put out feelers through the Italian banker Manzoni to suggest that Portugal might remain neutral on the basis of an agreement to limit the number of English and Dutch ships trading to Portugal in time of war.[2]

Diplomatic business had been interrupted in January and February by the illness of Mendo de Foios and Roque Monteiro, and of the king himself. The king's illness was perhaps diplomatic, for he had been obliged in the autumn to retire to Salvatierra to escape the importunities of Waldstein and De Rouillé, but he seems to have received Paul, whenever he could. On 8 February Paul

---

[1] S.P. 89/18, fo. 47, Paul Methuen to Vernon; Mayer, *op. cit.* p. 6.
[2] S.P. 89/18, fos. 35, 37, 55, 60, 63; Mayer, *op. cit.* p. 6.

told him of King William's satisfaction that he had not recognised the Pretender and said that war was inevitable owing to King Louis's breaches of the treaty of Ryswick. He also spoke of the new Parliament, which King William had opened with a speech of unusual warmth, ending with the words:

Let me conjure you to disappoint the hopes of our enemies by your Unanimity; I have shown and always will show, how desirous I am to be the common Father of all my people; do you in like manner lay aside Parties and Divisions. Let there be no other distinction heard of, but those who are of the Protestant religion and the present establishment, and of those who mean a Popish Prince and a French Government.

Pedro seemed impressed and was moved by the complaints regarding Spain. Paul again urged that if war arose from other causes than the Spanish Succession, and even if he could not take part in the glorious undertaking to liberate Europe, he should consider how much it was to his interest to keep his friendship with England. However, the king would not commit himself and he now asked France to send thirty ships, though it was put about that this was a ruse to make the French default, for he well knew that the French had not so many ships available. Paul was sceptical about this.[1]

On 21 March Paul told the king that the House of Commons had vigorously approved the Grand Alliance and had voted substantial sums for the armed forces by sea and land. Meanwhile King William had suffered his fatal fall and on 19 March he died. Owing to bad weather the news only reached Lisbon on 18 April, but this was at least a day before the news came by way of Paris, though Da Cunha had avoided the risk of his dispatch being held up by sending a message to Cunha Brochado a day before the event.

Da Cunha reported that the French believed the death of King William meant the end of the Grand Alliance and that Queen

---

[1] S.P. 89/18, fos. 52, 70; *House of Commons Journals*, XIII, 646–7.

Anne would not take up at once both the sceptre and the sword. In his memoirs he said that Louis XIV had sent a message to the United Provinces that the Republic had now recovered her liberty and was free to make peace. He added that France misjudged England but that the Dutch would have been satisfied if they had been left with the Barrier Forts.[1]

In his last dispatch before the news of the king's death Paul Methuen asked for instructions about Portuguese neutrality. In England it had almost become agreed that the neutrality of Portugal was acceptable, but Paul never received a reply, and when John Methuen was appointed to go on a special mission, he had orders to seek a closer alliance. Meanwhile King Pedro made no difficulty about recognising Queen Anne and, although Paul Methuen's new credentials had not come, received him formally on 2 May to announce Anne's accession. On this occasion Paul was accompanied by all the members of the Factory, dressed in black. On 8 May Methuen arrived, having made a good passage in H.M.S. *Winchester* in eight days.[2] As Methuen was on a special mission Paul continued to be minister and to conduct routine diplomatic business, but in practice he became subordinate to his father.

---

[1] Add. MSS 20817, fos. 290, 301–6, 313–14; S.P. 89/18, fo. 66, Paul Methuen to Manchester.

[2] Add. MSS 28590, fos. 6, 17, 19, John and Paul Methuen to Manchester.

CHAPTER 5

JOHN METHUEN DETACHES PORTUGAL FROM HER FRENCH ALLIANCE, MAY–AUGUST 1702

IT is not known how or when the decision was taken to send John Methuen back to Lisbon. It was probably mooted in King William's day and there is a suggestion that he was expected to carry on the negotiations single-handed. Count Waldstein's mission was officially ended and, although the Dutch minister Schonenberg was preparing to leave Madrid, Manchester thought he was returning to The Hague and Paul Methuen would travel with him to London. He suggested that they should both report to him there. But Schonenberg on his arrival in Lisbon, a week after Methuen, presented credentials to King Pedro, and Waldstein remained in Lisbon; so did Paul Methuen in the same capacity, for John Methuen at first only came on a special mission which was expected to be short.[1]

Before his departure Methuen had discussed the possibility of a Treaty of Alliance and Friendship with Da Cunha. In after years Da Cunha wrote that he had agreed on a Defensive Alliance, and that the idea of an Offensive Alliance only struck Methuen after he had taken the advice of an intermediary in Lisbon named Gomez da Palma, to whom Da Cunha had recommended him. He alleged that on return to England Methuen was accused by Nottingham of exceeding his instructions, but was supported by Godolphin and other ministers, who outvoted Nottingham.[2]

[1] Klopp, *Der Fall des Hauses Stuarts*, IX, 13; *Marlborough–Heinsius Letters*, ed. van t'Hoff (Den Haag, 1951), nos. 26–7; S.P. 94/75, Schonenberg to Manchester, 5 Apr. 1702; S.P. 104/196, fo. 244, Manchester to Schonenberg.
[2] L. T. de Sampayo, *O Instituto*, LXXVI, 6; S.P. 89/18, fo. 68.

Nottingham succeeded Manchester, after Methuen had left, and may have been inclined to take the Tory view that neutrality for Portugal was best, but Methuen's instructions, which he would not have shown to Da Cunha, clearly ordered him to invite King Pedro to join the Grand Alliance, and Da Cunha himself in his memoirs admitted this.[1] Schonenberg at his first audience followed Methuen in inviting King Pedro to adhere to the allied side.[2]

Methuen was instructed to seek an immediate audience with the king. He was to stress the importance of the Grand Alliance, to tell him that a great allied fleet would soon be coming and to ask permission for any number of allied ships to use Portuguese ports in addition to the six allowed by the treaties. If the king replied, as he had done hitherto, that he would do nothing contrary to existing treaties, he was to be told that besides the general engagements into which England had entered with her allies to withstand the united powers of France and Spain, England had a particular grievance on account of the recognition of the Pretended Prince of Wales as King James III, and if King Pedro inclined to that side it would be impossible to continue the old alliance with him; he was therefore to be invited to join the Grand Alliance, in which event the queen would use her good offices with the emperor to secure any particular desires or enlargements of territory wished by Portugal. An undertaking could be given that any losses to Portugal, arising from the failure to keep the engagements to France and Spain respecting the Cacheo Company, would be made good. Methuen was to demand an immediate answer, and if this was not forthcoming, to return to England by the same frigate that had brought him.[3]

From Methuen's minutes on the draft instructions it appears that he was responsible for making them more explicit. He

---

[1] Edgar Prestage, *Spanish Succession*, p. 16, quoting Da Cunha, *Instrucções a Marco Antonio de Azevedo Coutinho* (Coimbra, 1929), p. 42; Add. MSS 20817, fo. 336.
[2] Rijksarchief, The Hague, 7369, Secret, Schonenberg to States General, 30 May 1702.
[3] Add. MSS 29590, fos. 6, 434-9.

113

stressed that Waldstein had already made great offers, which had been rejected, and that to expect King Pedro to agree to admit the allied navies to his ports was to beg the whole question, and to commit him at once to the hostility of France; he would scarcely consent to do this without being sure that the allies would wage a vigorous war and that he would receive adequate and substantial advantages. He referred to the importance of the English communities in Portugal with property estimated to be worth £600,000. To guard these commercial interests, the existing 1654 treaty, which was very favourable, should not be altered, and Portuguese neutrality could not be tolerated, for during the last war the whole of the French trade had passed through Portugal with greater advantage to the Portuguese than they ever had in time of peace.[1]

Methuen's arrival in Lisbon was welcomed, and even Waldstein remarked that he was well liked. His rank of lord chancellor and the fact that he came on a special mission straight from the inner councils of Whitehall enhanced his personal prestige. The situation was nevertheless delicate. The Portuguese were still manning the forts on the Tagus, and the allied merchants were preparing to be evacuated in case of need. But the coming of the fleet was rumoured daily and the Methuens did their best to encourage this expectation.[2]

Before going further an account should be given of the principal persons with whom Methuen now had to deal. Waldstein has already been described. He had taken formal leave of the king and was eager to solicit preferment in Vienna; an added reason for departure was the pressure of family affairs occasioned by the recent death of his father the Imperial grand chamberlain. However, in spite of this he told Methuen that he had powers to negotiate and assured him of his co-operation. But he refused to do anything positive and instructions to him to invite Portugal

---

[1] Manchester Papers, P.R.O. 30/15/6, fo. 26.
[2] Mayer, 'Die Allianz Portugals', *Zeitschrift für die Österreichischen Gymnasien*, p. 6.

to join the Grand Alliance were only sent from Vienna in July, after Stepney had made representations.[1]

The Dutch minister Francisco Schonenberg had been many years in Spain, and had held credentials there from King William as well as from the States General. His family was of Portuguese-Jewish origin and had acquired Spanish nationality in Antwerp before moving to Amsterdam. His real name was Jacob Abraham Belmonte and his brother Francisco Jiménez Belmonte was Spanish Minister Resident in the Netherlands to King Charles II and afterwards to the archduke, King Charles III.[2] Methuen and Schonenberg might have been expected to disagree with Waldstein, but to work well together. They both had a commercial background, and the two maritime powers, though they were bitter rivals commercially, had common interests in the Peninsula. The two men tried to co-operate, and Methuen always obliged Schonenberg with small courtesies. But he kept his talks with the king secret, and before long Schonenberg was complaining to the States General and working on secret plans of his own.[3] Methuen had a weakness for being secretive and for plunging into schemes without sufficient consultation, but he had justification for believing that Waldstein neither would nor could co-operate fully, and that consultation with Schonenberg would only lead to delay. He had specific orders to work closely together with him, but he was obliged to talk freely to the king in order to keep the negotiation moving, and he had to respect the king's confidence, although he knew very well that anything he said was passed to the king's confessor, and was likely to filter through to the royal councillors and to a widening circle. He had also to report fully home, and Schonenberg was bound in the course of time to gather

[1] S.P. 89/19, Stepney to Hedges, 15 July 1702; S.P. 105/65, Stepney to Vernon, 12 Apr., and to Hedges, 26 July 1702.
[2] Künzel, *Das Leben und der Briefwechsel des Landgraven Georg von Hessen-Darmstadt*, pp. 353, 463; Rijksarchief 7369, 23 Apr. 1704.
[3] See Rijksarchief 7024 for a series of routine notes from Methuen, and 7369, 18 Aug., 18 Sept. 1702, for Schonenberg's views on Methuen.

the gist of his talks from London or The Hague, or, sometimes with malice aforethought, from the Portuguese themselves. Another difficulty was the temptation common to English and Dutch ministers to poach on each other's preserves, dating from the time when King William directed the foreign policy of both countries. The Methuens had sometimes spoken for the States General in Lisbon; and Stanhope, on reaching Madrid in 1690, found that Schonenberg had just received fresh credentials from King William. He made no personal complaint, for Schonenberg had paid him a civil visit, bringing gifts of wine and chocolate. But he found the situation peculiar and so did most Englishmen. Schonenberg was told not to interfere with Stanhope, who during Schonenberg's exile from court himself acted for Schonenberg, but after Stanhope's departure Schonenberg was again in charge of English affairs, and Aglionby, when he came to Madrid on a special mission, reported that he carried out his duties very well. In February 1702 King William refused a request of the States General to accredit Schonenberg to Lisbon, on the ground that he already had a minister there, but after King William's death he was appointed. He had formed the habit of writing directly to English ministers and to the navy, and showed an inclination to continue the practice.[1]

Schonenberg's dispatches were addressed to Fagel, the secretary of the States General, and were laid before that body. They had to be formal, and tended to be sparing in comment, but more specific in dates and details than Methuen's dispatches. Dutch instructions about routine, maritime and commercial, were businesslike, but questions of policy had to be referred to the various provinces and were often long unanswered. The Dutch were also slow payers. This applied to subsidies but also to

---

[1] For friction between English and Dutch ministers see M. Lane, 'Diplomatic service under William III', *Royal Historical Society Transactions*, 4th ser. x, 102–3; Add. MSS 9744, Stanhope to Blathwayt, 14 June 1690; Add. MSS 29590, fo. 66, Schonenberg to Nottingham; S.P. 94/75, Aglionby to S. of S., Apr. 1700; Add. MSS YY 17677, fo. 213, Vrijberg to States General.

Schonenberg's salary. Methuen was paid with tolerable punctuality but Schonenberg often had to wait. His salary was 10,000 guilders a year (the guilder was worth about 2s.) plus 12 guilders a day allowances, and some perquisites.[1] On one occasion after a long argument he received a 2 per cent commission on the advance of a subsidy from money due to the Dutch West Indies Company, and this was a fat sum of 17,000 cruzados or £2,500. But generally speaking Methuen with a salary as a minister of £5 a day, and from June 1703 as an ambassador of £10 a day plus £700 a year for extraordinary expenses, was better off.[2]

Difficulties between English and Dutch were bound to arise but they were exacerbated by the ill-feeling between the two men. Schonenberg was described as a very subtle minister by a detached observer, a nephew of Pepys, and there is no doubt that he was clever and devoted. But he was also smooth and self-seeking. In time of stress he could express himself sincerely and to the point, but he was usually high-flown and verbose. He was inclined to ask too much, while Methuen took a broader view and showed more candour, but was inclined to be fussily anxious and to promise too much. Both he and Galway thought Schonenberg an intriguer and a smart customer, and Sousa Pacheco, the Portuguese minister at The Hague, called him a strange character, sly, deceitful and to be treated with caution, for he made difficulties in order to get better terms for the Republic.[3]

On the enemy side not much was heard of the Spanish ambassador, the marquis of Capecelatro, but De Rouillé, the French ambassador, was an able man. He was inclined to be arrogant, and was as slow to take Methuen's negotiations seriously as the allies a year before had been to treat his own negotiations. He was now

---

[1] Waldstein had 2,000 guilders monthly (M. Landau, *Geschichte Kaiser Karl VI als König von Spanien*, Stuttgart, 1889, p. 116).

[2] Rijksarchief 7025, 23 July 1704, 22 Jan., 16 May 1705; Damião Peres, *Sucessão*, p. 11.

[3] Pepys, *Private Correspondence*, ed. J. R. Tanner (1926), pp. 143, 165; Damião Peres, *Sucessão*, p. 118.

instructed to go gently and he showed great patience. He suffered from the protocol laid down by King Louis, which prevented him seeing ministers who had not called on him first. This restricted him to the duke of Cadaval. Waldstein suffered from the same disability and saw no one but Roque Monteiro. However, De Rouillé had many contacts with Portuguese nobles who had married French wives, though the French merchants appear to have been less help to him than the Factory to Methuen, for they included many dubious characters who were estranged from their Embassy.[1] Both England and France had taken Portugal too much for granted, but the importance of English commercial interests obliged her to recognise the significance of Portugal. Louis XIV had always been more gracious to King Pedro than King William, and de Rouillé had begun to recommend concessions in 1701, but Versailles was slow to react vigorously, though in October 1702 a Treaty of Neutrality for Portugal was actually drafted.[2]

Methuen gained much by his ability to enter all doors with informality. The king greeted him like an old friend, but it was soon clear that he would not commit himself. He was now an elderly man, and his dark moods and illnesses and his alternations of energy and lassitude did not grow less. Also his ministers were less ready to face the risks of war and their influence on the king was stronger. He was ready to be persuaded by Methuen, but only if the guarantees were sufficient and his expenses were covered. The hedging and shifts of the Portuguese are easier to understand if it is remembered that they did not so much reflect the European situation, which was uppermost in the minds of European statesmen, as the position in Spain. King Pedro had consistently resisted French approaches until the spring of 1701, when Louis XIV obliged Spain to guarantee Portuguese integrity. He then made a sudden volte-face. He and his ministers had been born and

[1] Albert Girard, *Le Commerce français à Seville et Cadiz aux temps des Habsbourgs* (Paris, 1932).
[2] Legrelle, *op. cit.* IV, 279.

bred under the shadow of Spanish domination. Of late years the threat had been dormant but it had revived with the accession of Philip V. Security against Spain had again become a primary aim and the occupation or neutralisation of the frontier forts of Badajoz and Alcantara was stubbornly demanded throughout all negotiations. These towns were needed for defence, but it is interesting that Schonenberg reported on the economic aspect, saying that Portugal required concessions in Estremadura or elsewhere in Spain where there was corn and plentiful water, to remedy her own chronic shortages. King Pedro went so far as to say that the occupation of these places was a principal object of the alliance, and essential to the security of Portugal.

Portugal thought first of the defence of her Spanish frontier, but the protection of her ocean trade, from which the royal revenues were largely derived, was almost as important. Da Cunha believed that if Portugal remained neutral, Lisbon could again become a premier international port. But it was increasingly obvious that only the allies could protect the seaways and the homecoming of the Brazil fleet. The French gave specific assurances in 1701 and brought the Spanish treasure fleet safely to Vigo in 1702. But French naval weakness was apparent even before the destruction of the galleons at Vigo, and although it afterwards transpired that allied naval protection was incomplete Methuen gave assurances on this point in May 1702, and together with Schonenberg confirmed the allied undertaking in the autumn.[1]

The king's position was now improved by the possession of male heirs, who were growing up, but he was bereaved of his queen and had no family to advise him except his sister Catherine of Bragança. She had a number of priests and friars around her, and persons of Jacobite sympathies. An intercepted letter from Lady Tuke, one of her ladies in waiting, describes the situation from a Jacobite point of view. The ministers were said to be for France, but Methuen was moving the common people to favour

[1] Rijksarchief 7369, 5 and 13 Dec. 1702.

the allies by his propaganda and the distribution of pamphlets. She said that Queen Catherine, whatever her personal feelings, minded no business but her own. In fact the dowager queen kept out of politics and found it easier to be on good terms with Queen Anne than with King William or Queen Mary, both of whom she had actively disliked. Although she leaned towards the Jacobites, she was not pro-French. Her confessor was a Jesuit, and the Jesuits at this moment were inclined to be well disposed rather than otherwise.[1]

The foreign secretary, Methuen's old friend Mendo de Foios, was forced almost at once to resign by ill health, but lent his good offices when he could until his death in September 1703. His replacement, José de Faria, was less satisfactory and had a reputation for being pro-French. However, Roque Monteiro Paim now began to be called first secretary of state and to figure more in foreign affairs than Faria. He could do this as the king's private secretary, and later he was made a commissioner for the treaty negotiations, and was attached to Count Waldstein. He was not friendly at first, but he was a patriotic man, and after Portugal entered the Grand Alliance he was friendly both with Methuen and with Schonenberg. Most of the influential Portuguese were at the best lukewarm for an alliance, but Methuen's realisation that good offers to Portugal were essential, together with his long experience of Portugal and his friendship with the king, enabled him to make progress. Schonenberg was an abler man, but he would not understand that some eagerness in the other party was a necessary condition for driving a hard bargain. He believed both in bribery and the use of force, but the States General did not give him the resources to back either threats or promises. In achieving a cordial atmosphere Methuen was helped by Paul, who made friends among the younger nobility and the sons of ministers, and was able to double his father's part.

At the invitation of the king, Methuen asked for the marquis of

[1] Add. MSS 29588, fo. 179.

Alegrete to be attached to him. As the leading Councillor of State and expert on foreign affairs he was the only possible choice. Born in 1641 he was now elderly and often ill, and had outgrown the pro-Austrian tendencies with which he had formerly been credited, but he was prepared to join the allies if the terms were good enough.

The marquis of Arronches was now seventy-six and had recently lost by death his brother the cardinal archbishop of Lisbon, who had been a supporter of the treaty with France. The Conde de Alvor played no great part and the leading Councillors of State were still Alegrete and the duke of Cadaval. Cadaval was seventy but he showed no sign of flagging. He was described as perfectly willing to act as 'barber, apothecary, and jester, to keep the King's favour', but under easy manners he hid a great ambition and a deep sense of his importance.[1] He was regarded as a sinister figure by the allies and undoubtedly through his wife and through the nuncio he kept in touch with France and Spain. He was always, or nearly always, opposed to Portugal entering the war actively on the allied side. As commander in chief he no longer relished personally the idea of planning campaigns or taking part in them, but he also believed with justification that Portugal was neither prepared nor fit to engage in a major war, and that if she did so, she would risk loss and humiliation at the hands of powerful allies. Schonenberg described a Council of War held in July 1703, when fond hopes were entertained that a general rising in Spain would follow immediately an invasion by the Archduke Charles at the head of a German Catholic army. Cadaval showed himself sceptical but not uncooperative, and treated the practical problems of the probable date of arrival of the archduke, of the conditions for the campaign and supplies for the army particularly of horses and forage, with refreshing common sense.[2] When the emperor sent no troops and provided no other help than that of the archduke's person, as a kind of mascot for the allies, Cadaval

[1] Sloane MS 2294, fos. 5–6, 25.　　　　[2] Rijksarchief 7369, 20 July 1703.

lost any belief he might have had in this policy for Portugal, and he always felt that there was little difference between one king of Spain and another, as far as the interests of Portugal were concerned. He had been in touch with the party of the count of Oropesa and was not unfriendly to the Almirante de Castile when he reached Portugal, so he was not irredeemably committed to the side of France. But as time passed, his opposition to the war hardened, though he obstructed rather than resisted openly. He had many interests; he owned vineyards and farmed the tobacco monopoly; he had investments in the Brazil trade and the Setubal salt industry. Most of these interests would have prospered if Portugal had remained neutral, but were injured rather than served by her entry into the war.[1]

The king's confessor, Father Sebastião de Magalhães, was an old friend of Methuen. He had agreed to the French treaty, but had a genuine fear of French hegemony, and was now believed to be anxious to disclaim any responsibility, as he was afraid he might be blamed if there were an allied blockade, followed by bread riots, such as had occurred not long before in Madrid. As the repository of all the king's secrets his good offices were indispensable throughout Methuen's confidential audiences.[2]

The reports of Portuguese ministers abroad affected the negotiations. Both Sousa Pacheco at The Hague and Da Cunha Brochado at Paris had changing views in 1701; Pacheco became friendly to the allies but Brochado naturally reflected the views of Versailles and sometimes forwarded tendentious reports, such as the one of July 1702 that a French squadron from Toulon was on its way to Lisbon. Until the last he believed that Methuen's negotiations would fail.[3]

Luis da Cunha was the most influential minister abroad and his reports from London received particular notice from the king.

[1] Add. MSS 28946, fo. 200.
[2] Add. MSS 29590, fo. 28; S.P. 89/18, Methuen to Nottingham, 28 Nov. 1694.
[3] Coimbra MS 3008, fos. 28 ff. Brochado to Luis da Cunha.

Though more favourable to England than his colleagues, he believed in Portuguese neutrality, and only accepted entry into the war as a second choice of necessity. His Legation was suspect in London owing to the number of Jacobites and Catholics who resorted there. This was a consequence of his office, and personally he was careful not to involve himself in intrigues or with political parties. He was a man of some insight and integrity, but no friend of parliamentary government. Seeing the constant shifts of politics so closely, he was inclined to take a dim view of democracy, but on the whole he gave sound advice from the Portuguese point of view.[1]

Count Wratislaw, the new Imperial ambassador in London, was a hot-tempered man and according to Da Cunha hazarded his position by associating too closely with the Whigs, a mistake for which the Tories never forgave him. But his friendship with Marlborough proved useful to him. He was a cousin of Waldstein, and a supporter of the Archduke Joseph, but he was no particular friend of his cousin, though like him he aspired to take a leading part, and when difficulties arose in Lisbon proposed the removal of the negotiations to London.[2]

On the English side the duke of Marlborough came near to stepping into King William's shoes for the guidance of foreign policy. Plans for any Peninsular campaign diverted resources which he badly needed, but he supported the Mediterranean policy and recommended supplies and troops generously. He was sometimes glad to second for service in Portugal or Spain generals whose employment for one reason or another he did not welcome in his own theatre. Being ambassador at The Hague as well as commander in chief, he often discussed political questions with Heinsius and with Sousa Pacheco, and smoothed over Anglo-Dutch differences which arose in Lisbon.[3] Alexander Stanhope,

---

[1] Damião Perez, *Sucessão*, pp. 41, 57, 64, 73, 93, 141.
[2] Add. MSS 20817, fos. 246, 736.
[3] *Marlborough–Heinsius Letters*, no. 73.

the English minister at The Hague, had co-operated with Methuen when he was in Madrid, and had employed Paul as an attaché; he was still disposed to be friendly.

Owing to the difficulty of interesting the Court of Vienna in the Peninsula and the trouble with Waldstein, the intervention of the Legation at Vienna was often needed. The minister there was George Stepney, a poet and literary man; his excellent dispatches have been well preserved, and often give a clearer picture of the position in Lisbon than accounts written on the spot. But he was as strongly influenced by the Vienna point of view as Methuen was by that of Lisbon, and often criticised Methuen severely. Before he went to Vienna, he published an article in 1701, which already recommended an alliance with Portugal and the conveyance of Archduke Charles there by the allies. The emperor had encouraged plans for the archduke to go to the Peninsula, but after it was clear that the Archduke Joseph would produce no male heirs he became very averse to allowing his younger son to go to Portugal, and Stepney denied vigorously that he could ever be persuaded.[1]

On arrival in Lisbon, on 8 May, Methuen found the king was suffering his usual reaction after his return from a hunting trip. There was a delay of several days before he could obtain an audience. However, he managed to see the king more than once before either Schonenberg or Waldstein was received, and this was the beginning of the jealousy which upset the good relations between Methuen and his colleagues.

When Methuen had his audience, the allied declaration of war on France was still unknown, and could be spoken of as a contingency rather than as a fact. The king appeared very friendly and was forthcoming about the English merchants, saying that he had always been ready to protect their safety and was very glad to quiet their fears by assurances of his good 'correspondence' with England. However, he was wary of committing himself, though he promised to answer Methuen's inquiry about freedom

---

[1] *Somers Tracts* (1748), XI, 211, 'The Interest of England'.

for allied ships to use Portuguese ports within a week. Methuen's first report was optimistic. He admitted the strength of French influence, but thought that the Portuguese ministers were nervous of the consequences of their participation in the French treaty, and anxious lest they should lose the compensation payable to the Cacheo Company, a matter in which King Pedro was personally interested. Alegrete appeared to be well inclined, though Methuen complained that he was overmuch concerned with the king's honour, which he felt would be compromised by an early repudiation of the French and Spanish treaties.[1]

On 23 May the Paris mail brought fresh assurances from France and the promised reply about the use of the ports was not given. There was still no sign of the allied fleet, and the impression made by King William's last speech, by the change in the attitude of the House of Commons and by the stable beginning of the new reign had worn off. King Louis took no vigorous action and like the emperor was more interested in Italy, where the landing of King Philip in Naples had done something to offset the triumphs of Prince Eugène, than in Spain. But as long as action in Lisbon was confined to talk, the word of the French was as good as that of the allies; indeed there were already some French warships and galleys in Lisbon and there were constant rumours that more French ships were on their way.

The declaration of war in London was made with ceremony on 15 May. Queen Anne was styled queen of France, and King Louis, king of the French; there was no mention of King Philip V, but thereafter he was called the duke of Anjou in spite of the previous recognition. The declaration was based on the infringement of treaty rights by France and the injury done by the recognition of the Pretender, but mentioned the threat to the peace of Europe and the freedom of shipping and commerce caused by French domination of Spain. The argument, therefore, that England's war with France had nothing to do with the Spanish Succession could

[1] Add. MSS 29590, fos. 21, 28.

no longer be used, and it had to be accepted that Portugal would only be free from her new treaty obligations if the French and Spanish pledges to defend her were not kept. The news of the declaration of war reached Lisbon early on the morning of 28 May, and although Methuen had just been with the king, he was back again with him at ten o'clock.

Methuen again pressed for a reply about the use of the ports, but Pedro could only say that the French were bound to send him 'succours', but had not yet done so. Alegrete had been taken ill, but Methuen visited his bedside, and was assured that the French had not the ships available, and would be unlikely to be able to fulfil their commitments.

The news of the declaration of war did not fulfil Methuen's hopes, and he wrote home to urge that the fleet should sail soon and that a frigate should be sent ahead with full powers for Paul to negotiate. He also proposed that if the king made more difficulties the merchants should be called together and advised to leave Portugal. The king and Alegrete had always brushed aside any such proposals with assurances that in case of war the merchants and their property would be 'entirely protected without the loss of one shilling to any of them'. Methuen believed that even if the government were recalcitrant, the withdrawal of the merchants would provoke a violent reaction among the people of Lisbon. But he admitted that the Court was irresolution itself, and that it was impossible to give a clear account of so confused and uncertain a situation.[1]

Both Waldstein and Schonenberg had their first audiences on 31 May. Schonenberg was disgusted by the delay and by the lengthy scrutiny to which his credentials were subjected by the Council of State. Both he and Waldstein distrusted Portuguese intentions and several further conferences with Alegrete and with Methuen resulted in no further progress; Alegrete invited Methuen to stay until the fleet arrived, so that they could then discuss an alliance, but Methuen left again for England on 9 June.

[1] Add. MSS 29590, fos. 29, 30.

After Methuen's departure Schonenberg wrote directly to Manchester in rather pessimistic terms, saying that the Portuguese ministers were all for France, and hinting that the only way to win them over would be to offer them larger bribes than the French. In July he again pointed out to the king the great advantages that would accrue to Portugal if she joined the allies, and he hammered at his main questions, Would Portugal join the Grand Alliance and would she allow the allies to use her ports? But neither he nor Paul Methuen could obtain anything more from Alegrete than an assurance that the treaty with France would become void if the succours requested did not come, and that the four French men-of-war, which had joined the four galleys already in Lisbon, would not be regarded as 'succours'. Alegrete also began to suggest that it would be necessary for the whole allied fleet to come into the Tagus in order to disengage the king. This was contrary to Methuen's understanding that the appearance of the fleet in sight of the coast would be enough. Indeed the king had assured him privately that anywhere within a hundred leagues would be satisfactory. Paul Methuen and Schonenberg were both tempted to think that the Portuguese were only playing for time until the Brazil fleet was safely home. Paul wrote to Rooke to say that the sight of the fleet off the coast was all that was required and that the demand for it to enter the Tagus was inspired by the French, who hoped to avert an attack on Cadiz. John Methuen afterwards complained that Waldstein and Schonenberg had spoilt[1] the arrangement he had made with the king. There was some truth in this. Waldstein believed that a show of force would intimidate the Portuguese and wanted the fleet to enter the Tagus. He was reporting to Vienna at the time that the help of Portugal would make very little difference and was not required. Schonenberg was inclined to sympathise with Waldstein, and was in any case beginning his intrigues against

[1] Add. MSS 29590, fos. 22, 50, 53, 58, 64, 99; Rijksarchief 7369, 30 May, 5 June 1702.

Methuen. In July he wrote to Nottingham to ask permission to correspond direct with the English navy.

Both Dutch and English consuls had sent out warning notices, and Paul Methuen persuaded King Pedro to give orders to his provincial governors to assist the merchants in the event of their evacuation. The Spaniards now interrupted the mail service by way of Corunna, and Paul Methuen inaugurated the regular packet service between Lisbon and Falmouth. In view of what occurred later it is interesting to note that he particularly laid down that the packet boats should carry neither merchandise nor contraband.[1]

On arrival at Portsmouth on 13 June (o.s.) Methuen found that Rooke was still waiting for supplies and for the Dutch squadron to join him. He then hurried up to London to explain that he had not brought back a plain answer from King Pedro, as his instructions required, and to insist that the secret promise which Pedro had given him was sufficient. It was not easy for him to make his point, for many Tories favoured a policy of neutrality for Portugal and earlier in the year Marlborough had been inclined to agree with this point of view. However, it was decided that Methuen should return at once to Lisbon and should go together with Prince George of Hesse-Darmstadt, who was just leaving. He was provided with credentials as an ambassador, but his appointment as lord chancellor was also renewed, and he found it more convenient to continue on the same footing as before;[2] he did not take up his rank as ambassador until next autumn, after the treaty negotiations were over.

On reaching Portsmouth again Methuen found that the *Lime* was not available, and Hesse had already sailed in another frigate, the *Adventure*. He was obliged to wait, but he was increasingly worried, and uncertain whether his return to Lisbon without the

[1] Mayer, *op. cit.* p. 12; Add. MSS 29590, fos. 56, 66; Rijksarchief 7369, 30 May, 14, 15, 18 July 1702.
[2] *Cal. of Treas. Books* (19 May 1703). *Cal. of S.P.* (20 July 1702).

backing of the fleet would serve any useful purpose. Meanwhile Rooke and his old rival the duke of Ormonde were civil enough to him, though it is probable that they would not have been displeased to see Methuen relegated, and the Lisbon negotiations, possibly with the help of Hesse, take another direction.[1]

Meanwhile Hesse arrived in Lisbon. Nottingham had intended that he should co-operate with Methuen, but in the absence of Methuen he took up his residence with Count Waldstein, and was guided by him. Hesse appeared in many ways a very suitable emissary. He was a first cousin of the empress, and of her sisters the dowager queen of Spain and the late queen of Portugal. He had been favourably known to King William for his services in Ireland in 1691 and had served the late king of Spain in Catalonia. He had been viceroy there, and although his efforts to defend Barcelona had failed, he had been made a grandee of Spain and also a field marshal of the Empire. He had been spoken of to lead the Imperial forces to Naples, and also to accompany a German expeditionary force of 5,000 men, which was to be seconded to King Pedro for the purpose of invading Spain. Stepney had at first warmly supported this abortive plan and was still recommending that he should accompany any allied expeditionary force. Hesse was a young and glamorous prince and the emperor and empress were anxious to employ him. But all his qualifications for a high post and even the emperor's favour were not enough to overcome the jealousy of rivals. No military post could be found for him and efforts to provide him with a diplomatic post in Lisbon or with the fleet ran into the antagonism of Waldstein and of the duke of Ormonde. He was sent to London, where he submitted plans for the invasion of Spain, but the death of King William interrupted these, and he incurred the jealousy of the Imperial ambassador Count Wratislaw, who had not been properly informed of the nature of his mission. A move

[1] Add. MSS 17677, YY, fos. 112, 118, 121, 171, 173; Add. MSS 29590, fos. 44, 46, 48, 50; *HMC Downshire*, I, 814.

to send him to Lisbon was at first opposed by King Pedro on the advice of Da Cunha, who thought his presence would hamper the Methuen negotiations. Finally King Pedro consented to his coming, but the credentials, which were supposed to be on their way from the emperor, had not reached him; after some discussion of the protocol he was received personally by King Pedro, but only briefly and coldly, and the king spoke Portuguese, of which Hesse was ignorant, though both men were at home in Spanish. After this rebuff Hesse would have done well to be patient, but he was anxious to show his mettle, and Waldstein and probably Schonenberg were not averse to using him as their stalking-horse. In any case he began to distribute manifestos, in which he described himself as lieutenant general of the emperor and fully empowered to take possession of Spain in the emperor's name. He called upon the Spanish nobility and people to rise. His action evoked prompt and vehement protests from the Spanish and French ambassadors. Portugal could hardly condone such provocative conduct against two powers with whom she was still allied, and King Pedro sent him a polite note, accompanied by a present, which he refused, asking him to leave Portugal.[1]

Meanwhile the sailing of the fleet was still held up. Methuen had given Rooke an optimistic account of the state of the defences of Cadiz. Rooke read this with scepticism and already doubted his ability to succeed, though he did put forward the view, which was rejected at Cadiz, but afterwards agreed to be correct, that the only way to force the city was to land on the seaward side of the isthmus. Owing to bad management some of the transport ships had arrived empty, stores of butter and cheese had gone bad, and provisions for the landing force were short. He put to sea at last on 12 July, only to be forced back into Tor Bay by contrary winds. Finally he sailed; in addition to his misgivings Rooke was

[1] Add. MSS 17677, YY, fos. 173, 183; Add. MSS 29590, fos. 71, 87, 93, 100; Rijksarchief 7369, 18, 22 Aug. 1702; Mayer, *op. cit.* pp. 10–11; *Vernon Letters*, III, 209, 234.

a sick man and the day before he left the coast of England news came to him of the death of his young wife in childbirth. But he commanded a powerful force. Admiral Fairborne with sixteen English and eight Dutch ships sailed ahead of him to Cape Finistère, and Admiral Rooke himself had thirty English and twenty Dutch men-of-war with auxiliary ships and transports and 13,801 troops on board. At last he had a fair wind; he sighted the Portuguese coast north of Lisbon on 18 August and after approaching the mouth of the Tagus close enough to see the signal flares and all the Portuguese craft hurrying for shelter, he kept along the coast, passing Cape St Vincent on 21 August. He had already been joined by Fairborne's squadron and near St Vincent he was joined by the *Lime*, which he had sent into Lisbon with dispatches, and by two other ships with Paul Methuen and Hesse on board.[1]

Methuen had sailed in the *Lowestoft* on 31 July about a week before the fleet, and reached the Tagus on 8 August. He found that Paul Methuen had elicited an assurance that there was no need for the fleet to come to the bar of the Tagus, but he took the precaution of speaking to King Pedro and of pointing out that if the fleet was not entering the river, it was only because he had informed Queen Anne of the king's good intentions and of his desire to avoid anything which might look like the appearance of force. He even offered to send a message to Rooke to invite him to enter the Tagus, but the king assured him that this was unnecessary. This was just as well, as it would have been impracticable for the fleet to change its course.[2]

Methuen also had to complete the arrangements for Hesse's departure. He had full authority to do this, as Wratislaw himself had asked Nottingham to arrange for Hesse to join the fleet, and to put this right with Ormonde. Nottingham warned Ormonde that Hesse might be joining him, and authorised Methuen to

[1] S.P. 42/67, 13 and 20 June 1702; Navy Records Soc., *Journal of Sir G. Rooke* (1897-9), pp. 160-72.
[2] Add. MSS 29590, fos. 99, 100.

9-2

arrange for him to proceed, as soon as he thought he would be more useful with the fleet than in Lisbon. He therefore felt justified in bringing the *Adventure* down to the mouth of the Tagus, though the Portuguese had raised some difficulties, and in facilitating Hesse's sailing. He wrote at once to Ormonde and Paul Methuen went on board the *Adventure* to make Hesse comfortable. The Methuens believed that all was in order, but they were mistaken. Hesse complained to Ormonde that Methuen had sent him away in order to curry favour with the Portuguese, and had spoilt the plan he had concerted with Waldstein to avoid leaving Lisbon. He was not to be appeased and bore a grudge against Methuen for some years. Waldstein wrote to Vienna and to Wratislaw in London to protest against Methuen's lack of co-operation and Schonenberg wrote critically, though in less plain terms, to The Hague. Although in Vienna even Hesse's friend Von Kaunitz feared that he had done more harm than good and Stepney formed the Impression that he had been over-hasty, it was natural that the imperialists should try to gloss over an ignominious incident. Hesse even in his lifetime was a popular hero. Although at Cadiz he was kept at arm's length by the allied commanders and given a very subordinate position, when he arrived back in the Thames in November 1702 the postmaster took it for granted that he must be on a mission of importance and that the packet would have to be held up for a reply. His defence of Gibraltar and his heroic death at Barcelona enhanced this reputation and the legend grew that he had played a principal part in persuading King Pedro to join the Grand Alliance, and that like Methuen he had secret interviews with the king, who had treated him coldly only to throw dust in the eyes of the French. Such rumours were common and the Jacobite Lady Tuke was saying at the same time that King Pedro was deceiving Methuen and had a very good understanding with Louis XIV. The Hesse legend has, however, found a place in histories even in our own time. There is no evidence to confirm it. Hesse's views on the invasion of Spain played a considerable part in the councils of the allies, and his presence became the focus for various intrigues, but he only had an indirect influence on the Methuen negotiations.[1]

The fleet passed the mouth of the Tagus as soon as Hesse had sailed. The ships were some miles out to sea, but they were visible from the Portuguese coast and presented a brave sight. A year before, the Lisbon mob had threatened the English merchants as heretics, but they were now afraid that the French alliance might lead to a blockade and a want of bread, and instead of showing alarm they gave all the signs of love and affection, and even cheered the allies. Methuen wrote with satisfaction, 'I could have wished for the amusement of this Citty, who have been so far imposed on by the French, as to believe the Fleet would not come at all, that so great a fleet had passed in view, but I dare assure your Lordship that with the King and Court the effect is entirely the same in respect of being disengaged at present.'[2]

French warships entered the Tagus a day or two later and other French ships continued to cruise off the Portuguese coast, but on the next morning after Methuen had told the king about the passage of the fleet, the duke of Cadaval was delegated to inform the French ambassador that the alliance with France was void on account of the failure to provide the naval aid stipulated in the treaty. De Rouillé showed vexation and remarked that from this small spark there might arise a great fire. Cadaval took exception to this and replied 'that while it was a spark the Portuguese would blow it out with their mouths, and that if it were a fire, they would put it out with their hands'. The king, when he heard of the duke's stout reply, embraced him, and the tale was the talk of the town. Nevertheless, unlike the Spanish ambassador, who was furious, De Rouillé kept quiet and contented himself with the

---

[1] Add. MSS 29588, fo. 179; S.P. 84/224, Stanhope to Hedges, 8 Sept. 1702; *Cal. of S.P.* (1702–3), p. 288; Add. MSS 20817, fos. 346–8; *Rijksarchief* 7369, 27 Oct. 1702. For the Hesse legend *Theatrum Europaeum* (1715), XVI, 981; Lamberty, *Mémoires pour servir à l'histoire du xviiie siècle*, XII, 249.

[2] Add. MSS 29590, fos. 101–6.

dispatch of an express courier to ask for instructions. After some delay the reply came that he must assume a detached attitude and have patience. Meanwhile the Portuguese ministers reverted to their customary tactics of procrastination. Schonenberg was much less optimistic about the position in Portugal than Methuen, though he was more so about Spain. He congratulated King Pedro pointedly on 'his liberation by the coming of the fleet from the very harmful obligations to France and the scandalous treaty with France and Spain'. Pedro replied with some formality that he appreciated Schonenberg's zeal for the good of Portugal, and he would afford the fleet all facilities, but he refused to commit himself to join the allies. Schonenberg was not satisfied. He complained of Methuen's complacencies and, together with Waldstein, insisted that he must have written confirmation of the abrogation of the French alliance. Methuen had accepted the king's word as good enough, but on 6 September he persuaded Alegrete to repeat a verbal assurance twice in his presence, and eventually he obtained his written confirmation. Meanwhile the Portuguese gave one positive sign of their change of front by dispersing the forces which had been manning the banks of the Tagus, and by sending away their artillery to the Spanish frontier.[1]

[1] Add. MSS 29590, fos. 100, 108–9; Rijksarchief 7369, 29 Aug., 6, 18 Sept. 1702.

CHAPTER 6

PORTUGAL HESITATES TO COMMIT HERSELF FURTHER

THE repudiation of the French and Spanish treaties by Portugal without too open a display of force by the allies could be regarded as a triumph for Methuen. The presence of the fleet in the Tagus would have been awkward to handle and the delay would have cut down the few weeks of sailing weather still available for the siege of Cadiz. Nevertheless, a chorus of complaints had been sparked off by the Hesse incident and ministers in London were obliged to make up their minds either to back Methuen or to replace him.

Waldstein would have liked to see Ormonde made ambassador in Lisbon and there were rumours to that effect. He complained that Methuen had offered concessions without consulting him or Schonenberg, and had claimed to have authority to speak for the emperor. He was right in supposing that there was a plan on foot to place Queen Anne, if not Methuen personally, in charge of the emperor's part of the negotiations, and that Methuen had hinted something of the sort to King Pedro. Methuen had also distributed pamphlets written in Portuguese but printed in England; these did no more than explain the Allied case and call upon Spain to support the House of Austria, but in connection with them Methuen was described as ambassador of Great Britain, the emperor and the United Provinces. It is unlikely that Methuen was responsible for this, but, if his colleagues heard of it, it is not surprising that they were affronted. Schonenberg's grievances were less obvious but he was annoyed that Methuen had mentioned the subject of compensation to the Cacheo Company to the king and he was already suggesting that he would no longer be wanted in Lisbon and should be appointed Dutch ambassador to Habsburg Spain.[1]

In London Sir Charles Hedges, the new secretary of state, did not altogether see eye to eye with Nottingham, and although he arranged that all his correspondence should be copied to him, misunderstandings sometimes arose when Hedges was attending the queen at Bath while Nottingham was at Newmarket. For instance Hedges told Stepney on 11 August that it was too late to change Hesse's itinerary, although at the same time Nottingham was instructing Methuen to send him on from Lisbon to join the fleet. Hedges had doubts about Methuen. He also shared the apprehensions of the Admiralty lest the orders given to Rooke should result in his keeping the fleet at sea dangerously late in the season.

When Hedges received Methuen's report on the passage of the fleet, he had not yet heard from Wratislaw about Waldstein's complaints, but he had a general idea of the background. The question of Hesse's status had caused embarrassment in London, so the difficulties about him were understood, and in due course Da Cunha defended King Pedro's behaviour towards Hesse and incidentally Methuen's. It was known that Waldstein was hard to deal with, and Stepney had reported that care would have to be taken to prevent his falling out with Hesse. Methuen had pointed out that he would need to make better offers to King Pedro than Waldstein had already done before he left London, and the offer of compensation to the Cacheo Company had been authorised in his instructions and had originally in 1701 been an idea of Waldstein's own.[2]

[1] Rijksarchief 7369, 22 Aug., 18 Sept. 1702; Add. MSS 29590, fos. 96, 130; *HMC 7th Report*, pp. 763–4; S.P. 89/18, Stepney to Hedges, 18 Oct. 1702; Damião Peres, *op. cit.* p. 107. A Portuguese transcript of Methuen's pamphlet is in Coimbra MS 510.

[2] S.P. 100/10, Nottingham's minute of 6 Aug. O.S. and Wratislaw's letter of 29 Aug. 1702; S.P. 105/66, Hedges to Stepney, 11 Aug. 1702; Manchester papers at P.R.O. 30/15/26, fo. 26; Rijksarchief 7369, 16 Oct. 1702; S.P. 89/18, fo. 33; S.P. 89/19, Stepney to Hedges, 19 July 1702; Add. MSS 20817, fo. 38 and 29588, fo. 267; Douglas Coombs, *Conduct of the Dutch* (1958), p. 69.

Hedges decided that he would write rather stiffly to Methuen telling him that representations would be made in Vienna for fresh instructions to be sent to Waldstein, but in future he must be more open with Waldstein and Schonenberg and co-operate fully with both of them. He sent this letter unsealed to Warre, the under-secretary in charge in London, with orders to consult with Wratislaw, and not to send the letter off unless Wratislaw agreed to secure better co-operation from Waldstein. Though Wratislaw was himself a firebrand he was inclined to be sympathetic on this occasion. He defended Waldstein's point of view and said that neither he nor Schonenberg trusted King Pedro, but suggested that Methuen should be told that Waldstein was haughty and capricious, and would strongly resent being crossed or kept out of the picture, but would respond if Methuen treated him frankly. After consulting Lord Normanby, the only Privy Councillor left in town, Warre went back to Wratislaw, and told him that the king of Portugal had a particular confidence in Methuen, whom he had known for a long time, and had shown this by communicating to him, for the queen's ear alone, the secret assurance that he would declare himself free of the French alliance as soon as the Allied fleet arrived. For this reason the queen had chosen him for the negotiation, though 'he was old and at his ease', and their lordships had some difficulty in persuading him to accept. His reticence with his colleagues had been caused by the king restraining him to silence, and had been intended only for the public good and the emperor's interest, so there was good reason to excuse it. Wratislaw accepted this explanation as good enough for the past, but desired more open conduct in future.[1]

Hedges is credited with the remark that Methuen was more Portuguese than English. He certainly had some doubts about Methuen, though the remark can only definitely be attributed to a letter written some years later by Charles Montagu, Lord Halifax. On this occasion Hedges sent Methuen's original letter to

---

[1] S.P. 104/195, Hedges to Methuen, 11/22 Sept. 1702; Add. MSS 29588, fo. 219.

Stepney and a copy to Marlborough and asked for their comments. Later when it was established that King Pedro had definitely repudiated the French alliance Hedges's confidence in Methuen revived. At the same time Godolphin, who always had a good opinion of Methuen, circulated to the Cabinet an intercepted letter from Lady Tuke, a member of Queen Catherine of Bragança's suite to her brother at St-Germain, which suggested that Methuen was being duped by King Pedro but gave him full credit for being a redoubtable defender of the allied cause. It was agreed that Hedges's letter to Methuen had been appropriate and that Stepney and Stanhope should ask for instructions to be sent to Waldstein and Schonenberg to work closely with him, but that Methuen could not yet be authorised to speak on behalf of Waldstein.[1]

Waldstein had complained of Methuen direct to the emperor as well as to the foreign minister, and Stepney, though he was having his own troubles with the Austrian ministers and with his Dutch colleague, was inclined to be critical. He told Hedges that 'it was to be wished that ministers united in a common cause would not raise such unreasonable scruples, but would act openly and by concert for the service and interest of their country, since in matters of this nature there was ample field for everyone to know his share in the reputation to be acquired'. He added that he had 'tried to ensure that fresh orders were sent to Waldstein, but he already had leave to return to Vienna, and he believed he would soon take advantage of this in order to attend to his family affairs, for nothing would have kept him in Portugal so long, except the hope of a lucky turn enabling him to conclude a treaty to his reputation'. With some trouble Stepney had discovered that Waldstein had not hitherto been instructed to invite Portugal to join the Grand Alliance for fear of offending Spain. He thought

[1] Add. MSS 29588, fos. 179, 204, and 29590, fo. 106; J. Albrecht, *England's Bemühungen um den Eintritt Portugals in die Grosse Allianz* (Bremen, 1933), p. 34; *HMC Bath*, I, 155, Montagu to Rivers; S.P. 105/66, Hedges to Stepney, 13 Sept. 1702.

it unfortunate that Methuen had not been able to report specifically the terms asked by King Pedro, since, if they could have been communicated to the emperor, he might well have agreed to follow the recommendations of Her Majesty's government. The Court of Vienna had no notion of matters so distant, and would probably be very happy for the queen to undertake the responsibility for them.[1]

Stepney had seen a report from Wratislaw, saying that since their first quarrel Waldstein's first principle was never to agree with Methuen, and suggesting that the negotiations be moved to London. He did not care for this proposal or for another suggestion that all proposals made in Lisbon should be referred back. After hearing all sides of the story he began to move towards Methuen's point of view. Although fresh orders had finally been sent to Waldstein, he did not suppose he would remain in Lisbon to carry them out. He was mistaken in this, for Waldstein invited King Pedro to join the Grand Alliance on 16 September.[2] However, he recommended that England and the United Provinces should manage the negotiations, for although the emperor could never himself agree to the terms asked by Portugal, he had no objection to the allies doing so, provided that he was assured of the possession of Milan. He would therefore agree to the maritime powers promising in his name whatever they thought fit.[3]

In November Nottingham tentatively suggested that the negotiations might be moved to The Hague. But the Dutch had already instructed Schonenberg to begin them in Lisbon, and the Dutch ambassadors in London had agreed that it would be better for Methuen to make the first offers: if the Portuguese made them, they would inevitably become known to and bettered by the French. They also agreed that Dutch trade would never be safe as long as Portugal remained neutral, and that Schonenberg's

[1] S.P. 80/19, Stepney to Hedges, 25 Sept., 1, 28 Oct., 11, 15, 18, 19, 25 Nov. 1702.
[2] Rijksarchief 7369, 16 Sept. 1702.
[3] *Weensche Gezantschap's Berichten*, ed. C. van Antal and J. C. H. de Pater (s'-Gravenhage, 1934), II, 242–3, 246.

instructions, which might have been understood to condone neutrality, should be amended.[1] Nottingham now laid down that Methuen should carry on the negotiations in Lisbon in close co-operation with Schonenberg, but that Waldstein need not always be consulted. Wratislaw admitted that any concessions at the expense of Spain had better be made behind the emperor's back, and Bruynincks, the Dutch minister in Vienna, had fresh orders to support Stepney. On these lines there was now some hope of Allied harmony. The negotiations did indeed begin at the end of the year, though with many hitches.[2]

Before describing them some account must be given of the events at Cadiz. After the various plans for the West Indies had fallen through and, on grounds of impracticability, the emperor's urgent request for an expedition to Naples had been refused, the choice for an Allied attack lay between Barcelona and Cadiz, or possibly some other Spanish port. Cadiz had an imperfect harbour, but it commanded the Straits and was relatively accessible from England. It was also the home port of the Spanish American trade. In April Marlborough told Heinsius that Cadiz had been given priority. It did not take Louis XIV very long to hear of this, but apart from the removal of Leganez, the governor general, who was suspected of Allied sympathies, and sending a few French engineers, he did comparatively little to strengthen the defences. Allied reports estimated the garrison at about 2,000 and counted on a pro-allied rising, as soon as the fleet appeared. It seems that these reports were not far wrong, for French sources after the siege confirmed that the garrison had been small and supplies and munitions short. Nevertheless, Ormonde and Rooke did not accept them or decide on any plan of attack; they preferred to base their conclusions on the stories of a few fishermen whom they captured after reaching Cadiz. Their accounts varied, but from them the Council of War deduced that the garrison num-

[1] Add. MSS 17677, YY, fos. 249, 252-4.
[2] S.P. 80/19, Stepney to Hedges, 15 Nov. 1702.

bered 4,000 infantry and 1,000 cavalry, and the defences of Cadiz were stronger than had been represented.[1]

Cadiz was not an easy place to attack, as it was situated at the end of a narrow sandy point, bounded by the ocean on one side and a broad lagoon on the other. Access to the mainland led along an isthmus and over a narrow tidal channel, or across a series of sandbanks and marshes ending in the fort opposite the city across another channel. Across the bay it was defended by shallows and on the seaward side by surf. As soon as the Atlantic winds began to blow in autumn the seaward side became a dangerous lee shore.

Although both Ormonde and Rooke favoured an attack on the landward side of the isthmus, the navy now rejected it on the ground that the surf was too dangerous and the question of supply too difficult. They also rejected a plan to force the entrance to the lagoon. A third suggestion was adopted, which entailed a landing on the further side of the bay between the towns of Rota and Port St Mary, many miles from Cadiz by land.

The governor general of Cadiz boldly refused Ormonde's summons to surrender. The commanders of the other forts did likewise, but in fact offered little resistance until the allies were held up at Matagorda, the fort opposite and very near to Cadiz.

The landing force met with little resistance except from the surf, which cost them the lives of twenty-six men. They took St Mary's, which they found abandoned. St Mary's was full of warehouses and it was too much to expect that the invaders after a long and hot march, burdened with thick clothing and heavy equipment, would quench their thirst with the brackish water, which was all that was available. They plundered the unguarded cellars, and once the drinking and looting began, it spread to warehouses and dwellings and, worst of all, to churches.[2]

At Matagorda the allies were three miles from Cadiz, but for

[1] Add. MSS 29590, fos. 90, 145, and 38159, fos. 10–15; S.P. 105/66, fo. 28; Rijksarchief 7369, 18 July, 1 Oct. 1702.

[2] Add. MSS 38159, fos. 17–20; Anon., *History of Expedition into Spain* (1702).

practical purposes they were no nearer than before. The fort held out and the entrance to the channel between it and Cadiz had now been blocked by the use of sunken ships. It was decided that the attempt to take the city from the landward side must be given up and the troops were re-embarked. The navy were increasingly anxious lest they should be caught by an autumn gale. In spite of the opposition of Hesse, who said such an action would have a fatal effect on opinion in Spain, the navy decided to bombard the city, but bad weather prevented this too. Ormonde wrote urgently home for reinforcements and supplies and urged that another attempt should be made elsewhere, but after some days' futile discussion which followed the re-embarkation of the troops, the fleet finally left Cadiz in the last days of September.[1]

The looting of St Mary's did serious damage to allied prestige. Not only were the local people alienated but the shock spread through the whole Catholic world and especially to nearby devoted Portugal. The cry of sacrilege was a rallying cry for Catholic opinion and it was no help that some of the worst looters had in fact been Irish Catholic soldiers. The complaints of merchants were almost as damaging as the religious issue. A London merchant claimed that his agents had lost 25,000 dollars, adding: 'Our Fleet has left such a filthy stench among the Spaniards, that a whole world will not blot it out.'[2]

Ormonde had given strict orders that there was to be no looting, but until he was obliged by peremptory orders from London he took no disciplinary action against the offenders. Service opinion sympathised with them, and when courts martial were eventually held, officers like James Stanhope refused to give evidence. The navy were inclined to be critical of the behaviour of the forces ashore, but the sailors were not behindhand in taking their share when the opportunity arose, and captains of ships quarrelled over hogsheads of claret and connived at the sale of looted tobacco

[1] Add. MSS 29591, fos. 81, 91, and 38159, fos. 24, 29–30, and 28925, fos. 69, 115, 119.
[2] Add. MSS 29591, fo. 14; Cal. of S.P. (1702–3), pp. 297–303; HMC 7th Report, p. 766.

142

and snuff in Lisbon. However, the lesson of Port St Mary was not lost on the allies: Marlborough, by steady discipline and unremitting care for his men, so trained them that they were welcome in the lands they occupied; and in Portugal, Galway, though with less success, tried hard to diminish these abuses.[1]

The last word in the decision to leave Cadiz had rested with Rooke and the navy. Rooke was genuinely distressed by what he described as the shameful and dishonourable end to the expedition, but he had started out with grave forebodings and he was a sick man, so that at Cadiz gout prevented him writing even his own dispatches. His ships were running short of supplies and water, and an attempt to obtain these from Tangier was unsuccessful. It would not have been impossible to send some of the larger ships home and to winter somewhere in the area. Supplies could have been sent out and some of the supply ships he had with him actually returned home unused. But he was burdened with the need to victual a large land force and also had orders to detach a squadron to the West Indies and to give priority to supplying the ships concerned and a force of 2,000 men. Rooke made several proposals to his Council of War but they were all rejected. Ormonde refused to put his signature to the formal decision to sail home, but he took no other action.[2]

The failure was due partly to the lack of intelligence. The navy had insufficient boats to command the lagoons and Ormonde had no horses suitable to stand up to the climatic conditions and shortage of water on land. There was also little interservice co-operation. Rooke would not allow seamen to help with such slavish work as digging trenches and hauling guns. The most popular scapegoat was naturally the Spanish people. Not a priest or any Spaniard of note joined the Allies. Hesse had conferred with two Spanish noblemen from Madrid, who had given great assurances, but his promise of a general rising proved quite empty.

[1] Add. MSS 28925, fos. 131-2.
[2] Add. MSS 28925, fo. 69, and 29591, fo. 81, and 38159, fos. 30-1; S.P. 42/6, fo. 140.

143

Although the Council of War refused to accord him any status and Ormonde only backed him up to the extent of a half-hearted assurance that he was entitled to represent the emperor, his advice as a Spanish expert had been taken seriously. He was therefore generally blamed, though he indignantly retorted that it was vain to expect any Spaniards to join the allies unless they showed that their intentions were earnest by stopping over the winter and keeping a sufficient force in Spain.[1]

Although the fiasco of Cadiz caused profound heart searchings, it was generally assumed that the attack would be renewed, either at Cadiz or at some other place in Spain. In fact this was postponed; meanwhile the maritime powers were forced to commit themselves to an expedition based on Portugal and to depend to a much greater extent on Portugal joining the allies. But the lesson of Allied interservice and international lack of co-operation was not lost on Portugal. She was able to stand out for better terms and to refuse, even more firmly than in any case she would have done, to subject Portuguese forces to the command of foreigners. If an Imperial contingent had taken part, it might have been feasible to achieve agreement for the appointment of Hesse or of some acceptable Catholic as commander in chief, but all efforts to win seniority for an English general were vain. Furthermore, an expeditionary force in which Imperial or Spanish elements predominated could more easily have been based in Spain with a subsidiary front in Portugal. The failure at Cadiz reduced this possibility.

When the fleet was off St Vincent a Council of War was held to consider whether a squadron should be detached to winter in Lisbon, as Rooke's instructions of 20 July had suggested. This question was examined in the light of Methuen's latest reports. The position at Lisbon naturally reflected the latest news from Cadiz. This was scanty and, although Paul Methuen had done his best to assure a regular service between the fleet and the Algarve,

[1] Add. MSS 28925, fos. 171, 181.

144

King Pedro II of Portugal

Rooke sent no dispatches. This almost led to his missing the news that the Spanish treasure fleet convoyed by Admiral Château-Renault had gone to Vigo, but the bad news from Cadiz and that of Rooke's departure only reached Lisbon on 2 October, and the gap between the receipt of earlier optimistic reports and the news of the triumph at Vigo was considerably narrowed.

The Council of War turned down any plan to detach ships to Lisbon on the ground that Methuen's reports were not clear. In fact they were clear enough, though they reflected his own uncertainties, and his failure to obtain any positive response from King Pedro. The best that he could advise in the circumstances was that it would be quite possible to send an adequate number of ships to serve the purpose without infringing existing treaty rights, which allowed six English and six Dutch ships in each Portuguese port. By splitting the squadron between Lisbon and Setubal twenty-four ships could have been sent, but a combined Council of War, and two days later a Naval Council of War, decided that it would not be safe to leave any ships at the mercy of King Pedro. After he had the news of the abandonment of Cadiz, Methuen himself advised in the same sense, but his dispatch did not reach Rooke, nor did his renewed advice to send a squadron, given as soon as he heard the news of Vigo.[1]

The whole drama of Cadiz took place within six weeks and all parties were at cross-purposes owing to the slowness of communications. Paul Methuen's arrangements for a mail service to Lisbon by way of Faro twice a week failed to materialise and the prevailing north wind on the coast of Portugal held up ships bound for both Lisbon and the Channel. London was a little better off than Lisbon as the ministers received the first news of a setback in a dispatch from Admiral Hopson dated 26 September (N.S.). They had been living in a fool's paradise, and in

[1] Add. MSS 29591, fos. 90–4; Adm 1/4088, 2 July 1702; Add. MSS 38159, fo. 31; Mayer, 'Die Allianz Portugal's', *Zeitschrift für die Österreichischen Gymnasien*, p. 18. Navy Records Soc., *Journal of Sir G. Rooke*, IX (1897), 223–5.

response to Wratislaw's vehement requests for a squadron to be sent to the Mediterranean, they sent orders to Rooke on 1 September, as soon as Cadiz was taken, to send a squadron to attack the French on the coasts of Italy, and to proceed as far as the Adriatic before returning to Cadiz. They also ordered Rooke to detach ten ships to join Admiral Shovell in the search for the Spanish treasure fleet and to give priority to the dispatch of a squadron to the West Indies. This latter order was carried out and was given as a reason by the Council of War for not making any further attempt in Spain. As late as 24 September Ormonde was informed that in response to his requests hulks and supplies were being prepared for Cadiz, and reinforcements would follow. The frigate *Greenwich* delivered these orders in the neighbourhood of Vigo, but they were never considered in connection with the proposal to leave ships there for the winter.[1]

While hopes of success at Cadiz were still good, Methuen and Schonenberg began to discuss in general terms the possibility of a treaty of alliance. They emphasised that Portugal must agree to take an active part in the war and to set the Archduke Charles on the throne of Spain; at the same time England and the United Provinces would conclude a Defensive Treaty of Alliance with Portugal. In spite of the complaints which had gone home about Methuen, outward harmony between the allied representatives was preserved. Waldstein had his instructions to invite King Pedro to join the Grand Alliance and after a period of hesitation delivered the invitation to the king in mid September together with the news of the battle of Luzzara. Both the king and Alegrete assured Methuen that they had confidence in him, but told him that they trusted neither Waldstein nor Schonenberg, and they must have adequate guarantees before they could enter the alliance. These guarantees comprised cessions of Spanish territory and payment of compensation in respect of

[1] Add. MSS 29590, fos. 122, 124, 128, and 29591, fos. 2, 58, 79, 90, 92, 94, and 38159, fos. 30–5; Adm 1/4088, fo. 29.

the Cacheo Company. Methuen promised both and in talking of Spanish territory mentioned Vigo, which was a better harbour than Oporto. Schonenberg objected to the indemnity to the Cacheo Company and Waldstein would not hear of any concessions in Spain, saying that with the English and Dutch as allies the Archduke Charles had no need of the help of Portugal. He wrote directly to the emperor to recommend Methuen's recall and combined with Schonenberg in resenting the settlement arranged by Paul Methuen of the long-standing dispute about the merchants' debts. In accordance with this agreement money was being slowly remitted to England and, in 1704, 40,000 pieces of eight were sent.[1] These old debts had been the subject of standing orders for many years but Waldstein accused Paul of pocketing a large commission and of neglecting allied interests to obtain the settlement. He also accused the Methuens of trading in loot from Port St Mary. This story probably owed its origin to the fact that the frigates in which Hesse and Paul Methuen returned from Cadiz did sell some plunder, including church furniture and tobacco and snuff, in Lisbon. The infringement of the royal tobacco monopoly was almost worse than the sacrilege, and Methuen tried to buy back the tobacco and snuff in order to reimburse the king. The recriminations about the Port St Mary looting were many and long, but Methuen was able to tell the king about Queen Anne's decision to punish the offenders and to restore the stolen goods. King Pedro still had scruples whether he could agree to an alliance with such enemies of religion, but his confessor came to the rescue and quieted the royal conscience. However, Methuen was obliged to agree that allied troops should be subject to Portuguese law in matters of religion.[2]

In The Hague the Dutch were now coming to realise that a neutral Portugal might make inroads upon their trade and were

[1] Mayer, *op. cit.* pp. 14, 17–18; Add. MSS 29590, fos. 109, 130, 158, and 28056, fos. 35, 166; Rijksarchief 7369, 18 Sept., 4 Oct. 1702; Harleian MS 2264/12; S.P. 104/195, 7 Feb. 1700.
[2] Add. MSS 29590, fos. 141, 144, 161.

working towards an agreement with England for an embargo on trade with the enemy. Schonenberg thought that this would be a good thing, at least as regards Spain, and mentioned the subject to King Pedro in December. Nevertheless, the Dutch were conditioned to international trade and slow to bring themselves to the point. Although they agreed in principle to the embargo in February 1703, they did not pass the enabling decree for an embargo for one year until June. But they began interfering with Spanish shipping in the Straits, and Methuen was hoist at his own petard when a Dutch frigate seized some English-owned cargoes being carried in Spanish ships and Admiral Rooke could not interfere.[1]

When the ill news began to come from Cadiz, King Pedro became suspicious not only of Waldstein and Schonenberg but even of his own ministers, and Alegrete told Schonenberg that it would be dangerous for Portugal to join the allies. Methuen felt obliged to redouble his efforts and assured the king that if he entered the war with his full force, and undertook to receive the Archduke Charles and an allied army, he would be given full protection, and the allies would not make peace without him. He also mentioned Vigo, Pontevedra, Bayona in Galicia, and part of Estremadura lying on the way to Madrid, as possible concessions. The king was pleased, but said that Methuen must remain in Lisbon to conclude the treaty and carry out his promises, and he would like to be certain that Parliament would agree, as it was believed in Portugal that Parliament could disown a treaty, even after it had been signed. Methuen told the king that the queen would probably obtain parliamentary approval and requested in his dispatch home that the opinion of the Cabinet should be transmitted to him as soon as possible. He confessed that his offers might seem too great, but argued that the alliance would be worth the cost, and in any case France would offer the same terms or better. At the same time he answered the complaints about the

[1] Rijksarchief 7369, 16 Oct. 1702; Add. MSS 29590, fo. 122.

Hesse incident and said he hoped that he could now count on Schonenberg and that Waldstein would fall in with his views. This was too optimistic; however, Waldstein was sometimes more helpful and Schonenberg admitted that concessions were necessary, though he would never go so far as to specify them. Methuen had justification both in his instructions and in the circumstances for taking risks in his offers to the king, but he was not a master of that diplomatic double talk which might conceivably have enabled him to hint convincingly of offers without being explicit and to make his colleagues feel they were in the picture, without committing himself. Schonenberg, in an honest attempt to report objectively, said that neither he nor Waldstein understood Methuen, and he did not think they would make any progress by offering concessions to the Portuguese, but he was trying to smooth over the differences between Methuen and Waldstein. Nevertheless, though Schonenberg and Waldstein may have been tougher and more accomplished, it was only Methuen who made progress in persuading the Portuguese. But after the point of no return, which was perhaps his audience of 4 October, he was understandably anxious. 'Whatever effect', he wrote, 'my endeavours have from here, and if what I write to your Lordship is not perfectly and entirely a secret, all we can ever hope for is at an end, and I must appear no more at this Court, for not having communicated to the Ambassador and Mr Schonenberg my secret treating with the King, nor the whole matter to the Marquis or Alegrete. If the least word be known, there is an end and I must never see the King more.'[1]

Château-Renault, having avoided the attempts to intercept him, entered Vigo on 20 September. Methuen heard on 29 September that he had reached Vigo. Schonenberg also reported the news to the States General on 1 October, but seems to have taken no further action. Methuen forwarded the news and a plan of Vigo to Rooke by every possible route, but his messenger only reached

[1] Rijksarchief 7369, 4 Oct., 25 Nov. 1702; Add. MSS 29590, fos. 130–2, 139, 161

Faro in time to see the fleet passing in the distance and Rooke sent no boat ashore. A second messenger missed the frigates *Pembroke* and *Eagle* at Lagos. However, by a stroke of luck the chaplain of the *Pembroke*, who was a French-speaking Jerseyman named Beauvoir, ran into the French Consul in the street and was entertained by him. In his joy at the news that Château-Renault had safely arrived, he inadvertently dropped a broad hint which was picked up by the chaplain. Beauvoir then searched the town and found a courier from Methuen, who had left Lisbon before the news but had heard it in Faro. He hastened to tell the captain of the *Pembroke*. His ship was a poor sailer and in bad shape but he pressed all sail to catch up the fleet. He only did so on 16 October at a place north of Vigo, but a Naval Council at once decided to put about and a lucky change of wind to the north blew the fleet to the Spanish coast in twenty-four hours.[1]

The unloading of the galleons had been delayed by a claim for payment of duty by the director of the Cadiz customs and was still proceeding. The king of Spain's silver valued at three million pounds was mostly ashore, but much of the privately owned bullion and merchandise was on board. The men-of-war and the galleons were anchored at the head of Vigo bay behind a boom placed across the narrows, five miles above Vigo, at the fort and inlet of Redondella (see Plate 4).

The Allies succeeded in breaking through the boom and in capturing or destroying fifteen major French ships of war, three Spanish ships and seventeen galleons. Château-Renault escaped but the Spanish admiral and many French officers were taken prisoner. The spoils in plate and merchandise were considerable and included a quantity of snuff, for which the sale in London popularised the fashion. It was the treasure which struck the popular imagination, but it was the loss of a good third of the

[1] Rijksarchief 7369, 1 Oct. 1702; Add. MSS 29590, fos. 135–40, 146, 151; Anon., *History of the Expedition into Spain* (1702), pp. 101–5; Navy Records Soc., *Rooke*, IX, 227–30; J. C. de Jonge, *Geschiedenis van het Nederlandsche Zeewezen* (Amsterdam, 1840), IV, ii, 220.

French fleet which affected the course of the war most. The French still had their Toulon and Brest squadrons, and their privateers to harass commerce, but their capital strength in the Atlantic and the Channel was now inferior to that of the allies. The capture or destruction of the merchandise caused mixed feelings, for part of it was owned by Allied or Portuguese merchants. But part of the silver had been earmarked to pay the compensation due to the Cacheo Company. The French ambassador had hitherto been tempting King Pedro with hopes that this sum might still be paid. These hopes were now lost, and the obstinacy of Spain in refusing to meet other outstanding claims of the Cacheo Company for transactions in the West Indies furthered the allied cause, and probably influenced Alegrete, who in addition to his other duties was responsible for Portuguese finances.[1]

Throughout October Methuen passed anxious days until at last on 31 October the news of Vigo arrived. Even before this, affairs had taken a better turn; the war news from the north was favourable to the Allies, and though the number of French ships in the Tagus rose once to as many as eight their presence began to be discouraged, and by the end of October they had all left except for the four galleys which were laid up for the winter. Methuen wrote at once to inquire about Rooke's plans and informed London that Allied men-of-war, including the largest ratings, would be welcome in Lisbon. The king promised to find provisions for the fleet, and ordered the governors of the northern provinces to give all possible help. Methuen hoped that Vigo would be occupied and that Portuguese troops might perhaps assist. The Portuguese had been impressed by the recent arrival from Spain of the Almirante de Castile with a considerable suite, the first notable recruit to the Habsburg cause of all those promised by Hesse. Even Waldstein joined Schonenberg in urging Methuen to speak again to the king of the alliance. Hesse had recommended

[1] Navy Records Soc. *Rooke*, IX, 231–4; Mayer, *op. cit.* p. 17; Albrecht, *op. cit.* p. 32; Rijksarchief 7369, I, 27 Oct. 1702.

the use of Vigo and in all the Allied capitals as well as in Lisbon the general expectation was that Vigo would be occupied. Methuen had spoken of it to the king; and the Almirante of Castile, and also Alegrete, thought Vigo or Oporto would serve as a good base for an invasion of Spain. Supplies could have been brought with relative ease from England, Ireland or Portugal, and urgent needs could have been met by Admiral Shovell's squadron, which had been ordered to proceed from the Channel, where it had been waiting for Château-Renault, and which reached Vigo a few days after Rooke. But Rooke was determined to go home. Ormonde asked to be left in Vigo with a sufficient force of ships, men and supplies to winter there, but Rooke replied that he did not think any ships left behind would be any safer than Château-Renault had been, and in any case he could only leave five or six frigates and provisions for two months at most. He did not wait to receive Methuen's dispatch with its assurance of Portuguese help. Ormonde insisted no more and to the deep disappointment of Methuen Vigo was abandoned.[1]

[1] Add. MSS 29590, fos. 144–6, 151–3, and 38159, fo. 35; S.P. 42/6, fo. 140; Adm 1/4088, 4/15 Oct. 1702; *Cal. of S.P.* (1702–3), p. 255.

CHAPTER 7

PORTUGAL JOINS THE GRAND ALLIANCE, JANUARY–MAY 1703

ON his arrival back in London in the third week of November the duke of Ormonde was acclaimed as a popular hero, and according to Nottingham the queen asked that the fleet should return to Vigo. This was impracticable but there was a general desire to avenge Cadiz. An expedition to Spain remained the first item on the agenda for the Peninsula and was only relegated to a second place by the pressure of events.[1]

If an Allied force had wintered in Vigo or in Lisbon Portugal might have been encouraged to enter the war at once. The return of the fleet to England provoked a reaction, but the nobility and gentry now appeared to favour a war with Spain, and the king's advisers were friendly, with the important exception of Cadaval, who was definitely in opposition, and to some extent of Alegrete, who thought Portugal needed money and an army to enter a war, and should not venture to do so before the money was available and the army ready.[2] However, the war news was reasonably favourable to the allies. Dutch caution had cost the duke of Marlborough the chance of several victories in Brabant but he had driven the French back and had saved the United Provinces from the threat of immediate invasion. The defection of the Elector of Bavaria had made a deep impression on King Pedro, but the capture of Landau was a modest victory, which was built up by the maritime powers to increase the prestige of the Archduke Joseph and to divert the emperor from concentrating too much on Italy. Luzzara was claimed as a victory by both sides, but the fact remained that Prince Eugène had established an

---

[1] Add. MSS 17677, YY, fos. 239, 272.   [2] Add. MSS 29590, fo. 153.

Imperial army in Lombardy. In Vienna the news of Marlborough's occupation of Liège arrived simultaneously with that of Cadiz and offset it; Stepney had the good luck to be the first to announce the success, and the emperor was so pleased that at Court he advanced five steps to speak to Stepney and to congratulate him, which was an unheard-of condescension to a foreign envoy.[1]

Both in Spain and Portugal Catholic feeling had been gravely outraged by the excesses of the English and Dutch troops at Cadiz, but in Portugal it was the lack of co-operation between the allies and between the army and naval commanders which had the worst effect and most jeopardised the negotiations. It was realised that such weaknesses could disable the most powerful force and the Portuguese became all the more determined to manage their own affairs and to take no orders from foreigners. On the other hand even Cadiz had helped to prick the bubble of French naval prestige. In July the French had gleefully circulated leaflets offering a reward on behalf of the prince of Hesse to anybody finding and returning a lost fleet.[2] But a few days later Allied men-of-war covered the sea within sight of Portugal and, although Cadiz was not taken, the allies had shown that they could convey an army to Spain and bring it back again without loss or fear of the French navy. The arrival of the treasure fleet safely in Vigo had seemed a triumph, but it had not dared to enter Cadiz or Brest and had been destroyed in its port of refuge. A year before, the French had undertaken to convoy the Brazil fleet. This fleet was now ready to leave Brazil, but it was clear that it depended on Allied protection to bring it home.

As a neutral, Portugal could afford to sell her favours dearly but, as Methuen wrote, she could not afford to tolerate a Bourbon régime in Spain. This was her weak point. It was to her interest to stop the establishment of Philip V and the decisive question for her was the ability of the Allies to take Spain. She was more

---

[1] S.P. 80/19, Stepney to Hedges, 1 Nov. 1702; Add. MSS 29590, fo. 144.
[2] Add. MSS 17677, YY, fo. 214.

vulnerable than the allies, who could come to an arrangement. Portugal could not, and for this reason King Pedro wished to use as many Portuguese troops as he could muster, and to be able to count on two armies, one to invade Spain from Estremadura, and one from Cadiz. Methuen also favoured the use of Portuguese troops, as being cheaper to maintain, hardy, and close in religion and language to the people of Spain. He said that they had been brave and effective in their war of independence, when there had never been more than 3,000 Allied troops, and they would serve better than any others except the English, or perhaps some German regiments. In the event the Portuguese army fell far short of Methuen's expectations, but this was largely because they were never properly paid, fed, armed, or trained.[1]

The absence of King Philip in Italy until January 1703 had annoyed the Spanish grandees and it was generally believed that Spain was ripe for a revolution against him. These hopes had been proved false at Cadiz, but there were still constant rumours of disaffection at Madrid and a report received in Vienna listed sixteen grandees as pro-Habsburg, twenty as benevolently neutral, and only fifteen as pro-French.[2] Allied optimism was at last given substance by the arrival on the frontier at the end of September, and in Lisbon in October, of Juan Luis Enrique de Cabrera, Duque de Medina y Rio Seco and Almirante of Castile, with an imposing suite.

The Almirante was a wealthy grandee, described by Schonenberg as the greatest and best accredited nobleman in Spain. He had been prime minister, and head of the Imperialists, until he fell out of favour at the death of King Charles II. He was renowned for his magnificence, his fine house and collection of pictures, and for his gallantry with the ladies. In spite of his age he was still a great courtier and had at first some success with the new queen of Spain, the young daughter of the duke of Savoy, and with her confidante the princess of Orsini. He was offered the governor-

[1] Add. MSS 29590, fos. 153-4.   [2] S.P. 105/65, c. July 1702.

generalship of Andalusia, but it was known that he was in correspondence with Vienna, and his enemies prevented his appointment. He was too important to be disgraced, and with the approval of King Louis XIV, who thought he could be flattered or bribed into friendship, he was appointed ambassador at Paris. He did not think such a post was good enough for him and although he set out as if for Paris, he turned aside to the Portuguese frontier, which he reached during the siege of Cadiz, but before the allied failure was known. He had taken the precaution of sending away as much money as possible beforehand and of taking with him most of his valuables. He announced his arrival to the duke of Cadaval and was lodged by him at Belem in the house of the Conde de São Lourenço (San Lorenzo).[1]

The Almirante began by issuing a manifesto saying that he was not disloyal to King Philip and had only left Spain to be safe from his enemies. On 31 October he wrote to the queen of Spain, excusing himself and alleging the enmity of the French ambassador. In Vienna Counts Harrach and Mansfield told Stepney that he was slippery as an eel, and could not be trusted.[2] Stepney passed this observation to London, where he was long regarded with suspicion, but the Court of Vienna soon had a better opinion of him. It transpired that he had made no attempt to conceal his correspondence with the queen of Spain, and had indeed given Waldstein a copy of his letter to her. Although she was the wife of King Philip, she was also the daughter of the duke of Savoy, and at the moment she was suspected by the French of intriguing with her father. In fact the duke was in touch with the emperor and was on the point of joining the Allies. The Almirante's mediation with the queen could therefore be useful. How-

[1] Albrecht, *England's Bemühungen um den Eintritt Portugals in die Grosse Allianz*, p. 37; Marquis de Louville, *Mémoires* (Paris, 1818), pp. 50, 179–80, 234; *Recueil*, XII, ii, 73. The number of the Almirante's suite is usually given as 300, but Schonenberg only gives 50 including the count of Corzana (Rijksarchief 7369, 1 Oct. 1702).

[2] S.P. 89/19, Stepney to Hedges, 20 Dec. 1702; Künzel, *Das Leben und der Briefwechsel des Landgraven Georg von Hessen-Darmstadt*, p. 228, prints a letter from the Almirante to the queen of Spain saying the king of Spain's will was a forgery.

ever, it did not last for long, for in spite of the discretion with which he at first behaved in Portugal, he was soon proclaimed a rebel by King Philip and obliged to declare himself. King Pedro now had to decide whether he would treat the Almirante like Hesse, or whether he would offer him protection, which would mean committing himself. He chose the latter course, which was a great step forward to widening the breach between Portugal and France. At the end of the year Methuen reported that the Almirante was being treated with kindness, and was well received by the nobility, while the feeling against Spain was growing daily. In the long run Hesse's promises of support for the allies in Catalonia proved more valid than the Almirante's assurances about Castile and Andalusia, but the Almirante was taken much more seriously in Portugal than Hesse had been.[1]

The emperor began to regard the Almirante as his representative for Spanish affairs almost to the exclusion of Waldstein. Methuen found it useful to have an alternative channel to Vienna but the emperor also used the Almirante as a means to counter the lead which England was assuming in the negotiations. Methuen took the Almirante at his own valuation and reported that he was acting very prudently, and there was an understanding between them, though they could not meet openly until the position was clearer. Schonenberg and Waldstein also only conferred with him in secret. Both the Almirante and Waldstein had expected the Allies to begin a march to Madrid from Vigo. Schonenberg had much ado to explain the difficulties of sea communications in winter and the reasons why such a march had been impracticable. Schonenberg was pessimistic about the prospect of Portugal joining the allies and had several discussions with the Almirante and Waldstein, and also one with Hesse, when he passed through Lisbon, with a view to concocting some new plan. The Almirante had hoped to join the Imperialists in Andalusia. The failure at

---

[1] Carl van Noorden, *Europäische Geschichte, Der Spanische Erbfolgekrieg* (Düsseldorf, 1870), I, 39; Louville, *op. cit.* II, 35; Add. MSS 29590, fos. 144, 179.

Cadiz had foiled hopes of this, but he still looked forward to another and better organised expedition. He admitted that the emperor and most of his court set more store by Italy than Spain, but Schonenberg argued that an allied expedition to Spain would put France on the defensive in the Spanish dominions, would oblige Portugal to enter the war and would be cheaper than operations in Italy. He suggested that the emperor ought to persuade Queen Anne to send a new expedition to Cadiz or Galicia, for which the maritime powers would provide the transport and naval protection, while the land forces would all be raised by the emperor from the domains of the Catholic princes of the Empire and would serve under Imperial commanders. This would save money for the allies and avoid the difficulties and jealousies caused by English and Dutch participation and by differences of religion. If Portugal entered the war Portuguese cavalry from Estremadura could help to invade Spain in the spring.[1] Waldstein liked this and similar plans. He always promised that the emperor would send Imperial troops to make up half the allied contingent and he believed that Spain could be overrun without the need for help from Portugal or concessions to her. Schonenberg did not go as far as this, but he foresaw an easy conquest of Spain by a relatively small allied force with the help of Spanish dissidents. Methuen did not know of all these plans but he complained that his colleagues in talking to the Portuguese made the reduction of Spain seem far too easy. He believed that Portugal must be asked to play a greater part and was capable of doing so, but large concessions would be needed to compensate her. Methuen thought that he had converted Schonenberg to his point of view, and it is true that he had a more open mind than Waldstein on the subject, but he continued to express grave doubts to the States General about Methuen's policy and he never saw eye to eye with him.[2]

[1] Rijksarchief 7369, 16, 27 Oct. 1702.
[2] *Ibid.* 16, 26 Oct., 25 Nov., 13 Dec. 1702.

However, the Dutch ambassadors in London agreed that the negotiations should go forward and in November Methuen heard that his talks with the king had been approved. Schonenberg continued to hammer away at the question of the use by the allies of the Portuguese ports, and even Methuen did not altogether rule out the possibility that if Portugal conceded this point she might be allowed to remain neutral. However, he thought it would be fatal to admit as much to the Portuguese and reported in December that he thought he had talked the Portuguese out of ever mentioning the subject of neutrality. King Pedro told him that the French would prefer war to any agreement allowing the allies to use his ports, but in fact the French seem at least to have thought twice on the subject.[1]

Methuen was now embarrassed by the generous though vague assurances he had given the king in May about naval protection. Nottingham laid down that not only twenty-five ships but the whole allied navy would be available to protect Portugal, but Methuen must not commit himself to keep ships idle in the Tagus or to provide any specific number. Methuen promised not to commit himself but the point became very troublesome. However, he managed to confine himself to an assurance that enough ships would be kept in Portuguese waters to secure and defend the ports, coasts, and trade of Portugal. The Allies were to undertake convoys in each direction, but King Pedro was to keep fifteen ships available. The assurance about the ships for convoy duties in Portuguese waters was agreed in writing by Schonenberg.[2]

Methuen now continued his secret talks with the king, on the one hand stressing the urgent need for a positive reply, and insisting that he must soon leave for England, and on the other particularising and amplifying his offers. The sequence of events

[1] Add. MSS 29590, fos. 153, 159; Legrelle, *La Diplomatie Française et la Succession d'Espagne*, IV, 279; *Clarendon Corr.* ed. S. W. Singer (1828), II, 451. See also below, ch. 8, p. 195.
[2] Add. MSS 29590, fos. 154, 161, 169; Rijksarchief 7369, 5 Dec. 1702.

is hard to follow, as there was a double negotiation, one between the Portuguese ministers and Schonenberg and Methuen acting together, the other between Methuen and the king alone. Methuen's talks with the king were secret, but the gist of them was apt to leak, and in any case the substance of them came back to the Allied ministers as part of the Portuguese proposals. Waldstein only came intermittently into the picture, but he was always in touch with Schonenberg, and from the end of October with the Almirante of Castile.

In The Hague Heinsius had grumbled at the failure to leave any occupying force in Vigo but he agreed that Schonenberg must make further representations even at the cost of making concessions. In December Methuen and Schonenberg delivered identical notes, promising full support to Portugal if she entered the war, their good offices with the emperor to secure concessions, sufficient ships to protect Portugal, and an undertaking to make no separate peace. Schonenberg, who was anticipating good orders from Portugal for arms and munitions, promised that none should be delivered before she joined the Allies. In Vienna Stepney had been trying hard to convince the emperor that an alliance with Portugal was necessary and to persuade him to join in the embargo on trade. He also defended Methuen against Waldstein's complaints, and, after the arrival of the Almirante of Castile, Waldstein brought himself at last to offer a territorial concession and suggested that Portugal might have the Canary Islands and Buenos Aires. In December Roque Monteiro delivered to him a message from the king, asking him to co-operate and to persuade the emperor to send the Archduke Charles to Portugal. Waldstein insisted on having an explanation of Portuguese requirements in writing and would do no more than show his 'powers', and indicate verbally that the concession of the Philippines and Buenos Aires, and perhaps of the Canary Islands, might be possible. The Council of State then rejected Waldstein's offer and only the king still expressed his confidence in Methuen. However, Schon-

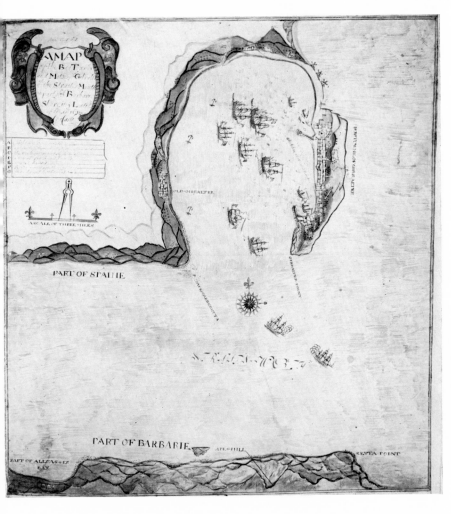

3   Map of Gibraltar made by Charles Carlile in 1700 (The original is coloured.)

4   The battle of Vigo Bay, October 1702, from an engraving by Anna Beck

enberg consented to carry on the negotiation with Methuen and this was agreed by Portugal. Waldstein at first objected, but after a stormy argument at Paul Methuen's house, in which Schonenberg played the part of mediator, Waldstein agreed not to interfere. Schonenberg was now agreeable to some territorial concessions, but he vehemently opposed Methuen's suggestions of expensive subsidies and supplies. Harmony might still perhaps have been kept if the two ministers had been able to negotiate jointly with the king, but the Portuguese insisted on their doing so separately.[1]

In his secret talks Methuen specified the territorial concessions likely, and discussed the numbers of men and quantities of arms to be contributed by Portugal and the allies. His proposal was that the allied forces should arrive in March and the archduke in the following weeks. The Council of State discussed Methuen's proposal and for a short time Methuen thought he had won them over and that even Cadaval would agree. But he was asked to put his offer in writing, and upon a promise of secrecy Paul Methuen handed it to Alegrete in a sealed envelope addressed to the king. Naturally the contents leaked, and indeed the gist of them was put into a note which Alegrete sent to Schonenberg regarding Portuguese requirements. These came under three headings: (i) adequate subsidies; (ii) adequate weapons, munitions and war supplies; (iii) compensation for the losses of the Cacheo Company. Schonenberg was persuaded to tell the king that he would negotiate in agreement with Methuen, but in his report to the States General he protested that the Portuguese demands were exorbitant. Methuen alternated between hope and despair, at one moment saying that he hoped to overcome the opposition of four or five great ministers, who were all that stood between him and success, and at another that these men had ruined his efforts, being 'all old men of seventy, in office since the King came to power,

[1] Mayer, 'Die Allianz Portugal's', *Zeitschrift für die Österreichischen Gymnasien*, p. 19; S.P. 80/19, Stepney to Hedges, 15, 19, 25 Nov. 1702; Albrecht, *op. cit.* p. 39; Rijksarchief 7369, 27 Jan. 1703; Add. MSS 29590, fo. 205.

timorous, irresolute in their councils, fearful of losing office, distrustful of Schonenberg and having a mean and light opinion of Waldstein'.[1]

Schonenberg had been busy with his own secret plans and his ambitions to be appointed ambassador to Habsburg Spain. He wrote to Marlborough about a plan suggested by the Almirante for a march to Madrid by way of Ciudad Rodrigo based on allied landings at Oporto or Viana. For this scheme the personal presence of the Archduke Charles would be required but he need not take an active part, and all Spain would declare for him. Marlborough discussed the plan in London, but it was decided that it would be better to wait until Methuen's views were known. Marlborough had some doubts about Portuguese intentions but he did not wish to go behind the back of Methuen, who he observed was at loggerheads with Waldstein, and perhaps with the Almirante and his henchman the count of Corzana, for they had wished to keep their plan secret and to confer with Schonenberg alone.[2]

The Oporto plan was not in fact very practicable, for although Oporto looked on the map very near to the frontier, the direct route lay over mountainous country unsuitable for the passage of an army, and the port was inadequate. Methuen at this very moment was trying to send a convoy of twenty ships to Oporto with a supply of Newfoundland fish but, 'not having the port of Vigo to friend, and the Barr being very dangerous', the ships dared not leave Lisbon and face the rough weather.[3]

In December a new trouble hindered Methuen. Alegrete had complained of New Christians and Jews taking refuge on English ships, and although Methuen issued strict orders that refugees must not be taken on board, twenty-six of them managed to embark on the frigates *Poole* and *Lime*, which were standing by to

[1] Add. MSS 29590, fos. 165, 173, 179; Rijksarchief, 13 Dec. 1702.

[2] *Marlborough–Heinsius Letters*, no. 73.

[3] Rijksarchief 7025, 28 Feb. 1703; Add. MSS 29590, fos. 167, 177, 180.

take Methuen home. There was an outcry in Lisbon, encouraged by the nuncio and the public inquisitor, and the king spoke in harsh terms of forbidding the ships to sail. The secretary of state told Methuen that he would not be received by the king unless he gave up the refugees. Methuen refused, but after taking up the question, over Faria's head, with Alegrete he was allowed to conduct the refugees ashore, on the understanding that they would not be molested or arrested within six hours of landing. Alegrete then intimated that the king would be willing to receive Methuen again. However, Methuen insisted on having a formal invitation to an audience; he had been firm but he still felt it wise to cover himself by suggesting to Nottingham that Da Cunha be told that he had been uncommonly easy and had shown so much compliance on account of the great desire of Queen Anne to show her friendship for King Pedro. Nottingham minuted the dispatch: 'speak with the Portugal Envoy accordingly'.[1]

Even now there were delays before the commissioners for the treaty were appointed. Cadaval was away at the frontier, and Alegrete and the king were ill. Methuen tried to secure the appointment of his old friend Mendo de Foios as a commissary, but the three Councillors of State, Cadaval, Alegrete and Alvor, and the two secretaries, Roque Monteiro and Faria, were chosen. Still nothing happened, until after many reminders the king signified his consent for the negotiations to begin. Methuen had expected that the Portuguese would suggest terms which bore some resemblance to those he had discussed with the king. But the opposition had been encouraged by a rumour that the Cardinal d'Estrées was on his way to Lisbon to win over the Court by joining the prestige of the Pope and the power of religion to the power of France and Spain. The Portuguese produced a project in forty-three articles, which was unanimously rejected as quite impossible by the three allied representatives.[2] Methuen said that

[1] Add. MSS 29590, fos. 156, 177–8.
[2] Copy of Portuguese project in Add. MSS 29590, fo. 450, and of Methuen's counter-project, fo. 201.

11-2

every single article in it had something amiss, being either excessive in quantity, where questions of arms, ammunition, money or troops were concerned, or physically impossible. Methuen in a two hours' audience persuaded the king to accept a counter-project in twenty-three articles, which he offered as a basis for negotiations, but it was generally expected that he would have to carry out his threat to leave Lisbon. Waldstein was uncompromising but allowed himself to be persuaded not to cancel the negotiations altogether, so that the way was not closed for a fresh start.

On 4 January Methuen received definite leave to return home if he could not obtain a satisfactory reply from the king. Although the ministers were proving so difficult, even Schonenberg was inclined to agree that King Pedro meant well. At an audience he spoke to Methuen of orders for tents and furniture in England, of the guns he had bought from two Italian ships in Lisbon, and of his intention to command the army himself. Methuen continued to hope that economic factors might help to encourage Portugal to join the allies. In the autumn he had written home to deplore the slump in trade, which had resulted from the spread of the war and the anxieties of the Portugal merchants. Very few goods had been shipped to Portugal and there was the greatest shortage of woollen goods that ever had been known. He urged that the Portugal merchants should be consulted and be assured that Portugal would continue her friendship and that they could safely remit goods and money and foodstuffs to Portugal. An adequate convoy should be provided to ensure that their ships arrived safely. With a flourishing trade the exchange, which had fallen, would revert to normal, and with plenty of foodstuffs Portugal would be encouraged. In the new year the promised convoy had not come but Admiral Leake had reached Lisbon with a number of ships from Newfoundland and some French prizes. Methuen made all the use he could of this and obtained leave for the fish on board to be sold in Lisbon, and for the prize goods to be freely exported, though he could not get leave for them to be sold in Portugal.[1]

At The Hague Heinsius was anxious to take positive steps in Portugal, but he found it difficult to move the States General either to declare the embargo on trade or to agree to an increase in the number of troops for Portugal. As it was getting too late to send the squadron proposed for the West Indies with any hope of it being available for Portugal in June, he toyed with the idea of diverting the ships and the troops on board to Portugal, but after discussion with Marlborough it was decided that this force could be better used in Flanders.[2]

By the end of January Nottingham had lost hope of Methuen succeeding, and, supposing that he was on the way home, addressed his dispatches to Paul. But he had been active in pressing the emperor, and Methuen would have liked the terms of a letter he addressed to Wratislaw. He expressed the queen's displeasure at the failure of the emperor to inform her of his negotiations with Bavaria and her fear that the same unhappy lack of co-operation would lose Portugal too, for, although King Pedro had shown his inclination to join the Grand Alliance, he had deferred his decision and made no other proposals, for no other reason to all appearance but the refusal of Count Waldstein to agree to anything that might be for the convenience or security of Portugal. Although the emperor had often been pressed to authorise Her Majesty to offer such terms to Portugal as she thought wise and reasonable, he had not thought fit to do it, but had instead given the authority to the Almirante of Castile in a manner showing little trust in Her Majesty's justice and prudence. The queen had no interest different from that of the emperor to incline her either towards Bavaria or Portugal, and there was good reason to fear that the emperor by his dilatory proceeding would give France the opportunity to treat with Portugal. He did not

[1] Add. MSS 29590, fos. 166, 179–80, 189, 191.
[2] *Marlborough–Heinsius Letters*, nos. 76, 80, 83, 86.

mention these things in order to complain of what was past, but in order to prevent the like proceeding in future, it being impossible[1] for the allies to carry on the war if they did not do so by united councils as well as by arms. It was visible to all the world that if Portugal and Bavaria could be brought to join the Grand Alliance, France could no longer resist the power of the allies, and that the House of Austria by giving up some parts of the Spanish dominions to these princes would soon be restored to the monarchy of Spain. He ended by expressing the queen's hope that the emperor would direct his minister in Portugal to agree to such terms as she thought fit, and that he would inform Stepney of the terms asked by Bavaria, so that she could try to win over the Elector.

The ministers in Vienna were taken up with various plans for permutations of territory, such as a scheme to give Naples and Sicily to the Elector in exchange for Bavaria. They furiously resented any suggestion of Partition coming from the Allies, because they could not openly give up any part of the Spanish throne, upon which all their claims depended, but in reality, as Stepney reported, they regarded the territory of Spain 'as a mere carcase, scarcely worth the having, unless accompanied with the dominions in Italy'. The younger Count Harrach once blurted out that if they could be masters of Naples and Sicily, they would willingly sacrifice the half of Spain and for that matter let England keep Cadiz and Barcelona. Stepney was genuinely shocked and said the emperor at least had some feeling for Spain and would never agree. Neither Mansfield nor Harrach would have had any real objection to the duke of Anjou keeping Spain, or to concessions in Spain being made at his expense, but they could not agree to any concessions being made in the name of the Archduke Charles.[2] They hoped that Spain would declare for the Habsburgs without the need for Portuguese help or the archduke's presence and were now reluctant to let him go to the Peninsula and

[1] S.P. 100/10, draft by Nottingham of 24 Dec./4 Jan. 1702–3.
[2] S.P. 80/19, Stepney to Hedges, 18, 25 Oct. 1702, and S.P. 105/65, 30 Aug. and 5 Apr. 1702.

particularly to Portugal, where he would be under the tutelage of King Pedro. They had failed to reach agreement on concessions to the allies in the West Indies, and there was hopeful talk in Paris that the Grand Alliance might founder upon this question and upon Dutch jealousy of English ambitions. However, the danger from Bavaria and the stubbornness of Portugal forced them to veer again and to agree to Nottingham's proposals. By then the treaties had neared conclusion and the Portuguese had gained many of their demands.[1]

Waldstein in a fit of exasperation said that Methuen's 'contemptible methods were only too well known to all here and he sought only to come out with advantage to himself' and 'that he had not only betrayed Austria and the United Provinces but also his own Queen'. Schonenberg was personally even more eager than Waldstein to outwit Methuen, but officially he was more circumspect and he tried to calm Waldstein. He confined himself to the remark that Methuen was an odd man, neither fish nor fowl, and too much attached to his own interests, while the quarrels with Waldstein were most vexing. Methuen on the other hand observed that Waldstein's attitude was most mysterious; either the emperor did not want to make an alliance with Portugal and place his son on the throne of Spain or he was ill served by his ambassador.[2]

Such bickering between diplomatic ministers was not peculiar to Methuen. Imperial ministers everywhere were apt to be highfalutin. Stanhope had trouble with Count Harrach, and even the able and genial Stepney found Von Kaunitz trying. In London Wratislaw made himself very awkward, and at one time refused to correspond with Hedges, and insisted on writing only to Nottingham, until he was called to order. Stepney's difficulties with his Dutch colleagues were due more to the delays of the States General than to any personal quarrel, but he often complained, and, as already mentioned, English and Dutch ministers were

[1] S.P. 106/67, fos. 390, 423, 448; Coimbra MS 3008, fo. 13.
[2] Mayer, *op. cit.* pp. 22, 24; Rijksarchief 7369, 5 March 1703; Add. MSS 29590, fo. 173.

tempted sometimes to encroach upon each other's preserves. Even the French, though they had the best diplomatic service, were not exempt from such broils; their affairs in Madrid were jeopardised by the quarrels between the Cardinal d'Estrées, his nephew the Abbé, and De Louville, who had been seconded as gentleman in waiting to the king. Perhaps they contributed to the mistake by which a project for a treaty of neutrality with Portugal, dated 22 April 1703, was addressed to the Cardinal d'Estrées in Madrid and never reached Lisbon. The cardinal had expected to come to Lisbon and had written to tell King Pedro he would be coming, but the visit did not materialise, nor did a counter-offer to Waldstein's offers, the suggestion that one of King Pedro's small daughters should be betrothed to the duke of Berry.[1]

The Portuguese project was duly discussed in London and rejected and Methuen's counter-project was accepted. Da Cunha and Pacheco argued earnestly that the Portuguese demands were just and reasonable and afforded no ground for supposing that King Pedro was insincere. It was customary in Portugal to begin bargaining by asking for too much but the tenacity with which the Portuguese persisted with many of their original demands showed that, reasonable or not, they were regarded as essential. Nottingham discussed Methuen's project with Da Cunha on 16 February and the latter undertook to convey Nottingham's views to Lisbon, though he refused to make any concessions. In Lisbon Methuen's project was eventually accepted as a basis for negotiation.[2]

Methuen cut out the demand that all the allied troops should be Catholic but conceded that they should be subject to Portuguese law in religious matters. Matters exclusively affecting the Dutch were shelved for consideration with the Triple Defensive Treaty. The dangerous Portuguese requirement that their entry into the

[1] S.P. 80/19, Stepney to Nottingham, 15, 19 Nov. 1702; Albrecht, *op. cit.* p. 36; S.P. 105/67, fos. 1, 158, 229, 328; Coimbra MS 3008, fos. 16, 18; Louville, *op. cit.* I, 347, 369–70, II, 25; *Recueil*, III, 214; Add. MSS 29590, fo. 209; *Marlborough–Heinsius Letters*, no. 86.

[2] *Cal. of S.P.* (1702–3), p. 570; Add. MSS 17677, WWW, fo. 83; Add. MSS 29590, fos. 213, 215–16.

war should be conditional on all the provisions for bringing allied forces into the Peninsula being completed was rejected, for this would have exposed the Allies to the risk of the treaty being abrogated in the same way as the recent French treaty. The Portuguese demand that the number of the forces to be kept by the allies in Italy, Brabant and the Rhine should be specified in the treaty was obviously absurd and impracticable.

The core of the negotiations concerned the size of the Portuguese and allied forces and the amount of the subsidies. The Portuguese regular army was fixed at 15,000 men without difficulty but there was long argument about the Portuguese auxiliary forces. Methuen had mentioned a figure of 8,000 in November and this was the number in his project. Schonenberg began by refusing to pay any subsidy for the auxiliary forces and proposed 3,000 and an allied army of 18,000. This meant a quota of 6,000 for each of the allies, and Waldstein at one point thought the emperor could provide 8,000. The Portuguese project asked for 15,000 and proposed to furnish auxiliary forces to a maximum of 20,000. For their upkeep they asked an initial payment of 1,000,000 cruzados and an annual payment of 500,000 patacas. Methuen offered 4,000,000 cruzados for 8,000 men and a further 400,000 cruzados for their upkeep until the end of 1703. He suggested 12,000 for the allied force and this figure was accepted. He evaded King Pedro's request for thirty ships by promising a sufficiency of ships to protect Portuguese trade. He included an undertaking that the allies would bring the archduke to Portugal and would make no separate peace. A year or two before, the emperor had wanted to send the archduke, but now he refused to consider it, and Nottingham asked whether the archduke could be omitted. Methuen replied that it was impossible and in February the Council of State decided that the coming of the archduke was essential.[1]

[1] Add. MSS 29590, fos. 207–9. Copies of the Portuguese project are in Add. MSS 29590, fo. 450; S.P. 106/67, fo. 391 (a German version); and Rijksarchief 7369, 27 Jan. 1703. Methuen's 23-article project is in Add. MSS 29590, fo. 201.

By the end of January Methuen had had no less than three farewell audiences with King Pedro. These resulted in his finally giving a more satisfactory answer about Methuen's project and, further, in his persuading Methuen not to leave at a time when fresh proposals were on foot in both London and The Hague. One of these proposals was a new plan sent by Schonenberg to The Hague for a combined force of Imperial, English, Dutch and Portuguese troops to advance from Oporto, backed by another force of 4,000 cavalry to be landed between Cadiz and Barcelona, but this was turned down by Portugal. Schonenberg was having his own troubles with a long-standing dispute about the Setubal salt[1] and also complained that he was having increasing difficulty in preventing an open break between Waldstein and Methuen. There was a bad quarrel between them at a conference held with Faria, but Waldstein was induced to withdraw and was understood to agree to the Almirante carrying on with the negotiations. The Almirante now hinted that some concessions in Spain might after all be possible and he reported to Vienna that he did not think Methuen was pandering to the Portuguese but if anything was too stiff with them. However, he thought Schonenberg was the ablest of the three envoys and the most likely to be able to conclude a treaty.[2] Schonenberg now also withdrew his objections to any concessions in Spain and, after a further threat of Methuen to return home, unexpectedly softened on the subject of the subsidies.

It was now 20 February and the Portuguese knew that their own project had no chance of being accepted. They were also encouraged by the arrival at last of the convoy from England, for which Methuen had asked, and the safe homecoming of an exceptionally rich Brazil fleet. Schonenberg estimated that it consisted of 86 ships (one from Goa) with 46,000 chests of sugar, 30,000 rolls of tobacco and 600 pounds of gold for the king. Methuen reckoned 95 ships and a value of £1,500,000. Soon he was able to report that he had put off his departure on account of

---

[1] Rijksarchief 7369, 25 Nov. 1702. [2] S.P. 80/20, Stepney to Hedges, 7 Apr. 1703.

Schonenberg's change of attitude and that the main points of the Quadruple Treaty were on the way to being settled. The Portuguese had stepped up their demands to 4,000,000 cruzados for an auxiliary army of 13,000 men. Schonenberg agreed to a figure of 1,500,000 and Methuen offered to go to 2,000,000 on his own responsibility if the States General refused to pay the extra 500,000. Finally the Portuguese agreed to an annual payment of 1,000,000 patacas plus an initial payment of 500,000 patacas to be made when the treaties were ratified.[1]

It was now found that Waldstein had not after all delegated his responsibility to the Almirante, though Roque believed he had done so and had informed the Council of State. He returned to the discussion with an offer to add Sardinia to his list of concessions. Finally he granted everything except Badajoz; King Pedro offered to relinquish three places in Castile, but still insisted on Badajoz. Methuen again threatened to leave, and it was settled that the remaining points should be left to the arbitration of Queen Anne and the States General. The King then allowed a small reduction in the subsidies and agreed that the allies should not be responsible for convoying the Brazil fleet beyond the Atlantic islands. He was in fact not anxious to encourage the appearance of allied warships in Brazil. Waldstein then again raised some points which were believed to have been settled, and refused to agree to the Acts of Renunciation of the Succession required of the emperor and the Archduke Joseph in favour of the Archduke Charles. Methuen and Schonenberg threatened to conclude the treaty without him. Alegrete returned from the cure he had been taking, but instead of signing the treaty, he raised fresh difficulties and all three envoys threatened to leave. There was a further fracas with Waldstein in the presence of Roque Monteiro and Faria, and Methuen was accused of saying that Queen Anne would bring the emperor to

---

[1] Add. MSS 29590, fos. 201, 206, 209, 219; Rijksarchief 7369, 10 Feb., 5 March 1703, and 7025, 28 Feb. 1703; Albrecht, *op. cit.* pp. 47, 63; S.P. 80/20, Stepney to Hedges. The cruzado was worth 2s. 6d. and the pataca 2s. See Appendix 2.

reason and half Spain could go to Portugal without hurting any English interest. Schonenberg and the Almirante tried to make the peace, and it is interesting that the emperor himself in an audience with Stepney attributed an analogous remark about Spain to the Almirante. Stepney had been trying to convince the emperor that it was unsuitable to employ a Spaniard in a negotiation which involved such large concessions to Portugal, and Queen Anne was obviously the person best qualified to handle this delicate matter. It was then that the emperor replied that in the view of the Almirante the Spanish nation would rather part with their kingdom than remain under the French yoke.

King Pedro was now anxious for a settlement, but Cadaval had recently assured the French ambassador that he was not yet engaged to the allies, and the Opposition ministers hoped for fresh French offers. Although both treaties were already being drafted and put into Latin, they raised five new points. They asked for an increase in the subsidy if the army spent more than six months in the field in any one year, for twelve ships specifically to be provided for the protection of their coasts and trade, and for the allies to use their good offices to secure compensation for the Cacheo Company and to accept responsibility for the archduke to pay this as king of Spain. The other two points regarding the Setubal salt and Portuguese claims in China only affected the Dutch.[1]

Methuen had another 'final' audience with the king on 3 April, and told him that if the negotiations were broken off he must not expect any further friendship from England or the United Provinces. The king seemed to be inclined to yield on all points except that of the Setubal salt, which Methuen felt was capable of being settled and in any case only concerned Schonenberg. Nevertheless, Methuen reported that he had decided to leave Lisbon with the next convoy, unless the treaty was signed, as he could do nothing with Schonenberg in his present humour.

[1] Albrecht, *op. cit.* pp. 46–7; Mayer, *op. cit.* pp. 23–4; S.P. 80/20, Stepney to Hedges, 10 Feb. 1703; Add. MSS 29590, fos. 220–1, 226, 230; Rijksarchief 7369, 20 March 1703.

Waldstein was adamant, and the Portuguese only seemed to be playing for time. He did not sail until 11 April but took no further action before leaving.[1]

On 4 April Schonenberg had agreed with Methuen in contesting the five points and in concluding that the 'frivolous chicanery' of the Portuguese ministers was proof that the king had no further intention of entering the alliance. He complained to the States General that he had received no guidance as to their policy, and that the Portuguese were saying that their demands had been accepted in London and The Hague, so it was only the Lisbon envoys, and particularly himself, who were holding up the treaties. However, after a long sitting with the Portuguese he believed that the outstanding points affecting the Dutch could be left to be settled at The Hague. He added that Methuen had wanted to concede the three remaining points, but even at the risk of being blamed he had held out, for he considered that in their zeal for the common cause the States General had now accepted burdens enough and could go no further.

Schonenberg then missed a mail, which accounts for the complaints made that he had failed to keep the States General informed. His next dispatch was dated 28 April and in it he said that Methuen had told him that he had orders to attend the opening of Parliament in Ireland in his capacity of lord chancellor and that he must leave, but Paul had full powers to carry on. Methuen had insisted on leaving in spite of Schonenberg's protests and those of the Portuguese Court, but with the agreement of Paul Methuen he had settled the three outstanding points. He had undertaken that six months' subsidy would be paid, irrespective of the length of time the army was in the field, and that a sufficient number of ships would be left to guard Portugal during the absence of the fleet. As for the Setubal question he had agreed with Roque Monteiro to leave it to be settled in The Hague.[2]

---

[1] Rijksarchief 7369, 4 Apr. 1703.
[2] Rijksarchief 7369, 28 Apr. 1703; S.P. 84/224, fo. 404, Stanhope to Hedges.

Methuen had been anxious to explain his difficulties in London and also to confirm his claim to retain his lord chancellorship. He had spoken of it in his correspondence with Lord Rochester, and as long as he was lord lieutenant Rochester had kept the place open for him. But the duke of Ormonde succeeded Rochester in February and there was already talk of Sir Richard Cox succeeding Methuen. There was also a move to recall Methuen and to transfer the negotiations to The Hague. Indeed, although Da Cunha said that it would be preferable to leave Methuen to conclude the negotiations, which were already so far forward, a dispatch dated 2 March instructed Methuen to request that full powers be given by King Pedro to Sousa Pacheco at The Hague. This dispatch reached Lisbon after Methuen's departure. As matters were taking a better turn, Paul Methuen, after informing Schonenberg, took no action on it. After his father's departure he had seen the king and formed the impression that he was friendly enough and the Portuguese now wanted the alliance more. Pedro had expressed regrets for the departure of Methuen but had been reassured on being told that Paul had full powers. Paul, however, refused to make any concessions which had not been approved by his father, and asked the ministers not to attempt any innovations.[1]

Waldstein reported to Wratislaw that Methuen had fled to avoid his irresponsible conduct being brought to light, and that he and Schonenberg were breaking off the negotiations and leaving Lisbon. The news of Methuen's departure was greeted with astonishment in the Allied capitals, for the last news from Da Cunha and Wratislaw was that the treaties were almost signed. Furthermore, ministers in London had just received the emperor's letter of 12 March entrusting the queen with the handling of his Peninsular affairs, and were therefore feeling optimistic.[2]

Vrijberg, one of the Dutch ambassadors, recorded his impres-

[1] Add. MSS 29590, fos. 232–3. *Clarendon Corr.* pp. 451, 455; Add. MSS 17677, WWW, fo. 165; S.P. 100/37, fo. 56, Da Cunha to Nottingham.
[2] S.P. 105/68, fo. 126, Hedges to Stepney; S.P. 105/67, copy of emperor's letter to Queen Anne.

sions of Methuen's unexpected arrival. As soon as he heard of it, he hurried over to consult Da Cunha and Wratislaw, and found them puzzling over Waldstein's report. Da Cunha had not heard of the envoy's intention to leave, but had been instructed to complain of Methuen; however, his latest information was that King Pedro had conceded the disputed points, so he was at a loss to explain Methuen's departure. In fact Da Cunha was not altogether 'au fait', for although the king had been conciliatory, at the time of Methuen's departure the ministers were still holding out. As no letter had come from Schonenberg, Vrijberg, in spite of the lateness of the hour, went on to call on Nottingham, whom he found equally perplexed. However, Methuen was there and he was able to ask him whether it was true that Waldstein and Schonenberg were leaving. Methuen replied with apparent unconcern that four days before his departure they had been determined to leave, but just before he himself left, Schonenberg had made progress on the disputed points and had asked him to stay on. There was no reason for either of his colleagues to leave now, and they both knew very well that Paul had full powers to conclude the treaties, but Schonenberg had refused to believe he was going, which was no doubt his reason for omitting to write.[1]

Methuen had some difficulty in explaining himself to the Cabinet. Hedges told Stepney that they were all at a loss what to think, but he hoped the situation would be saved, if only the emperor would undertake to send the archduke to Portugal. Stepney criticised Methuen severely, in private, saying of the disappointment in Portugal, 'That business is in the dark still, as the person always is, who has had the management of it. Methuen's reasons for returning were light and trivial. A man of less appearance of gravity and sense might have made a better hand of the whole affair.'[2] Stepney was not a malicious man and his opinion cannot be taken lightly. However, good diplomatist as he was, he

[1] Add. MSS 17677, WWW, fos. 180–1; Rijksarchief 7369, 28 Apr. 1703.
  S.P. 105/68, fos. 220, 248; fo. 248 from Stepney to Shrewsbury, private, is printed in
  HMC Buccleuch, II, 659.

was not immune from error; he was wrong on the subject of the archduke's coming, for instance, and Hedges thought his expressions about it very strange. But even if he was right, Methuen could have retorted that he had left Paul behind with full powers and with less appearance of gravity to make a better hand of the whole affair.

The fury of Methuen's colleagues was largely inspired by the fact that he had actually done what they would have liked to do. Most of the envoys engaged in the treaty negotiations were reaching the end of their patience. Stepney found the Austrian ministers very trying, and would have come home if he had not been warned that in the present state of party politics it would have been unwise. Progress in Vienna was impossibly slow, and even Prince Eugène, who was a royal prince and a popular hero, had to submit fifty memorials to obtain his needs for his army in Italy, and was still kept waiting. In London Wratislaw was actually packing his bags to return to Vienna, for he too had fallen out with everyone and was at the end of his tether. Only a nagging ambition had kept Waldstein in Lisbon, and Schonenberg complained that he had no money, that the Portuguese were insincere, and that he could not elicit satisfactory answers from the States General. Methuen was exceptional, not in being moved by private considerations, but in acting on them.[1]

Nevertheless, the upshot tended to show that Methuen's official reasons for leaving Lisbon were good. He was able to explain in London how it came about that the treaties were blocked, when everybody believed they were on the point of conclusion, and to convince Da Cunha that further concessions were impossible. In Lisbon the king was persuaded by Methuen's departure that he must now agree or lose the treaties, and in London the ministers, who might have objected to Methuen's latest concessions, were rattled into agreeing. Even Wratislaw,

---

[1] S.P. 105/68, fos. 98, 114, 116, 183, 344, 360. Wratislaw had made himself uneasy in London and wanted to woo a rich widow in Vienna.

who had threatened to tell Waldstein to break off the negotiations if a squadron were not immediately sent to Italy to help Prince Eugène, moderated his tone. Stepney too agreed that the negotiations were easier to manage in London. But they would not have progressed if the Methuens had not been a team, if John had not been able to leave Paul to act for him, and if Paul had not been of of the calibre to rise to the occasion.[1]

Paul Methuen met his heavy responsibilities calmly and successfully. He was still only thirty-one and De Rouillé had spoken of him as a man of small consequence, who thought of little but his pleasures. He liked to pose as a fashionable spark with an elegant taste in wine and women. There is no reason to doubt that he was normal in the enjoyment of both, and in spite of his Continental upbringing, which made him appear affected in English eyes, he later reached the top of the best London society. He always preferred social life, and the arts and more gentlemanly sports to business, but this did not prevent him from being shrewd, industrious and competent. Marlborough, whose opinion of John Methuen was reserved, said that from all he had heard of Paul he was an ingenious young man. His dispatches were able and concise, and in his personal relations he must have had character and charm. It was easier for him to make friends with Waldstein and Schonenberg after his father had gone, and he was placed in a good position to hold his own by pleading his inability to make any more concessions, but the conclusion of the treaties was still a big task, and he completed it with success.[2]

Schonenberg now felt a great urge to justify himself and worked very actively to settle the two outstanding points which concerned the Dutch, the Far East and the Setubal question. He believed he had settled both and relegated them to form two secret and separate articles of the Triple Defensive Treaty. The States General refused to ratify either article, and they were to

[1] S.P. 100/10, 23, 24 Apr. 1703; S.P. 105/68, fo. 268.
[2] Legrelle, *op. cit.* IV, 207; *Marlborough's Despatches*, ed. Sir G. Murray (1845), II, 214.

harass Schonenberg for some time yet, but for the time being they were out of the way. He was more successful in his settlement of Articles 5 and 7 of the Quadruple Treaty. To the surprise of Paul Methuen he agreed that the subsidies should begin from the date of ratification of the treaties, and not from the declaration of war or the commencement of active service, but he won his point that the subsidy should not be raised if the Portuguese troops served longer than six months in any one year. He also persuaded Waldstein and the Almirante to agree to an instrument by which the Almirante pledged the archduke to pay his share of the subsidies as soon as he was on the throne of Spain.[1] Although Schonenberg now took a greater part Paul Methuen's role was by no means negative. He received embarrassing instructions to persuade King Pedro to declare war as soon as the archduke was proclaimed king of Spain, instead of waiting until he came to Portugal. However, he felt able to ignore them, as both Waldstein and the Almirante were now convinced that King Pedro would never invade Spain without the archduke and that it would be fatal to give him any ground for supposing that the archduke would not come. The Portuguese were still insisting on twelve ships being permanently available for their protection, but Paul managed to use the phrase 'a sufficient number of ships', while allowing it to be understood that twelve would be regarded as a suitable number, and securing agreement that they need not be kept in the Tagus. Waldstein continued to promise that the emperor would provide 6,000 men, but it was already clear that he would not pay his third part of the subsidies, and Paul assisted Schonenberg in obliging him to give a written undertaking that the emperor would honour his obligations before the treaty was ratified. Roque Monteiro tried hard to manoeuvre Paul and Schonenberg apart, but Paul refused to agree to any point separately.[2]

[1] Rijksarchief 7369, 5, 28 Apr. 1703; Add. MSS 29590, fo. 236.
[2] Add. MSS 29590, fos. 232–5, 261.

On 28 April Waldstein reported that the treaty was now certain to be concluded, or at least would be in any other country than Portugal, where events were unpredictable. After lengthy discussions of protocol regarding the order in which the plenipotentiaries' names should be written and the precise manner in which the archduke should be received as king of Spain, the treaties were drafted and put into Latin. Roque Monteiro took some days longer than he had promised, and insisted on waiting for the packet boat, in case there were any final points raised by Da Cunha, but at long last, after four hours of going over the documents, on the evening of 16 May the Offensive Quadruple Treaty and the Defensive Triple Treaty were signed. Schonenberg wrote a congratulatory letter to Nottingham, though to Heinsius he complained that he could have got better terms if Methuen had been more helpful. Waldstein left at once in the flagship convoying the Dutch Setubal fleet, but was captured by the French. He was lucky to escape alive, for the Dutch captain Van Roemer Vlacq was determined to blow up his ship if the French boarded her, and took no notice of Waldstein's protests that he carried dispatches to the emperor and was too important to be allowed to die. He was saved by a chance shot which mortally wounded the captain, whereupon he took charge and arranged a surrender. It was a year before he was exchanged for Marshal Villeroy, a prisoner of Prince Eugène, but luckily he had sent the treaty itself on the packet boat to England in charge of his secretary. His arrival in Vienna might have persuaded the emperor to send his quota of troops to Portugal, for he was personally pledged to provide 6,000 men, and according to Schonenberg would have done his utmost to fulfil his promise.[1]

The conclusion of the treaties was received with satisfaction in the allied capitals, and in Lisbon the arrival of eleven cornships in

---

[1] S.P. 105/68, fo. 210; Add. MSS 29590, fos. 262, 265; Albrecht, *op. cit.* p. 62; Add. MSS 17677, WWW, fos. 210, 259; Jonge, *Geschiedenis van het Nederlandsche Zeewezen*, IV, ii, 261–75; Rijksarchief 7369, 20 June, 30 Aug. 1703. The treaties are printed in Borges de Castro, *Collecção de Tratados*, pp. 140–87.

early June showed the people of Lisbon the value of allied friendship, the more so as there was another shortage and attempts to
control the price of corn were breaking down.[1] But there were
still great obstacles to the treaties being ratified. Articles 19 and 20
of the Quadruple Treaty, which gave the command of allied ships
in the Tagus to Portugal, were bitterly resented in London, and in
The Hague too. Nottingham said that Parliament would see him
hanged if he agreed to such articles, and ordered Paul urgently to
tell the king that England had never allowed any foreign prince to
command an English ship. Paul was in a dilemma, for the
Portuguese stuck to their point through three meetings of the
Council of State and could show a good precedent in the 1661
treaty, which allowed the earl of Sandwich to give precedence to
the Portuguese when he came to Lisbon to fetch Queen Catherine
of Bragança. Paul had no choice but to yield and to offer to accept
the responsibility if the queen refused her ratification. Da Cunha
thought the Portuguese ministers had purposely insisted on the
flag privilege in the hope of preventing ratification. Finally, after
Godolphin had explained the advantages of the treaties the
Cabinet advised the queen to ratify them with the hope that some
solution of the disputed point might ultimately be found.[2]

In Vienna the slow pace of the Court was enough in itself to
delay ratification for the full three months of grace. There were
also three questions outstanding, the acts of renunciation to be
signed by the emperor and the Archduke Joseph, the departure of
the Archduke Charles, and the payment of the emperor's third of
the subsidies. Another difficulty was to find a form of words to
cover the fact that, in spite of all that had been said about 'Partition', the emperor was reserving the duchy of Milan as a portion
for the Archduke Joseph. The solution adopted at Waldstein's
suggestion was to refer to Charles as 'King of Spain and the
Indies', and to use the term 'Kingdom of Spain and the Monar-

[1] Rijksarchief 7369, 2 July 1703.
[2] Add. MSS 29590, fo. 292. E. Prestage, *Portugal and the War of the Spanish Succession*
(Cambridge, 1938), p. 15.

chies under it' in the acts of renunciation, a wording which excluded the duchy of Milan. Until the last Stepney protested that the emperor and the empress would never agree to let Charles go to Portugal; nevertheless as a result of the secret negotiations with Savoy they had already agreed that he could go to Italy, and from this point they were gradually brought to consent to his embarking in Trieste for Spain or Portugal, and ultimately to his travelling direct to Lisbon from Holland with the allied fleet. The duke of Molés, who had been appointed Spanish ambassador to the emperor just before the death of the king of Spain, now acted as an intermediary for the Habsburgs with the Almirante. He strongly objected to the archduke putting himself into the hands of King Pedro until at least one Spanish province had declared for him, but Charles himself welcomed the prospect and at last, as a result of Allied pressure, on 30 June his journey was arranged. Queen Anne defrayed his travelling expenses, and, as Stepney put it, the archduke was more obliged to the queen than to his own parents, for they only brought him into the world as an archduke, whereas Her Majesty was going to place him on a throne.[1]

Stepney pointed out that the emperor could not possibly provide a bodyguard for the archduke of more than 2,000 men. He was inclined to blame Methuen for giving the impression that 6,000 men would be available, but Nottingham told him that it was not Methuen's fault and there was nothing to be done. In fact the emperor was able to contribute neither men nor money. This had already been realised in Lisbon, but it came as a shock to the States General. They refused to accept responsibility for a cent more than their quota, though they withdrew their objection to ratifying the treaties on this ground. Paul Methuen and Schonenberg had extracted an undertaking from the Almirante and Waldstein that the archduke would accept the responsibility, but

---

[1] S.P. 105/68, fo. 126, Hedges to Stepney, and fos. 211–13, 254, 356, Stepney to Hedges, and fos. 446, 458 to Nottingham; S.P. 80/20, Stepney to Hedges, 23 May, 4 July 1703. Da Cunha in Add. MSS 20817, fo. 390, said the improved prospects in Savoy were a factor in King Pedro's decision to enter the alliance.

Queen Anne undertook to advance the money, and finally the emperor endorsed Waldstein's and the Almirante's promissory note.[1]

Waldstein's copy of the Quadruple Treaty reached Vienna on 30 June, but a Breslau paper arrived the next day containing a copy of every article, and a Jew named Machado told Stanhope in April that he had seen the drafts of both treaties, so in spite of all the secrecy observed there had been a leakage. The ratifications left Vienna just within the prescribed three months and reached England in time for Methuen to take them back with him to Portugal. They had one final adventure in Harwich, where a customs officer impounded them in mistake for a piece of dutiable lace.

Bad weather and the interruption caused by Methuen's departure had interrupted Schonenberg's reports and the States General complained that the treaties had been huddled up without their consent. Heinsius had no complete copy and said he could not base a decision on only snips and parcels. A copy of the Triple Treaty was hastily forwarded to him from London and copies of both treaties followed on 5 June. The lack of information was perhaps a matter of form rather than of substance, but it put the States General in a bad humour, which was not lessened when they knew the terms, which they considered far too generous. However, the States of Holland ratified on 25 July and the other provinces followed slowly, until by 28 August all the provinces had signed except Guelderland, for which the States General accepted responsibility.[2]

Methuen sailed for Lisbon again from Portsmouth on 15 September. He would have preferred to continue as lord chancellor of Ireland, and at first the queen insisted on this as a

---

[1] S.P. 105/68, fos. 338, 397, 458, Stepney to Nottingham, and fos. 310, 386, 401, 443 to Hedges; S.P. 80/20, Stepney to Hedges, 20 June, 4 July; S.P. 84/224, Stanhope to Hedges, 26 June, 31 July, 3 Aug. 1703; Add. MSS 29590, fos. 235, 260; Rijksarchief 7369, 16 May 1703.

[2] S.P. 84/224, Stanhope to Hedges, 8, 22 May, 27, 31 July, 28 Aug. 1703; Add. MSS 17677, WWW, fos. 191, 206; *Marlborough–Heinsius Letters*, no. 112.

compliment to King Pedro. However, the duke of Ormonde raised very strong objections and Methuen was then appointed ambassador to Portugal, as from 18 June. He was prevented by an attack of gout from going to Windsor to kiss hands and when he reached Lisbon he presented his credentials without making a state entry or any special ceremony. His failure to make a splash vexed some of the Factory, who accused him of parsimony. A quiet and inexpensive entry suited Methuen's taste, but there were real difficulties of protocol in the way of a state entry, and Methuen made up for any lack of ambassadorial splendour by the proofs of the advantages he brought with him. He had not only the ratifications of the treaties, but a credit for 60,000 pieces of eight to finance the purchase of corn in London and letters of exchange for the two-thirds of the sum of half a million patacas due to be paid by the queen and for payment of several monthly instalments of the annual subsidy.[1]

Schonenberg had been the recipient of many inquiries regarding the coming of the ratifications and of the money for the subsidies. Purchases of corn had been facilitated also in Holland, and Pacheco had been authorised to buy 8,000 helmets and 3,000 cuirasses there, which paralleled an order placed in England, according to Luttrell, for 10,000 broadswords, an abundance of 'baggonets', and firearms to the value of £19,000. But Schonenberg had no money to advance as Methuen had, and no promotion to bolster his prestige. His request to the States General for the rank and salary of ambassador received no reply, and it was mortifying for him that Methuen brought the ratifications, delivering the emperor's ratification to the Almirante of Castile, and the Dutch ratification to him by the hand of Paul Methuen.[2]

---

[1] Add. MSS 17677, WWW, fo. 304, and 29590, fos. 317, 353–4, 376, 396; *Cal. of S.P.* (1703–4), pp. 24, 27, 40, and *Cal. of Treasury Books* (1703), pp. 71, 294, 353.
[2] Rijksarchief 7369, 2, 18 July, 22 Aug., 22, 23 Oct. 1703; Luttrell, *Brief Account*, V, 325, and VI, 304.

CHAPTER 8

JOHN METHUEN'S COMMERCIAL TREATY OF DECEMBER 1703 AND ITS BACKGROUND

WITHIN a few weeks of his return to Lisbon Methuen concluded the commercial treaty which was to make his name famous. At the time the Quadruple Treaty, by which Portugal joined the Grand Alliance, was rightly regarded as the most important of the three Methuen treaties, though after the Treaty of Utrecht it became obsolete. The Triple Treaty was intended to be a subsidiary to the Quadruple Treaty, and to cover subjects affecting the maritime powers and Portugal, but not the emperor. But it had an importance of its own, for its scope extended beyond immediate war aims; it was styled a Perpetual Defensive Treaty and gave permanent guarantees to Portugal against attack by Spain or France. It also tidied up a few old outstanding questions and the commercial treaty could properly have been included in it. In 1712 it was appreciated that the Triple Treaty had become the most important treaty for Portugal and there was talk of renewing its guarantees in the form of a new Anglo-Portuguese Treaty, in view of the fact that the 1654 treaty was mainly a commercial treaty and the Triple Treaty itself included the Dutch. However, this suggestion came to nothing and the Triple Treaty was largely forgotten until Pombal invoked it in 1761 to seek aid against Spain. The Commercial Treaty came into the limelight in 1712 and the appreciation of its value proved a sufficient guarantee that England would continue to protect Portugal.[1]

John Methuen negotiated his treaty very rapidly. He produced

[1] Coimbra MS 2974, Cunha Brochado to Mendonça de Corte Real, 12 July 1712.

it like the conjurer to whom he had been compared, with a speed and economy of paper unknown in Portugal and rare in diplomatic history. The merchants concerned were pleased, but other events filled the public eye, and ten years passed before the treaty was widely discussed and the name of Methuen became a household word. The Whigs, who in 1713 voted for trade with Portugal rather than France, soon came into power and stayed there a long time. During their first years of government Anglo-Portuguese trade reached unprecedented heights; and they naturally attributed this to their own wisdom and foresight, and praised Methuen to the skies. The treaty did not in fact cause the trade, but it kept the way open for it. Like a minority party at an election it turned the balance at a crucial moment and fortified the vested interest in Anglo-Portuguese trade. It would be a mistake to follow the Hanoverian Whigs in magnifying the significance of the treaty, but it would be equally wrong to rate its importance too low.

The background of the treaty extends for at least a generation, but there is little on paper about its immediate antecedents. Methuen had discussed the subject in London before returning to Lisbon, but he never referred to any specific instructions. This has led to discussion whether the Portuguese were the first to broach the matter; the question was on the agenda both in England and Portugal, but it was the English cloth trade which stood to gain most directly, and there is no reason to doubt that Methuen began the negotiation.[1] The Portuguese had latterly been ready to consider any proposal linked with concessions for their wines but the English clothiers had shown the more positive interest, together with the wine importers, and the 'Portugal merchants' in London, who were concerned with both imports and exports.

The first object of Methuen was to persuade the Portuguese to lift the restrictions on the import of English cloth. From the Middle Ages the trade had been vital to England and it still was.

[1] Sampayo, 'Para o Tratado de Methuen', *O Instituto*, LXXVI, 6; Add. MSS 29590, fo. 380.

Defoe boasted that not a monarch in Europe or even in the East was not proud to flaunt his cloak of scarlet of English wool. Defoe glorified the trade to show that it need not fear competition, but in fact the journals of Parliament in recent years had been full of petitions against foreign and Irish competition and against foreign restrictions. The government made desperate efforts to stop the 'owlers', who carried on a lucrative trade in raw wool in exchange for French silks and brandy. They believed that without stocks of English raw wool the foreign trade could not compete and, in 1689, 299 riding officers were appointed in the coastal counties of England, and in Middlesex and Surrey, to curb the 'owling'. Smuggling was most active on the coasts of Kent, Surrey and Hampshire, but the largest proportion of officers and the biggest seizures were in the three counties on the Scotch border.[1]

The difficulties of the woollen cloth industry went back further than the memory of Methuen and were due partly to a loss of markets and partly to a change of fashion. The market in north and central Europe for heavy woollen cloths had shrunk notably and in the second half of the seventeenth century the valuable French market was closed by the protectionist policy of Colbert. Also the old white broadcloth, which had been the staple of the English industry, had gone out of fashion, as had to some extent the old and somewhat monotonous heavy woollen cloths. On the other hand the decline in exports was offset by an increase in home consumption and by new developments. Improvements were made in the dyeing and finishing trade, and great advances were made in the production of worsteds, of the materials known as the new draperies, and of fine woollens. While many old-fashioned clothiers fell on evil days enterprising men such as John Ashe and Paul Methuen made fortunes. The new worsted industry took root in the west country and other districts, but the one spectacular

[1] Sir R. Lodge, 'The Methuen Treaties', *Chapters in Anglo-Portuguese Relations*, ed. E. Prestage (1934); Defoe, *Plan of English Commerce* (1728), pp. 161, 163, 176, 181, 276; John Smith, *Wool* (1747), II, 166.

success in the seventeenth century was the manufacture of Spanish or medley cloth from fine Spanish wool. The headquarters for this was a district on the borders of Gloucestershire and Worcestershire, which included Bradford-on-Avon in Wiltshire.[1]

The worsted industry included worsted proper, and the new draperies, such as perpetuanas, serges, shalloons and stockings. The worsteds were made by a different process from that used for heavy woollen cloths and used long-staple wool. This was coarser than short-staple wool and came from sheep pastured on rich grasslands, fens and marshes, while the short-staple wool grew on the smaller mountain and downland sheep; short-staple wool was closer and finer and predominated in England before enclosure became general in the Midlands. With the rise of the worsted industry long-staple wool came into fashion, and, being little grown abroad, became a staple of the smuggling trade, especially from Romney Marsh, which was noted for its production.[2]

The new draperies and worsteds were lighter and gayer than the old heavy cloths and were acceptable in the warm climates of the Mediterranean and even in Brazil. They were welcome in Portugal, though their high price restricted their sale in so poor a country. However, Lisbon was the entrepôt for exports to Mediterranean countries and particularly for Brazil, and it was the proceeds of the Brazil trade, together with the export of some Portuguese fruits and wines to Spain, which financed Portuguese purchases of English textiles.

At the time of the Restoration the cloth trade was looking for new markets, and expansion of trade to Portugal and Spain was particularly welcome. Both countries opened up prospects of vast overseas markets, though English merchants could only trade with South America through intermediaries. They hoped as a result of the 1654 treaty with Portugal to share in the trade with Brazil directly,

[1] P. J. Bowden, *The Wool Trade in Tudor and Stuart England* (1962), pp. 43, 48, 49; G. D. Ramsay, *The Wilts Woollen Industry* (1943), pp. 116–18.
[2] Charles Wilson, 'Cloth Production and International Competition in the 17th Century', *Economic History Review* (Dec. 1960); Bowden, *op. cit.* pp. 26–41, 195–6, 213–14.

but they never succeeded in doing so to any appreciable extent. Nevertheless, after the marriage of King Charles with Catherine of Bragança and during the war after which, in 1668, Portugal at last won a grudging recognition of the independence of her Crown from Spain, trade with Portugal flourished. The expulsion of the Jews and New Christians had deprived Portugal of her commercial class. The Portuguese had no notion of buying goods at their source and were content to leave foreign trade to the English, French, Dutch, Italians and Hamburgers. A few Portuguese statesmen and particularly the Jesuit Father Antonio Vieira urged that the Jews should be allowed back again, and some New Christian artisans were introduced, but the ban was never raised officially, and although some Jews and New Christians remained and even engaged in commerce, the foreign merchants took the lead and were near to having a monopoly in external trade. The English communities in Lisbon and Oporto flourished and many merchants made fortunes and were able to retire to England.[1] Although the Portuguese Jews had been expelled, they still had an influence, for they settled in European ports, particularly in Amsterdam, and in the West Indies, and with their wide experience and international connections, they played an important part as traders and as bankers. In time of war they traded with both sides and were much implicated in contraband activities.

The boom in trade with Portugal did not last long. She began to suffer from economic stringency as a result of the cost of her war against Spain and a decline in the Brazil trade due to the competition of the English, French and Dutch West Indies in the production of sugar and tobacco. She also shared with other Catholic countries such as Spain a reaction against the Reformation, which resulted in a mood of austerity, intensified by her desire to vindicate and strengthen her independence. In addition her more progressive statesmen were influenced by the protec-

---

[1] *HMC Dartmouth*, III, 23. The number of firms in the Lisbon English Factory was 60 after the Restoration, 20 in 1672, and 12 in 1700, but there had been some take-over bids by the larger firms.

tionist doctrines of Colbert. These various motives produced a series of 'pragmatical decrees' aimed at the restriction of luxury goods and of the tendency to extravagant display, which was a national Portuguese weakness.[1] These decrees were issued from 1660 onwards, but it was not until 1677 that they began to cause serious alarm in England. The 1677 decree prohibited a number of luxury articles such as silver buttons, gold and silver thread, etc., and prescribed moderation in dress, and simplicity in funerals. It also forbade the wearing of foreign coloured cloth and laid down that persons clad in it would not be received at Court. However, the prohibition mainly concerned the new coloured cloths, and fine woollens such as Spanish cloth, and did not apply to the coarser woollens or to all the new draperies or worsteds. It was more injurious to the French trade in luxuries such as lace and ribands than to the English trade in cheaper fabrics. Furthermore, the decree was an internal regulation and did not at first affect the customs, so that it was left to public opinion and to fashion, or to local authorities, to control offenders and to administer the rules laxly or vigorously at will.

Although the decrees were always framed as sumptuary laws with a strong moral flavour, the later decrees had a pronounced economic trend. The decree of 1686 introduced new prohibitions covering hats of foreign manufacture and black cloth, and forbade the clearance of prohibited fabrics through the customs. Attempts were made to set up factories to make cloth at towns such as Covilhão and Porto Alegre, which were away from the coast with its foreign influences. Some New Christian artisans were brought from Andalusia, and with the help of the Portuguese ambassador in London plans were made to bring expert workmen and machines from England, and also Huguenot and Dutch artisans. However, the efforts of the ambassador were stopped

[1] For the text of the pragmatica see *Collecção das Leis Extravagantes* (Coimbra, 1819), pp. 79, 163, 178, 262, 339, 344. Pepys, 24 Feb. 1667, said the king of Spain dressed very plainly in a cloak of Colchester bays.

as soon as they were detected, and the Portuguese Inquisition steadfastly opposed the use of the services of Jews or heretics. In any case the new industries could only make the cheaper qualities and try to 'produce on a factory scale fabrics which were already homespun by peasant industries. The attempt to introduce workmen from Colchester indicates a plan to make worsted products, but Portugal did not have the long staple wool necessary for this. Spanish wool of very good quality was grown in the mountains but Portugal did not have the skills to make Spanish cloth, though this wool was probably used to make hats, which were protected by the decrees and continued to be manufactured at Braga in the north even after the Methuen Treaty.[1] The pragmatical decrees therefore gave little real protection to the attempt to found Portuguese industries, as the coarse cloths, which alone could be manufactured in Portugal, could still be imported, and at the worst of times there was always some loophole left open. But they hampered English trade badly and the threat remained that they might become more severe. Accordingly the Portugal merchants submitted a memorial to Parliament in 1677, in which they pointed out that the damage already done to English trade was serious and might easily become more so. They suggested that some inducement ought to be offered to persuade the Prince Regent Pedro to modify the decrees and that a reduction of the duties on Portuguese wines might serve this purpose. At this period Portuguese wines were classed with the sweet wines of Spain and paid £4 a ton more duty than French wines. This was a result of a recent large increase in the duties on all wines. Parliament had been toying with ideas for its own brand of pragmatical decrees; corpses were to be buried in English woollens, and there had been a provisional ban on the import of Canary wine on the ground of its cost in English bullion and of French wines on account of the unfavourable balance of trade with France. Neither prohibition

---

[1] *Cal. of S.P.* Coventry to Attorney General, 5 Sept. 1678; J. L. de Azevedo, *Épocas de Portugal Económico* (1929), p. 413; Bernardino José de Senna Freitas, *Memórias de Braga* (1890), IV, 422.

lasted for long but the notion that wines were a most profitable source of customs duty had come to stay; the high duties were to remain and become ever higher. It was not profitable to import Portuguese wines at the existing rate of duty, but the idea that it might be advantageous to take them instead of French wines was already conceived.[1]

Parliament paid no attention to the merchants' plea for the reduction of duties on Portuguese wine but the Council of Trade in the next three years made persistent efforts to negotiate in Lisbon a new treaty with Portugal. They alleged that the treaty contained various defects and omissions, and was above all 'indecent' on account of its references to the lord protector, the usurper Cromwell. In fact the treaty was very favourable to England and became more so with the passage of time, as the valuations on most of the types of cloth imported were fixed and the duties charged did not increase with the market value of the fabrics, which appreciated considerably. But the Portuguese much preferred to keep the old treaty and whittle down its privileges in their own way rather than sign a new treaty, in which they might be obliged to dot the i's and cross the t's, and remove the very loopholes in its strict observance in the interest of England, which the English merchants desired. Accordingly after two years of vague assurances, which came to nothing, the prince regent ultimately in August 1680 informed the English plenipotentiary that he would be very glad to remove the 'indecency' by substituting the name of King Charles for that of Cromwell, and to see that justice was done in any case of infringements, but that he was not prepared to alter the treaty itself, which he regarded as good enough, having been very carefully drafted, and having lasted for twenty-six years.[2]

---

[1] Burney Coll. British Museum, 806, m. 11.

[2] *Cal. of S.P.* XVIII, 510, XXI, 437; Add. MSS 35101, fos. 251, 267; Sampayo, *Instituto*, p. 15, reports a statement by Da Cunha that a bay valued at 0·15 for customs purposes would fetch 0·27 in the market; *HMC Finch Papers*, II, 102; *House of Commons Journals*, IX, 703.

Soon after this the import of Portuguese wines was stimulated in quite a different way by the prohibition of French wines. This only lasted for four years and there is reason to believe that a great deal of French wine still entered England either by being falsely declared in the customs or by being smuggled. But the large-scale trade in Portuguese wine had begun and after a brief interval during the reign of James II was to be renewed on a more solid basis and to continue. The trade in wine greatly improved Portugal's trade balance with England and from 1690 her position as a neutral in the European war brought to her a measure of prosperity. Consequently the pragmatical decrees, which had been constantly renewed and reaffirmed, after reaching their highest point of severity before 1690, were slowly relaxed after that year. Even as late as 1700 foreign visitors were struck by the extraordinary uniformity and sobriety of Portuguese dress in Lisbon, but the wine trade had restored to the English Factories a measure of their former prosperity and had eased the conduct of a substantial trade with and through Portugal overseas. French wines continued to be prohibited in England and at the end of the war they were only admitted upon payment of crippling discriminatory duties. There was always the fear on the Portuguese side that French wines might again be admitted on equal terms with Portuguese wines and on the English side that the pragmatical decrees might be tightened up to become a total prohibition, but neither fear was realised, nor in spite of various *démarches* was any positive step taken to negotiate a new Anglo-Portuguese agreement.[1]

There is no record in Methuen's dispatches that he ever discussed the modification of the pragmatical decrees during his first mission in Portugal, but he must have done so, for in October 1696 the new Portuguese minister in London had instructions, if he were approached on the subject, to say that he would be glad to consider any fresh proposals, but the subject had already been

[1] Additional duties of £8 and of £25 a ton were imposed by W. & M. Acts 4 and 5, Caps. 5 and 7, W. Acts 7 and 8, Cap. 20, and the new subsidy of 1699; C.O. 388/3, fo. 186.

discussed with Methuen.[1] Da Cunha always maintained that if the English duties were not reduced, as in any case they ought to be in accordance with the existing treaties, the pragmatics ought to be extended to include the coarser fabrics, which could be manufactured in Portugal. He boasted that on his way to take up his post he himself had worn a suit of Portuguese cloth made in Covilhão. Although he distrusted the House of Commons, whose aim he believed was to forward English manufactures and ruin those of Portugal, he thought an agreement was feasible, for while France would sacrifice her wines rather than her manufactures, England would pay more for her wine rather than lose her exports of woollens. Also he thought that the English public had become accustomed to the sweet Portuguese wines, and would not care to go back to the sour dry French wines. This is an interesting remark, as although there was an increasing demand for wines which were sweet and strong, the aim of wine merchants until recently had been to make their wines as much like claret as possible, and by no means all Portuguese wines were sweet. Indeed much was green and sour, and the dark heavy wine, which was the prototype of port, was apt to be turbid and bitter. The port-a-port described in 1693 in Dr William Salmon's *Compleat Physician* was 'a very strong-bodied wine and a strong stomatick, but not very palatable'. However, the deprivation of French wine during the war had done much to hasten a revolution in taste, which was also fairly general, having its counterpart even in France. In aristocratic circles dry wines were still appreciated but for general sale the vintners tried to sweeten wines, even if they were not sweet by nature. Furthermore, although Da Cunha had served as a magistrate in Oporto and must have known Oporto well, he was a Lisbon man and may have had the Lisbon wines in mind. These wines were sweet and they were more fashionable than port-wines.[2]

[1] Sampayo, *O Instituto*, LXXVI, 2.
[2] Da Cunha, *Obras*, I, 102, or *Testamento Político*, p. 37 (both Lisbon, 1820); Sampayo, *Instituto*, pp. 4, 6; Dr W. Salmon, *Compleat Physician* (1693), p. 926.

Da Cunha was ready to discuss an agreement, if the duties on French and Portuguese wines were equalised, that is to say, if the extra £4 payable under the 1677 and 1685 acts was removed. At the moment French wines paid heavy extra duties of £8 and £25 a ton under two other acts, but the Portuguese do not seem to have felt able to rely on this differentiation remaining permanent. However, he felt he could count on France refusing to agree to a commercial treaty with England, so when the Portugal merchants approached him in December 1697 he did not give them any hope of easy terms. But in 1700 he suggested to Methuen, when he was in London, that an agreement might be made if the duties on Portuguese wines were stabilised at a fixed rate. Methuen replied that this was impracticable, as any reduction would have also to cover Spanish wines, but there was no reason to grant an equal favour to Spain, as there were no woollen manufactures there. However, Methuen took advantage of the permission which had been given to him to write to Mendo de Foios, to consult him on the subject, and had the reply that if he wished to treat on the basis of a lifting of the embargo on English coloured cloth in return for concessions in favour of Portuguese wine, he should obtain plenary powers for the purpose. It was clear that Portugal would grant nothing without reciprocal concessions from England. There are then gaps in the Portuguese archives, but nothing seems to have occurred until October 1702, when Methuen was seeking to open the negotiation for his political treaties. Da Cunha then reported an interview with Nottingham, and recommended that Portugal, who held the balance between the powers, should drive a hard bargain and, if she preferred to stay neutral, should allow English ships the use of Portuguese ports in return for concessions on Portuguese wines and for Portuguese citizens residing in England.[1] Methuen was inclined to think that France would never contemplate any compromise allowing the use of Portuguese ports by the Allies, but Da Cunha thought otherwise, and seems to have had

[1] *Cal. of S.P.* (7 Jan. 1701); Sampayo, *Instituto*, pp. 5–6, 8–9.

some grounds for his belief. Methuen more than once reported rumours of new French offers. Some of them were based on mutual trade concessions, and one alleged to have been made during the Methuen negotiations was to take Brazil (fine) sugar and tobacco from Portugal, but Portugal preferred to conclude an agreement with Methuen.[1]

Although there is no mention of the subject in Methuen's Lisbon dispatches, the Portuguese evidently remembered the question, for in their proposal in 43 articles submitted in January 1703 the following two articles appeared:

Article 32. England shall allow the import of Portuguese wine to England and her dominions at a rate of custom's duty no higher than that paid by French wines, and Portugal shall allow the import of English cloths.

Article 33. English and Dutch Trade shall be on the same footing as before 1650.[2]

Article 32 was more favourable to England than Methuen's own treaty except for the extension of the right to export Portuguese wine direct to the American colonies, which hitherto had only been allowed to wine from Madeira. But Article 33 would not have suited England or the United Provinces. It would have left them their judge conservators and some of their privileges, but would have taken away a number of advantages given under the 1654 and other treaties.

The project was perhaps drafted by Joseph Faria, who remembered that Portugal paid £4 more duty a ton on her wines than France between 1681 and 1685, when he was in London, but did not reckon on the permanence of the later acts discriminating against French wine. There is no mention of the United Provinces in the article about wine. Probably Schonenberg had said no Dutch concessions were possible, for he afterwards excused

[1] Add. MSS 29590, fos. 159, 289; *Somers Tracts* (1748), XIII, 297.
[2] Add. MSS 29590, fos. 159, 209; *Somers Tracts* (1748), XIII, 297. Copies of the Portuguese project are in Add. MSS 29590, fo. 450; S.P. 105/67, fo. 391; and Rijksarchief 7369, 27 Jan. 1703.

himself to the States General for the advantages won by Methuen in his commercial treaty by saying that he knew very well that if Methuen gained good terms for England, Portugal would be bound under existing treaties to give the same advantages to the Dutch. As the whole question of Anglo-Dutch treaty relations was in the process of being brought up to date in London, Methuen could be regarded as stealing a march on Schonenberg, but in view of Schonenberg's statement his sin was perhaps excusable.[1]

A paper in Da Cunha's handwriting, which he probably gave to Lord Nottingham, is evidently an attempt to justify the Portuguese project and contains some more exacting demands. Da Cunha had struck out Articles 32 and 33 and had inserted a new article guaranteeing the same privileges to the Portuguese in England and the United Provinces as were enjoyed by the English and Dutch in Portugal. This article was inserted as no. 15 in the Triple Defensive Treaty. Schonenberg made use of it to justify his argument that Portugal must give the Dutch the same freedom for their woollen fabrics as that granted to the English by the Methuen treaty. Many years later the same article was invoked by the marquis of Pombal to obtain better treatment for Portuguese merchants in England.[2]

Methuen's first reference to his Commercial Treaty was made in his dispatch of the 11/22 November 1703.[3] He reported his suggestion to the king of an agreement to allow the importation of Portuguese wines, at a rate of duty always lower than that on French wines, in return for the free admission of English cloth. The king was willing, but as usual referred Methuen to Alegrete. Alegrete replied that Da Cunha had orders to speak in London on the lines proposed, but it was not enough that the duties on

---

[1] Rijksarchief 7369, 5 Aug. 1704, secret. For the Anglo-Dutch treaty, see S.P. 108/341.

[2] Add. MSS 29590, fos. 215, 478; Rijksarchief 7369, secret, 5 Aug. 1704 to the States General and 11 Aug. 1704 to Secretary Fagel.

[3] Add. MSS 29590, fo. 380.

wine should be a little lower. They agreed to talk it over again. Methuen observed that an agreement would be well worth while, for it would improve the balance of trade by as much as £100,000 a year in favour of England.

Da Cunha took no further steps in London, but advised Lisbon, as he had always done, that the embargo on cloth should not be raised. However, the next that he heard was that the treaty had already been signed. Indeed Methuen wrote already on 7 December that he had agreed on the terms with Alegrete, and that as there was a great need for cloth in Portugal, the formalities would be cut to a minimum in order to save time and expense. All that would be required would be to make a writing in the form of a treaty, and for the queen to ratify it; the merchants in England could then be confident that their cloth would be freely admitted from that time.[1]

The treaty, which was very short, was signed by Methuen and Alegrete on 27 December and forwarded to London at once. There is no mention of it having been referred to the Council of State, but Methuen had won over Alegrete and Cadaval, the principal councillors. The procedure may have been eased by the death on 15 September of the acting secretary of state, Joseph Faria, who had never been very helpful, and his replacement, on the recommendation of Methuen's friend, the king's confessor, by the bishop of Elvas. The titular secretary of state, Mendo de Foios, who had been ill for some time and was soon to die, was now dropped, but Elvas does not seem to have had the same authority. He was styled second secretary, while Roque Monteiro began to be called first secretary and to take a leading part in foreign affairs. He was already the king's secretary and a commissioner for the treaties. He now became more friendly to the Allies, and the change benefited Methuen.

The definitive text of Methuen's commercial treaty was in Latin. The following is the version in English submitted to the

[1] Add. MSS 20817, fo. 400, and 29590, fos. 380, 384.

House of Commons. It differs in one or two small points from the Board of Trade version usually quoted.[1]

Article 1. His sacred royal Majesty of Portugal promises, in his own Name, and in the Names of his Successors, that there shall be admitted at all times into Portugal, woollen cloths, and other the woollen manufactures of England, no otherwise than they used to be, before they were prohibited by Pragmatical Sanctions, upon this Condition nevertheless:

Article 2. That her sacred royal Majesty of Great Britain be obliged in her own Name, and in the Name of her Successors, at all times to admit into England, Wines gathered from the Vineyards belonging to the Portugal Dominions, as that at no time, whether there be Peace or War, between the Kingdoms of England and France, any more shall be demanded for such wines, directly or indirectly, on account of Customs or Impost, or upon any other Account whatsover, than what shall, after deducting a third part of the Customs or Impost, be demanded from a like quantity of French Wine, whether such Wines shall be imported in Great Britain in Pipes, Hogsheads or any other Vessals; but if at any time this Diminution of Duties, to be made as aforesaid, shall in any manner be attempted, and the same shall be infringed, it shall be right and lawful for his sacred Majesty of Portugal to prohibit again Woollen Cloths and other the Woollen Manufactures of England.

A final article laid down that the agreement must be ratified within two months of signature.

Methuen acknowledged that he had acted without instructions and sent home a short history of the whole question, which was laid before Parliament with the treaty. He stressed the care that he had taken to avoid committing Parliament to any new concession or the use of any phrase to which exception might be taken. He affirmed that the clause about Portuguese wines was in line with the proceedings of Parliament for the past twelve years and asked that the treaty be laid at once before the queen. He was clearly nervous lest there should be some hitch in the House of Commons. Although the idea was gaining strength that Parliament should be consulted on matters of foreign policy, and had become familiar

[1] Printed in *House of Commons Journals*, XIV, 289–90, 20 Jan. 1704. The Board of Trade text is used by Adam Smith, Hertslet, etc.

even to King Pedro, treaties were not yet submitted to Parliament as a matter of course, unless they involved changes of taxation. Commercial treaties usually involved customs duties and therefore fell within the province of the House of Commons. This fact, together with the difficulty of agreeing with the Dutch, perhaps accounts for the frequent omission of commercial questions from the multilateral negotiations of the time.[1]

Methuen had practical as well as political reasons for needing an early reply. He had alerted his friends, and large consignments of cloth were arriving in the Portuguese customs. An increase of imports was also desirable to provide currency to pay the allied troops, and to finance the subsidies smoothly and punctually without a loss on exchange. Methuen made anxious inquiries by every mail. A reply came quickly from Hedges saying that the treaty had been laid upon the table of the House and had met with general approval, but after this a long spell of bad weather delayed the receipt of the ratification until 22 April. King Pedro was as good as his word and signed a decree raising the embargo on 26 April. Even the usual time lag between Lisbon and Oporto was overcome, for Luttrell reported on 27 May that cloth was being freely admitted there. King Pedro's ratification was dated 2 May, though it was apparently not signed until October. The preamble states: 'As our treaty of friendship lays down there should be freedom of trade between the two countries, it is convenient that we should add to our old treaties and to those recently signed a new agreement to increase our mutual trade·' A copy of Alegrete's full powers with a silver skippet appropriately adorned with a figure of Ganymede, Jove's cup-bearer, with an original copy of the ratification and of the articles of the treaty is in the Public Record Office. Another original copy of the articles has found its way to the University of Michigan at Ann Arbor.[2]

[1] See above, p. 83/4; Add. MSS 29590, fo. 391; *Royal Historical Journal*, 4th ser., x, 1927. The reference fo. 384 given there by Sir. R. Lodge is to an earlier letter on the same subject.

[2] S.P. 104/108, 18, 20 Jan. 1704; Add. MSS 29590, fos. 411, 417; S.P. 89/18, Methuen to Nottingham, 22 Apr. 1704; S.P. 108/393 and 389.

The treaty attracted little publicity at the time. The merchants kept quiet and there was no point in drawing attention to a matter which might cause contentions in Parliament or arguments with the Dutch. The French in due course made as much propaganda against the treaty as they could, and some of it found its way into the history books. They put it about that Methuen had bribed the Portuguese and had flattered them with the idea that they were empire-builders and soldiers rather than traders, and could dispense with industry and live on the riches of Brazil.[1] They also predicted that English trade would languish after the war owing to the shoddiness of English goods. Occasional instances justified this allegation, for in 1715 the Lisbon Factory complained of the quality of Colchester bays. Other critics of the treaty, including Da Cunha, blamed the treaty for the decay of Portuguese industry. This was generally believed in England as well as Portugal, and even by Methuen himself. Yet in another place Da Cunha ascribed the decay of the Portuguese woollen industry, or rather its failure to develop, to interference by the Inquisition with the New Christian artisans and entrepreneurs, and Colonel John Richards, who visited Fundão and Covilhão in the autumn of 1704, gave the same reason. This was undoubtedly one factor but the government interest in promoting these industries had slackened after the death in 1690 of the count of Ericeira, the statesman principally interested in them, and there was not the same incentive to push Portuguese industry either during the relatively prosperous time of Portuguese neutrality in the 1691-7 war or during the boom resulting from the entry of Portugal into the War of the Spanish Succession and the payment of subsidies to her. Porto Alegre was occupied by the enemy, and the other centres were in the area invaded and devastated in 1704. Further, from 1700 onwards the influx of gold from Brazil provided Portugal with the bullion to pay for her imports. These factors had

[1] Francisco Antonio Corrêa, *Tratado de Methuen* (Lisboa, 1930), pp. 6, 29; J. L. de Azevedo, *op. cit.* p. 401.

more to do with the stagnation of Portuguese industry than the Methuen treaty, which in any case only affected the new draperies and woollens, which were not made in Portugal. Only a few local industries survived, such as the making of hats at Braga and of linen at Guimarães. The Portuguese had a natural aversion to industry, which even Pombal could not remedy, so that even eighteenth-century visitors marvelled at the astonishing dependence of Portugal upon imports for even the simplest manufactures.[1]

Another allegation against the treaty was that it encouraged the replacement of corn-fields by vineyards to a degree hurtful to the subsistence of the people. This also was widely believed, and Da Cunha sometimes referred to it, and so did Methuen. Yet Da Cunha himself recommended the export of wine, and the sudden increase of wine exports from Oporto occurred some time before the Methuen treaty. It is true that Lisbon exports rose considerably after the Methuen treaty, but after a few years they fell again, and the shortage of corn was a regular phenomenon much earlier. Portugal, in fact, had been short of corn since the early sixteenth century, and only grew nine months' supply in a good year and six months' supply in a year of bad harvest. Da Cunha had urgently asked to buy corn in London in 1699 and the Portuguese were very conscious of their chronic shortage, so that in 1704 Colonel Richards said the newly landed English troops were obliged to camp on the damp sand in order to save a most thin and miserable crop in the neighbourhood of the Tagus. In later years Pombal restricted the planting of vineyards, but specifically applied his rule only to level ground suitable for corn-growing in the Alemtejo, and exempted ground more suitable for vineyards. No doubt new vineyards were planted in the first flush of the new wine trade but it is unlikely that enough of them were made on good corn-land to effect a substantial reduction of the acreage.

[1] J. L. de Azevedo, *op. cit.* p. 413; Add. MSS Stowe 467, fo. 15; Coimbra MS 2974, Da Cunha Brochado to Mendonça de Corte Real, 13 Sept. 1702; S.P. 110/89, fo. 37.

Certainly the rocky hillsides of the Douro, which were best for growing port-wine, would not grow corn, and although the green sour wine of the Minho was cultivated on rich soil, the vines were mainly trained up arbours and trees at the sides of the fields, and did not interfere with the cultivation of maize or other crops.[1]

So many people abused Methuen's treaty for various and sometimes opposing reasons that it became necessary to invent somewhat abstruse causes for his extraordinary success in persuading the Portuguese to accept an agreement so disadvantageous to them. The Whigs by boasting of the extraordinary advantages of the treaty to them encouraged the notion originally spread for propaganda purposes by the French that Portugal had been exploited. It was necessary to suppose either that Methuen had been a genius or that he had used some sinister means to accomplish his ends. He was accused of having bribed Alegrete and of having provided handsome dowries for the nieces of the king's confessor. It is true that Alegrete's son married a daughter of the duke of Cadaval during the negotiations. Perhaps Methuen gave a wedding present. Also there is a record of Methuen being granted one lump sum of £2,000 from secret service funds for services connected with the political treaties. But there is no evidence of any expenditure connected with the commercial treaty or any suggestion that Alegrete or any of the men around King Pedro could have altered the decision for the sake of a bribe, even if they had wanted to do so. On the other hand Methuen at the end of 1703 was for a short time in a very favourable situation. The Archduke Charles had just been proclaimed king of Spain in Vienna and the doubts about his coming had been stilled. King Pedro looked forward to invading Spain at the head of an army predominantly Portuguese and to betrothing one or more of his children to members of the Imperial family. Methuen could take

[1] Da Cunha, *Obras*, I, 104, and *Testamento*, pp. 37–8; Stowe MS. 467, fo. 48, and 468, fos. 33, 38; *Coll. of Parl. Debates* (1741), V, 155; J. H. Elliott, *Imperial Spain* (1963), p. 180; A. Guerra Tenreiro, *O Douro, Esboços para a sua História Económica, Conclusões* (Oporto, 1944), pp. 54–5, 99; S.P. 89/18, fos. 235–6.

credit for bringing these ambitions within reach and above all he held the purse-strings for the payment of the English and Imperial shares of the subsidies. Within a few days of his treaty he actually paid out 500,000 dollars.[1]

As Da Cunha wrote, it was natural that King Pedro should wish to please Queen Anne, and Alegrete and Cadaval had nothing against a treaty which would help the export of wine, as they all owned vineyards, and in fact an immediate result of the treaty was an increase of trade in Lisbon wine, though the Oporto trade tended to decrease as a consequence of war conditions. The nobility were glad to be able to buy the latest fashions in English coloured cloth and there were special reasons for encouraging an increase in trade and in the circulation of money at the outset of a war to be undertaken on Portuguese soil with the help of powerful allies. Normally the Portuguese would have met their requirements by easing the application of their regulations. They much preferred to do this rather than to commit themselves to a permanent recognition of foreign liberties and privileges, and had consistently followed this policy for a generation past. But it was convenient and even necessary to agree to the treaty for the time being and in future it was to prove a valuable guarantee for the continuation of the trade in wines, which no other country was likely to be able to afford. There is no ground for surprise at Methuen's success at this moment, but he would not have seized this opportunity, which was quite a brief one, if he had not had a long experience of Portugal and a personal knowledge of the wine and cloth trade and of the merchants in London and Portugal engaged in it. His mention of the attitude of Parliament for the past twelve years shows that he had closely followed the subject. It is not known whether he gained any direct personal advantage either from investment

[1] Azevedo, *op. cit.* p. 400. Methuen had £5,583 silver and £1,272 gold plate issued to him (Harleian Misc. 2284/12, 9 Jan. 1710). This was for the use of his Embassy but he could have given some of it away for presents, though in theory he was due to return it at the end of his mission (Add. MSS 28056, fos. 2, 29).

in the cloths specially shipped to take advantage of the treaty or from any profit made by his brother's mills at Bradford-on-Avon. It is likely at least that the trade of the Bradford district benefited, for although the Spanish cloth and medleys, in which it specialised, formed a small part of Anglo-Portuguese trade, they were among the articles freed from restriction by the Methuen treaty, and the imports to Portugal rose from 107 pieces in 1701 and 486 pieces in 1703 to 3,005 pieces in 1704 and 3,647 and 2,386 pieces in the two succeeding years.[1]

Methuen also took a personal interest in wine-growing and had a vineyard at his quinta. Towards the end of his first mission he wrote to James Vernon: 'Our vintage is not likely to be great, but very good, and I hope to see my wines made before I leave this place, and to bring into England soe good for my friends, as to credit the wine of this place.'[2] He often sent gifts of wine to the great men in London, to Secretaries Trenchard and Hedges (both men with Wiltshire connections), to Vernon, to Halifax, to Godolphin, to Shrewsbury, and once at least to Marlborough. Unfortunately we have no record of the recipients' opinions, though Lisbon wines were quite fashionable. Oporto wines were much less so, and Bolingbroke, who preferred burgundy and champagne, when he received a present of Portuguese wine, promptly passed it on to a parson friend.[3] But Methuen praised the red Barra Barra from Santarem and a red Lisbon wine became known as 'Methuen'. In later years Paul Methuen was said to have given his name to 'palhete', little Paul, a sort of vin rosé made from a mixture of red and white grapes, but this is probably a legend, made up when the name of Methuen was famous, for 'palhete' actually means straw-coloured, and a bill for some 'palhete' bought by Methuen as early as 1706 still exists. Methuen also had some family interest in the wine trade for he had a son-in-law, named Humphrey Simpson, who was an importer. But

---

[1] See Appendix 3, p. 364.   [2] S.P. 89/17, Methuen to Vernon, 20 Aug. 1696.
[3] C.O. 389/20, Henry St John to a Rev. Sir.

it is unlikely that he drank much wine from Oporto or indeed in his second mission much wine at all. He suffered too much from gout, and was obliged to follow a régime, though Paul, according to Da Cunha, had the thirst normal for his time.[1]

Many of the arguments for and against the treaty were only thought of in after years, when the treaty came into the limelight. Methuen showed great adroitness in making it appear that England conceded a favour without involving Parliament in the grant of a single penny. It is true that in anticipation of the treaty a proposal to lay a new duty of 1s. a gallon on all wines was dropped, but almost immediately afterwards another duty of a third of a subsidy was approved and in the following year (1705) a duty of two-thirds of a subsidy was imposed, so that the total increase amounted to £3 a tun or 3d. a gallon. The only gesture expressly made to help the Portuguese trade was an increase in the charges on French prize wines, which in the first years of the war were not subject to the full additional duties.[2] At the end of the war, when both sides were thoroughly disillusioned, the Portuguese representative Da Cunha Brochado, like his predecessor Da Cunha, severely criticised both the Methuen treaty and its creator, although this was the very time when it proved its worth to Portugal. The treaty owed much to Methuen's skill, but there was no reason to be surprised that King Pedro agreed to it. He had great sympathy for the sumptuary side of the pragmatical decrees, and had taken the lead in enforcing them, but the new cloth mills had not been a great success, and in 1704 he was anxious to expand trade to the utmost for the supply of his armies and the increase of his customs revenue. The Church, which exercised so great an influence in Portugal, did not favour industries which involved the employment of heretics, and, in so far as it had an interest in the

---

[1] According to an MS at Corsham Court, Methuen bought a cask of palhete from William Browne for $29.700.

[2] Luttrell, *Brief Relation* (4 Dec. 1704). The Essex baymakers protested against the 1s. duty (*House of Commons Journals*, XIV, 278, 343). The subsidies were Anne 2 and 3, Cap. 9, and Anne 3 and 4, Cap. 5.

subject, probably preferred free trade. Neither the secular clergy nor the religious orders were large consumers as individuals, but corporately they needed an immense yardage of cloth to dress with seemliness, and the best materials for the purpose were the new draperies. The Dutch exported from Leyden a special cheap sort of says, called 'monniken says', for the Carmelite monasteries of Italy, and Defoe spoke of the Italian clergy wearing black bays, and the nuns fine says and long ells of English worsted. He also based hopes for trade on the Portuguese colonisation of Africa, where they were inducing the naked savages to wear light worsteds within five degrees of the Equator. The Jesuits controlled the trade with Brazil and required such materials to clothe themselves and their converts. It was in 1760 that the Abbé Baretti spoke of the export of Exeter serges for the use of monks and nuns in Catholic countries, and remarked that many fantastical speculators would like to see the religious orders abolished, but if it were not for these other fanatics who composed these orders, Exeter would be but poorly. But Exeter serges were already known in Portugal in 1703, so it is likely that the same consideration applied.[1]

It is difficult to assess the immediate results of the Methuen treaty. The figures in Appendix 3 show an increase in the import of new draperies, but much of the general increase can be attributed to war needs. The increase of consumption in Portugal was larger than the figures show, for the pre-war imports included many goods re-exported to Spain during the interruption of Anglo-Spanish trade. But there is no doubt that in the long run Methuen's hopes were justified. The war boom passed and was followed by a slump, but after the Treaty of Utrecht the trade in both wine and cloth was stabilised at a higher level.

The embargo on cloth had applied to all countries, but it was the Dutch trade which was most affected by the advantage given

---

[1] Defoe, *Plan of English Commerce* (1743), pp. 138, 185, 187; C. Wilson, *op. cit.* p. 217; Joseph Baretti, *Journey from London to Genoa* (1770).

to England. As soon as the Methuen treaty came into force, the States General acted with relative promptitude and by a resolution dated 30 June instructed Schonenberg to claim the same privileges. He made repeated and strong representations, particularly invoking Article 15 of the recent Triple Defensive Treaty, which accorded reciprocal privileges to English, Dutch and Portuguese. He was very sore when the Portuguese would not accept his arguments, the more so as he had already been warned by the States General that he must not allow Methuen to secure preferential treatment for the English in the West Indies. In 1704 it was realised that allied naval forces could not be extended to cover a powerful expedition to the West Indies as well as to Italy, Spain or Portugal, and the plan to conquer or occupy territory in America was given up. The fate of Admiral Benbow had not been a happy precedent, and West Indian service had proved unpopular with officers and men to the point of mutiny. However, although the emperor had not so far been induced to concede trade privileges to the English and Dutch, it was still hoped that some or all of the Spanish possessions might declare for King Charles, and that the emperor would become more amenable. Schonenberg had discussed the question with the Almirante and had helped to forward a letter to the governor of Cartagena, calling on him to offer his allegiance. He was enabled to take a leading part by the fact that his brother, the Baron de Belmonte, was Spanish Minister Resident at The Hague and had now declared for King Charles. Schonenberg sent the letter to Amsterdam by a fast galley to be forwarded by his brother.[1]

Methuen had also been negotiating with the Almirante of Castile and had agreed to accept a lien on Spanish customs duties paid by English merchants as security for a loan made to the Almirante to pay Spanish deserters. He hoped to go further and submitted a proposal to Nottingham for an advantageous commercial treaty with Habsburg Spain. His plan was ignored for

[1] Add. MSS 38159, fo. 24; Rijksarchief 7369, 23 Apr., 31 May 1704.

some time but a treaty on the same lines was concluded in 1707 by James Stanhope. Methuen was warned that the Almirante could not be trusted, but insisted that he was more intimate and familiar with him every day and used to visit him alone in his country villa and garden. He attributed the talk against the Almirante to the gossip of Count Wratislaw and the jealousy of Schonenberg, who could not bear to see him on such close terms, or to think that he should be concerned in the affairs of Spain. The Almirante was deeper than Methuen supposed, and Schonenberg equally believed that he enjoyed his sole confidence, for the Almirante used to chaff him about the Methuen treaty, and assure him that as long as he had any influence he would never allow the English to have any favours in Spain to the prejudice of the Dutch.[1]

The king and Roque Monteiro assured Schonenberg of their esteem and affection, and of their willingness to negotiate, but they insisted on the same terms as those agreed with Methuen, and added that the queen of England would be offended if they showed special favour to the Dutch. Schonenberg argued that the Dutch duties on wine were much lower than the English ones, but Methuen supported the Portuguese contention that the Dutch could not expect a free entry for their cloth without giving something in return. Schonenberg admitted that the concession asked would not cost much, but he was afraid that any preferential rate would injure the Dutch trade in French wines. This trade was openly renewed in June 1704, when the Dutch failed to extend their twelve months' embargo on enemy trade, and Queen Anne took advantage of it to buy in Holland large quantities of French wine for the use of her Court, though officially the English ban on trade with France lasted until the end of the war. Actually Portuguese wines even at a reduced rate of duty never penetrated the Dutch market to an extent which affected the French trade, and the Dutch trade in woollens was relatively unimportant. Pacheco

[1] Add. MSS 29590, fos. 382, 403, and 28056, fos. 23–7, 34–6, 40; Rijksarchief 7369, 5, 11 Aug. 1704.

May it please Your Lordship.

I am not honoured with any letter from Your Lordship since mine of the 28th past by the last Packetboate, in wch I acquainted Your Lordship, that Monsr Schonenberg and I, had the day before adjusted and setled every word of both the Treaties in Portuguese with Roque Monteiro, so that nothing farther remained to be done but the putting them into Latin. The next day after the Packetboats departure being the 29th Last, the German Ambassador having retired that the Articles of the Offensive Alliance, in which the Emperor his Master was so much concerned, should aloe be read before him and the Almirante of Castile for their approbation, we met the same afternoone at the Almirante's house for that purpose, Count Waldstein, Monsr Schonenberg and my self together with Roque Monteiro, and spent severall hours in redding them over and discoursing of them, but without making any alteration excepting in one point alone, which was done by the Almirante's meanes and at his desire. This was that whereas it was setled before in the tenth Article, that for the horses the King of Portugall was to furnish us with for our Cavalry, we were to pay forty milrees for each horse for the Troopers, and sixty milrees for those that were for the Officers, and but thirty milrees for those that were for our Dragoons, and forty for those designed for their Officers; the Almirante represented to us, that unless our Dragoons were as well mounted as the other, they would not be able to engage the spanish Cavalry, whose horses were generally very good; and therefore desired that the horses for y' Dragoons might be as good and of the same price as the others, which was agreed to. So every word of the Treaty as well as of the secret Articles belonging to it, being approved by the German Ambassador and the Almirante; Roque Monteiro promised to send us faire Copies of both the Treaties in Portuguese, and order them to be put immediately into Latin, that no farther time might be lost, and that they might goe secure by this Packetboat which he therefore desired me to detaine, that she might carry them.

The R^t Hon:^{ble} The Earle of Nottingham.

5   Paul Methuen's report of the signature on 11 May 1703 of the two Methuen Political Treaties

6 Original copy of Methuen's Commercial Treaty of 27th December 1703

found that the deputies in the States General whom he consulted showed very little interest. There was no vociferous wool lobby in the States General, such as there was in the House of Commons. But for Schonenberg it was a matter of prestige to have the same treatment as Methuen and also of personal concern, for he had probably told his Amsterdam friends that all would be well, and in March 1705 three or four cargoes of Dutch cloth were held up in the Portuguese customs. The Methuen treaty became an obsession with him; he wrote that the English were doing their best to ruin the commerce and navigation of Holland, and painted a dark picture of Methuen treaties being concluded everywhere, with Spain, Denmark and even France or the Levant.

The States General were not as indifferent as Schonenberg feared, but the mail carrying a resolution taken by them in December was lost at sea, and Schonenberg only obtained a private copy through a Dutch merchant in March. By this time the question had become entangled with the general question of the payment of the Dutch subsidies, which by January 1705 had fallen five months in arrear.[1] Schonenberg had hitherto been able to parry Portuguese reproaches by insisting that he must wait until he received a detailed muster roll of the Portuguese troops provided, but in February the musters were produced and this excuse for delay no longer held good. The Portuguese protested that they could not carry on the war without money, and even Schonenberg was forced to admit to the States General that he was at a loss to think of further excuses, and to entreat them to consider his account of the money due to Portugal, and no longer to leave him in complete abandon.

In December the States General had based their claim to most-favoured-nation treatment on the 1654 rather than on the 1703 treaty. Schonenberg fell back on this alleged breach of a treaty obligation to defend himself, but in May when the arrears of monthly payments amounted to nine, the queen regent, Catherine

---

[1] Rijksarchief 7369, 7 Jan., 28 Febr., 7 March, 7 May 1704; 7370, 28 Feb. 1705.

of Bragança, remonstrated with the States General and told Schonenberg she would have to withdraw the Portuguese army if the money were not paid. She also took Methuen to task, saying that Queen Anne should keep the Dutch up to the mark, or pay the subsidies herself, and informed the States General that the cloth question had nothing to do with the subsidies, which were a matter of international good faith, or with the Methuen treaty, which was a reciprocal agreement with England. However, out of her friendship for the States General, she would be pleased to treat for a similar cloth agreement if they wished.[1]

Methuen denied all responsibility for the Dutch subsidies and at The Hague Stanhope pointed out to Heinsius that Portugal was under no obligation to give free entry to Dutch cloth as a result of the Methuen treaty. He condemned the intransigence of Schonenberg, and the hurt done to the war effort by the arrears of payment amounting to half a million cruzados. Pacheco had told him that Schonenberg already had the bills to pay the subsidies, but had been ordered not to pay a penny until the Dutch cloth was admitted. This was not altogether true. Schonenberg was using his claim about the cloth to justify his arrears, but in August, when Roque Monteiro told him that according to Pacheco a quarter of a million cruzados had been remitted, he had not yet received any notification. Indeed Methuen seems to have had the news before Schonenberg, and promptly took credit for it with Queen Catherine as due to English good offices.[2]

At their own deliberate pace the States General paid up some arrears and agreed to the Portuguese terms for a commercial treaty. The Dutch also arranged a loan of one million crowns, which Da Cunha had tried in vain to borrow in London. Money could always be raised in Amsterdam, even by the French, provided that the interest was secured. In this case the Portuguese gave the Dutch a lien on their customs and had to pay 1 per cent

[1] Rijksarchief 7370, 25 May, and 7025, 16 May 1705; Borges de Castro, *Collecção de Tratados, Supplemento*, ed. Biker, x, 182.
[2] S.P. 89/18, fos. 191, 195, 218, 227.

more than the normal rate of interest in Holland. These Dutch facilities often caused jealousy in London.

The treaty was signed on 4 August. It is a little confusing that Catherine signed herself both 'Queen of England' and 'Regent of Portugal'. She is often referred to by both titles in Roque Monteiro's correspondence and sometimes is just called Her Britannic Majesty. In return for the free entry of the Dutch cloth, the Dutch reduced the duty on Portuguese wines to a third below that payable by French wines and undertook never to raise the duty. But the Dutch ratification was slow in coming and the Portuguese refused to speed the formalities, as they had done for Methuen; the embargo was not lifted until 12 February 1706.[1] In order to conciliate the Portuguese, Schonenberg was obliged to use his own credit to make advances on the subsidies; after the Portuguese had asked for 300,000 cruzados, Schonenberg offered 100,000 and 20,000 more in ten days' time. Only this unusual gesture secured the release from the customs of cloth which had been held up for almost a year.[2]

The succession of King Charles as emperor in 1711 and his departure from Spain changed the whole situation and placed the Methuen treaties in danger. The Tory government in England was inclined to pull out of Gibraltar and Port Mahon, and to make a trade agreement with France which would include, if possible, guarantees that the advantages won by the 1707 treaty with Spain should not be lost. There was talk of Portugal leaving the Grand Alliance but Cunha Brochado, the Portuguese minister in London, pointed out that England could send a fleet to Rio, and it was imperative to preserve good relations with the powers controlling the sea. England also had some scruples about her obligations to Portugal, and Lord Dartmouth assured Brochado that her interests would still be defended. Brochado suggested a new Anglo-Portuguese treaty, which would meet the desire of

---

[1] The treaty is printed by Borges de Castro in *Collecção de Tratados*, II, 211.
[2] Rijksarchief 7370, 28 Aug. 1705, and 7026, 3 Jan., 12 Feb. 1706.

Portugal for a 'barrier' against Spain, and would replace the Triple Defensive Treaty and the old 1654 treaty. He reported to Lisbon that trading privileges in Brazil would probably be sought, but there was no reason to fear territorial demands, as the English were traders and not conquerors.[1]

The new treaty did not materialise. Parliament legalised the import of French wines in 1711 but Portugal had little to fear as long as her wines paid about £23 a ton customs duty compared with £50 paid by the French. However, in May 1713 a provisional reduction of the duties on French wines was proposed and, under Articles 8 and 9 of the commercial treaty with France, most-favoured-nation privileges were to be granted which would have abolished the preference enjoyed by the wines of Portugal. Brochado protested, but refrained from using the obvious threat that Portugal would be obliged to reimpose the restrictions on English cloth. He was soon saved the trouble of doing so by the vociferous complaints of the English merchants.[2]

The queen had ratified the French treaty by virtue of her prerogative on 24 March 1713, but the consent of Parliament was required for the financial commitments made in Articles 8 and 9, and the treaty specified that this should be obtained. Government bills were seldom rejected, and at first all went smoothly, as the Whigs felt themselves too weak to resist, and abstained from attending the first reading. Then petitions against the bill began to pour in. They were numerous from the Colchester baymakers of East Anglia, from the West Country and Wiltshire makers of serges and worsteds, and from those engaged in the triangular trade in codfish with Newfoundland and Portugal. The weavers of Nottingham, the makers of hats and worsted stockings, and the Spitalfield silkthrowers swelled the chorus. The Portugal and the Spanish and the Italian merchants submitted a petition to the

---

[1] Coimbra MS 2974, Cunha Brochado to Mendonça de Corte Real, 12 Aug. 1710, 5 May 1711, 12 July 1712.

[2] Coimbra MS 2974, Cunha Brochado to Corte Real, 23 May 1713.

House of Lords and gave evidence there. Although brandy was a prime commodity for smuggling, the distillers had done well since the prohibition of French brandy, and the distillers of Chester now protested to their member Shakerley. The Scots were up in arms against the new Malt Tax and rallied in force to the opposition.[1]

Although the Tories had brought the question to a head and it had become such a party matter, some pains had been taken by Parliament to examine the problem objectively. The House of Commons had in July 1711, ordered the inspector general of customs Charles Davenant to produce import and export statistics. This was no easy task, and Davenant was reputed to be a lazy man, but his predecessor William Culliford had been compiling records since 1690, so he was able to submit a convincing set of figures to Parliament.[2] For the general public the theme was well ventilated for the Opposition in the *British Merchant* by Henry Martin, and for the Government in *Mercator*. Addison and Steele touched on the subject in the *Spectator*, the *Tatler*, and the *Guardian*, so that it became a hot and burning controversy argued in coffee-houses and taverns and at street corners, and elaborated in plays.

Owing to the abstention of the Whigs the first reading of the bill was passed on 30 May by 146 votes to 12. The second reading took place on 4 June. Now the Whigs voted, and mustered 135 votes for the Opposition against 202 votes for the Government. Brochado reported that the upshot was still uncertain and that the power of the Court and its obstinacy were so strong that he did not think it would desist from pushing the bill through. He also mentioned the wide belief that the commercial treaty was linked with plans to bring over the Pretender and to send discharged soldiers from Marlborough's armies over to France to build up an

[1] Davenport, *European Treaties* (Washington, 1934), III, 219; D. A. E. Harkness, 'Eighth and ninth articles of Commercial Treaty with France of 1713', *Scottish Historical Review*, XXI (1923-4), 211. G. M. Trevelyan, *England under Queen Anne* (London, 1930-4) III, 257, speaks of the port-wine interest in Chester, but this appears to be a slip.
[2] *House of Commons Journals*, XVII, 362-7, 397.

invasion force. The third reading was on 18 June.[1] Paul Methuen
was not yet back in the House after losing his seat at Devizes, but
James Stanhope, an old friend of the Methuens, and the negotiator
of the commercial treaty with King Charles III of Spain, spoke
eloquently for the opposition and three of the four Tory members
for London had been persuaded by the merchant interest to vote
for it too. The Scottish members joined in, and Aislabie, one of
the lords of the Admiralty, and Francis Annesley, a commissioner
of the public accounts, spoke against the bill. The deciding vote,
which lost the motion, was attributed to Sir Thomas Hanmer, a
wealthy Tory squire, who had lately been in Paris, where he had
been courted by the Jacobites but had not been convinced by
them. He was a true Tory, and married to the widow of the duke
of Grafton, but he represented an Essex constituency where the
clothiers were strong. He said that after maturely considering the
allegations of merchants, traders, and manufacturers he was convinced that the wool and silk manufacturers of the kingdom would
be greatly damaged and the number of poor generally increased
if the bill were passed. He would never be blindly led by the
ministry, nor was he biased by what might weigh with some men,
fear of losing the elections. The principles on which he acted were
the interest of the country and the conviction of his judgement,
and upon these two considerations he voted against the bill.
Hanmer's speech made a great impression and carried with it a
number of Tory votes; the bill was rejected by 194 votes to 185.[2]

Brochado was jubilant and wrote that all the fair hopes that the
Court had given to the people of the great advantages of their
mysterious negotiation were turned to smoke, and they were left
without a French treaty of commerce, it being understood that it
was better to have no treaty than to keep one which did so much

[1] Coimbra MS 2974, Brochado to Corte Real, 6 June 1713; *House of Commons Journals*,
XVII, 354, 402, 430.
[2] For Stanhope's treaty and separate article about trade with the West Indies see Lamberty,
Mémoires pour servir à l'histoire du XVIIIᵉ siècle, IV, 192–7; G. M. Trevelyan, *op. cit.* III, 256–8,
William Cunningham, *Growth of English Industry and Commerce* (1882), pp. 31–3, 414–15.

harm to England and so much good to France. He added that the general joy exceeded that even for the peace.[1]

Parliament thanked the queen for making the commercial treaty, but Bolingbroke's creation was buried for ever. The Tories had taken thought, and now that the Pretender had made it clear that he preferred his religion to a throne, they concluded that the Church of England and the rule of Parliament were worth the loss of a God-appointed king, even at the cost of a Hanoverian monarch and a possible return of the Whigs. They may have felt that they were ruined by the Land Tax, and that claret was preferable to port-wine, but they all had a younger brother or cousin in trade, and trade with Portugal was a reality, while that with France was only an aspiration. Moreover, when there was a good harvest the export of corn to Portugal helped to keep up the price. So the 'whimsicals' were formed. For once the moderates forced out the extremists. It could be argued that the turning-point, when England decided to jettison the Stuarts, and to embark on her eighteenth-century course, was reached with the rejection of Articles 8 and 9 of the commercial treaty with France, rather than on the proverbial day of the death of Queen Anne.

It had been a close thing. Defoe told Harley that it had been a blunder to allow the issue to become a party question, for, if the government had kept quiet, Parliament in the search for funds would automatically have taxed Portuguese wines and would have forced the Portugal merchants to prefer the treaty.[2] Bolingbroke mingled an aristocratic disdain for the proletarian petitions and the multitudes of papers, over which he had moiled, with a deeper emotion. He genuinely believed that the revival of trade with France would unite England and France in a lasting friendship and secure the peace of Europe. Many years later the historian

---

[1] Coimbra MS 2974, Brochado to Corte Real, 19 Apr., 4 July 1713. For a cynical comment on Hanmer's real motives see Lady Mary Wortley Montagu, *Memoirs* (1777), I, 96.
[2] *HMC Portland*, II, 287; *Coll. of Parl. Debates, 1668–1771*, VI, 104–5.

Lecky agreed with Bolingbroke with fervour. He said there could be no shadow of rational doubt that the enormous market which the English cloth manufacturers would have won in France immeasurably outweighed any advantages England received from the trade with Portugal, and he blamed the mercantile theory then in fashion for deluding the people of England as to their true interest. The idea that by a commercial treaty the long wars with France might have been avoided is attractive, but there is little ground for belief that after so long an intermission England would have been allowed to capture the French cloth market, and to beat on their own ground French manufacturers and the well established Dutch. The French had shown no wish to take such a course in the preceding years, and Matthew Prior, commiserating with Bolingbroke on the failure of their hopes, complained that the French were growing colder towards us, and that with the exception of the people of the Garonne, who were in danger of being the losers but had in fact sold their wine that year to the Dutch, the rejection of Articles 8 and 9 was received in France with great indifference.[1]

Further, although the value attributed by the mercantilists to the import of bullion was excessive, at a time when England was not long past a serious currency crisis and London was seeking to outstrip Amsterdam as a banking and financial centre, the possession of a sufficiency of the most acceptable means of exchange was of great importance. There was a chronic stringency, principally of silver, which was constantly drained to India by the East India trade, but later of gold. This need was perceptibly eased by the imports from Portugal. The export of gold from there was prohibited, and the Portuguese steadfastly refused to modify their law, which enabled them to keep the whiphand for use in case of need in spite of the raising of the embargo on cloth. They used the law when some firm displeased them, or it was politically con-

---

[1] *Bolingbroke Letters and Correspondence*, ed. G. Parke (1798), IV, 137–8, 141, 149, 197, 264; Lecky, *History of England*, I, 143–5.

venient, but normally gold was taken out by the packet-boats and by warships without interference. As Brochado observed, the extraction and acquisition of gold was the most precious ambition of trade; people and princes would stop at nothing to get gold. Portugal could not keep the prohibition strictly, because if England or any other power did not get Brazil gold, and lost hope of getting any, it would go to fetch gold with less respect and more force. Perhaps the winking at some smuggling of silver served to keep the Indies in Spanish hands. For the same reason he thought it unwise for Portugal to complain of individual ships entering Brazilian ports illegally except in very general terms, particularly as they were usually ships of the East India Company, over which the English government had little control.[1]

In practice it was England which had the monopoly of smuggling bullion, for the Dutch and Hamburgers, who also needed precious metals, had not the same facilities and received their share by way of London. Most of the metal was Brazilian gold, but there was less stringency in Portugal with regard to silver, and some silver also found its way out. Much of the bullion was taken to the Bank of England for minting, but Portuguese coins were common currency, and already in 1713 merchants in Exeter used little else. Stanhope and Charles Montagu, speaking of the Methuen Treaty, said no Portuguese gold was imported before 1703, but in the three years 1710–13, 3,550,008¾ cruzados were coined by the London mint.[2]

It was the interests of the cloth trade which saved the Methuen treaty, but it was the connection with port-wine, which was afterwards remembered. In 1715 the term port-wine was beginning to be used for wine shipped from Oporto, but could still be used indiscriminately to cover all Portuguese wines. The better types of wine from Oporto were described as bright, fresh, and

[1] Coimbra MS 2974, Brochado to Corte Real, 15 July 1710.
British Merchant, xx, 24. Sampayo, *Instituto*, p. 22; T. S. Ashton, *Economic History of England in the 18th Century* (1953), pp. 171–2.

strong and were table wines. Much green wine was also imported and this had to be sweetened or fortified in one way or another. The wine from the Douro, which was the predecessor of true port-wine, was already used for this purpose and was also sometimes imported in its natural form. The birth of port-wine, as we know it, that is, of wine fortified during the pressing with brandy used to stop fermentation, is usually attributed to the year 1720 or thereabouts, but it had been common practice before to mix brandy with wines, and to fortify cider. Port-wine as we know it was a much later invention, when the art of maturing wine in the bottle had been perfected, but for most of the eighteenth century something which was called port-wine was the principal wine used by the English people.[1]

[1] For a reference to medieval port-wine see E. J. García Mercadal, *Viajes de Estranjeros por Espanha e Portugal* (Madrid, 1952), p. 273, and for early history of Douro wines, Guerra Tenreiro, *Douro, Conclusões*, p. 9.

CHAPTER 9

PREPARATIONS FOR A PENINSULAR WAR, JUNE 1703–MAY 1704

As soon as the treaties were signed Nottingham instructed Stepney that the archduke's presence in the Peninsula was an indispensable condition for the queen's ratification. Stepney long doubted whether the emperor would ever spare his son or would agree to allow him to travel by way of Holland and the Channel instead of from Italy. However, he put his back into the task of 'struggling with a very perverse people, who will not understand or pursue their own interest' and 'of trying to remove those fond notions, and to convince the Ministers that the way to Holland was the plain and natural road, unless they would expose the hopes of their family to an accident in the Mediterranean like what Waldstein met with in the Ocean'. At last the ministers agreed. There were earnest discussions about protocol in Lisbon, and in Vienna it was decided that the new 'Catholic King' must leave as soon as he had been proclaimed, to avoid insoluble problems of precedence between himself and his brother Joseph, 'King of the Romans'.

English ministers were inclined to be sarcastic about the 'darling archduke', but the behaviour of his parents was not only natural but justifiable for reasons of state. Princes as important as Charles could not be allowed to hazard their lives, and, although in the event he escaped with nothing worse than seasickness and some attacks of dysentery, the dangers of the journey and of the campaign in the Peninsula were serious. Only two lives stood between him and the Imperial throne, and Charles was likely to be next heir after his brother, for the last hopes of the 'queen of the Romans' bearing a son had been given up. The empress wrote with reason to her cousin Prince George of Hesse that sending him away was a sacrifice to the common cause. In fact it was not long before his father and his brother died; he was only to return to Vienna as emperor.[1]

The archduke was barely eighteen years of age and he was still escorted by his tutor, Prince Anton Florian von Lichtenstein. As a tutor he had done his duty well, for the boy spoke Latin, Italian, passable French and some Spanish, as well as his native German. His manners were excellent, though rather stiff. He was good-tempered, shy, and very anxious to do the right thing; Galway thought in 1704 that he had much good sense for a man of his age and anxiety to do well. But it was not until 1705 in Barcelona that he showed some independence of spirit and courage; in Portugal he was uneasy under the tutelage of King Pedro and often unwell. He developed some kingly qualities, but he was always obstinate and attached to protocol, and remained wholly, and in the eyes of the Allies fatally, under the influence of his German advisers.[2]

These gentlemen were generally condemned but they were in a difficult situation. Their training imbued them with a profound reverence for the importance of the emperor and a conviction that other crowned heads were second class. None of them had any notion of the painful processes of democracy, involving constant consultation and deference to other people's opinions. Even an outstanding man like Prince Eugène had a short way with allied troops under his command. Discussing the coming campaign with Stanhope at The Hague in 1708 he said: 'I also had auxiliary troops under me in Italy and no one ever thought of asking me what I was going to do, and when the actual day came I made them fight without probably their expecting it.' When Stanhope

---

[1] S.P. 105/68, fos. 126, 385, 397, 454, 458; S.P. 80/19 and S.P. 89/21, Stepney to Hedges, 11 Nov. 1702, 20 June 1703; *HMC Buccleuch*, II, 659–64; Borges de Castro, *Tratados*, II, 89; Künzel, *Das Leben und der Briefwechsel des Landgraven Georg von Hessen-Darmstadt*, p. 237.

[2] Add. MSS 28056, fo. 172; S.P. 84/226, Stanhope to Hedges, 23 Oct. 1703; Voltes Bou, *El Archiduque Carlos de Austria* (Barcelona, 1953), pp. 31–3 ff., describes the archduke's court at Barcelona.

remarked that the English and Dutch always feel their liberty, Eugène replied: 'Very good, but I say again that it is not the way to get anything done or to make the least progress.' So also Prince George of Hesse, though a good soldier and a better mixer than Prince Eugène, had an authoritarian streak and was unable to win the liking of the English troops under him at Gibraltar.[1]

Charles did not have Hesse with him in Portugal, and only one notable Spaniard, the Almirante de Castile, who soon fell out of favour. His advisers were all German and the leader of them, and apparently the worst, was Lichtenstein. Lichtenstein was a good deal more than a tutor. He had been ambassador in Rome and was well connected; his relative 'Prince Lichtenstein the Rich', according to Stepney, owned a country house as large as Chelsea Hospital. The diatribes of Peterborough against him can be taken with a grain of salt, but Paul Methuen was also very critical, and he was generally described as alternately arrogant and pusillanimous, irresolute, obstinate, and nearly always wrong. John Methuen once put in a good word for him, saying that during the hard times in Lisbon, when King Charles and his Court were pawning their silver, he put aside his German arrogance and behaved tactfully with both Spaniards and Portuguese. But his conversion was short-lived, for normally he quarrelled with everybody.[2]

The unhappy influence of King Charles' German entourage was not fully apparent, until he came to Portugal. In England the young king made a better impression than had been expected and it was only the long delay in his arrival which caused disappointment. He left Vienna on 15 September 1703. The allies had wanted to bring him to Lisbon in time for the autumn campaign and had been pressing for his departure, but now it was their turn to stall, for they were not ready and the Dutch feared the cost of en-

---

[1] Basil Williams, *James Stanhope, 1st Earl of Stanhope* (Oxford, 1932), p. 69; Add. MSS 28056, fos. 258, 268.
[2] Add. MSS 28056, fos. 101, 260; S.P. 105/64, fo. 32.

tertaining him. So he did not reach Holland until the end of October, and after more delays was held up for a further month by the great storm of 27 November, which raged up the Channel, destroying houses, wrecking ships, and killing under his own roof the bishop of Bath and Wells. The squadron waiting to embark the king was dispersed and in France there were hopes that the allied navy had been destroyed. The loss and damage were serious and Admiral Rooke took almost a month to make ready again. King Charles at last reached Portsmouth on 26 December, where he was met by Hesse and the duke of Somerset. He spent the night at Petworth and continued to Windsor to visit the Queen.[1] All the Court and especially the ladies were in the greatest excitement and he was reported to be 'beautiful, well-shaped and his mien and address very graceful and proper'. Queen Anne did her best to make a good showing and startled him by offering her cheek to be kissed in the English fashion. The fairest ladies in their finest dresses and loveliest jewels pressed around him. The ball was deemed to fall short of the standards of Vienna but nevertheless to be a magnificent spectacle. Charles spoke little and was too shy to pay the ladies the compliments they deserved. Officially he was perfect. He was judicious and obliging, and did not presume on his rank as king to snub Prince George by refusing to sit at table with him, as King Philip, duke of Anjou, had done with the duke of Savoy. He behaved towards the queen with dignity and respect, and they conversed graciously. Da Cunha remarked that the ministers present took little interest in what they said, owing to the youth of the one and the mediocrity of the other. Handsome presents were given to the ladies in waiting, and Charles achieved an act of gallantry by pulling a ring off his finger and handing it to the duchess of Marlborough together with the queen's jewel, which he had held for her while she was washing her hands. Though he contrived to look pleased with everything, he was not seen to smile once during his three days at Court. Only

[1] S.P. 84/226, Stanhope to Hedges, 23 Oct. 1703; Add. MSS 29568, fo. 166.

one human trait is related of him: he still had a schoolboy appetite. Admiral Rooke remarked that on board the flagship he ate dinner enough to keep a Lazarus for eight months.[1]

The short visit to England had passed off well, but the misfortunes of the royal voyage were not yet over. A good wind took the archduke in sight of Finistère, and Hesse was sent ahead in a frigate to give Lisbon the good news of his coming, but a gale drove him back to the English coast, so that he did not reach Lisbon until 11 February. When the fleet did not follow Hesse's arrival the wildest rumours flew around Lisbon, and, prompted by the French, Cadaval and his ministers suggested to King Pedro that he ought to send a message to the fleet that the treaties had been broken and therefore the alliance was annulled, and the fleet must turn back. The king stood firm but he was cast into a deep melancholy by the sudden death from smallpox of his eldest daughter aged eight. In spite of her youth he had planned a great marriage for her, possibly with King Charles himself, and the blow to his ambitions was as great as to his affections. He retired to his room and remained for thirty-six days without even seeing a light.[2]

The king finally sailed up the Tagus, with a fair strong wind, which had brought him from England in thirteen days, so that he 'bounced' in unannounced and took Lisbon by surprise.[3] A month earlier Portuguese preparations to receive the fleet had been well forward, but now many of the supplies had been sold to save them from going bad, and all was at sixes and sevens. Also the French ambassador was still in Lisbon, and Portugal was still at peace with both France and Spain. There were more protocol troubles, and the Almirante of Castile was inclined to recommend King Charles to defer landing until the situation was clarified. However, the French ambassador finally left, and after a last-

[1] Add. MSS 20817, fos. 482–3, and 29568, fo. 166; Burnet, *History of His Own Time* (1823), v, 82; *HMC Portland*, IV, 78, Charles Goring to Robert Harley.

[2] Add. MSS 28056, fo. 46; Künzel, *op. cit.* pp. 306–9.

[3] Stowe MS 466, fos. 23, 27.

minute discussion everything was done to give Charles a royal welcome as the rightful king of Spain. King Pedro emerged from his mourning and the orders for illuminations, fireworks and general rejoicings were put into effect. Even Methuen, who had been most dejected, and bed-ridden with gout, said that everything done by the king of Portugal for the king of Spain had been respectful, noble and kind. 'I have lived My Lord,' he wrote to Godolphin, 'to see ye day so much desired. The King of Spain safe here and received by the King of Portugal with all the kindness which can be imagined and the King of Portugal resolved to carry on this enterprise with vigour, but I my self ill of a fever and taken violently with the gout the same day the fleet appeared. So I have had no share of the public joy but may assure Your Lordship I have had a double share of all the trouble such a hurry brings with it because every one hath known where to find me in my bed.'[1]

The gala landing of the king, and the presence of the fleet, animated the Portuguese for a while with enthusiasm. But most of the fleet soon sailed again and the Germans around King Charles were discontented from the outset. The very warmth of their reception in England had spoilt them, and they had not the discretion to hide their complaints. If they made a bad impression during the first warmth of Portuguese hospitality, worse was to come. The next weeks were to bring many disappointments. The troops had been long on board and there was much sickness, and few hospitals to care for it. The Portuguese did what they could, and Methuen worked hard to move the men to better quarters up country, but many of the English were delayed in a damp unhealthy camp near the river.[2]

There had already been several ups and downs since the conclusion of the treaties. A high point had been reached with the

---

[1] Add. MSS 28056, fo. 40. Da Cunha, Add. MSS 20817, fo. 470, thought the expense of King Charles's reception was extravagant.

[2] Rijksarchief 7369, 24 March 1704; S.P. 89/18, fos. 85–7; Add. MSS 29590, fo. 317, and 29595, Nottingham to Heinsius, May 1703; Julian S. Corbett, *England in the Mediterranean* (1904), p. 237.

Lisbon March ye 12. 1704

40

I have lived my Lord to see ye day I so much desired. The K. of Spain safe here & received by the K. of P. with all the kindness which can be imagined and the K. of P. resolued to carry on this enterprise with vigour. but I my self was ill of a feavour & taken violently with the gout the same day the fleet apeared off. So I have had no share of the publick joy but may assure your Lords.p I have had a double share of all the trouble such a hurry brings with it because every one hath known where to find me in my bed

I pray my lord beleive me the K. of P. is so willing to accomodate every thing & so impatient to have our men on shoare in order to be gon to the frontiere of Spain that his ministers doe on their part all they can. Some little stops & delays & change of opinion & want of agreeing or rather speaking together have been on our Part. but every thing will doe well very soon These matters for three days have been treated between two Dukes who the K. of P. saith seem to desire the same thing & agree well together. I doe not say their measures agree with the K.s hast

The disappointments & losse may excuse necessary arms & ammunition not being now come but indeed my lord if the same want of every thing yt is requisite continue there is no hope of carrying on the service. English souldiers sent to conquer Spain without arms would be a pretty Entremes on a stage at Madrid

Count Wratislow writing again to the Almirante to the same purpose & more hath given me much trouble but I have now agreed with him but the papers are not signed. your Lords.p must immediately begin to remitt ye mony for my drawing all of it here will have great inconveniences Mr Morris is arrived but hath brought no bills with him but comes to me to have mony to subsist the army. wee are in debt to the K. of P. he wants mony extreamly. our monthly payments are now double & there must be two months advance by the treaty. I cannot write now for I am just got up but hope to be well soon & wee have this day another packet boate to dispatch at leasure. by which I have no letter from my Lord Nott. If your Lords.p doe not immediately remitt a good summe wee shall be at a full stop. I am my Lord your Lords.ps most humble & most Obedient servant Jo: Methuen

7   John Methuen's 'Nunc Dimittis': his letter to Lord Godolphin on the arrival of the Archduke Charles in Lisbon and his proclamation there as King Charles III of Spain

8a   The Archduke Charles, King
Charles III of Spain, and later
Emperor Charles VI

8b   Sir Paul Methuen, Knight of the Bath:
detail from a portrait by Joseph Highmore

arrival of a convoy of corn ships and supplies in July, and in August Admiral Shovell's fleet had anchored off Cascais at the mouth of the Tagus. King Pedro had ridden down to look at the ships through his spy-glass and many of the Portuguese nobility had been entertained on board and invited to take part in a cruise up the Mediterranean. The fleet, in response to Wratislaw's repeated requests, had sailed as far as Italy, but achieved no visible results. However, the indirect results were appreciable, for a principal object of the cruise had been to encourage the duke of Savoy, and the duke joined the Allies on 25 October. Also, the Toulon fleet expected that Shovell would soon be reinforced and did not dare to put to sea during the whole summer.[1]

King Charles had originally been expected in October and the Almirante of Castile had hoped to persuade King Pedro by great promises of a Spanish rising to occupy Ciudad Rodrigo. Colonel Richards thought that a great opportunity had been missed to invade Spain while the country was disunited.[2] In September there had been a rumour that Spain had taken the initiative and had declared war on Portugal but, although the country was more united after the return of King Philip from Naples in January, Spain did not feel strong enough to declare war until April 1704. There had been rumours of troop movements near the Portuguese frontier, but Portugal had no cause for alarm until the New Year, when French troops began to arrive and the duke of Berwick assumed command at Madrid, which he did in February.[2]

Methuen stoutly affirmed his trust in the sincerity of King Pedro, but the French reported that he had been anxious and alarmed. Paul Methuen and Schonenberg failed to prevent him receiving in September the new French ambassador, the marquis de Châteauneuf, or to persuade him to tell the ambassador to leave; when Hesse arrived in February he began packing, but when

---

[1] Add. MSS 28056, fo. 23; Stowe MS 467, fo. 55; S.P. 84/224, fo. 520; Hon. A. Stanhope (Mahon), *History of the War of Succession in Spain* (1832), p. 82.

[2] Coimbra MS 3008, fo. 94: Da Cunha Brochado did not finally leave Paris until 1704; Add. MSS 20817, fo. 435, and 29590, fo. 381.

the fleet failed to appear he stayed on, and did not leave Lisbon before the arrival of King Charles. The Spaniards had taken a more aggressive line and their ambassador left at the end of November and was exchanged at the frontier for Diogo de Mendonça.

Even Methuen reported that 'the King's long illness, the death of his daughter and the disappointment so often of the Fleet and of the King of Spain gave great handles to work on a superstitious prince'. In March the French offered to bring the duke of Anjou at the head of an army to the frontier, if the king put off the Allied fleet; many of his ministers wavered but he remained staunch and indeed showed himself more active and practical than most of his Court in furthering the plans for the mobilisation and equipment of his army.

Methuen's prestige was now enhanced; at home Godolphin was always cordial and Hedges showed signs of thawing. Schonenberg had not won much credit for his share in the treaties, and was very sour. In January Methuen wrote: 'I am unwilling to trouble you in writing the inconveniences Mr Schonenberg's conduct causes here, and that the only obstacle I apprehend to our advantageous settlement of Spain is from him, choosing rather by my own patience and industry to overcome it.' However, Schonenberg had instructions to defend Dutch interests and he was justified in his suspicions of Methuen's dealings with the Almirante of Castile.[1]

Both men cultivated the Almirante in the hope of obtaining an advantageous agreement with Habsburg Spain. Methuen submitted suggestions for a commercial treaty to Nottingham, which had no immediate result, but in 1707 became the basis of the treaty concluded by James Stanhope, which gave advantages to England in Spain and the West Indies, but made no mention of the Dutch. The Almirante on his side was out to get what he could. He was very short of money, for by February 1704 he was reputed already to have spent 80,000 pistoles. He had brought his

[1] Rijksarchief 7369, 7 Jan., 20 Feb. 1704; S.P. 89/18, fo. 121; Add. MSS 28056, fos. 36, 46.

jewels, plate and Old Masters from Spain, but the upkeep of the first two hundred volunteers and other expenses soon consumed his private fortune. Methuen arranged for him a loan of £40,000 secured on the duties paid in Spanish ports on wool and tobacco, and in November Schonenberg proposed a similar loan at a rate of 6 or 8 per cent interest to be secured on the export duties in Bilbao and Cadiz on wool, wine and oil, and also on fruits and other commodities. However, Schonenberg's proposal was held up in The Hague in spite of representations by the Imperial envoy there and by Schonenberg's brother, the Baron Belmonte, who had been appointed Minister Resident by King Charles.[1]

Although Methuen was personally canny in money matters, he was more generously disposed than Schonenberg, and was also in a better position to help. Schonenberg agreed that some effort should be made to encourage the recruitment of Spanish volunteers and that they should be paid a dollar a day, which was more than the Portuguese got. But he undertook no responsibility for raising the funds required. Methuen exerted himself and by the end of May had advanced $80,000, using his own credit to find the money. He also warmly defended the Almirante against insinuations made by Count Wratislaw that he had failed to pay the volunteers. However, there were limits to what Methuen could do, and as soon as the remittances showed signs of drying up, the Almirante began to complain to Godolphin about Methuen and relations became cool.[2]

The old grandee with his wealth and prestige had done much to bring over the Court of Portugal during the negotiations. He promised that Spain almost to a man would rise in favour of King Charles, and Schonenberg, Waldstein, and Hesse, all of whom considered their experience of Spain entitled them to speak with authority, were equally optimistic. Methuen was not much less so,

[1] Rijksarchief 7369, 5 Aug. 1704; Add. MSS 29590, fos. 382, 403. For the 1707 treaty see Lamberty, *Memoires*, IV, 192–7; Künzel, *op. cit.* p. 308.

[2] Add. MSS 29590, fos. 374, 381, and 28056, fos. 1–5, 23–7, 34–6, 40, 52, 70; S.P. 89/18, fo. 107; Rijksarchief 7369, 7 Jan., 23 Feb. 1704.

15-2

although he complained that they made the conquest of Spain seem too easy to the Portuguese.

The degree of allied optimism about Spain is surprising in view of the facts that anti-German demonstrations had encouraged the late king of Spain to make his will and that both King Pedro and King Louis thought the Spanish people favoured France. However, King Louis observed that the people had no power to assert themselves without outside help and it is true that the Almirante's friends, the nobles of Castile, resented French domination and had been alienated by the departure of King Philip to Naples.[1] In Catalonia and Aragon the desire for home rule and the hatred for Castile worked for the Allies and in Andalusia the Almirante looked at first for support to the nobles, and Methuen always believed that the merchants of Cadiz and Seville, whose trade was being ruined, would oppose King Philip. The Almirante might have been proved right if the Allies had not prejudiced their cause by so many hesitations and failures; King Charles's allies, the Catalans and the Portuguese, were hated in Castile, and when it came to the point the nobles disliked the Germans even more than the French. The Almirante had attributed to all Spain the resentment he felt personally for slights put upon him, and his prestige fell as his prophecies were discredited. It was too late for him to turn back. He was a vain and opinionated man, who brooked no rivals and cared for no plans which he had not originated himself. He did not become easier as his hopes failed, and he died in June 1705 a disappointed man. But in Portugal he was regarded as more responsible even than Methuen for her entry into the war, and Soares da Silva, whose gossipy memoirs throw a rare light on Lisbon feeling, described the Great Admiral as 'the cause, origin, and fount, of all this martial fuss' and his death as 'leaving hanging by one thread all the plot, which he had spun'.[2]

---

[1] Legrelle, *La Diplomatie Française et la Succession d'Espagne*, II, 565; Add. MSS 34335. fo. 69.

[2] Soares da Silva, 'Memorias, 1701–15', *Gaçeta em Forma de Carta* (Oeiras, 1931), p. 39.

The Almirante's demands were an added problem to those derived from the treaties. In February the Dutch were still disputing the article about the treatment of Portuguese missionaries in the Far East and had settled the Setubal salt and Malacca harbour dues questions with the utmost difficulty. England was still boggling at Article 15 of the Quadruple Treaty, which gave King Pedro the command of allied forces in Portugal. The treaty with France had gone by default at the instance of the Allies and they could hardly afford now to default on their own treaty commitments.[1] There was no dispute about the terms agreed for the subsidies but their punctual payment raised practical difficulties. Luckily Methuen had good relations with merchants and bankers in London, and with the Factory and also with Italian and New Christian men of business in Lisbon, and contrived to find money when the remittances from London were delayed. Until the arrival with the fleet of Thomas Morrice, as paymaster to the forces, he was responsible for all payments, and afterwards he paid the subsidies and all payments to the Almirante for King Charles, He had brought with him letters of credit to pay the English third and the emperor's third of the half-million dollars due upon the mobilisation of the Portuguese forces and several monthly instalments of the annual subsidy of a million dollars.[2] The Portuguese claimed that they had been ready since August 1703 and after some argument the allies agreed to begin payment as from 1 November 1703. Schonenberg asked the States General to begin remittances but in the meanwhile excused himself on the ground that the disputed articles of the treaties had not yet been ratified. Methuen paid up before the end of 1703. He even paid some instalments ahead of time, explaining that 'the desires of the Portuguese being rather according to the necessity they were in than the sums that were precisely due, and that want of money was so great that there would have been danger of losing the

---

[1] Albrecht, *Englands Bemühungen um den Eintritt Portugals in die Grosse Allianz*, pp. 76–7.
[2] Rijksarchief 7369, 23 Oct. 1703, 22 March 1704. (Portuguese dollars or patacas.)

wheat for the army, if he had not allowed some advances'. In fact in January there had been an urgent need to collect all the grain and barley in Estremadura to turn it into the flour required by the army. Methuen even tried to borrow 100,000 crowns from the Setubal salt money due to Schonenberg, which was still in a chest in the king of Portugal's hands.[1]

The Dutch were by nature punctilious, but they were short of money, and they were glad to take advantage of the available excuses for delay. But even when the articles of the treaty were settled and the Portuguese had proved their mobilisation by production of the muster rolls, no money was sent from Holland, and after long argument the first payments were only made from the 850,000 cruzados Setubal salt money due to the Dutch and collected from the salt tax, but still held in deposit in Portugal. The Portuguese threatened at one time to embargo this sum to meet a claim by the Cacheo Company in respect of a Portuguese ship taken by the Dutch in the West Indies, but they credited it to the Dutch subsidy account and in the end the States General agreed. A further complication was the death in April 1704 of the Dutch Resident, de Famar, who had handled the Setubal moneys; he left his affairs in great disorder and had deducted for himself the customary 2 per cent allowed by the company; after persistent claims Schonenberg was eventually reimbursed this sum. The use of the Setubal salt money enabled the Dutch to avoid remitting any cash in the first half of 1704. Their payments to Portugal were thus well ahead of those to Savoy, where the English envoy had paid 460,000 crowns of the subsidy of 600,000 crowns due to the duke but the Dutch owed 228,000 of their quota of 300,000 and the Dutch minister, 'a plain and impolite' man, told the duke that there was no obligation to pay before the treaty was signed.[2]

---

[1] Add. MSS 28056, fos. 33, 47, 52, 66.
[2] Rijksarchief 7369, 7, 20, 26 Jan., 23 Feb., 22 March 1703, and 7025, 22 Jan., 6 Feb., 7 March 1705, and 7026, 19, 29 Apr. 1706; Add. MSS 28056, fos. 33, 72.

Methuen spaced out his transactions in order to save losses on exchange, and was proud that he only paid 6s. 2½d. for the milreis. The milreis was used for computing large sums though there was no coin of that denomination; it was worth 2½ cruzados or Portuguese crowns and normally 5s. 9d. in English money, though in 1696 it had gone as high as 7s. 6d. The increase in trade in cloth and wine eased Methuen's problems; the imports of cloth created credits in Lisbon; in London the credits for wine could be diverted to pay the subsidies and the Portuguese purchases of war supplies. Methuen recommended friends in London to discount Portuguese bills, for Da Cunha sometimes spent as much as three-quarters of the monthly subsidy in England. Methuen also used the opportunity to collect the old merchants' debts and in May hoped to remit 40,000 pieces of eight on account. He often assumed heavy personal responsibilities. In January 1704 he advanced through Lisbon friends 250,000 crowns to buy wheat, to be repaid without loss on exchange when the money came from London, and in 1705 according to Luttrell he advanced £37,000 to King Charles. The figure mentioned in Parliament was 35,596 milreis only, but even so this was a large sum.[1]

In spite of the payments which he received, King Pedro soon ran out of money even for his most pressing needs, so Methuen was constantly plagued, and 'he was torn to pieces' to find money for King Charles. Meanwhile Pacheco was much criticised for some of his extravagant purchases at The Hague, where he ordered for King Pedro tents, calashes, sumpter cloths and rich equipages. Richard Hill described them as fit for the tastes of a Persian monarch and observed that the indolence or tranquillity of Pacheco would make one believe he was quite ignorant or careless of the failure to pay the emperor's third, which was giving their lordships in the cockpit so much preoccupation.

[1] S.P. 89/17, Paul Methuen to Vernon, 18 Feb. 1696; S.P. 89/19, Methuen to Hedges, 25 May 1705 (among 1706 letters). For Portuguese money see Appendix 2 and H. E. W. Fisher, London Ph.D. thesis (1961), on Anglo-Portuguese trade. Luttrell, *Brief Relation*, v, 619; *Coll. of Parl. Debates, 1668–1741*, VI, 76.

Stanhope wrote that King Pedro had ordered four large rich coaches, two rich royal tents of six rooms, and saddles and harness all richly embroidered, so that it appeared he did not intend to carry away much of his subsidy in specie. These fashions of the Field of the Cloth of Gold no doubt added to the delay in getting the king's baggage on the move. In the critical days of the Beira campaign of 1704 the army was never ready to move before nine o'clock and the full heat of the day. However, such splendours appealed to the taste of Lisbon. Soares da Silva described with relish the magnificence of the hangings of green velvet for the tents with a great gold flower on the insets, and silver on the fringes, and the arms of Portugal in the centre, with splendid saddles and thirty-three saddle cloths, all different, of velvet and so shining, you could not tell whether they were of beaten gold and silver or of thread.[1] All the nobles and their ladies in Lisbon went to see this wonderful sight, and the nuncio went three times. It must be admitted that such extravagances were good propaganda for the public. At The Hague these purchases had the opposite effect, but Pacheco probably intended to emphasise the sincerity of Portugal in preparing for war, as well as to satisfy Pedro's ideas of what was fitting for a king on campaign. Other purchases by King Pedro were sensible enough. He ordered 3,000 cuirasses, 7,000 helmets and various munitions in Holland and in July increased his order for bread from 40,000 to 50,000 rations. Large orders for grain were also placed in England, and Methuen was consulted about purchases of saddles, arms and equipment. Some orders were placed through contractors, some through Da Cunha. Methuen helped the purchase of artillery and arms, and arranged for a credit of £10,000 to be given through the London agent of a Lisbon merchant named Antonio Vas Coimbra. Some of the money

---

[2] Richard Hill, *Diplomatic Correspondence*, ed. R. W. Blackley (1845), 1, 243. Hill was on a mission at The Hague, before he went to Turin. S.P. 84/224, fo. 503; Add. MSS 28056, fo. 169; Soares da Silva, *op. cit.* p. 17. According to Agnew, *Henri Massue de Ruvigny, Earl of Galway* (1864), p. 109, some of this equipment was taken by the enemy at Castelo Branco.

was ill spent, and Schonenberg complained of Methuen's complacency but the latter's attitude at least produced progress. Contretemps could be avoided in neither England nor Holland. The king found he only had a third of the arms he needed from Holland and had to order more, while the muskets from England for three companies were found to be without bayonets and the pistols for whole troops of dragoons failed to arrive. Methuen showed considerable and unbureaucratic independence in his efforts to get things done, but he appreciated the use of the exact accounting which Whitehall asked of him, and tried to secure vouchers for all his payments. Schonenberg insisted on seeing the Portuguese muster rolls before he would pay subsidies for their troops, and Methuen held up payment for the 1704 campaign, due to begin from 1 May, until the 1703 accounts were settled. The muster rolls gave details of Portuguese units and their commanders and of the number of men in each unit; the reality probably fell short of the statistics, but so, often, did the numbers of the English units, and Methuen seems to have done what was practicable to keep a check.[1]

By February the king had already spent the half million dollars advanced for the mobilisation of his army. His request for a loan of a million crowns could not be met, but both Schonenberg and Methuen hoped that the arrival of the Brazil fleet would ease the situation, and also the recovery of a large sum of silver from a Spanish galleon from Buenos Aires which had been driven ashore by a Dutch frigate in the Algarve. Nevertheless, Methuen had to find 50,000 crowns to enable the king to leave in May for the front. The army paymaster had no funds and Methuen had to borrow through his friend John Milner and to pay 6s. 3½d. for the milreis, the highest rate he had yet paid, though reasonable in the circumstances.[2]

---

[1] Add. MSS 28056, fos. 40, 46, 52–3; S.P. 89/18, fos. 126, 128; Rijksarchief 7369 has a copy of the muster roll dated 22 Apr. 1704.
[2] SP. 89/18, fo. 94; Add. MSS 28056, fo. 54.

The campaign was ready to begin and it was expected that the fleet would protect the coast of Portugal and would also make a diversion by landing a force on the coast of Spain. Wratislaw, the Almirante and Lichtenstein had all been pressing for this, but a reinforcement had to be found for Rooke's 2,000 marines. There was talk of Savoy providing 5,000 men, and Nottingham told the Savoy minister that King Pedro might supply 3,000 men. The Almirante had apparently approached King Pedro, but he lost interest when Hesse took the matter up, and neither Schonenberg nor Methuen seems to have been informed. However, in April Rooke asked for 2,000 men, and both ministers tried to further the plan. The king had professed willingness and there was talk of embarking the troops at Oporto or the Algarve, but when Rooke returned to Lisbon from his cruise in the Straits, the troops were neither ready nor likely to be so in the near future. Rooke had orders to sail for the Mediterranean at once and could not wait to take the Portuguese on board.[1]

Articles 17–18 of the Quadruple Treaty stipulated that in the absence of the fleet an adequate force must be left to guard Portugal and a verbal understanding had been reached that twelve ships would be a reasonable number. England provided no ships before the fleet arrived, but six Dutch ships under Van Almonde came in the autumn of 1703. At the king's request they cruised in the Straits, and they drove a Spanish galleon ashore in the Algarve. Rooke had orders to clear up the naval questions arising from the treaties, but he reported that he could not seek an explanation of Articles 19–20, which placed English ships in Portuguese waters under Portuguese command, because Methuen was ill, and in any case he doubted whether he should broach the subject before King Pedro declared war on France. King Pedro had issued a manifesto giving his reasons for recognising the archduke as king of Spain and for deciding to free Spain from French domination.

[1] S.P. 89/18, fos. 89, 100, 108; R. Hill, *op. cit.* pp. 90, 92–4; Rijksarchief 7369, 23 Apr. 1704; Künzel, *op. cit.* pp. 313–18; S.P. 89/88, Methuen to Rooke, 13 Apr. 1704; Klopp, *Der Fall des Hauses Stuart*, XI, 305–9.

This resulted in a Spanish declaration of war, but in spite of pressure from the allies to fulfil this treaty obligation King Pedro never himself declared war on France.[1]

Rooke crossed out the instruction in his orders to leave the agreed quota of ships in Lisbon. He discussed the question with Methuen, who had explained that it would be hard to change the treaty but some compromise might be possible. They agreed to leave the question pending until Rooke returned from his cruise. Methuen had already asked the captain of the *Panther*, the ship which brought Hesse, to do some cruising for Portugal, and he thought that the question could be solved if the Portuguese requests could be channelled through him or Schonenberg. Rooke had already been told of Methuen's views by Hedges in November, and Methuen expected this procedure would be acceptable and was delighted when, after Rooke sailed, the Portuguese addressed their request for a convoy to him. The treaty itself offered a loophole, for it only gave the Portuguese seniority in missions of purely Portuguese interest, in which the Portuguese provided the larger force. Also the king had been dissuaded from appointing a Portuguese admiral and this removed one difficulty. But the navy never admitted that they were bound by articles 19 and 20 of the treaty: nor were they ever given discretion to vary their orders in order to meet urgent requests from Methuen or the Portuguese.[2]

Rooke was back in the third week of April. He had taken three Spanish prizes but sighted neither the French nor any Spanish galleons. He found awaiting him in Lisbon fresh orders to go to Nizza in Savoy, where a French attack was expected, and determined to sail as soon as possible, though he agreed to embark a Portuguese force of 1,500 men, if they could be ready at once. The two kings pressed for some ships to be left behind, and as the

---

[1] S.P. 89/18, fo. 90; Borges de Castro, *Tratados*, II, 199.
[2] S.P. 42/67, fos. 56–8 (see Appendix 4); *Cal. of S.P.* (2 Nov. 1703); Rijksarchief 7369, 7 Jan. 1704; Borges de Castro, *Tratados*, II, 144–7, 177; Add. MSS 29590, fos. 420–1.

Dutch admiral had not received any orders to sail to the Mediterranean, he was inclined to defer to their wishes. At a council on board the flagship the Almirante, Hesse, Lichtenstein, Methuen and Schonenberg all asked Rooke to wait for the Portuguese troops and to send a reconnaissance force only to Nizza, which could be reinforced if the French were found to be attacking the place. As Rooke demurred the Almirante suggested that the navy should hold another Council of War; the admirals adjourned to another room and after a long discussion sent back a message to the princes and plenipotentiaries through Paul Methuen 'junior', as Schonenberg pointedly phrased it, that they would send a written reply later. As Rooke was ill with gout and their presence was evidently unwelcome, the ministers went ashore, where they learnt later from the Dutch admiral Callenborg that he had tried to dissuade the English, but they had insisted on sailing at once for Nizza, after which they agreed they would try to help Hesse in Catalonia. They were then summoned to the palace to be told by Alegrete that the king considered that the departure of the fleet without his consent would be contrary to the treaty and a breach of faith. He demanded a categorical reply to his two points regarding the security of Portugal and the observance of the treaties. Methuen took the initiative in replying and said that the Allies earnestly desired to keep the treaties and to find a satisfactory solution, but the Portuguese must admit the absolute necessity to obey the queen's orders to go at once to the Mediterranean, which was the only place where the French fleet would come and where the safety of Portugal could be preserved. He added that while the Portuguese had been talking, the allies had been acting by taking the right measures for the protection of Portugal. Cadaval retorted that if Rooke left, the protection of Portugal would devolve on the Channel squadron, which was too far away to prevent the French attacking Portugal, or intercepting the Brazil fleet. After this Schonenberg, Methuen and the Dutch admirals again tried to persuade Rooke to wait a few days, to leave a few ships behind, or at least to guarantee a landing in Catalonia. Callenborg offered to leave two ships, if Rooke would leave three, and argued the danger of angering the king, and the jeopardy to the whole costly Spanish expedition, which depended on good relations with Portugal for its success. He added that Rooke must accept the entire responsibility, for the discouragement to the Spanish rebels would be very great and his decision might affect the whole fortunes of the war. Rooke replied that he had written home to ask for reinforcements but he must sail at once. The Dutch were mortified at being reduced to the role of mere spectators, obliged to obey Queen Anne's commands, but there was nothing the disgruntled ministers could do except return ashore and break the news to the Portuguese. The whole fleet put to sea on 8 May and at the same time news came from Castelo Branco that the enemy had crossed the frontier and taken Salvaterra, but this came as a positive relief to the allied envoys, for the outbreak of hostilities at least committed Portugal definitely to war.

Methuen's visits to the flagship cost him a severe chill; he was laid up for some weeks and had to give up his plan to go to the front. Paul went instead and Methuen was left to cope with the Portuguese ministers, who came early in the morning to his bed-side, crying that no regard was paid to the treaties or to the safety of their country, and that the fleet had sailed without even taking the troops needed to support a landing. King Pedro had planned to leave on 8 May; he did not go until the end of the month, but he received Admiral Rooke's message politely and took no notice of the general panic. Schonenberg had planned to go to the front too, but his plea to the States General for his expenses to be paid remained unanswered and he decided to remain in Lisbon. Before his departure King Pedro showed good will by dismounting some of his troops to provide horses for the allies and by handing back to their owners two small ships recovered from Spanish privateers.

[1] Add. MMS 28056, fo. 66; S.P. 89/18, fos. 109–12; S.P. 89/88, Methuen to Rooke, 6 May 1704; Rijksarchief 7369, 8 May 1704.

Methuen wrote staunchly to Godolphin that he was doing his best to appease the king, and to regain his health by a strict diet and a régime of asses' milk, but his private feeling was one of despair. The ships' captains took no notice of his requests for convoys and in another letter he wrote: 'My Lord, I think myself obliged to write not to desire any increase of power for myself, but that the truth may be known, and I do it more freely, because I have desired Your Lordship to lay my humble request before Her Majesty that she will please to recall me from her service, which I hope Your Lordship hath done and will continue, for I find every day myself less able to carry on the service and with more reasons to return home.'[1]

The French Brest squadron passed down the coast in sight of the mouth of the Tagus on 22 May. After sending in a scout under English colours to see whether the Allies were still in the river, they continued, as Methuen had predicted, to the Mediterranean, but the Portuguese were convinced that they had been left defenceless and in grave danger. Meanwhile Hesse was persuading Rooke to land 1,000 English and 400 Dutch marines at Barcelona, while he sent a herald to summon the city to surrender. But the viceroy, Velasco, had forestalled the insurrection, which Hesse so confidently expected, by arresting three of the leading conspirators. There was no response to the summons and the troops were obliged to embark. Rooke was willing to wait for a few days for Admiral Shovell, but there was no sign of him, and he continued along the coast to get into touch with the duke of Savoy, and to detach a small force to reconnoitre Toulon. He ordered a rendezvous at Hyères, whence he expected to sail to Nizza and Villafranca, but on 6 June the *Charles* galley urgently dispatched from Lisbon on 23 May by Methuen warned him that the Brest squadron under the Comte de Toulouse was on its way through the Straits. A Council of War decided to turn back to meet the enemy, who were soon sighted near Minorca. Both

[1] S.P. 89/18, fos. 114–15; Rijksarchief 7025, 7 June 1704.

fleets were becalmed in sight of each other for two days, but the French did not try to engage, and Rooke would not risk being caught between the Brest and Toulon squadrons. The Brest squadron, which had been reinforced by six ships from Cadiz, was in itself equal to Rooke, and the French ships were clean, while those of the Allies had been at sea the whole winter and were foul. Rooke therefore retreated to the Straits, where Admiral Shovell joined him on 28 June.[1]

Methuen had no news of Rooke for thirty-six days, and it was the end of June before Zinzerling, Hesse's secretary, arrived from the Straits with first-hand news of the fleet. It was very difficult for the allied representatives in Lisbon to defend Rooke's departure and his apparently futile cruise. Rooke's earlier orders contemplated the defence of Nizza, if it were attacked, and a few of the commanders, including Hesse, knew this. But the full purport of the secret orders held by Rooke were known to him alone. They concerned the southern thrust to support Marlborough's Grand Design to march to the Danube and were only divulged to Godolphin and necessarily to Richard Hill, the English minister to Savoy. Rooke was told to disregard all previous instructions and objections of the ministers of Portugal, and all other persons whatsoever, in order to support the duke of Savoy,[2] who was to march to the relief of Nizza and with the help of the fleet to continue to Toulon. In the inner councils of England the great naval base of Toulon was regarded as the most desirable of all objectives and from 1704 to 1707 secret plans were constantly made to concentrate on a combined attack on Toulon or on operations in Italy at the expense of a contraction of operations in Portugal on which so much money was being spent. The co-operation of the duke of Savoy was essential. He occupied a key position geographically and was incidentally a grandson of Charles I and a

---

[1] S.P. 89/18, fo. 117; Rijksarchief 7369, 23 May 1704; Künzel, *op. cit.* pp. 418–26; Corbett, *op. cit.* pp. 239–52; R. Hill, *op. cit.* I, 108.

[2] Add. MSS 28056, fos. 76, 78; Rijksarchief 7369, 1 July 1704.

possible alternative candidate to the English throne. But he was an incalculable prince and as much a rival as an ally of the emperor, the other claimant for help in Italy. Where Marlborough was concerned there was the touch of genius, but the secret plans became nevertheless too complicated. A note written by Rooke at the end of April 1704 showed that his agenda was much over-loaded; no less than ten objectives of varying practicability and importance were included in his orders. Before he was ordered to Toulon, an attack on Cadiz, Gibraltar or some other Spanish port still headed his programme, but alternative plans comprised not only Nizza and Toulon, but Tuscany, Naples, Sicily, and even the Adriatic as far as Venice and Buccari.[1]

Unfortunately the duke of Savoy was not at all disposed to play the part assigned to him. The French had called off their attack on Nizza and were concentrating on Italy, where the duke must confront them. On the day after Rooke left Lisbon fresh orders left London saying that the Toulon plan was impracticable; he must prevent the junction of the Brest and Toulon fleets, join Shovell and carry out a diversion on the coast of Spain to help King Pedro and King Charles. Contrary winds prolonged the crossing of the Lisbon packet to twenty-two days and these orders only reached Rooke on 7 June in the Straits. Methuen observed that if the orders had come sooner Rooke might have embarked the 2,000 Portuguese and 400 Spaniards for an attack on the Spanish coast and satisfied King Pedro. Marlborough was already on his way to the Danube when he heard the disappointing news, and said he was glad that Rooke had been reinforced and had fresh orders to co-operate with the Portuguese, as he feared the allies would make little progress without naval help.[2]

Methuen hoped to persuade Shovell to embark the Portuguese troops and he assured Schonenberg that he could solve the

---

[1] Klopp, *op. cit.* II, 223–4; S.P. 42/67, fos. 56–8. For Rooke's secret orders see Appendix 4.
[2] Corbett, *op. cit.* pp. 247–8; R. Hill, *op. cit.* I, 6/7, 83; S.P. 89/19, fo. 122; *Marlborough's Letters and Despatches*, ed. Sir G. Murray, I, 298.

difficulty of the convoys. But Shovell was as adamant as Rooke and refused to leave a single ship in Lisbon, though he promised to leave orders for any ships reaching Lisbon subsequently to be at Methuen's disposal, and to detach a convoy for the Brazil fleet as soon as he reached the Straits. Two English ships and one Dutch were in fact sent. Meanwhile Schonenberg arranged with Admiral Callenborg to send six Dutch ships home with a convoy to be available for the autumn convoy and for service at Lisbon next winter. Rooke was much annoyed and it transpired that his anger was justified, for, while those at home thought he had sixty ships to meet the French, he now had only fifty-two and had lost the margin of superiority, which he might have kept for the battle of Malaga.[1]

[1] R. Hill, *op. cit.* I, 97; Rijksarchief 7369, Schonenberg to Callenborg, 21 June 1704, and 7370, 17 March 1704; Add. MSS 28056, fo. 104.

CHAPTER 10

THE FAILURE OF THE CAMPAIGNS IN PORTUGAL IN 1704

KING PEDRO, followed by King Charles, reached the Portuguese headquarters at Santarem at the end of May. The Portuguese army had been under arms since the previous autumn; under the treaties it was not anticipated that they should serve for longer than six months in the year and they were not used to being absent so long from their homes and fields. Little had been done to train them, and they were scarcely readier in the spring than they had been in the autumn, when conditions had been more favourable for them to filter into Spain and to rally Spanish dissidents to join them; now the enemy had been reinforced by French troops and was ready to confront them.

In spite of the muster rolls produced for the allies the Portuguese were never up to strength. Penalties for desertion were seldom enforced and the Portuguese colonels were paid according to the number they could muster at the end of the campaign. They positively preferred their men to remain at home, where they suffered no casualties, but could be counted for the quota.[1] This system conduced to a humane economy of life, but not to military efficiency. The best regiments were probably those in which a local leader commanded men personally known to him, for the army was still organised on a local and feudal basis. Even the English army had some similar characteristics, though the process of turning it into a professional force had gone further. English regiments were still recruited by their titular colonels, and in Portugal and Spain Lt.-Col. St Pierre and officers of the Royal Dragoons had to engage in long correspondence with their

---

[1] Add. MSS 28056, fo. 82, Schomberg to Methuen; Stowe MS 468, fo. 77.

Colonel, Lord Raby, then minister at Berlin, to get his decision on regimental questions and particularly on promotions.[1] Absenteeism was common and James Stanhope and the earl of Galway had to take severe measures to remedy it. But if the Portuguese had little experience of active warfare or logistics, they knew how to fight hunger, sickness, nakedness and the heat of the sun, which were often more formidable enemies than either Frenchman or Spaniard; the conventional soldiers, educated to the standards of the north, could fight to the death in correct formation on a battlefield, but they could not cope with hopeless disorder, the constant failure of rations, and the lack of practically everything which they thought essential for the conduct of a proper war.

The allied force was supposed to consist of 8,000 English and 4,000 Dutch. Each country accused the other of being short of its complement, and sickness had taken a heavy toll during the long immurement on board ship. Many of the Portuguese supplies had gone bad during the weeks of delay; their hospitals were inadequate and the camping grounds at Lisbon were mostly in unhealthy spots near the river. The duke of Schomberg showed no inclination to move from Lisbon, until the desirability of doing so was forced on him, but the Dutch made better arrangements to move their men up country to Abrantes, Castelo Branco or the Beira. The English eventually got away to the Alemtejo. A few Allied sappers, engineers, and technicians had arrived, but the generals and senior officers promised by Article 14 of the treaty for the training of the Portuguese were conspicuous by their absence. The king was much upset, and it was decided that the Allied generals must receive Portuguese rank and take over these duties. It had been anticipated that Schomberg would be troublesome about his rank and there had been talk of sending Lord Portmore in his stead, who might be more amenable. Schomberg

[1] Rijksarchief 7025, 11, 12, 21, 24 March 1704; Add. MSS 29590, fos. 421, 429–30; S.P. 89/18, fos. 85, 87, 126; Add. MSS 31134, Lt.-Col. St Pierre to Lord Raby.

insisted on the rank of captain general and Methuen saw no harm in his receiving this. He now took umbrage at the idea of being given the Portuguese rank of Mestre de Campo, but he was cajoled into accepting it, though he took further offence when the Dutch general, Baron Fagel, was also given it. The Almirante's suggestion that some Spanish officers should be appointed was rejected by King Pedro and it was not practicable to fit Prince George of Hesse into the hierarchy. He had to be content with his appointment by King Charles to be vicar-general of Aragon, which, he remarked, would give him kingdoms and provinces to govern, if God gave him luck. His jurisdiction would cover Catalonia, Aragon and the Balearic Islands, but his actual command, until he became governor of Gibraltar, was limited to sixty Spanish volunteers.[1]

Hesse was the most promising of the generals and it was unfortunate that he could not be employed, but the appointment of Schomberg had been recommended by Methuen at the suggestion of King Pedro, who remembered that the duke's father had been a hero in the war against Spain and had left a Portuguese title to his son. The Portuguese generals and statesmen dated from that time and thought fondly of the old duke for a saying attributed to him 'that with a handful of Portuguese he could conquer the world'.[2] In command of a well-supplied army in conditions with which he was familiar, Schomberg might have been adequate, but he was a hot-tempered man and better at action than at patient diplomacy. Methuen expected that his fault would be 'too much heat and overforwardness'. It was not surprising that he quarrelled with his colleagues, and particularly with the old count of Galveas, who as governor of arms in the Alemtejo was his Portuguese senior, but he was not expected to be irresolute and reluctant to fight. It is possible that his reluctance was partly political, and that he had received some hint that his

---

[1] Add. MSS 9721, fos. 142–3, and 28056, fos. 52–3; Künzel, *Das Leben und der Briefwechsel des Landgraven Georg von Hessen-Darmstadt*, p. 313.
[2] Sloane MS 2294, fo. 19.

troops might be required to re-embark for the Mediterranean with the fleet, but it is more likely that he was merely suffering from a fit of the sulks, and from the dismay produced in a professional soldier by the first sight of Portuguese conditions and by the great gap between the resources promised on paper and those he actually found. The Dutch general, Baron Fagel, suffered much the same reaction. He concealed his resentment at being subordinate to the Marquis de Minas tactfully enough to earn the approbation of the Portuguese, but the despair he expressed in his reports was complete. In the first place he had no experience of mountains. He could not conceive how a campaign could be fought among them and thought that a mountain range in Guelderland would solve for ever all Dutch problems of defence. After reaching the front he wrote that he had never seen anything so miserable as the Portuguese cavalry and that all would be lost if the king did not take the advice of the allied generals.[1] He could not bear to contemplate the lack of commissariat arrangements and protested that it was like trying to climb a high tower without a ladder or to embrace the moon with one's arms. He was no leader of forlorn hopes and protested that he could not resist a powerful and superior enemy without an adequate force, but on his own terms he was anxious to fight. His second in command, Van Frisheim, with whom he was on bad terms, had a combative spirit but no particular ability. The English senior officers for the most part were equally cast down by conditions so utterly different from all they had learnt in their military textbooks. Many of them felt sick, and James Stanhope, one of the best of them, was incapacitated early in the campaign and had to be brought back from Porto Alegre on a stretcher to Lisbon, where Methuen looked after him until he was fit to travel to England. John Jason, an officer of the Royal Dragoons, writing in August, hoped he was now seasoned for Portugal, as he had had fever and been delirious for several days. He lamented the death of a comrade and said all

---

[1] Rijksarchief 7369, 23 May 1704.

were sick first or last, and those who had been to the West Indies thought them a 'healthfuller' place. Portuguese food disagreed with English stomachs and did not help our men to think well of our allies. So Jason wrote, 'Pray God grant you never see this Hellish Country. Everybody is weary of it. I heard General Wyndham swear ye other day he "believed they'd starve our Horse first and then Us".'[1]

The failure of the Allies to provide a single first-class general was keenly felt and Methuen often lamented it. But the imagination of a Peterborough or the genius of a Marlborough was required and such qualities were hard to find. Marlborough was naturally inclined to appoint to the Peninsula men whom he could himself spare. Their fault was not so much their inability as their failure on account of rank or temperament to fit into the hierarchy. This was a fault which beset every nationality. There were not only perpetual quarrels between the allies about their ranks and powers but between officers of the same nationality. Fagel fought with his second in command, Van Frisheim, and other Portuguese generals were jealous of Minas. Lord Portmore, a friend of Hesse and something of a favourite with King Pedro, returned to England in disgust when Galway succeeded Schomberg over his head.[2]

The Portuguese generals were hampered by their inexperience and their obsolete organisation. The best of them was the Marquis of Minas. He was not over seventy, as has often been said, but he was born in 1644 and took part in the siege of Elvas at the age of thirteen. He was a gallant, hot-headed man, and, although Fagel was critical, Galway found in him many redeeming features. His obstinacy in adhering to the plan to march into Castile by way of Ciudad Rodrigo was much condemned, but the scheme was sound in itself and only made impracticable by events beyond his control. His relative, the count of Atalaya, was a brave cavalry

---

[1] Rijksarchief 7369, Fagel to Schonenberg, 31 July 1704; Add. MSS 31134, fo. 43, John Jason to Lord Raby.
[2] Add. MSS 20817, fo. 739; Add. MSS 28056, fo. 138, letter from Brigadier Hugh Wyndham.

leader and was succeeded by his son. Many of the Portuguese officers had courage and goodwill, but they were touchy and had no knowledge of modern war. A few were against the war or even in contact with the enemy. The count of Galveas, as governor of arms in the Alemtejo, was a man of great importance, for he was senior to Schomberg; he had had a distinguished career but he was getting far too old, and Schomberg had no use for him. The duke of Cadaval combined the office of governor of arms in the Estremadura with that of minister of War. He was opposed to the war and to the futile sacrifices which he thought it represented for Portugal, but he was a man of good sense. He took a realistic view of Portuguese resources, and in 1705 observed that so far from allying herself with England and Holland, Portugal was not in a position to confront the most inconsiderable prince in Lombardy.[1]

One of the gravest problems facing the allies was the shortage of horses. King Pedro was engaged by the treaties to provide 5,000 horses for his own forces and to furnish 2,000 to the allies at their expense. In the autumn he believed he had mustered his quota and in May 1704 Roque Monteiro produced a list of 2,010 horses with their provinces of origin, headed by the Alemtejo with 717. But there was no proper stabling in Lisbon and during the winter many both of the Portuguese horses and of those brought from England had sickened, died or disappeared. Horses were scarce everywhere and Louis XIV also faced a shortage; in Portugal the French ambassador was rumoured to have bought or spirited away as many horses as he could from Estremadura.[2]

King Pedro knew about horses and often discussed the subject. He requisitioned all those available, including those of the nobility and clergy, but was obliged to admit that he still had too few. Even the Almirante of Castile concerned himself and wrote a long

---

[1] Coimbra MS 3008, fo. 123.
[2] Rijksarchief 7369, 22 Apr. 1704; Luttrell, *Brief Relation*, IV, 475; S.P. 89/18, fo. 127; Add. MSS 29590, fos, 333–5, 355; *Quadro Elementar*, II, 124.

letter in his great handwriting to Methuen.[1] The nearest place where horses could be bought was Morocco. King Pedro hoped to procure 1,000 there and the Moroccans spoke of the sale of 6,000, but the French intrigued to prevent it and the sale of horses to Christians was said to be contrary to the religion of Islam; whatever the reason, the efforts of all the allies failed to produce any horses from Morocco. Plans to buy horses in Germany fell through and Da Cunha's purchases for King Pedro in England were thwarted by lack of money, grooms, shipping and convoys. Horses came from Ireland but many of them died on the voyage or were not up to standard.[2]

Many of the Portuguese horses were small, starved-looking animals. They were tough and could live on little, and were good enough to carry small, lightly equipped men at a mule's pace over the mountains. They were not strong enough to carry heavy northerners, nor were they fit for a cavalry charge or even for reconnaissance at any galloping pace. On the other hand English chargers were little use for the mountain tracks of Portugal; they served well enough for the Alemtejo or the plains of Castile, but even there they suffered from the heat and the lack of forage. The English and Dutch cavalry, and even the dragoons, insisted on large horses, which could carry heavy weights and make some speed. The Portuguese horses and their riders often lived to fight another day, but they were not an offensive weapon. They tried to charge once at the fatal battle of Almanza, but in general a charge was too much for them. Only in the later stages of the war in Spain, by which time they had acquired Spanish horses, were some Portuguese squadrons led by the younger count of Atalaya able to give a good account of themselves.[3]

The French owed much of their success to their superiority in cavalry but they too had their difficulties. They lost many Spanish

[1] S.P. 89/18, fos. 115, 138, 141, 146, 199.
[2] S.P. 89/18, fos. 115, 138, 141, 146, 199.
[3] Stowe MS 468, fo. 41; Klopp, *Der Fall des Hauses Stuart*, xx, 387; Voltes Bou, *El Archiduque Carlos de Austria*, pp. 219, 229, 235–6.

horses in 1704 because they did not realise that they required barley and could not live on natural forage. This fact and many losses from heat contributed to the petering out of the French advance. But after this setback they soon regained their superiority in cavalry. In February 1705 Galway reckoned that he could only count on 3,000 indifferent mounts to face 6,000 good horses of the enemy. In 1704 King Pedro tried to help by dismounting some of his own men to mount the English and the Dutch, but the Portuguese horses were inadequate and the shortage was never overcome.[1]

The lack of good horses also contributed to the weakness of allied intelligence. Ormonde had some horses on board at Cadiz, but for want of forage and water was able to make little use of them, and without means for a rapid reconnaissance his troops were blind and slow. Throughout the war the Allies showed a striking inability to obtain a good knowledge of the country in which they were fighting, or to obtain accurate information of the strength and resources of the enemy. The Methuens appreciated this need more than most, and actively sought information about military and naval movements and the defences of places to be attacked. They understood the use of maps, and the reports they obtained were valuable, though sometimes too optimistic. Their agents were usually merchants or persons of some judgement, though they might be politically biased. Admiral Rooke and the navy preferred to use their own agents and were inclined to give too much credence to stray fishermen and peasants; the accounts they extracted were often garbled, and exaggerated the enemy's strength, as much as the Methuens' reports minimised it. The navy denied all knowledge of the terrain at Cadiz, though many of them had wintered there, and even a keen soldier like Hesse was not altogether dependable on the subject of the fortifications of Barcelona, though he himself had been responsible for them. An instance of this curious ignorance occurred during the Beira

[1] Add. MSS 28056, fos. 242–5.

campaign. Although Almeida was an important fort and near the frontier river Agueda, no one could indicate where the river was fordable. Fagel claimed to have taken pains to ascertain the facts, but when the question of crossing the river arose, he was obliged to make a personal reconnaissance with Galway and Paul Methuen; in the face of some enemy fire Fagel insisted on retiring, so they returned not much wiser than before. Perhaps faulty liaison with the Portuguese was to blame in this case, for more seemed to be known about the Agueda at a Council of War in Lisbon than at Galway's headquarters.[1]

In any case trained and lightly equipped scouts seem to have been unknown and generals often had to go out themselves to look for information. On the Allied side Peterborough was the only general who was always well informed. He had the advantage of fighting in friendly Spain, for although Portugal was an ally the armies there had won such a bad reputation by plundering that the peasants were likely to kill at sight any soldier of either side whom they found alone. But the Allies were welcome in Catalonia and Aragon, and Peterborough took great pains to profit by this situation. His conquests of the ladies and his capacity for making friends with priests were very helpful to him, but he spared neither time nor money, and the result was that he was never at a loss and he always knew what the enemy were doing. He also grasped the essential feature of Peninsular warfare, which was to forget the standards of northern Europe and even on occasion the ordinary rules of military prudence. In the Peninsula, when a general had nothing, it was very possible that the enemy also had nothing. The brave imaginative man with nothing could always beat the prudent man with nothing. No other Allied general had this flair, and the only English officer who began seriously to learn this lesson was Colonel John Richards.

Richards was a gunner, and had seen service in Poland and

---

[1] Add. MSS 28056, fo. 168. The duke of Berwick perhaps referred to the same incident in his *Memoirs* (1779), p. 235; Rijksarchief 7369, 21 Sept. 1704, Fagel to Schonenberg; S.P. 89/18, fo. 152.

Greece. He was precluded from holding an English commission by his Roman Catholic religion. At the request of Da Cunha he was seconded to serve under King Pedro. He was given the rank of brigadier but for some time received only the pay of a major. He served in the Beira throughout 1704, and in the Alemtejo in 1705, and left a diary of his experiences. Like other foreign officers he was at first horrified by all he saw. He shared the belief that the Spaniards would rise, of their own accord, in favour of King Charles but thought that the Portuguese, though friendly, were ignorant of war and had no means to supply themselves. He wrote that there were no horses, mules, or guns, and scarcely half a dozen officers with experience of war, or one who had slept under a tent. But he did not spare criticism of his own people. He complained that the troops had been kept so long on board and alleged that the Dutch had made better arrangements than the English for the care of their men. He was tempted to volunteer to embark with Hesse and blamed Methuen for the muddle about the Portuguese landing force. He regarded Methuen as a man of the long robe, good for delivering long harangues but not for dealing with military preparations. No one knowledgeable, he said, had been consulted. However, as time passed he learnt to take things more as he found them and no longer to blame in particular either the Portuguese or Methuen. His own pay and status gradually improved and he realised that Methuen was not responsible for the difficulties with King Pedro arising from the articles of the treaties. His observations are of interest not only in themselves, but on account of the persons to whom they were addressed; he wrote habitually to his brother Michael, and to James Craggs, junior, who was a nephew, but also sent reports to Nottingham, Godolphin, Hedges and occasionally to Marlborough.[1]

Richards had heard that the attack would be made on two fronts in Portugal, and sustained by a landing in Spain. However, at a late stage the main effort was diverted to the north, while

[1] Stowe MS 468, fos. 10–24.

Schomberg's army in the south was weakened by the detachment of forces to man the forts at Castelo de Vide and Porto Alegre. The fleet made only a half-hearted landing at Barcelona, and in the north Minas had a large army but neither the arms nor the munitions for a protracted thrust. He could have reached Ciudad Rodrigo if King Pedro had not hesitated to commit the first act of war, but he had only just crossed the frontier when he received urgent orders to turn south to resist the enemy invasion.[1]

As one of the few Catholic and Portuguese-speaking Allied officers Richards had already been accepted as universal guide and counsellor. He left Lisbon on 23 May to join the army in the Beira at Almeida, travelling two days by boat to Abrantes and then overland. After leaving the valley of the Tagus he passed through country of increasing poverty, where it was scarcely possible to find even the most ordinary necessities. He joined Minas on 2 June and found him on the point of retiring. He was reluctant to do so, and Richards agreed with many of the Portuguese, who would have liked to ignore the king's orders and thought the retreat was a great mistake.[2]

But the initiative had already been taken out of allied hands by the enemy, whose main force, led by the duke of Berwick and King Philip, had crossed the frontier north of the Tagus. The first Portuguese fort, that of Salvaterra, was not important in itself and in no condition to be defended; the Portuguese commander was so overawed, when he learnt that he was facing His Catholic Majesty, that he apologised for not having surrendered earlier. Most of the English were south of the Tagus with Schomberg, and it fell to Fagel, who was in the main path of the enemy's advance, to bear the brunt of the attack. He had been on the point of marching northward to join Minas. Fagel complained that the Portuguese did not seem to want to defend their king, and that they retired before the enemy appeared, or surrendered without

[1] S.P. 89/18, fo. 111; Rijksarchief 23 Apr., 8 May 1704.
[2] Stowe MS 468, fos. 26–30, 36, and 467, fos. 1–2.

firing a shot. The duke of Berwick was equally astonished and said he met with little resistance where he expected it, but much more in the villages and open country. A regiment of marines which had orders to reinforce Fagel advanced, according to his account, only two hours each day and halted within a league of him on the very day on which one of his four Dutch regiments was surprised by an enemy force and driven back with heavy casualties and the loss of thirty officers. Fagel with a small party saved himself by a rapid retreat; he was criticised for having failed to retreat in time and to obey the orders of Minas to join him under the guns of Penamacor. Richards said that his general-ship had not been worthy of himself or the men under his command, but that he had made a brave defence and retreat.[1]

While Fagel was retreating towards Abrantes the enemy advance was diverted to give support to their army south of the Tagus and to besiege Castelo de Vide and Porto Alegre. At the latter place Stanhope's regiment had been obliged to capitulate, after the bishop had surrendered half the city. Schomberg con-sidered that Castelo de Vide was indefensible, and would have withdrawn the English garrison if Galveas had not prevented him. Richards believed that Castelo de Vide might have held out and according to Berwick the Portuguese commander was inclined to resist, until he was intimidated by threats of a wholesale massacre and rape of the women. Berwick said the Portuguese stopped the English resistance by throwing their powder down a well. Richards did not mention this story.[2]

Meanwhile, Minas marched almost to Castelo Branco to con-front Berwick if he returned across the Tagus. Richards on joining him found great disorder in the army. The Portuguese straggled rather than marched and the confusion at every alarm was incredible. A Dutch sentry who called out 'Wer da?' ('Who

[1] Rijksarchief 7369, 23, 29, 31 May 1704, and 7025, 29 May 1704; Berwick, *op. cit.* pp. 216–17; Stowe MS 468, fo. 27.
[2] Berwick, *op. cit.* pp. 218–19, 222; S.P. 89/18, fos. 133–4; Add. MSS 28056, fo. 108; Stowe MS 467, fos. 4–7.

goes there?') was shot in error. After a few days in Spain they entered Portugal near the fort of Penamacor and reached the small fort of Monsanto held by a French garrison. They were drawn up before the walls and Richards urged Minas to retire to the shelter of a clump of trees, where he could direct the battle like a general. But 'the brave little good old man answered that he must fight and would fight' and he plunged into the battle at the head of his men and was sorely wounded, and would have been cut to pieces but for his armour. Meanwhile the cavalry of his brother-in-law, the count of Atalaya, was in danger of being worsted, but Richards brought his artillery up and made the enemy retire. Two days later the garrison capitulated after hearing news of the Allied landing at Barcelona. Though cheered by this success a shortage of bread almost caused a mutiny in the Portuguese army; however, they advanced until they were faced by a large enemy force. Fagel and Paul Methuen were anxious lest Minas's impetuous temper and keen desire to vindicate the Portuguese might lead him to some rash engagement with Berwick's superior force, but Richards persuaded him to retire his main force to the protection of the guns of Penamacor. At the same time he was able to cut off some French convoys, capturing a number of waggons with silver, while the peasants took several hundred horses. Berwick did not retaliate and did no more than send a messenger with fifty pistoles for the French taken at Monsanto, and apologies for not sending a regular 'trumpet', because he would have been murdered by the Portuguese peasantry.[1]

To the surprise and relief of the allies the enemy retired in July over the Tagus, burning their stores and their pontoon bridge at Vila Velha. King Philip soon returned to Madrid. Political intrigues, Spanish-French differences, and the fear of an insurrection were partly responsible, but Berwick had not originally intended to fight through the hottest part of the summer or to

[1] Stowe MS 468, fo. 33, and 467, fos. 7–8; Add. MSS 28056, fo. 92; Rijksarchief 7025, 21 June 1704.

advance beyond Abrantes. His success might have tempted him to do so, if the inertia of Tzerclaes, his commander south of the Tagus, had not held him back. However, his army was short of food and he had lost many of his French horses from the heat and of his Spanish horses from lack of barley. His waggons were useless in a country which had no roads, and much of his bread had been left half-baked, to add to the weight, and had gone bad.[1] In spite of their victories the French were harassed and exhausted, and though they had wasted little shot on the towns they had taken, they were short of munitions and the forays of Minas and guerilla attacks had taken their toll. The reasons given by Berwick were enough to account for a retreat which seemed to the allies nothing short of providential. He blamed Schomberg for not attacking in the Alemtejo, but thought that Minas's plan to advance from the Beira was the best, as Ciudad Rodrigo, which was the only obstacle on the way to Madrid, could not have been defended. Richards remarked that with bread and artillery and a few officers they could have made a glorious campaign. Paul Methuen took the same view and pointed out to King Pedro that his forces would have been superior to those of the enemy if he had not split them into three and dissipated them to garrison various forts. Paul Methuen estimated that Berwick had fourteen French, three Spanish, two Walloon and one Irish battalions, and 9,000 cavalry, and Minas nineteen Portuguese and two Dutch battalions, and Fagel five Portuguese and two Dutch battalions. He reckoned the allied cavalry with a few dragoons to total 5,800, 1,800 with Minas, 1,000 with Fagel and 3,000 with Schomberg. Roque Monteiro maintained that the Portuguese had 9,000 men with Schomberg or Galveas, but Schomberg denied this, and Paul estimated there were nine Portuguese and six English battalions south of the Tagus. The Portuguese accused the English of being much below complement, and Richards admitted that after the campaign the six English battalions had dwindled to

[1] Berwick, *op. cit.* pp. 228–33; Add. MSS 28056, fo. 124; Rijksarchief 7369, 23 July 1704.

2,250 men, but he also claimed that the Portuguese were well below establishment. All were agreed that the Allied cavalry were much inferior.[1]

All the ministers and generals now tried to find a scapegoat. It was easy to pick on Schomberg, for he had quarrelled with everybody except the enemy. Paul Methuen had a long heart-to-heart talk with the king, who met his reproaches patiently. He had no need to accuse Schomberg as Galveas had been technically responsible. Galveas complained that Schomberg had refused to take orders and had done nothing but magnify the strength of the enemy. Further he had appropriated all the mules to look after his immense personal baggage and had kept no discipline, allowing his men to plunder freely. Schomberg on his side alleged that Galveas had refused to allow him to concentrate his troops and to withdraw them from the indefensible fortresses. He replied indignantly to the criticisms of him passed on by Methuen that surely he, as the man on the spot, 'was a more proper judge than those who reasoned in their closets', and 'the Portuguese Ministers would do better to study good and effectual methods than to make unfounded statements about their resources and constant complaints about the non-performance of allied treaty obligations'.

Galveas had been a gallant cavalry leader in his time and had been wounded twenty-two times in the war against Spain, but he was now over eighty and King Pedro made little attempt to defend him. But it was clear that Schomberg must go, and Da Cunha dropped a hint in London to that effect. Godolphin acted at once, sending the queen's coach to Rockley in Hampshire to dig the earl of Galway out of his retirement. Galway protested that he was old and far from well, and in any case reluctant to accept an appointment which would discredit Schomberg. But Godolphin insisted that he was the only man to reconcile 'the

[1] Add. MSS 28056, fos. 86–90; S.P. 89/18, fos. 124–8; Stowe MS 468, fo. 46, and 467, fo. 2.

jarring humours of Portugal'. He sailed at once and was in Lisbon on 11 August.[1]

Galway was an old friend of Methuen from his Irish days and there was no question of his good will or character. He was honest and brave and very patient and understanding with the Portuguese. It was hoped at first that he would work well with the Dutch but unfortunately he fell out with Fagel over questions of seniority. Many had great hopes of him, but there were doubts of his capacity. It was said of him that he might have been a good general if his father had not moved him from the army to serve in diplomacy, and that he had turned out a fine courtly gentleman but not more of a statesman than a general. He was not lucky in his record, but he was perhaps the best choice for Portugal. He was more successful than Schomberg and he proved better than any other allied general in the Peninsula except Peterborough, and possibly James Stanhope.[2]

King Pedro suggested that Paul Methuen should go to London to explain his difficulties, as this could be best done by someone who had been on the spot, but he did not wish to offend Da Cunha. Paul did not go until the following year but Methuen recovered sufficiently to travel to Santarem to see the king and he sent home a long report on the reasons for the allied lack of success. Richards also sent home separately two reports, which contained some criticisms of Methuen but agreed in the main with his findings.

Methuen referred to the delay in the ratification of certain articles of the treaties and the disputes regarding them. There had been delay in the arrival of supplies and munitions; they had only arrived with King Charles and could not be sent ahead of him to the front. In January there had been 400 landing craft and 500 mules ready for the disembarkation, but the failure of the fleet to come had disrupted these preparations. There had been the king's

---

[1] Add. MSS 28056, fos. 80, 88, 109.

[2] *Memoirs of Marquis of Ailesbury* (Roxburghe Club, 1890), p. 39; Agnew, *Henri Massue de Ruvigny, Earl of Galway*, p. 108; Add. MSS 31134, fo. 99; Stowe MS 467, fo. 70, and 468, fo. 73; Rijksarchief 7025, 18 Aug. 1704.

illness and his own, and the chronic shortage of money occasioned by the increase in prices and the vast excess of expenditure over what the Portuguese had reckoned. The allied officers and crafts-men promised had not been sent, and, on landing, the army had suffered from bad quarters and sickness. Nevertheless, Methuen could not acquit Schomberg of blame, for whatever his shortages he had nothing to fear from the sorry army of Spaniards under Tzerclaes facing him. He hoped that he had succeeded in smooth-ing over the trouble made by Rooke's departure, but he had as yet no news either of Rooke or of the ships he promised to send, and it was an insuperable difficulty having no allied ships in Portugal.[1]

Later Methuen forwarded his suggestions for the future. Corn to the value of 100,000 dollars had rotted on shipboard in London the previous autumn for want of a convoy. This year a convoy must be ready in time and the cost of the corn ought to be deducted from the subsidies and paid directly to the merchants at a good rate of exchange. Horses must be bought in England, Ireland or Morocco and sufficient officers and recruits sent to restore the army to its full strength. These recommendations were agreed by Methuen, Schonenberg and Richards and all accepted in principle. Nevertheless, the arrangements for sending corn became even worse and a parliamentary inquiry at the end of the war found it was cheaper to buy from the Dutch, who procured it from the Baltic. Enough horses were never forthcoming and the provision of officers to train the Portuguese was perpetually held up by disputes about their pay and their religion. The English Tories objected to the employment of Galway's Huguenots, even when the Portuguese agreed to having them. Cevennois refugees were turned down and sent to England, and King Pedro would not have the Spanish officers proposed by the Almirante.[2] The

---

[1] Stowe MS 467, fos. 44 ff.; S.P. 89/18, fos. 126 ff.; Add. MSS 28056, fos. 86, 102; *Courant* newspaper, 20 Jan. 1704.

[2] *Coll. of Parl. Debates, 1688–1741*, V, 135; Add. MSS 20817, fo. 434, and 28056, fos. 113, 128; Stowe MS 468, fo. 84.

Portuguese soldiery were good material, brave, reliable and cheap. Richards and Methuen appreciated their good qualities, as Wellington did a century later. Some of the young Portuguese officers were eager for glory, and under the inspiration of leaders of the right calibre might have infused spirit into their men. But the Portuguese did not take kindly to new ways and with nobody to guide them they made no progress in the art of modern war. Furthermore, they seldom received either regular rations or pay, and the Portuguese refused to allow the allies to undertake the direct payment of their subsidised auxiliary troops.[1]

New contractors were appointed in 1704 but they were no better than the old ones. The Portuguese did not care to employ New Christians or foreigners but they had not the capital or the experience to do the work themselves. Nor did the contractors have an easy time. Convoys were late and payment slow. The Dutch in particular took umbrage when the contractors pestered them to settle their accounts. Later in the war English merchants obtained contracts to supply bread, barley, straw and clothing to the Portuguese army, but they too were prevented from fulfilling their contracts by difficulties in obtaining payment.[2]

However, for the time being there was a general atmosphere of good resolutions. The French retreated before Minas could organise a counter-attack, but he was eager to do so, and he and Fagel rallied and concentrated their forces. Methuen wrote to Galway to encourage him and to try to discount some of the pessimism of his own reports. Minas was anxious to concentrate his forces at Almeida for a new offensive towards Castile and this plan was accepted, though Richards observed that Minas consulted no one about this favourite project and it was unfortunate that his judgement was taken for gospel. His plan was still a good one, but, as Fagel so clearly grasped, everything depended on adequate supplies, and the difficulties in the Beira were greater than

[1] Rijksarchief 7369, 16, 21 Sept., and 7370, 3, 19 Dec. 1704; S.P. 89/20, 8 Aug. 1710; S.P. 42/47, fo. 10; Adm 1/4089, 7 Aug. 1703, etc.
[2] Add. MSS 28056, fo. 122.

they had been in the spring. The wells and rivers were dried up with the heat, and war and looting had stripped the province of corn and food as far south as the Tagus. The very reinforcements to the army increased its needs and the approach of the two kings with their swollen suites unnecessarily increased its burden.

However, the ministers in Lisbon did their best. The English regiments in the Alemtejo joined Minas after a long forced march through the worst heat of the summer. Some of them passed like a flock of locusts through Viana, and recruits were landed at Oporto and taken directly through the mountains to Almeida. Fagel arrived there with his Dutch and found little was ready; he complained that with nothing one could do nothing, and the Grand Army did not know how it would subsist, for Minas was ransacking the villages for bread. He was doing all he could to bring his horses and men into good condition, but he was convinced it was too late in the year to prepare a campaign.[1]

King Pedro lingered on the way and reached the Upper Beira at the end of August. King Charles, who had spent an unhappy summer in conditions of positive poverty, was delayed by an attack of dysentery, but followed by a different route. Old King Pedro, though irresolute in Council, was as keen as Minas to fight, and Paul Methuen told his father that his spirit and invincible obstinacy made attendance on him a post of real danger. He insisted on Richards bringing all their artillery with them and the army crept ponderously forward to the banks of the Agueda within sight of Ciudad Rodrigo. There was little water in the river but the steep banks made the passage difficult. The news of Blenheim had just come to give the allies heart and the Portuguese talked boldly of fighting and destroying their enemies, but Paul Methuen wrote gloomily that they were in very ill condition and wholly ignorant of the number of the enemy. In short he did not think that anything was ever undertaken with less reason or hope

[1] Rijksarchief 7369, 1, 7, 23, 31 July, 11, 12 Aug. and 14 June 1704; Stowe MS 467, fos. 59, 66.

of success than their enterprise there. However, Galway still did not despair, and Paul admitted that the Portuguese displayed a measure of fortitude and suffered the lack of bread more patiently than the English or Dutch.[1]

The crucial decision to advance or retreat was taken on the banks of the Agueda on 6 October. The Almirante firmly recommended an advance into Spain on the ground that there was not enough food in Portugal to keep them. Galway recommended a retreat, as in order to advance they must beat the enemy first, and neither their men nor their horses were in good enough shape to do this. Galway also feared that the Portuguese would make peace if it was accepted that they could no longer sustain their armies, but all present including Cadaval opposed the Almirante's argument. The proposal to attempt a crossing of the Agueda was opposed by all the generals except Minas and Marialva, though Fagel claimed afterwards that he had agreed to it with some reservations, and Van Frisheim, who did not attend the Council, maintained that he would have agreed to an advance. King Charles, when asked for his views, said he could only conform to the opinion of so many experienced generals. King Pedro told him to reflect well, for they had all come hither for his service, and the way back was the road to Germany and not to Madrid, but Charles answered that although they were already at Madrid he would never hazard the lives of so much nobility against the judgement of their generals. King Pedro was cruelly upset at having to turn his back on the enemy and lingered near Almeida a few days longer to toy with the idea of returning to the Agueda or of following up a mad scheme to march sixteen leagues southwards to attack Alcántara. He fully intended to bring up his army to full strength and to try again in the spring, but soon after his return to Lisbon he suffered the reaction habitual to him after a spell of country life and then succumbed to an illness, from which he never recovered. At first he had an affection of the throat, which

[1] Stowe MS 467, fos. 59–62; S.P. 89/18, fo. 152; Add. MSS 28056, fos. 149, 157, 159.

he seemed to overcome, but towards the end of the year he had a 'bastard apoplexy', and after frequent blood-lettings became so weak that his life was despaired of, and an embargo was placed on ships leaving Lisbon to prevent the bad news spreading. Partly at the instigation of Methuen, Queen Catherine, who had already acted as regent during the king's absence on campaign, was reappointed.[1]

The allied troops now moved to winter quarters, the Dutch to Tomar and Santarem and the English to Abrantes. Methuen said that Cadaval had tried to put the English in a miserable part of the Beira but he and Galway arranged for their transfer to 'warm and fruitful country'. However, they endured a wet and weary march to get there, and would have starved if it had not been for the plenty of chestnuts in the mountains, which was all they had to eat.[2]

The inexperience, lack of confidence, and prudence of the generals perhaps saved the Allies from a major disaster, possibly from a success. Berwick admitted that Ciudad Rodrigo could not have held out. He had been ordered to remain on the defensive and to take no risks. At the last minute he had leave to attack but according to his account the Allies retreated in good order and gave him no opportunity. Like the Allied generals, he judged by European standards, according to which neither side had the strength to win, and he probably did not realise the extent of the Allied shortage of food. But his own position was undermined politically, for the French ambassador wished to direct military policy over his head and to take away troops for a siege of Gibraltar. At the request of the queen of Spain he was soon to be replaced by Marshal Tessé, upon whom the queen counted to help her arrange the return to Madrid of her friend the Princess Orsini,

[1] Add. MSS 20817, fo. 527, and 28056, fos. 115, 168, 172, 178–9, 180, 188, 220, 268; Rijksarchief 7369, Fagel's and Van Frisheim's reports of 12 and 29 Oct. 1704, and Schonenberg's audience with the king of 19 Nov., and 7370, 7, 29 Jan. 1705; S.P. 89/18, fos. 178, 210, 213, 217. Richards repeated the old tales against the habits of the king and the saying 'Qui no paga la putana, paga el medico'.

[2] Stowe MS 467, fos. 63, 66–7.

who had incurred the displeasure of King Louis and been recalled to Paris. Tessé, who was a friend of Berwick, asked the queen how he had offended her, and she admitted that she had only dismissed him 'because he was a great devil of an Englishman, who always went his own way'.[1]

The French now transferred a number of troops to meet commitments at Gibraltar and elsewhere, but the Portuguese were in no mood to take advantage of the situation. They were increasingly suspicious of Allied good faith and reluctant to advance into enemy territory, except to take fortresses which they might hope to keep. Finally, the breakdown of the king, who had been the great supporter of the war, took the heart out of any Portuguese enthusiasm. At first Methuen and Schonenberg had great hopes of Queen Catherine's regency, but whenever the king recovered a little he was inclined to interfere and the queen could not rule with vigour. In spite of this there was a rumour that the king had made a will making his sister regent in the event of his death, but according to the constitution his fifteen-year-old son was of age to succeed, so this suggestion only antagonised the Court and afforded fresh material for the intrigues of the duke of Cadaval and the anti-war party.

Methuen's own position was shaken by rumours that he was to be replaced by Galway. He was anxious to give up his post but he did not agree that Galway would be able to combine the functions of general and ambassador. A redeeming feature was that Methuen and Galway worked in close harmony. Methuen arranged for Galway to take part in all the Councils of War, and persuaded the Portuguese to agree to hold weekly meetings of all the generals and ministers to plan the next year's campaign. Galway in return told Godolphin that Methuen was an honour to his employment, who spent far more on entertaining general officers and persons of quality than the queen gave him, and that Paul was a man who served the queen well and merited an independent post.[2]

---

[1] Berwick, *op. cit.* pp. 223, 250.   [2] Add. MSS 28056, fos. 210, 216, 226.

Galway worked to improve the discipline of his troops, which had been a subject of complaint by King Pedro. Among other offences his men were found to have used their leisure time in winter quarters to make counterfeit money. Galway dealt severely with them but refused to hand them over to the Portuguese courts. The Allies claimed the privilege of administering their own justice but had little machinery for doing so. Richards was astonished to note that there were no provost marshals to bring looters to book. The Dutch were said by him to be particularly bad offenders and to be encouraged by their officers. The result was that any soldier found alone was likely to be murdered by the peasants. Galway tackled the problem firmly and methodically and made some progress, but he was pessimistic about the main prospect. When ministers in London wrote to him optimistically after the victory of Blenheim, he replied with a jeremiad. He admitted that the inability of the French to reinforce their army in Spain improved the allied position, but pointed out that the enemy had 6,000 good horses for their cavalry against 3,000 indifferent ones on the allied side. It was true that the Allies had more infantry but his own forces consisted only of 3,000 infantry, 600 unmounted dragoons and 200 or 300 ill-mounted cavalry; he had no authority over the Dutch whatsoever and the Portuguese regiments consisted largely of untrained boys and were far short of their complement. The French infantry equalled the combined English and Dutch contingents, and, if sieges were planned, the Allies were short of engineers. Therefore, though at the queen's command he would remain to do his best, he was sure that many could do better, and he would be only too glad to be replaced and to return home.[1]

Galway kept on good terms with the Portuguese but his relations with Baron Fagel were increasingly strained. Fagel had a low opinion of the marquis of Minas, but he also kept on good terms

[1] Add. MSS 28056, fos. 242–3, Galway to Godolphin, 23 Feb. 1705; S.P. 89/18, fo. 199; Stowe MS 467, fo. 15.

with the Portuguese, who found it convenient to use him to offset the English and thanked him for his services. He too had been talking of returning home, but he produced in the autumn a careful report, summarising the reasons for the failures of 1704 and describing the terrain for the 1705 campaigns, and the means of communication, the possibilities for defence and attack, and the best locations for stores.[1] Fagel was a capable soldier, but he was slow, and he was determined not to sacrifice Dutch lives in fruit-less ventures. He was not personally a very easy man and as he refused to take orders from any English general, he came to be regarded by the English as obstructive and even defeatist. He had some justification for his attitude, as he had arrived in Portugal before Galway, had an equally long military experience, and though his contingent was nominally only half the size of the English contingent, he had suffered fewer losses in 1704 and in fact at this time had nearly if not quite as many men. However, England was the senior partner in paying for the war and Galway was a man of rank and prestige; it was likely therefore that Galway would receive the most powerful backing. Schonenberg loyally supported Fagel, and Galway remarked that Schonenberg was more trouble than all the States General put together. Indeed the States General agreed that King Pedro should be asked to antedate Galway's commission as Mestre de Campo to give him seniority to Fagel. Fagel agreed to sacrifice his private interest, but his relations with Galway scarcely improved and, in spite of the Portuguese wish to keep him, English pressure for his removal continued. Nevertheless, he did not go until the end of 1705.[1]

If Galway's relations with Fagel were poor, Methuen's with Schonenberg went from bad to worse in spite of the fact that in many respects their outlook was similar. They had agreed in the argument with Rooke about naval protection, and in their work to prepare for the 1705 campaigns they had much in common,

[1] Rijksarchief 7369, 16 Sept., 17 Nov. 1704, and 7025, 29 Jan. 1705; S.P. 89/18, fos. 167, 179, 191; Fagel, *Account of the Campaign in Portugal, 1705* (London, 1708), p. 3.

though Schonenberg tended to plan with the Almirante for a march to Madrid, while Methuen generally thought in terms of a march into Andalusia after the capture of Badajoz. But Methuen's commercial treaty rankled with Schonenberg and he lost no opportunity to impute to Methuen sinister designs against Dutch trade. Methuen was equally suspicious of Schonenberg, sometimes without much justification.[1]

Personal jealousies accentuated Anglo-Dutch differences in Lisbon but there were serious divergencies elsewhere too, and at the end of 1705 Marlborough said that the Dutch were very divided, though he hoped they were mostly still in favour of the war.[2] As soon as the threat of invasion was diminished differences between the provinces asserted themselves and Amsterdam in particular was anxious to renew her international trade without being restrained by any embargoes or blockades. Schonenberg hoped to secure Dutch interests in Spain through his friendship with the Almirante of Castile but he kept up a cordial correspondence with Hesse at Gibraltar and also cultivated Lichtenstein. Methuen was inclined to think an attack on Andalusia would be the best method to put Charles in possession of his kingdom and aimed at an advance under Galway, which would establish English influence independently of Portugal in Cadiz and 'above all ensure that Gibraltar remained in English hands'.[3]

However, Methuen and Schonenberg agreed in feeling some sympathy for King Charles personally and in working to free him from Portuguese tutelage. Of all those who had been disappointed in Portugal in 1704 King Charles was perhaps the worst off. He was an awkward and expensive guest; the enthusiasm for him had long vanished and the apprehensions felt in Vienna about putting him in the hands of King Pedro had been justified. The proud and rigid Germans of his small Court found themselves in a country

[1] S.P. 89/18, fos. 138, 167; Rijksarchief 7370, 7 May 1705.
[2] Add. MSS 28056, fo. 389.
[3] Rijksarchief 7370, 8 Dec. 1704, 6 Feb., 7 March, 8 June 1705; Fagel, *op. cit.* pp. 8–9; S.P. 89/18, fo. 229; S.P. 89/19, fo. 191.

which they disliked, where they commanded neither money nor respect. They behaved badly and Lichtenstein showed small consideration for the foibles of King Charles's Spanish partisans. King Charles himself evoked sympathy and compassion. Instead of playing the star part he had been relegated to the wings. The Portuguese could not afford to entertain him royally and they were estranged by his German suite. Even in the first days at Santarem he was in an unhappy situation. The heat confined him to the small house which was the best that could be offered; he had few visitors and was reduced to amusing himself by playing cards with his servants all day, and shooting at the bats and swallows in the evening. The water was contaminated and in July produced an epidemic of dysentery, which prevented him following King Pedro northwards for some days. He might have hoped to find relief in the activity of a campaign after so much enforced idleness, but there was little action, and the weeks he spent with the army brought neither solace nor success. The winter was equally miserable amid his quarrelling Court and brought comfort only to the Lisbon pawnbrokers, who were acquiring his jewellery and silver. Galway was sympathetic but had no funds to help him. Both he and Methuen recommended an advance by Queen Anne, and tried to ensure for King Charles a share in the silver from the two galleons from Buenos Aires confiscated by the Portuguese in Rio. Schonenberg was also sympathetic but took no practical steps; Methuen tried to arrange a loan from Lisbon merchants and eventually advanced 100,000 cruzados on the security of the silver, to be deducted from the subsidies.[1] When it was clear that King Charles stood no chance of being allowed by King Pedro to take part in the 1705 Portuguese campaign both English and Dutch were glad to further the plan for him to accompany Peterborough on the expedition with the fleet.

[1] Künzel, *op. cit.* pp. 350, 359–60, 461, 501; S.P. 89/18, fos. 227, 245.

CHAPTER II

OPERATIONS IN 1705 AND THE PART
PLAYED BY THE NAVY

A PRINCIPAL aim, perhaps the principal aim of the maritime powers in drawing Portugal into the Grand Alliance, was to deny the use of Portuguese ports to France. They were reluctant to undertake a Peninsular War on land but were obliged to do so in order to win over Portugal. It might have been easier for Portugal to supply a squadron to defend her coast than to catch up on her arrears of military experience, but King Pedro thought first of his land frontier with Spain and was anxious to raise a large army even at the cost of Allied subsidies. Naval service in Portugal had no prestige and he only undertook to provide ten ships, while the Allies were expected to provide any more necessary.

The Allies were ready to protect Portugal by sea in return for her alliance, but only in a general way. Methuen gave this assurance in May 1702, but when the time came for more detailed negotiation he was expressly ordered to give no promise for any specific number of ships to be detailed to convoy the Brazil fleet and to serve in Portuguese waters under Portuguese command. Methuen temporised as well as he could, but he was obliged to yield something. An article was included in the treaties which stipulated that enough ships would be placed at the disposition of Portugal for the protection of her coasts and of her trade. The Methuens managed to evade naming any definite number, but Paul Methuen had to let it be understood that twelve would be a likely figure and that the actual number would be settled by agreement with King Pedro.[1]

Neither Parliament nor the States General wished to agree to these terms and the English Admiralty was even more obstinate

[1] Add. MSS 29590, fo. 292.

than the Dutch on the subject of the flag privilege. Methuen could only hope that he might succeed in effecting a compromise, and he might have done so if Lisbon had become the main base for Allied operations. Lisbon was well placed for a squadron which had orders to patrol the Straits or to intercept the Toulon or Brest fleet, and was an excellent base for any expedition going to Cadiz or Andalusia. It was also quite a convenient half-way house on the way to the West Indies. On his first arrival in the spring of 1704 Admiral Rooke prepared to use Lisbon as a base for the first purpose. He left his flagship and several other ships to be refitted, while he proceeded to the Straits. But on the receipt of orders to proceed into the Mediterranean he refused to leave any ships behind to guard Portugal, causing the shock to Portuguese feelings which has been described above.[1]

Lisbon was not so good a base for operations in the Mediterranean. It was often hard to get into the Straits when the Levant wind was blowing in the summer, and hard to get back to them when Atlantic gales came in the autumn. The way from Lisbon to the next safe port in the direction of the Mediterranean was far. Cadiz was outside the Straits and very exposed in winter; Gibraltar was just inside but had no room for careening more than one or two ships at a time and only offered full protection from westerly winds.[2] It was exposed to southerly gales, and gusts from the east were liable to swirl round the rock. The nearest alternative to Lisbon therefore was Cartagena or Port Mahon. So in November 1707, when Gibraltar was in allied hands and Port Mahon was about to be taken, Paul Methuen could still write: 'If we lose Portugal, we cannot without the use of this harbour (Lisbon) carry on any design on the continent of Europe, unless we are masters of Cadiz.'[3]

The neglect of Portuguese local requirements, which the Allies

[1] S.P. 42/67, fo. 58a. See p. 236, above.
[2] Nevertheless, a hulk for careening could have rendered great service, as, according to *HMC Finch*, II, 105, it did in 1681.
[3] Bodleian Add. MSS D 23, fo. 69, Paul Methuen to Bishop of Salisbury; Corbett, *England in the Mediterranean* (1904), II, 256.

were obliged by the treaties to supply, had a very bad local effect, but could be justified on grounds of high strategy. The Allies, and particularly the English, decided to concentrate on containing the French fleet and from May 1704 priority was given to the master plan for an attack on Toulon or an expedition to Italy. Nevertheless, the project for a joint expedition to the West Indies was on the agenda at least until August 1705 and a further attack on Cadiz appeared at least as probable as one on Barcelona or some place further afield. So there were always good reasons for going ahead with the development of the shipyards at Lisbon, but the English Admiralty was most reluctant to give priority to plans for this, and was very slow to take any action whatever.

The Admiralty was dominated by Tories, who felt a profound distrust of the Portuguese and found it hard to contemplate close co-operation even with the Dutch. But administrative difficulties and the natural slowness of a bureaucracy to adapt itself to new conditions perhaps played a greater part than political prejudices. Nottingham himself had realised as early as July 1702 the need to provide for possible bases overseas, but his approaches to the Admiralty were met with the rejoinder that only Admiral Rooke could decide what was required, when and if he captured a foreign port. Nevertheless, Nottingham asked in September that supplies and hulks should be sent to Cadiz, and next year, in June 1703, he advised Prince George's Council to consult Methuen about naval requirements in Lisbon. Methuen said there were storehouses in Lisbon, and King Pedro could be helpful but was not in a position to furnish many supplies, as his resources were very limited. Some stores could be bought from Danish salt-ships in Lisbon, but hulks and most of the stores would have to be sent from England. The Admiralty went slowly to work and equipped a hulk named the *Consent*, but this craft lost both anchors in the great storm of the autumn of 1703 and did not reach Lisbon until 1704.[1]

[1] Rijksarchief 7025, 22 Oct. 1703; S.P. 42/6, fo. 109, and Adm/1/4088, 2 July 1702; Adm 3/17, 14 Dec. 1702, and 3/18, 16 June, 17 July 1703; J. H. Owen, *War at Sea under Queen Anne* (Cambridge, 1938), p. 46; Add. MSS 29590, fo. 383.

Methuen complained that nothing had been done and this was the more vexing as the Dutch had six ships in the Tagus and had appropriated the only available hulk. In fact neither ships nor instructions reached Lisbon in the autumn of 1703. On the other hand Schonenberg was ordered in October to find storehouses and to arrange facilities in the shipyards, while Admiral Wassenaar arrived in November with the six Dutch ships due under the treaties and two storeships. The result was that when Admiral Leake arrived with Rooke's fleet he formed the impression that Methuen was inefficient compared with Schonenberg. Later he grew to appreciate Methuen and called Schonenberg 'an artful designing man', but his understanding never included those to whom he referred as 'those dambed Portuguese'. Furthermore, his complaints to Rooke of the unsatisfactory conditions in Lisbon strengthened, if this were possible, the admiral's antipathy to wintering abroad and to the use of Lisbon in particular.[1]

King Pedro, to do him justice, was always ready at Methuen's request to assist, but he could not produce hulks or warehouses or supplies from out of the air. The navy did not appreciate this and were only confirmed in their profound distrust of the Portuguese; they disliked being referred to them for help, but were yet indignant when prompt help was not forthcoming. King Pedro on the other hand soon found that he could not get the assistance to which the articles of the treaty entitled him. As soon as the fleet arrived he asked for a convoy to take some supply ships to Viana and Oporto. This was very necessary, as four or five privateers were waiting off Vigo and Portuguese vessels could not even sail the sixty miles between Oporto and Figueira de Foz without danger of being captured. Methuen was told that no ships were available but the *Tiger* would be detailed for a convoy as soon as she had been careened and should be ready in a week. This proved impossible and Methuen began his long series of fruitless protests, in which

[1] Rijksarchief 7025, 18, 22 Oct., 20 Nov. 1703; de Jonge, *Geschiedenis van het Nederlandsche Zeewezen*, II, 249; Add. MSS 5441, fo. 17; Owen, *op. cit.* p. 47.

he urged the importance of preventing Portuguese ships falling into the hands of the enemy, and pointed out that his request should have priority, being only what Her Majesty was obliged to do by the treaties.[1]

Methuen had an acrimonious correspondence with Rooke in July about the use of the fleet, but the navy ignored their treaty obligations towards Portugal, and in February 1705 Leake could still write, 'I had never sight of the Articles of the Treaty, or else had not given Your Excellency this trouble.' He was inclined to think that Methuen was interfering with matters outside his province and often became impatient. In reply to a protest about another failure to provide a convoy, he wrote

I don't know, how easily it may be believed Ships can be cleaned, victualled and fitted for service at this place, but because Your Excellency seems to be surprised that Ye Ships are not ready, I shall only take leave to tell you that I want no pain to forward me in my Duty, and as to my providing a convoy for Viana, will comply thereto as soon as possible, but at present ye Swallow only wants a Bolt Sprit and all sorts of stores, neither has she above 30 men belonging to her, but what she has had out of other ships to keep her in safety.[2]

Methuen on the other hand could with justice argue that he was familiar from the time of his first mission with the problems attending the refitting and careening of ships in Lisbon and had given repeated and ample warnings to the Admiralty. But all his applications, and those of Nottingham and Hedges supporting them, remained unanswered, so that he could never hear from the officers either of the Admiralty or of the navy of their desires or intentions. If he had known in good time, he could have found storehouses and hulks, and had them at less expense, before the cost had gone up. The Admiralty were in fact moving, but very slowly. In response to a reminder from Nottingham they

[1] Add. MSS 5437, fos. 47–8; Add. MSS 5441, fos. 19, 23.
[2] Add. MSS 5441, fo. 17; Add. MSS 5437, fo. 100; Navy Records Soc., *Life of Admiral Sir John Leake*, I, 313; and see p. 275 below.

appointed a victualling officer to Lisbon in January 1704 and a year later a naval commissioner, with both of whom Methuen was satisfied, but the provision for the maintenance of Leake's squadron in the winter of 1704/5 was insufficient and the shortages were rendered more acute by the needs of Gibraltar, for which departmental responsibility was not settled until June 1705.[1] In 1705–6 the supply of Barcelona was added to the burden and the requirements of Lisbon rose to a peak. Thirty ships were expected to winter there and a number more put in for repairs. The English and Dutch were still jockeying with each other for place and Admiral Wassenaar wrote from Barcelona anxiously hoping that he could reach Lisbon in time to find boats and pontoons to careen his ships before they were appropriated by 'Messieurs les Anglais'. In November 1706 Admiral Shovell was still complaining of the lack of storehouses and hospitals.[2]

Methuen established quite cordial relations with Leake who did all he could for the good of the service, but he had many quarrels with individual captains. For the most part, in refusing requests from him they were only obeying orders, but some of them were slack and lingered over the fleshpots of Lisbon when they should have been at sea, or went prize-hunting when they had other duties. One of them was Captain Legge of the *Antelope*, who was eventually court-martialled. He was accused of hunting prizes instead of carrying out orders to cruise off Cape Spartel, of failing to complete a mission to Tangier with stores for Gibraltar, of missing convoy duty with the Brazil fleet, and of failing to have his ship ready to sail on an urgent mission for Methuen.[3] The complaint made by Methuen was not proven, and he was acquitted of all the charges save one. Nevertheless, he was dismissed the service and no doubt the case served to embitter Methuen's relations with the navy. Methuen became increasingly testy in his

[1] *Cal. of S.P.* (26 Nov. 1703); Adm 3/19/2, 27 June, 18 July 1704; Adm 3/20, 22 Feb., 24 June 1705.
[2] Rijksarchief 7370, 23 Oct. 1705; S.P. 42/67, 24 Nov. 1706; S.P. 104/208, fo. 20.
[3] Add. MSS 5441, fo. 238; Rijksarchief 7025, 20 Oct., 19 Nov. 1704.

latter days of sickness and worry, and he found naval captains most unresponsive to his wishes.

Methuen was not the only minister or general to complain of the navy. At Cadiz the bad relations between the services were notorious. Peterborough once wrote: 'God grant the ignorance of seamen and their self interest never prove our RUIN; our squadron is gone a galleon hunting. I think in the present exigency, I would not have lost a day's sayle to have them loaded with silver.' Peterborough always needed to be taken with a grain of salt, but other generals sounded the same note. The capture of Port Mahon, for instance, was a naval objective of the first importance, but it was left to Brigadier James Stanhope to take the initiative, and but for the good luck that his brother was in command of one of the ships available, he would never have persuaded the captains to transport his men from Spain to Minorca.[1]

By June 1704 Admiral Rooke was entering the Straits again to meet Admiral Shovell. He had failed to prevent the junction of the Toulon and Brest fleets, but as yet Portugal had come to no harm as a result of his departure. However, the two kings were pressing Paul Methuen at Santarem for ships to be detached to protect the Brazil fleet from a threatened attack by fifteen French privateers. King Pedro claimed that Da Cunha had been specifically promised a convoy of eight ships, but Paul Methuen denied this and argued that in any case there was no danger from privateers, as with their Toulon and Brest fleets fully manned the French did not have so many available. He was beset by all the ministers, 'who were more hot than sensible about the Brazil Fleet and the Spaniards worst of all'. 'Lichtenstein signalised himself by the vain ostentation of his tongue and showed in a long Italian harangue much more his knowledge of that language and the volubility of his tongue than his depth of understanding or experience of state affairs.' Nevertheless, Paul thought he was on

[1] Add. MSS 28057, fo. 91; Basil Williams, *James Stanhope, 1st Earl Stanhope*, p. 77.

good terms with them all and claimed particular credit for still being on speaking terms with Lichtenstein.[1]

Among the ministers there were many points of view. Cadaval wanted to attack Cadiz, Lichtenstein Italy. Some thought Rooke should act at once, others that he should wait for Shovell. Shovell arrived in Lisbon on 15 June, and, refusing to leave any ships there, joined Rooke on the 28th. As soon as this news was received the two kings formally asked for an attack on Cadiz or Port Mahon or some other Spanish port.[2] Schonenberg recommended to Admiral Callenborg a token landing at Cadiz supported by a bombardment and King Pedro also favoured a bombardment. Methuen heard that the merchants of Cadiz, with their trade at a standstill and heavy war taxes to pay, were ripe for a revolt and he entreated Rooke to attack, telling him that a landing force of 2,000 Portuguese veteran soldiers was ready in the Algarve for him to embark. He said that he was ready to venture his life on the project and appealed to Rooke's sense of glory. Rooke had heard a similar story about Barcelona and was sceptical. His Council of War rejected the proposal as preposterous, and in his reply Rooke said that if His Excellency cared to venture his life with the 2,000 Portuguese, he should come along and his Flag Officers might agree to land some marines with him, but no sailors, for such was not their business. His own opinion was that Cadiz was better defended than Barcelona, for he had been told by captured boat-men that 8,000 or 9,000 citizens were ready to take up arms to de-fend their properties, and he was sure that if the kings two consulted their generals, they would agree with his point of view.[3] There is no means of telling whether Methuen or the boatmen were right. Hesse and Schonenberg and the majority of King Charles's court believed that the Allies had many sympathisers within the

[1] Klopp, *Der Fall des Hauses Stuart*, XI, 305–9; Add. MSS 28056, fos. 99–101.
[2] Adm 1/4089, fos. 4–15; Künzel, *Das Leben und der Briefwechsel des Landgraven Georg von Hessen-Darmstadt*, pp. 335–40, 355.
[3] R. Hill, *Diplomatic Correspondence*, I, 126, 448–55; Rijksarchief 7369, 21 June, 23 July 1704; Add. MSS 28056, fo. 117.

city. They all agreed that Cadiz should be attacked, and few or none now had the scruples about bombarding Cadiz previously held by Hesse, but few thought that a naval bombardment would be enough to reduce the city without support from a landing force.[1]

After Shovell had joined him, Rooke held several Councils of War to decide how he could comply with the wishes of the two kings and the latest orders from Hedges, which also demanded action. The Council decided that neither Cadiz nor Barcelona could be attacked without a landing force, but that the French fleet must be engaged, wherever it could be found, at Cadiz or elsewhere. On 28 July (N.S.) the views of the two kings, of Hesse, Methuen and Hedges were all considered and, in spite of the fact that the French fleet was reported in the neighbourhood, the decision was taken to bombard Gibraltar and to land a force there under the command of Hesse.[2]

Gibraltar had been mentioned as an alternative to Cadiz in Rooke's orders, and in a letter to Hesse King Charles now spoke of it with San Lucar as a possible objective, but without enthusiasm, for though it would be easy to take, it would be hard to hold. However, any foothold in Spain was better than none for prestige purposes, and it was the only objective which was immediately practicable and which would satisfy the demands for action which were reaching Rooke from all quarters. Gibraltar was naturally a very strong place and Rooke had no siege equipment, but it was known that the garrison was small and the defences had been neglected. It could be attacked from Tetuan, where the fleet was anchored, in a very short time, and this was essential in view of the lateness of the season and still more of the proximity of the whole French fleet. The decision was justified, for after a naval bombardment the force of 2,000 English and 400 Dutch marines stormed the place without serious loss except that of a hundred men from the explosion of a magazine.[3]

[1] S.P. 89/18, fos. 143–4.
[2] Künzel, *op. cit.* pp. 335–54; Rijksarchief 7369, 1, 10 July 1704; Add. MSS 5440, fos. 85, 191, 195, 197.   [3] *Cal. of S.P.* (1702–3), p. 109; Künzel, *op. cit.* p. 337.

Leaving 2,000 marines as a garrison Rooke crossed to Tetuan to water his ships, but returned at once to Gibraltar when he had news that the French were approaching. He embarked 900 marines and sailed towards Malaga, but owing to a fog missed seeing the French, so that when they were eventually sighted and engaged they were between him and Gibraltar. The fleets were evenly matched; Rooke had a total of two more ships and his middle-sized ships were as powerful as many of the larger French ships, but he had fewer three-deckers and small craft. The French also had twenty galleys to help in manoeuvring, and being fresh from port were in much better shape than Rooke. The battle consisted of a long exchange of broadsides, which damaged many ships but sank none. Rooke suffered most and exhausted his ammunition, which had been depleted by the bombardment of Gibraltar, but, after the battle was broken off, the French passed him in the night without re-engaging him and retreated up the Mediterranean. Both sides claimed the victory, but Rooke's claim was perhaps the better, for Gibraltar was safe and the Allies were left in command of the Straits.[1]

In spite of a further demand from the two kings for a demonstration against Cadiz, and a rumour that Ceuta might declare for King Charles, Rooke took no further action and sailed home in September with the first favourable wind. The Portuguese were disappointed, but he had already detached two English and one Dutch ships to convoy the Brazil fleet before Malaga, and he now sent Leake with five ships to Lisbon.[2]

Hesse was left with something under 2,000 men to hold Gibraltar. He asked for 2,500 and suggested they should all be English and Dutch: if there were any Portuguese among them, they would quarrel with the Spaniards. Methuen disagreed. He wanted a majority of English troops, but thought the Portuguese would co-operate with the Spaniards better than the English or Dutch and strongly recommended the acceptance of the two

[1] Corbett, *op. cit.* pp. 264–76.   [2] S.P. 89/18, fo. 151; Add. MSS 28056, fos. 98, 100.

Portuguese regiments who were still waiting in the Algarve. Paul Methuen inspected them in December and described them as 'very good men, old soldiers, who had served in Ceuta, at the beginning of the siege'. Rooke at one time had himself asked for the Portuguese and had offered to ferry them, and the administrative difficulties about their payment from the Portuguese subsidy had finally been settled. But although ships were detailed to transport them as late as February 1705, the exigencies of the service always prevented it, and in the end they had to be marched back to the Alemtejo.[1]

Leake could not get back to Gibraltar before November and no reinforcements came from England before December. By then Hesse's garrison was reduced to 1,200 fit men, though he had 2,600 mouths to feed. Hesse was also having trouble with the marines, who resented serving under the flag of King Charles and the military government of the Conde de Val de Soto, an old Irish comrade of Hesse named Nugent who had won a Spanish title serving in Catalonia. Relations had been strained from the beginning, when Admiral Byng, whose men had taken the mole, began removing all the stores and wine, including some cannon with Hesse's own initials on them made for him in Barcelona. In Lisbon Schonenberg complained that the English ministers behaved as if they meant to hold Gibraltar for England, and that Methuen was intending to replace Hesse by an English governor. Methuen did not try to do this, but, when Val de Soto was killed in action in November, Galway firmly recommended Brigadier Shrimpton, an English officer, as his successor. Hesse agreed to this but he tried to encourage the Dutch to offset the predominance of the English and have the Dutch senior officer, Colonel Tulkens, given equal rank with Shrimpton.[2]

Methuen was one of the first to appreciate the importance of

---

[1] S.P. 89/18, fos. 144, 151, 202.
[2] Künzel, *op. cit.* pp. 376, 465–6, 493, 524, 526; Rijksarchief 7369, 8 Dec. 1704; Fagel, *Account of the Campaign in Portugal, 1705,* pp. 8–9; S.P. 89/18, fo. 147.

Gibraltar and already in mid-September said it ought to be in English hands and English troops should be sent to relieve the two Portuguese regiments which he was expecting to go there. Schonenberg also referred to Gibraltar as the 'Key to the Straits' and was anxious to strengthen its defence, but he could not advance money or stores without authority, as Methuen with the co-operation of Galway took the responsibility of doing. However, Hesse still bore a grudge against Methuen and blamed him for shortcomings which were not his fault, although Methuen protested that no one had been more earnestly concerned than himself to provide for Gibraltar and Hesse's personal service. There was no question of this during the siege and Galway gently scolded Hesse. Methuen thought of going to Gibraltar himself. Eventually Paul went, and succeeded in melting Hesse personally, and in making him joke about his troubles with the English garrison, though he did not cure them.[1]

Samuel Pepys had appreciated the value of Gibraltar years before, and Marlborough told Hedges that the place might be of vast use and that no expense should be spared to keep it. The merchants trading to the Mediterranean were overjoyed at its capture and diplomatists posted in the area, such as Richard Hill at Turin, agreed with Schonenberg and Methuen, but Galway was sceptical and so in general were statesmen at home. Godolphin remarked: 'I do not know, whether this place can be held, and what use it can be to us.' Da Cunha thought Gibraltar was kept more as a trophy than for its use, and there was talk after the war of trading it back to Spain; but by that time the siege of Gibraltar in 1704 and 1705 had become a legend, and both Parliament and people warmly defended its retention in English hands.[2]

Methuen wrote urgently to Rooke to ask for troops and stores and to point out the importance of Gibraltar as a base. Rooke as

[1] Rijksarchief 7369, 18 Aug., 3 Dec. 1704; Künzel, *op. cit.* pp. 502, 534, 567.
[2] A. Bryant, *Samuel Pepys* (Cambridge, 1938), I, 162; Add. MSS 20817, fos. 553–6; Coimbra MS 2974, 17 Apr., 21 June 1712; R. Hill, *op. cit.* I, 143.

usual complained that Methuen's letter was far from clear, but he did his best to make the Admiralty send supplies of ropes, sails and medicines without delay. But it was a long time before anything could be dispatched, and meanwhile Methuen had to find supplies locally. He had a shipload ready in September, and in October he dispatched Captain Legge with two frigates and the engineer, Captain Bennett, who was to play a staunch part in putting Gibraltar's defences in order. Unfortunately the September shipment could not proceed owing to the French blockade of Gibraltar, and Captain Legge for the same reason did not go further than Tangier, where he unloaded some of the stores. However, it was suspected that it was not the French that deterred Legge from going to Gibraltar but a desire to go prize-hunting. He did in fact take three French ships loaded with fish from Newfoundland and was charged with this in his court martial. Meanwhile Hesse blamed Methuen for the failure of help to reach him. Hesse was also chronically short of money, but Methuen arranged for him to receive out of the Portuguese subsidy a sum of 50,000 crowns originally intended for the defences of Port Mahon if it were taken, and honoured the Dutch share of payments, which Schonenberg could not or would not defray.[1]

Leake was back in Lisbon on 22 September and set about refitting his ships. There was a great shortage of everything and it took a month or more to clean two or three frigates, although the crews worked hard to help each other out. Meanwhile Admiral Pointis had twenty ships to blockade the Straits. Leake mustered fifteen ships, by retaining four which were about to take Schomberg with a convoy to England, but he resisted pressure to sail until the beginning of November, when the arrival of a Dutch convoy brought up his squadron to number twenty-three English and Dutch ships.[2]

---

[1] Künzel, op. cit. pp. 479, 500, 514, 520, 554; S.P. 89/18, fos. 144, 151–3, 177; Adm 1/48, Log of H M.S Antelope; Rijksarchief 7369, 29 Oct. 1704; MS at Corsham Court for payments to Hesse.

[2] S.P. 89/18, fo. 17. Künzel, op. cit. pp. 508, 526.

Bad weather had dispersed the French, so that Leake only found five in Gibraltar bay, which he ran ashore or destroyed. But he arrived only just in time to foil an assault, which might easily have been final. He at once landed 300 men, who were soon reinforced by a further party of English and Dutch, to work on the fortifications under the direction of Captain Bennett. Leake did not have the same objection to his men doing 'slavish' labour as Rooke, and his sailors went ashore with shovels. The plan to fetch the Portuguese troops from the Algarve had to be given up, and Leake was often driven out of the bay by bad weather, but he was able to repair the gaps in the defences, and to stay until December. He then sailed for Lisbon but left enough men to bring the garrison up to 2,000 again.[1]

Leake had planned a rendezvous with a convoy of twenty transports and four men-of-war under Captain Legge, which after various irksome delays had left Lisbon on 10 December. Legge saw a number of ships off Cape Spartel and began towing his ships towards them, but when he was quite near he realised they were French and his squadron hastily scattered. Three or four transports with half the Dutch Walloon regiment and several English companies and two men-of-war were blown back into the Tagus. The remainder straggled into Gibraltar, but there was no news and great anxiety in Lisbon until Leake returned on 22 January.

In spite of the contretemps at Cape Spartel, Hesse now had a substantial reinforcement including a regiment of Guards, but the enemy, although they were short of powder and were suffering from the winter, showed no sign of raising the siege. In spite of his good resolutions to co-operate with Brigadier Shrimpton, who had succeeded Val de Soto, Hesse was still having trouble with his English officers. The men were good material but the officers were inclined to be a drunken lot and to have trade union rules about fighting, particularly under a German commander. Hesse

[1] Adm 51/4184 and Adm 1/48, Logs of H.M.S. *Expedition* and *Antelope*.

was an honest attractive man, but he was inclined to be wasteful of lives and obstinate; the English did not share his enthusiasm for counter-attacks, and there was much prejudice against him on account of the part he had played in bringing about the court martial of Brigadiers O'Hara and Bellasis for looting at Cadiz.[1]

In February Marshal Tessé succeeded the duke of Berwick and was ordered to go to Gibraltar. He was a courtier as much as a general, and would have vastly preferred the view of the prince of Condé's swans on the lake at Chantilly to that of Leake's ships in the Straits, but his appointment underlined the importance of the siege. His report enlarged on his difficulties and the shortage of guns and powder, which, in the absence of a road, all had to come by sea from Cadiz. In October Hesse estimated that the besiegers numbered 7,000 including the marines landed by Pontis. Tessé sent reinforcements of 4,500 men, but by January the marines had been reduced to 1,700 and many Spaniards had deserted or withdrawn. Tessé had perhaps more men than he represented and a superiority in numbers for most of the siege, though smaller than allied accounts claimed. However, after Leake brought a reinforcement in the spring the garrison had probably at the end of the siege as many or more fit men than Tessé.[2]

When Leake returned to Gibraltar on 21 March he had seven English, four Dutch and eight Portuguese ships. Methuen was not a little pleased that he had persuaded Queen Catherine to send eight Portuguese ships. He arranged for competent seamen to be appointed as captains and for a conference to settle any difficulties about the flag privilege or other obstacles to co-operation. But Leake was unenthusiastic. He grudgingly allotted the Portuguese a place in the line of battle, but professed his inability to translate naval orders into Portuguese or to devise signals which would be understood. The difficulty was genuine, but the Portuguese were

[1] Künzel, op. cit. pp. 483, 530–6, 553, 567.
[2] Tessé, Mémoires et Lettres (Paris, 1806), II, 142, 147, 152; Lettres, ed. Comte de Rabuteau (1886), pp. 233, 236–7.

a seafaring people, and it was unlucky that greater efforts were not made to enable them to play a part. This was their second try to help at Gibraltar, but it had little more success than their offer of troops from the Algarve.[1]

Pointis had resumed his blockade, but it had constantly been interrupted by bad weather, and communications with Gibraltar had not been entirely cut. Leake found five sizable French ships in the bay, of which he took three and forced the other two ashore. The pursuit of the French man-of-war *Lis* led to confusion. She should have been captured, but the English attackers were at cross purposes, and the Portuguese in a manful effort to engage fired in error at H.M.S. *Pembroke*. The *Lis* escaped only to be driven ashore and burnt. Leake was driven to the north-east and took some days to work his way back, and the same gale lost several anchors and blew two of the Dutch and four of the Portuguese back to the Tagus. Leake landed a force as soon as he could reach Gibraltar and bombarded the enemy, who began to take away their artillery and show signs of withdrawal, which after some hesitation they completed in the course of April. Hesse was burning to counter-attack, and the Dutch were willing, but the English refused, and their decision was confirmed by the combined Council of War. Hesse complained of the English officers to Galway and was indignant at the failure to take the opportunity to attack, when the enemy had lost their morale and were at a disadvantage. Methuen praised Hesse, but thought he had shown undue animosity, and there was a general feeling that he was inclined to be too free with English lives.[2]

Methuen again wrote to stress the importance of Gibraltar and

---

[1] Künzel, *op. cit.* pp. 544, 551; Rijksarchief 7370, 17 March, and 7025, 17 March 1705. Add. MSS 5440, fos. 104, 109; Add. MSS 28056, fo. 250. According to Boxer, *Golden Age of Brazil, 1695–1750*, p. 365, several famous Portuguese captains took part. See also for the Portuguese point of view Soares da Silva, 'Memorias, 1701–15', *Gaçeta em Forma de Carta*, pp. 34–5.

[2] Künzel, *op. cit.* pp. 556–7; Add. MSS 5440, fos. 111–14, and 5441, fos. 23–4; Rijksarchief 7370, 7 May 1705; S.P. 89/18, fos. 229, 244–5, 250; John Drinkwater, *Siege of Gibraltar* (1785), p. 16; Add. MSS 28056, fo. 260.

to urge that it should be kept, for if it were fortified, it could be made impregnable. The Dutch continued until 1713 to provide part of the garrison, but they refused to pay any part of the cost of the siege or of the transport of the troops there, and Methuen reconciled himself to this in the hope that England would now have the prior claim to control Gibraltar. He also stressed the part which he personally had played in the preservation of Gibraltar, and claimed that if he had not assumed responsibilities outside his province the place would have been lost twice over. In spite of all his complaints of the navy he had received all possible help from Leake, and also from Galway, but he could justly claim credit for persistence and initiative. The supply of Gibraltar was the one great service rendered by Lisbon as a base, and during the winter much of it had to be scraped together from Portuguese resources. The enemy losses were perhaps less than the 10,000 claimed, but the French navy had been defeated in their own sea, the enemy losses had been considerable, and the blow to French prestige suffered at Gibraltar was very great.

There was the usual delay before the good news reached Lisbon on 24 April. Paul Methuen was present at the relief of Gibraltar and after one final attempt to bring over the Portuguese from the Algarve, he crossed to Tangier to try to conclude with the emperor of Morocco the negotiations which Hesse, the English representative Delaval and lately the English Jew Israel or Jezrael Jones had begun. The object of these negotiations was to foil French manoeuvres, to buy corn and horses, and possibly to put an end to the Moorish siege of Ceuta, which had been proceeding for years in a desultory way, and to arrange that it be taken over by King Charles or possibly by England. There had been a great deal of muddle about these negotiations and this was not helped by the failure to arrive both of Paul Methuen's credentials and of the presents so essential for eastern potentates. Methuen bought presents in Lisbon and the credentials came and were forwarded, but Paul Methuen's mission produced little result except a fund of stories about Africa, upon which Paul later dined out in London. Methuen also went to great trouble to look after the Moroccan ambassador when he arrived in Lisbon sick and almost destitute, and to see that he was well received in London, but nothing came of it except the redemption of a few Christian slaves for cash payments.[1]

However, Paul had at least succeeded in making friends with Hesse, who told King Charles that Methuen could now be used as an intermediary to raise funds, instead of the Almirante, and that he was now on good terms even with Lichtenstein. He also said that Methuen could easily be kept sweet by the flattering suggestion that he would be welcome as ambassador at Madrid. In spite of his ill health and his repeated requests to resign his Lisbon post, it appears from a letter of Paul that he never gave up this ambition.[1]

During the winter the effort to prepare the spring campaign and to avoid the mistakes of 1704 was an equal preoccupation with Gibraltar. At first it looked as if Queen Catherine, as regent, might put backbone into the war preparations. She began well by dismissing two colonels for absence from their regiments, and Schonenberg was pleased that she relied on Roque Monteiro, who was now his friend, and on Jesuit confessors, who were well disposed. But her firmness was mainly displayed in a quarrel with the Dutch about their arrears of subsidy, and the Jesuits involved her in a dispute with the nuncio about the payments of their order to Rome, which according to Schonenberg resulted in her renouncing the regency in September when King Pedro refused to expel the nuncio. In any case the king, after he had recovered a little, constantly interfered, so that as Diogo de Mendonça put it, 'the Queen was Regent but Alcantara governed'. No one knew

---

[1] S.P. 89/18, fos. 142, 150, 234, 246, 269–70, and 89/19, 19 Feb. 1706; Rijksarchief 7370, 6 Feb. 1705; Künzel, *op. cit.* pp. 474, 504, 507, 536; *Cal. of Treas. Books*, xx, 77, 539–41, 650.

[2] S.P. 89/18, fos. 245, 250; *Marlborough's Letters and Despatches*, II, 574, Paul to John Methuen.

whether the king gave orders or his sister, and from the Allied point of view the regency was a disappointment.[1]

Galway pleased the king by his attempts to improve discipline. The Portuguese regiments were always short, and desertions were common and little punished, but it was not easy for the Allies to protest effectively, when their own quotas were so wanting. In addition to the losses by sickness and the capture of whole regiments in 1704, there was absenteeism; in May 1704 there were forty-nine officers who officially failed to join their regiments. Galway took stern measures but was never able to bring his regiments up to complement. The Dutch were in rather better case and Schonenberg was able to make up for their other short-comings by claiming that they were not far short. Fagel and Schonenberg were eager to remedy the defects of their army but they were determined to maintain Dutch independence and this brought them into conflict with Galway and gave an opportunity to the Portuguese anti-war party to profit by their quarrels. It proved almost impossible to agree on a plan of campaign; Fagel and the Almirante tended to prefer a plan to invade Castile from the north, while Methuen and Galway looked towards Badajoz and Andalusia. However, after the relief of Gibraltar Methuen began to interest himself in Barcelona and to be less unfavourable to the Madrid plan. Fagel was sympathetic to the plans for the defence of Gibraltar, as long as the Dutch had a share in them, but was jealous of the English taking the lead there.

Methuen tried to obtain the supreme command for Galway, and Fagel reluctantly agreed to his commission being dated later than that of Galway, but King Pedro gave the count of Corzana the same rank, so that the upshot was that the three generals took weekly turns to command under the general orders of the Conde de Galveas, the governor of arms for the Alemtejo. However,

---

[1] S.P. 89/18, fos. 211, 217–18; Add. MSS 28056, fos. 273, 287; Künzel, *op. cit.* p. 561; Rijksarchief 7370, 9 Sept. 1705; Coimbra MS 3008, fo. 112, Diogo de Mendonça to Luis da Cunha. Alcántara was King Pedro's summer palace.

Methuen succeeded in obtaining access for the generals to the Portuguese Council of War, and in freeing them from its tutelage while they were at the front.[1]

Galway, though a sick man and no outstanding general, was tactful and inspired respect by his integrity and honesty. Fagel was by no means incompetent, but he was obstinate, and Methuen and Galway made up their minds that it was impossible to work with him. However, in London Da Cunha resolutely opposed the appointment of Galway as commander in chief on the ground that this would reflect on Portuguese prestige, though he did once agree that Hesse might be acceptable. Godolphin and Marlborough persuaded Heinsius that Fagel must go and the States General wrote to King Pedro and King Charles on the subject. Sunderland also raised the question at The Hague when he passed through on his way to Vienna. Fagel himself was not unwilling to return home to attend to his private affairs, but his friends in Holland fought for his credit and in Portugal Cadaval entreated him to stay. The result was that he remained until the end of the year.[2]

In spite of these quarrels and of delays in the convoys and arrangements with the new army contractors, a force of nominally 20,000 men was mustered south of the Tagus by the end of April and a smaller force of 3,000 men under the Marquis of Minas north of the river. Until the last moment King Pedro still hoped to lead the army, but was prevented by ill health. He refused to allow King Charles to join the army without him, and although the English and Dutch felt much sympathy for the young king, who threatened to go to the front in defiance of King Pedro, he was obliged to stay in Lisbon.[3]

Although the Portuguese, except for Minas, favoured an advance on Badajoz, Fagel's plan for a march by prudent stages

---

[1] S.P. 89/18, fos. 90, 104, 152, 196, 198, 363; Add. MSS 28056, fo, 246; Rijksarchief 7370, 7, 17 May, 7 June 1705; Künzel, *op. cit.* pp. 562, 575.

[2] Add. MSS 17677, XXX, fos. 68, 72; Add. MSS 28056, fo. 283; Rijksarchief 7025, 14 June 1704, and 7370, 8 June 1705.

[3] S.P. 89/18, fos. 245–7; Rijksarchief 7370, 7 May 1705; Add. MSS 28056, fo. 268.

towards Alcantara was accepted. Minas took Salvaterra, which was the last town held by the Spaniards on Portuguese soil, and with it 300 prisoners. Galway captured Valencia de Alcantara. This success was published in the *London Gazette* and annoyed the Portuguese by giving the whole credit to the English. The next objective on the road to Madrid was Alcantara itself. Methuen believed he had persuaded the Portuguese to order an advance, but Fagel and other generals decided that Alcantara was too far and determined to attack Albuquerque instead. It was again Galway's week and beginning on a Monday he managed to take the town, although it was a strong place. Now it was agreed that Badajoz should be the next objective and Methuen persuaded Queen Catherine to order the army to cross the river Guadiana in spite of the opposition of the Conde de Galveas. Some Irish deserted, but some Spaniards came over to the Allied side, and a Portuguese battalion fought well. But the heats of summer now set in and the Portuguese insisted on retiring to summer quarters, alleging as an additional reason the depletion of the army by the drawing off of regiments to sail with Peterborough.[1]

Peterborough arrived in Lisbon on 20 June and immediately became the centre of interest. Later he took credit for accomplishing the hard task of getting 'an old minister to draw bills in his favour, and a general to part with troops under his command'. This was unfair to Methuen and Galway, who were tired of disappointments in Portugal and generously sacrificed men and troops to help Peterborough in his new and more hopeful project. The Portuguese naturally resented the removal of reinforcements to another theatre. Their interest flagged still more and Methuen had to be more and more peremptory to keep their army in being. His friend the king was failing in health and his relations with the Portuguese became strained and far from cordial. However, England was strong enough to maintain her pressure. In spite of

[1] Künzel, *op. cit.* p. 562; Coimbra MS 3008, fo. 122; S.P. 89/18, fos. 243–7, 254–9, 262–8, 279; Add. MSS 28056, fos. 260–8, 279; Stowe MS 467, fo. 75; Rijksarchief 7370, 7, 17 May 1705.

Schonenberg's efforts the Dutch were losing ground. After 1705 they too fell short of their quota for their army and, though they sent a strong squadron to the Mediterranean in 1705 and 1706, they tended to be elbowed out of the Mediterranean picture by England, who paid little regard to Dutch interests. Schonenberg had hitherto been able to profit by his qualifications as an expert on Spain, but his contacts were in Madrid rather than in Catalonia, and after the departure of King Charles from Portugal his influence diminished.[1]

Anglo-Dutch interests tended to diverge as soon as the immediate danger of a French invasion was removed, and this divergence was encouraged by the failure of the Dutch in June 1704 to renew their participation in the embargo on enemy trade. In Portugal they had always resented their costly commitments to pay large subsidies, and were more interested in the everyday protection of their commercial interests than in the pursuit of a grand strategy for victory in the war as a whole. It was not only in Portugal that relations were strained. While Sunderland was protesting about Fagel, and Stanhope was arguing about the Methuen commercial treaty, Harley went so far as to suggest that the English troops might be withdrawn from Flanders if the Dutch did not co-operate better with Marlborough.[2] Such a threat was scarcely serious, but it marked a new determination on the part of England. The Dutch responded and the alliance was saved, but henceforward England was the dominant partner in Portugal and Spain.

Methuen's personal position was strengthened by Whiggish progress in the government at home, but he had provoked resentment among both Portuguese and Dutch and had to combat much ill will. This took shape in exaggerated rumours of his illness and impending departure and other incidents to damage his credit. One of them was a personal matter. It will be remembered that Methuen had taken Sarah Earle, the wife of John Earle, the

[1] Add. MSS 28056, fo. 25; Coimbra MS 3008, fo. 114.
[2] De Jonge, *op. cit.* pp. 553–4, Douglas Coombs, *Conduct of the Dutch*, p. 111.

elderly consul general, to be his housekeeper together with his other 'cousin', Ann Browne. This ménage was generally accepted. Peterborough found it rather amusing and the Portuguese made jokes about it. Galway and Paul Methuen used in writing to send their love to the ladies, and Paul in a letter from Gibraltar referred to them affectionately, saying: 'Kind love to my cousins at the Quinta, who delighting so much in bloody scenes and tragical deaths, would be much more pleased than I am, to see those which pass here every day.'[1]

John Earle made no complaint until December 1704, when John Methuen appointed John Milner, another leading member of the Factory, as consul general in his stead. This decision resulted from a complaint from Admiral Rooke that no proper steps had been taken to round up naval deserters, a duty which fell within the consul's province. Earle then wrote a long and pathetic letter to Hedges, in which he summed up all the current gossip against Methuen. After speaking of Methuen's abduction of his wife and accusing him of defrauding him of some property he had owned near Bath, he alleged that Methuen only kept one ramshackle coach and failed to keep up his dignity as ambassador, that he provided no furniture or facilities for the chaplain to hold divine service, and that he had falsified the muster rolls of the Portuguese army.[2] There is some evidence to disprove the last two charges at least, for he obtained furniture from the Treasury for the chapel in 1703 and the muster rolls and payments are well supported by vouchers, and lists, which he submitted, while Schonenberg sent copies of them to The Hague. Earle's letter in his neat precise writing with its stuttering conclusion pleading that 'Her Majesty would be soe soe gratiously pleased, soe gratiously pleased to continue him in the Consulship' makes sad reading, but the

[1] Add. MSS 28056, fo. 256.
[2] S.P. 89/88, Rooke to Methuen and reply, 13 Apr. 7 May 1704; Earle to Hedges, 21 Nov., 13 Dec. 1704; S.P. 89/18, fo. 152. *Cal. of Treas. Papers* (1703), p. 374. A history of the chaplain question is in S.P. 89/20, 1 Aug. 1710, and the muster rolls are in S.P. 89/88 and copies in Rijksarchief 7369 and 7370. See also S.P. 89/18, fo. 333, and S.P. 89/19, Milner to Hedges, 10 Jan. 1706.

Lisbon Factory, usually so ready to voice a grievance, made no protest in Earle's favour. It is probable that he had indeed outlived his use, and there appears to have been no reaction from Hedges, though Hedges does seem henceforward to have encouraged John Milner to write to him and thus to provide an alternative channel of communication with Lisbon.

More important was the scandal of the French prisoner, which arose in 1705 and upset Methuen very much. One of Methuen's troubles was the propensity of the navy to put their prisoners of war on shore. They had no room for them on board and captains were indignant at the idea of their ships being used as gaols. The Portuguese picked these men up and had no means to treat them properly. The French usually behaved well to English prisoners, but were liable to take reprisals if their compatriots were ill fed and neglected in Portuguese prisons. Methuen wished to prevent these difficulties, for he regarded prisoners as valuable currency to be used for the redemption of much needed soldiers and sailors in enemy hands. He corresponded freely with the competent officials in Cadiz and Vigo, and used the communications he established to cover his intelligence work. At least on one occasion a ship going to Cadiz with prisoners for exchange planted an agent there who came back with a report.[1] Such correspondence with the enemy was liable to misinterpretation. In arranging the repatriation by land of a batch of French prisoners Methuen issued identity documents to enable them to get travel passes from the Portuguese. A French sailor was picked up near the frontier with one of these papers signed by Methuen and alleged that he was travelling on important business for him. The story soon circulated that a letter found on him gave information of Allied plans and details of the forces under Peterborough, though a note from Roque Monteiro to Methuen shows that in fact nothing of importance was found on the man, and, as Methuen pointed out, countless small craft were always leaving Portugal for the Straits,

[1] S.P. 89/18, fos. 220, 239; S.P. 104/108, Hedges to Methuen, 13 Nov. 1705.

so there was no need to use a prisoner to take a message nor means to prevent messages passing. But the story soon grew that the sailor carried a letter from Methuen to King Philip or a letter from Madame Amanda. Madame Amanda, alias Elvas, was arrested later on a separate charge. She was a sister of the French consul, and the only woman of education ever taken by King Pedro for a mistress. Her daughter by him married a son of the duke of Cadaval and she herself kept a kind of salon in Lisbon, frequented by literary people and friends of France. She was undoubtedly a spy and corresponded with D'Aubenton, the French naval attaché in Madrid. The story of her arrest and of Methuen's connection with the French sailor was the talk of the town and was related by the Lisbon diarist Soares da Silva. The Portuguese anti-war party and the pro-French faction were glad to use this opportunity to discredit Methuen. So was Schonenberg, who was fighting the last stages of his battle about the commercial treaty and was anxious to shift to other shoulders the resentment felt against the Dutch for their failure to pay their subsidies.[1]

Methuen's Portuguese friends rallied to him, and Alegrete wrote a letter, copied to Da Cunha, absolving him of all blame. Nevertheless, Methuen was distressed and asked for a thorough investigation to be made. He particularly complained that Schonenberg abetted these calumnies and requested that Stanhope should be informed at The Hague of the truth and should pass it privately to Heinsius. Hedges answered that Godolphin and the Cabinet looked on it as an idle, malicious story, and not only the Lords, but the queen also, were satisfied that it was false.[2] He added that he had copied the correspondence to Stanhope and had asked him to speak with Heinsius, but he thought that otherwise the best course was to take no further notice, for he had only heard the

---

[1] S.P. 89/18, Methuen to Hedges, 26 Sept., 3 Oct. 1705. *Diary of a French Merchant*, Rawlinson MS at Bodleian 423. See also R. F. Michel, *Les Portugais en France* (Paris, 1882), p. 73; Soares da Silva, *op. cit.* pp. 42–4.

[2] S.P. 104/109, Hedges to Methuen, 9 Oct. 1705.

story from one person in England and he had it from Schonen-berg. It was lucky for Methuen that the war news at the moment was good and that the awkwardness of the Dutch was much in evidence. A year later, when Godolphin was out of office and Rivers served the story fresh from Lisbon with further garnishings, the great men in England paid more attention to it. But by then Methuen was dead.

CHAPTER 12

THE CAPTURE OF MADRID IN 1706
AND THE DEATH OF METHUEN

THE earl of Peterborough reached Lisbon on 20 June 1705. His appointment as joint commander of the expeditionary force with Sir Cloudesley Shovell caused surprise. However, he was a favourite of the duchess of Marlborough and had been designated in 1702 to lead the proposed expedition to the West Indies. He had no experience as a general, but he was a good political choice to promote harmony between the army and navy, and to override the undeniable claims to the command of Charles or the prince of Hesse.

Even before the death of the Almirante of Castile left a gap in King Charles's advisers the friends of Hesse were trying to secure promotion for him. Zinzerling suggested he might return to Portugal, and if he wished to do so he ought to cultivate Schonenberg, in the vein of the Spanish proverb: 'Let the miracle be done, even if a Jew has to perform it.' Da Cunha was inclined to support Hesse, and at one moment Peterborough half-heartedly agreed, on the understanding that no post given to Hesse interfered with his own command. Hesse came to Lisbon for consultation, but he returned to Gibraltar without any new appointment, and when he joined Peterborough it was as as a plain volunteer.[1]

King Charles told Peterborough that he would rather die at the head of one of Queen Anne's regiments than remain inactive. Peterborough thought the king's presence would be an asset and was delighted to find that Methuen agreed and had received orders to further his departure. King Charles was overjoyed to accept Queen Anne's invitation to join the fleet and to escape from

---

[1] Klopp, *Der Fall des Hauses Stuart*, XI, 488–9; Künzel, *Das Leben und der Briefwechles des Landgraven Georg von Hessen–Darmstadt*, p. 353.

Portuguese captivity; nevertheless he travelled as Peterborough's guest; there were still many difficulties and he ran the risk of finding himself a first-class passenger rather than a king proceeding to his kingdom.

Peterborough plunged into urgent discussion with the Portuguese about the objectives of the expedition and the nature of the help Portugal could give in any attack on a Spanish port. According to Methuen, he was 'employed every hour, night and day, in hastening all he could, and in addition to the fire expected of him showed a life, spirit and resolution, which cut out all pretexts for delay'.[1] Peterborough for the time being was equally pleased with Methuen, reporting that Methuen did not flatter the Portuguese, and, however much his heart was set on his Portuguese treaties, he did not in the least palliate the conduct of Portugal, to deceive the Government. He would have felt bound to enlarge upon the follies of Lisbon, but having seen Methuen's last letter he could safely leave it to him to write long dispatches. He told Godolphin that he had expected to find Methuen a cautious minister in view of 'the agreeable establishments' he had in Lisbon and the intimacy he enjoyed with the king, but far from being over-inclined to complacencies with the Portuguese, Methuen sacrificed his private inclinations perfectly and with courage to the public good. So he recommended that Methuen be supported with a high hand. 'You may give your ambassador great authority, which he knows how to use and with advantage among such people.' As far as Godolphin was concerned, the advice fell on good ground, for he always held Methuen in high esteem.[2]

Peterborough had a low opinion of the Portuguese and confessed that he had exceeded his instructions in making promises to them, because he was sure that whatever offers he made, they would contribute nothing but words. The Portuguese were at no time amenable to being hustled, but they now had reason for procrastination. They were owed nine months' subsidies by the

[1] Add. MSS 28056, fos. 285, 293.   [2] *HMC H. of L. Report*, VII, n.s., 363, 500–6.

Dutch and they could not get satisfaction on the perennial question of a convoy for the Brazil fleet. The queen dowager roundly asserted that there could be no autumn campaign until the Dutch paid up. Also they viewed as a betrayal of their cause plans to move King Charles and many of the Allied forces away from Portugal up the Mediterranean.[1]

The Allied plans were as ambivalent as the year before. Peterborough and Shovell had secret orders to concert an attack on Toulon with the duke of Savoy, and if the weakness of the French or the strength of Savoy allowed, to develop the plan under colour of attacking Barcelona. Nobody in Lisbon knew of the secret orders save Peterborough and Shovell, but Toulon and Italy were obvious objectives and had often been discussed. Count Maffei, minister of Savoy in London, had conceived of an attack on Toulon the previous year, independently of the English ministers. There had been correspondence on the subject with Richard Hill at Turin, and Alexander Stanhope had a copy of the secret orders at The Hague. Also there had been leaks, for Marshal Tessé heard of a plan to attack Toulon from an agent in Galway's entourage and told Versailles.[2]

Therefore, when the Portuguese opposed the Barcelona plan they may well have suspected that the expedition might go further than Barcelona and outside their sphere of interest. However, the Barcelona plan was not only a smoke screen; it had a life of its own, which raised its own difficulties. Mitford Crowe, a former resident of Barcelona, had been empowered to treat with the dissident leaders of the 'State of Catalonia'. Galway approved his mission, but suggested that it ought to be kept secret from the Almirante of Castile, who opposed all plans not of his own making, but would in any case disapprove of the references to

---

[1] S.P. 89/18, fos. 273–6; Coimbra MS 3008, fo. 117, Cunha Brochado to Da Cunha, 8 July 1705.

[2] Klopp, *op. cit.* XI, 223, 487. Tessé, *Mémoires et Lettres*, II, 169; R. Hill, *Diplomatic Correspondence*, I, 196; S.P. 89/18, fos. 226, 270. Stanhope's copy of the secret orders is in S.P. 94/5 and they are printed in *HMC H. of L. Reports*, VII, n.s., 363.

Catalan privileges which would be bound to figure in any agreement with local Catalan leaders. The Almirante got to hear of the mission and expressed no disapproval, but he developed a sudden enthusiasm for the alternative plan to concentrate on an invasion and landing in Andalusia, rather than on a Barcelona landing to support a Portuguese-based march on Madrid. Peterborough tried to win Schonenberg over to the Barcelona plan, but he refused to be blandished and insisted that even if the allies had an initial success, the Catalans were a fickle and difficult people, whose support would entail a heavy commitment. Galway was helpful and readily sacrificed troops, supplies and precious horses for Peterborough. Yet Peterborough in his own mind had no wish to go to Barcelona at all and doubted the feasibility of taking the city. Even Hesse, who had been the most vehement advocate of the Barcelona plans, wavered and recommended a landing at Alicante instead. This proposal had good points. There was a good harbour nearby and it was a better starting-point for Madrid than Barcelona. Also, the district was rich in supplies and no resistance was to be expected there.[1]

During these discussions Peterborough was embarrassed to receive a request from the duke of Savoy for help and news that he was hard pressed by the enemy and could not invade Provence. Further, Hedges sent him a dispatch in cypher, which arrived mutilated, instead of writing en clair by the packet-boat, so he had no guidance from London. He realised that the Toulon plan might have to be called off but warmly recommended an expedition to Naples. Prince Lichtenstein, who aspired to be viceroy, liked the Naples plan, but King Charles wanted a landing in Spain, and Godolphin wrote recommending Barcelona. As a report from Crowe announced that he had reached an agreement with the Catalans, and other news from Catalonia was favourable, Peterborough was almost reconciled to forgo his cherished

[1] Add. MSS 28056, fo. 245; S.P. 94/75, 24 June, 12, 28 July, 11 Aug. 1705; Rijksarchief 7370, 28 June 1705.

expedition to Italy before he left Lisbon. As a letter from Hedges saying that the orders to go to Catalonia were 'very right' reached him at Gibraltar, the question was settled.[1]

Peterborough took from Galway two dragoon regiments, a Dutch regiment and some horses, and at Gibraltar embarked some trained men in exchange for the recruits just come from England. Methuen advanced money and negotiated a loan through the Italian merchant Manzoni. He also advanced 57,000 dollars to King Charles and borrowed 20,000 dollars to equip a regiment of Spanish volunteers. On the day that the fleet sailed the Portuguese Council of War at last voted for an attack on Badajoz, on condition that Methuen advanced two months' subsidy payments. King Pedro was too ill to give the orders but his confessor persuaded Queen Catherine to do so.[2]

Paul Methuen accompanied King Charles with the rank of minister. After calling at Gibraltar the fleet reached Altea on 10 August. Whether from curiosity or loyalty, the people flocked to see King Charles and the prince of Hesse. A Levant wind then held up progress and the fleet did not reach Barcelona until 22 August (N.S.) The neighbouring town of Sitges had defied the Allies and there was no sign of welcome, but on the 23rd 3,000 men landed. The grass had been fired to destroy any forage but they met with no opposition. However, all the Councils of War decided that a siege was impracticable and King Charles was obliged at last to assert himself and to lobby all the generals individually to persuade them to take any action. Peterborough was much embarrassed, for he still hankered personally to go to Italy and fresh orders received on 6 September instructed him to give all possible aid to the duke of Savoy. Nevertheless, he felt he ought to support King Charles and vote in the Councils of War in favour of a siege. Colonel Richards was consulted and did not altogether rule out an exploratory attack, but gave it as his opinion

[1] S.P. 94/75, 30 May 1705; R. Hill, *op. cit.* I, 219, 220, 232; *HMC H. of L. Reports*, VII, n.s., 494.
[2] Add. MSS 28056, fos. 295, 304.

298

that on purely military grounds a siege was impracticable. A plan to march to Tarragona was then agreed and Richards and Stanhope were detailed to consult the navy. The admirals thought it was too late to go to Italy and, partly from resentment against the command of Peterborough, partly from sympathy for the young king, were inclined to help. It was now that Peterborough was rescued from his dilemma by the idea gathered from some deserters that an attack on the outlying fort of Monjuich might be practicable. The story of this feat of arms is well known but its success would have been impossible if Peterborough had not been in a position to give all the necessary orders personally. The whole affair was arranged in thirty hours and King Charles and Paul Methuen were only informed at six in the evening, when the troops were already leaving for their long night march.[1]

The fall of Monjuich did not materially weaken the defences of Barcelona, but the effect on morale was immense. The Miquelets or Catalan rebels began to join the Allies and with the help of the navy the resolution to attempt the siege was taken. The city capitulated comparatively quickly and the whole of Catalonia except the town of Rosas came over to the Allies. Nevertheless, Paul Methuen was not happy about the situation, as there was much bad feeling between the Allies, and no movement to join King Charles in Castile or Andalusia. When the news after a month's delay reached Lisbon, Schonenberg observed that he had always said that it would not be hard to take Barcelona, but that keeping it would be a different matter. Nevertheless, the situation was transformed and for better or worse the allied war effort was now centred there.[2]

The death of Hesse at Monjuich was a great loss. Paul Methuen said 'the love of the Catalans for him was greater than it could be

---

[1] There is a good description of Monjuich in Philip Woodruff, *Colonel of Dragoons* (1951), p. 291; and Captain Carleton, *Memoirs* (Oxford, 1840), though not authentic, has a basis of fact. See also Add. MSS 31134, John Topsham to Lord Raby; Stowe MS 471, *H. of L. Reports*, VII, n.s., 223, 495.

[2] *Marlborough's Letters and Despatches*, II, 571; Rijksarchief 7370, 468, fos. 108–9, and 467, fos. 34–6, 10 Nov. 1705.

represented and would have enabled him to improve any success on our side much better than could well be done by anybody else'. In England a Tory wrote: 'Scarce will Barcelona compensate for the loss of Hesse.' It may well have been true, for his rank and close relationship with the empress won him universal prestige, and he was the only one of the king's German entourage who was well liked. Though a gallant soldier, he had perhaps more enthusiasm than judgement but, as his biographer Künzel pointed out, he was known in Spain not only as a friend and a brave soldier, but as a good Catholic and one of the few personalities to offset the impression that King Charles was the creature of English and Dutch heretics.[1]

Admiral Shovell sailed for England soon after Barcelona was taken. Paul Methuen went with him to report the news in Lisbon and in London, and to try to raise supplies. Although both King Charles and Peterborough spoke very well of him, neither recommended him to continue as minister. The king recommended James Stanhope, and Peterborough Mitford Crowe. Paul obtained a promise of powder and troops from King Pedro and was well received by Queen Anne after his fourteen years' absence from England. She gave him the choice of posts at Lisbon, Barcelona or Savoy. He chose Savoy and Stanhope succeeded him at Barcelona, though retaining his army command. Stanhope's assignment was no sinecure for he had to try to keep the peace between Peterborough and the king's German advisers. Galway had refused an invitation to come and had recommended the count of Corzana, but King Charles favoured no Spaniard except the Miquelet Cifuentes, who was a gallant but eccentric character and loathed by Peterborough.[2]

Meanwhile the Portuguese autumn campaign had petered out. In July Methuen had obtained the compliance of Schonenberg and

---

[1] Künzel, *op. cit.* p. 210. Hesse was brought up as a Lutheran but became Catholic in order to serve in the Imperial army (Add. MSS 28056, fos. 297, 331, 337, 387; *HMC Cowper*, III, 65).

[2] Klopp, *op. cit.* XI, 507–10.

Fagel to besiege Badajoz and the Council of War had agreed, but August passed without any move being made, and the Portuguese began to say it was too late in the season. Methuen had to tell Queen Catherine that unless he received satisfaction he would have to report that the Portuguese planned to do nothing. The queen was already near her last illness and thoroughly tired of the regency. She was also vexed with her brother for his refusal to support her in a quarrel with the nuncio on behalf of her favourite Jesuits. On 21 September she gladly relinquished the regency to King Pedro, who was very ill but rallied enough to summon the Council of State and four secretaries to consult in his bedroom. It was there that at last unequivocal orders for the siege of Badajoz were given. The army crossed the Guadiana with 16,000 foot and 4,000 horse. Methuen hoped, if the city fell, to persuade the Portuguese to advance towards Seville and Cadiz in the spring. He still believed that the merchants in Cadiz would join the allies. It is true that the French had trouble there and Tessé thought much needed to be done for the defences, but he cannot have rated the danger of an insurrection very high, for he did not recommend the evacuation of civilians.[1]

Any prospects of success at Badajoz were destroyed by a chance shot, which took off Galway's hand and made amputation below his elbow necessary. Although the States General had at last agreed that Fagel should be superseded, King Pedro and Cadaval had retained him. He was still at hand and, to do him justice, was behaving like a proper soldier, for the shell which wounded Galway grazed his sleeve. Galway was obliged to hand the command over to him, and he abandoned the siege at once upon the unexpected appearance of Marshal Tessé with enemy reinforcements. A chance to counter-attack was missed, but the retreat over the Guadiana was ably covered by Galway's friend the Marquis de Montandre. Immediately afterwards the Portuguese,

[1] S.P. 89/18, fos. 321, 325, 330, 333; Rijksarchief 7370, 19 Sept., 1 Oct. 1705; Tessé, *op. cit.* pp. 174–80.

as old custom demanded, dispersed rapidly to their homes and the vintage, preferring, as an English commentator put it on a similar occasion, 'to tread the grapes rather than to trample on the enemy'.[1]

Fagel was generally blamed and the Portuguese held an inquiry. However, his defence, which was translated and published in England, was not unconvincing. He had consistently opposed the siege and was very conscious of the weakness of the Allied forces, but an intercepted letter from Tessé showed that he equally lacked confidence and might have been daunted by a spirited resistance. The prime cause of the Allied defeat was the failure of their intelligence. They were taken by surprise by Tessé and did not know until the last moment on which bank of the river he was marching. Consequently it was impossible for them to deploy their forces across the river to face the enemy.[2]

The capture of Badajoz was a principal Portuguese war aim and the possession of the city had always been a condition on which the king insisted absolutely. The failure there was as great a disappointment to the Portuguese as to the Allies. Portuguese inertia had given Methuen just cause for complaint but the Portuguese too had many well-founded grievances. Alegrete, when taxed by Methuen, retorted that Portugal was exhausted by the war, but her armies had taken three places in the year, although the Allies only had 4,000 men in Portugal instead of the 12,000 required by the treaties, and the Dutch had not paid their subsidies.[3] It was true that the Allied quota, which had never been full, had been further depleted by the diversion of reinforcements to Gibraltar and Barcelona, but circumstances had changed and the Allies' case by land was arguable. Their failure to meet their naval obligations was harder to defend except in the most general sense that the French fleet was held in check and convoys were eventu-

---

[1] A. Boyer, *History of the Reign of Queen Anne, 1703–13*, IV, 156/70; Agnew, p. 115; S.P. 89/88, fo. 7.
[2] Fagel, *Account of the Campaign in Portugal, 1705*, pp. 10/19.
[3] S.P. 89/18, fo. 305.

ally available, though not on request as the treaties required. Alegrete had been specially anxious to obtain a convoy for the Brazil fleet, which promised to be unusually valuable, as it would carry much gold from the new Brazil mines and the silver from the two Buenos Aires galleons, and comprise three ships from Goa instead of the normal complement of one. Alegrete asked for six ships in May 1705 and was promised three, but the ships were not sent, and in October Paul Methuen was still complaining in the strongest terms to Admiral Shovell, who only detached the ships when he passed the Straits on his voyage home. In November Methuen was still receiving reports that they had not gone and the subject was very sore, as he was having the greatest difficulty in supplying Gibraltar and Barcelona. He wrote to Hedges that the captains of the least of Her Majesty's ships made it a point of honour to refuse doing whatever he desired, and that Gibraltar, which he looked upon as being of the greatest importance to England, would be lost if more care were not taken. He had recently reached a deadlock with a certain Captain Hooper of the *Flamborough*, who refused a request to convoy the outward-bound Brazil fleet to the Canaries, on the ground that he had Admiral Leake's orders to take some cloth to Gibraltar. Methuen offered to make alternative arrangements for the cloth but Hooper was adamant and Methuen said that, if he was justified, Da Cunha should be told that Her Majesty's ambassador had no authority in the matter, and then he would no longer be blamed.[1]

Hedges replied that he was sorry that Alegrete harassed Methuen with so much warmth when the queen was at so vast a charge, beyond what she was obliged to, to maintain her superiority of strength in seas so distant for the security of all. Her Majesty had the protection of the Brazil fleet as much at heart as could be desired, and what could be done would be done. Eight ships had been ordered to be detached, as soon as the immediate operations in the Straits were completed, and there was no reason other than

[1] S.P. 89/18, fos. 222, 244, 305, 310, 337; Add. MSS 28056, fo. 339.

some rumours for believing that the French had any ships in the Atlantic strong enough to threaten the Brazil fleet. It was not prudent to detach the ships if it meant weakening the fleet at a critical time, and in his opinion no misfortune could equal what might befall the fleet of England for want of ten ships of war. He ended by advising Methuen that he ought to think it a happiness that he had no powers to give orders to the navy, but only to use his endeavours to persuade in pressing occasions. In other words, Methuen would do better to behave like a good civil servant, and not take such things to heart and try to assume other people's responsibilities. It was in fact impracticable, even if it were advisable, to give ambassadors and generals authority over the navy, and the command given to Peterborough, in an attempt to solve the problem of interservice co-operation, and to quiet the clamour aroused by the quarrels at Cadiz, was not a success. However, the navy slowly realised that convoy duties must be given a higher priority, and began to attend to them in their own way, but not at the orders of any shore authority. In November 1705, when Methuen was worrying about supplies, Sir William Jumper made his own arrangements, independently, to send three ships to Barcelona.[1] But Methuen continued to protest that the captains refused to fall in with his plans, and the rumours about French ships in the Atlantic were not always unfounded, as their attacks on Rio de Janeiro four years later amply demonstrated.

The Portuguese had done little to strengthen their navy and had become unnecessarily dependent on the allies, who were fully occupied in containing the Brest and Toulon fleets, and might have expected Portugal as a maritime power to cope with local enemy privateers. But the breach of the treaties was undeniable, and when in the spring of 1704 the Brest fleet passed down the coast and the Allies had no ships within striking distance, Portugal had reason to complain. They could also have pointed out, though

[1] S.P. 104/109, Hedges to Methuen, 12 March 1706; Add. MSS 28056, fo. 383.

there is no record that they did so, that the French in the days of their alliance had been more forthcoming, for they had kept six ships in the Azores, and had promised that Château-Renault with twenty-five ships would wait to provide a convoy.[1]

The winter and spring of 1705–6 were spent in the usual struggles to procure money and supplies and in arguments about the Brazil convoy. The needs of Barcelona and Gibraltar made the calls on shipping heavier than ever. Alegrete pleaded that Portugal was exhausted by the war, but Hedges retorted that he could not believe he was serious, for the English trade was very beneficial to Portugal, and the subsidies and the money spent on their armies could not be a disadvantage. This was obvious to English eyes, but war profits went largely into the pockets of foreign merchants, and the king did not know where to turn to enlarge his traditional revenues. He had given up the use of the Cortes to vote new taxes and the most he could do was to raise a local 10 per cent subsidy from the Lisbon Senate and to exact a quarter of a million dollars from the French merchants as the price of permission to continue their residence in Portugal.[2] The Dutch defaulted on their subsidies and even Methuen sometimes fell into arrears. The money was largely earmarked for purchases abroad or for supplies before it was received and the cost of all commodities had risen steeply, so that the sources of income would have been swallowed up even if the administration had been incorruptible and efficient. Alegrete's complaints of stringency were well founded, and both Methuen and Schonenberg agreed that they were.

Leake had a hard passage from Barcelona against the wind and could do little to supply Gibraltar; the Dutch had lagged behind in the hope that the Balearic Islands would declare for King Charles and were in still worse case. Leake had to divert three Gibraltar supply ships to help them and to put into Gibraltar

[1] *Os Manuscritos da Casa de Cadaval respeitantes ao Brazil*, ed. V. Rau (Lisboa, 1958), II, 61–2.
[2] S.P. 104/108, Hedges to Methuen, 9 Oct. 1705; Borges de Castro, *Tratados, Supplemento*, X, 171.

himself. He reached Lisbon finally on 27 January.[1] There were now twenty ships at a time in Lisbon in need of service, but in spite of all Methuen's representations and the appointment by the Admiralty of a victualling agent and a dockyard representative, facilities for refitting ships were still very short. There were few ships in the Tagus throughout the winter and scarcely any provisions; Methuen found fresh food for the sailors with the greatest difficulty and was obliged to borrow the king's bakery and ovens to make a supply of rusk. No convoy arrived before 22 March. By intense efforts and by concentrating only on the most essential work Leake was ready to sail on 8 March with six-teen ships, but few of them had been careened and they were not fit to face any long period of rough weather or contrary winds.[2]

The frigates *Gloucester* and *Expedition* had gone to Rio de Janeiro in the autumn to convoy the Brazil fleet homeward, but Alegrete considered that they ought to be reinforced to escort the Rio, Pernambuco and Bahia fleets over the last part of the voyage from the Azores to Lisbon. On 20 February Admirals Leake and Wassenaar discussed the Portuguese demands with the ministers and Alegrete followed this up with a memorandum, in which he appealed to the treaties, and hinted that in the event of the allies refusing to honour their obligations, the king might be driven to ask the French for protection. Methuen believed this was more than an idle threat, for the marquis de Châteauneuf, latterly ambassador in Lisbon, was at Badajoz and the duke of Cadaval was reputed to be in touch with him through the nuncio. He had told London of the exceptional value of the Brazil fleet and had been authorised to tell Leake that the claim under the treaty was correct and that he had been expressly ordered by the queen to assure King Pedro that her obligations to him would be punctually performed. The English merchants usually had to give credit for

[1] Rijksarchief 7025, 18 Aug. 1704, and 7370, 28 Febr. 1705; S.P. 89/18, Methuen to Hedges, 29 Jan. 1706.
[2] S.P. 89/19, Methuen to Hedges, 19 Feb., 22 March 1706; Add. MSS 28057, fos. 13, 45; Navy Records Soc., *Life of Admiral Sir John Leake*, II, 10.

their cloth until the Brazil fleet brought in a supply of money, and no doubt this consideration also weighed with Methuen. He estimated that the fleet would be carrying cargo to the value of a million sterling, and that if the fleet were lost all Portugal would be undone, and there would be no longer an alliance with England or means to carry on the war. Alegrete also pointed out that the Allies would still be responsible for breaking the treaties, even if by a lucky chance the fleet came in safely without a convoy.[1]

Methuen's difficulties were now enhanced by news from Cadiz that the Spanish treasure fleet was preparing to sail to America, and by the fact that the navy were more interested in taking prizes than in protecting Allied property, and that ministers in London were also inclined to favour an attack on the galleons. On the other hand the Portuguese, and more than anyone the king, thought only about the safety of the Brazil fleet and had mixed feelings about the Cadiz galleons, in which some of them, and also Allied merchants trading under Spanish names, had cargoes. Methuen persevered with his protests about the convoys, but at the same time he had to respect naval feeling and the wishes of the home government. He temporised by holding up the transmission of Alegrete's memorandum until a Naval Council of War had already met and decided to attack the galleons. The Dutch admiral shared the views of his naval colleagues, but Schonenberg defended or tried to make the Portuguese believe he was defending their case for the detachment of a Brazil convoy.[2] At the last moment a compromise was agreed by which four English and four Dutch ships were to be detached as soon as the attempt against the galleons was completed. Methuen used the opportunity to extract from the king the positive order to the marquis of Minas to take the field, for which he had long been asking. Difficulties then arose about the rendezvous for the convoy with the Brazil fleet and the signals to be used. The Portuguese were

---

[1] Add. MSS 5441, fo. 71; Add. MSS 28057, fo. 48; S.P. 89/18, 23 Feb. 1706.
[2] Add. MSS 5441, fo. 71, and 28057, fo. 107; Rijksarchief 7370, 4 March 1706.

20-2

reluctant to reveal the secret sailing orders of the Brazil fleet and some of the hitches were no doubt promoted by the anti-war party.[1] A final crisis was caused by the muddle over the embargo on ships leaving the Tagus. This had been imposed at Leake's request to prevent the enemy learning of the proposed attack against the galleons. It had not worked very well and Methuen had already protested about two ships slipping out.

Methuen only received the Portuguese instructions about the rendezvous at 2 a.m. on 6 March, but he translated them and sent them down to Leake before sunrise. Leake dropped down the river but was obliged by contrary winds to anchor just outside the bar. King Pedro was fretting about the Brazil fleet and in a fever for Leake to sail. But next morning, when the wind changed and the Falmouth packet hoisted sail, she was fired on by the nearby fort of St Julian. Leake was further out from the shore and took no steps to find out what had occurred, but when he weighed anchor early on the next morning, 8 March, the fort fired again. He was dissuaded by the Dutch from forcing a passage and having dropped anchor, sent a messenger ashore. Methuen heard what had happened by 8 o'clock and, after sending urgent messages to St Julian and also to the superintending fort at Belem, went to see the king, who was most indignant and said it was the greatest carelessness of which he had ever heard.[2] Whatever the reason for the firing, a mistake or conscious malice, the upshot was a further delay of twenty-four hours before Leake sailed. He cleared the Tagus on the morning of 9 March but reached the Straits too late to intercept the galleons. He actually passed them, but they were too far off to see; and the frigate *Lime*, which was within sight of both fleets at once, had orders not to speak to any ships she met, and, being uncertain of the identity of either fleet, kept silence. Admiral Wassenaar was the first to learn about the galleons and the whole squadron put about and sailed in hot

[1] Add. MSS 28057, fo. 48, and 5441, fo. 72.
[2] S.P. 89/19, Methuen to Hedges, 8 March, 26 May 1706 and Mr Johnson's report of 25 May.

pursuit, but the galleons were nineteen hours ahead with a strong wind behind them and Leake had to give up the chase. At a time when Anglo-Dutch relations were often strained, Admiral Wassenaar's note to Admiral Leake on the subject makes pleasant reading. 'I am very sorri of this great misfortune. One day sooner would have done our business. I shall not sleep all night and am afread this niews will make you verri uneasi, butt I could not forebear of letting you know itt, as soon as I had itt and remain etc. Pray excuse me broken English.'[1]

Leake took some days to work back to Gibraltar against the wind, and in view of the news that Barcelona was being besieged with the help of a strong French squadron, he decided to take the ships detailed for the Brazil convoy up the Mediterranean. By the time this news reached Methuen, on 21 April, Leake had been reinforced by Admiral Byng and by an Irish convoy, so that the news was most embarrassing to him, but Leake could not be sure that these reinforcements would come in time and even with the eight ships he was scarcely equal to the French, so his decision to keep the eight ships was fully justified.[2]

Despite all these mishaps the Brazil fleet arrived safely at the end of May. Duguay-Trouin, the famous French privateer, was waiting for them fifteen leagues from the Rock of Lisbon with three ships, including the *Jason*, a new well-found ship of guns specially built for privateering. There were six Portuguese men-of-war convoying the fleets and from Trouin's account he did not have the best of the encounter, though he was reluctant to admit it. He succeeded in taking one man-of-war, but inflicted no more casualties and, after a running fight had taken him almost to the bar of the Tagus, was obliged to give up and continue to Cadiz. The Pernambuco and Bahia fleets, consisting of some 200 sail, came safely in, and two days later the Rio fleet arrived under the protection of the *Expedition* and *Gloucester*. John Milner described their arrival.

[1] Add. MSS 5441, fo. 96.   [2] S.P. 89/19, Methuen to Hedges, 22 Apr. 1706.

Their whole Brazil Fleet, those from Rio too, are safe arrived here and prodigious rich, bringing a vast quantity of gold; what is upon the King's account comes to 60 or 70 pounds and 'tis believed not one quarter of what is come is quintad, that is marked for the King, who has one fifth; the mines improve every day yielding still greater quantities and not above four feet in the ground; 'tis so great an encouragement that they fear 'twill destroy the sugar trade, ye people are all running to ye mines; we are upon all accounts pleased with the good arrival, since if they had come to any misfortune after our promising eight men of war for convoy we would have been uneasy.

The captains of the two frigates were received by King Pedro and thanked. As a happy sequel for Methuen they agreed to help him by reinforcing an escort of two ships which was convoying 150 merchant vessels to England.[1]

Now that the war had been diverted to Catalonia Methuen was thinking of an agreement to modify the treaty, so that the Portuguese would have less troops and less subsidy. The Portuguese on the other hand tended to turn from a policy of passive obstruction to positive defeatism and Methuen had to be increasingly peremptory. His relations with Alegrete were no longer cordial and he seldom saw the king, who, like himself, was in a decline. There were rumours of peace feelers by the Dutch, and Methuen spoke of the malicious and villainous proceedings of Schonenberg, while Galway said he could not have been worse if he had been specially chosen by the king of France. Marlborough was inclined to agree and asked for his recall, opposing his transfer to the Court of King Charles on the ground that he would do as much harm there as in Lisbon. But Peterborough compared him favourably with Methuen, and Milner was won over to do so, as soon as Methuen was dead.[2]

---

[1] *Du Guay de Trouin, Memoirs of*, ed. Henri Malo (Paris, 1929), pp. 142–52; Soares da Silva, 'Memorias, 1701–15', *Gaçeta em Forma de Carta*, pp. 64–5; S.P. 89/19, Milner to Hedges, 4 June 1706; Owen, *War at Sea in the Reign of Queen Anne*, p. 65.

[2] Klopp, *op. cit.* XII, 37–8, 47, describes the Dutch attitude and Marlborough does so in Add. MSS 28056, fo. 389. See also *HMC Bath Coll.* I, 80.

The packet-boats were falling into disrepair and a bad winter delayed the convoys. Until the Brazil fleet arrived money was very scarce. The Dutch were again in arrears with their subsidies, and Methuen fell two months behind and was obliged to borrow 50,000 milreis from the paymaster, Thomas Morrice, though he too was having difficulty in finding cash to pay the troops. The Portuguese troops were six months in arrears, but all attempts to pay them direct or to ensure that the Allied money reached them were unavailing. Methuen tried to send £40,000 to Barcelona in specie to enable King Charles to set up a mint, but was foiled by the difficulty of communications and the death of his agent the Italian Jewish banker Manzoni. He then tried to arrange for Jewish merchants in Barcelona to make advances there against credits given them in London. Meanwhile Peterborough, who understood nothing of higher finance and mocked at Methuen's idea that money could be found in Barcelona, was crying out for money and fulminating against Methuen for incompetence.[1]

After the capture of Barcelona Peterborough had soon fallen out with King Charles's German councillors and he was glad to take the opportunity to go to Valencia to confront the Spanish force which was counter-attacking there. He found much less support than he had been led to expect, but, although the people of Valencia were loth to take up arms, they would always help him with information and supplies. By displaying extraordinary energy, imagination, and courage he bluffed the Spaniards into retreat, and made himself the master of Valencia. He then wrote a series of desperate letters crying out for men, money and supplies. Methuen was doing his best, but it was March before he got the frigates *Panther* and *Tiger* through to Denia with money. Richard Hill also sent 120,000 crowns in gold to him from Genoa. But Peterborough spent all he received easily enough in buying horses and equipping men, and fell even further out of favour

---

[1] Add. MSS 28056, fos. 394, and 28057, fos. 45, 89, 91, 103, 107; S.P. 89/18, fo. 301, and S.P. 89/19, Methuen to Hedges, 19 Feb. 1706.

with King Charles by failing to pass on to the king the remittances sent by Methuen. On the contrary he urged the king to leave Barcelona and to join him in a march on Madrid, but refused to divulge what troops, forage, or provision for baggage, and what money, he had by him for this purpose.[1]

At the beginning of April Barcelona was besieged by a powerful army under Tessé and a French squadron of thirty ships. Peterborough, however, refused to reinforce the garrison. He was still eager for any reinforcements which came by sea to be landed for his march on Madrid and he insisted on regarding the besiegers as besieged, as in a sense they were, for they were surrounded by hostile Miquelet rebels and were dependent for their food on supplies brought by sea. The French wasted time and energy in reducing Monjuich but even so Barcelona was very near to falling. Admiral Leake was held up by contrary winds, and doubtful whether he was in any case strong enough to face the French. He waited until 4 May, by which time Admiral Byng with thirteen ships and the Irish convoy had joined him. King Charles had already taken the decision to escape from Barcelona, but to the last moment Peterborough was anxious to have the land force disembarked first, so that Leake could concentrate on attacking the French squadron. Even Peterborough believed that Barcelona could only last three days longer, but one morning when they had come to within twenty miles of the city the fleet woke up to find Peterborough had joined them in a row-boat and his flag as admiral and joint commander-in-chief was flying alongside that of Leake. Peterborough's commission, in fact, had lapsed and although a new commission to act together with Leake was made out, it was never issued to him, but he genuinely believed that he was in command. Nevertheless, Leake would not send a detachment ahead, as Peterborough wished, but proceeded with all his force. He was in the nick of time to save the city but twenty-four hours

[1] Add. MSS 28057, fos. 23, 29, 91, 105; S.P. 89/19, Methuen to Hedges, 9 March and 7 Apr. 1706.

too late to catch the French fleet. If he had come suddenly from the sea with the sea breeze, he could have won a decisive victory, but the French had hurriedly cut their anchors the night before, and Paul Methuen described how in the early morning he saw the last of them vanishing in the distance. Tessé could still perhaps have taken the city by a determined attack, but in a few days he began to retire and, by doing so, provoked guerilla attacks, which inflicted heavy losses and obliged him to leave behind much of his artillery and supplies. As he began his retreat the sun offered a total eclipse; King Philip crossed into France and the omens seemed indeed good for the allies.[1]

It was now mid-May and Galway's army had just retreated from its first abortive march towards Madrid. By dint of constant efforts the allied army had been galvanised into action about a month before. The task had not been easy. It had been doubtful whether Galway would be sufficiently recovered from his wound to take command at all but he did so in the New Year, and, although Methuen could not secure his appointment as commander in chief, he and Minas were given the rank of military governor of whatever province they found themselves in, despite the protests of the other Portuguese military governors. Now that Catalonia was in Allied hands Galway and Methuen were united in desiring a march on Madrid, but at this point King Pedro had a fancy to attack Galicia, and Minas wanted to take up the Badajoz plan again, on the strength of inside information he believed he had of disaffection in the city. Through a misunderstanding Methuen believed that Galway had voted for this too and supported the Badajoz plan in the Council of War; the misunderstanding was near to breaking the harmony between Methuen and Galway, but the mistake was discovered in time

[1] *Marlborough's Letters and Despatches*, 1845, II, p. 571 n. Paul Methuen to his father; MS at Corsham Court, Paul Methuen to duke of Shrewsbury, 12 Oct. 1710; Navy Records Soc., *Admiral Leake*, II, 10; Add. MSS 5441, fos. 101, 110; Rijksarchief 7026, Lichtenstein to Schonenberg, 1 May 1706; Mahon, *History of the War of Succession in Spain*, II, 178; Add. MSS 28057, fos. 150-4.

and orders were issued for an advance to Alcantara. The duke of
Berwick had resumed his command in Spain but his army was
much depleted to reinforce the siege of Barcelona, and the important fortress of Alcántara was taken by the allies on 14 April
without too much difficulty and with the capture of 5,000
prisoners. The Portuguese behaved well and made so good a
march that they were near to capturing Berwick. Minas was
jubilant and anxious to march to Madrid, but Methuen had great
difficulty with the Council of War in Lisbon. He threatened that
Galway's forces would be withdrawn and no more subsidies paid
if the army stopped at Alcántara; Schonenberg would not back
him up and there was loud complaint by the Portuguese of his
peremptory tone, but with the help of Paul Methuen, who was
on his way from London to join the fleet and could confirm that
Methuen's strong line had the backing of his government,
Methuen won his point. The council now raised the standing
complaint that the Allied troops were pillaging churches, but
Minas reported that there had been some looting and he had given
strict orders to stop it, but the Allies had not been worse implicated
than some Portuguese.[1]

In spite of increasing reluctance on the part of the Portuguese
generals the army now advanced as far as Almaraz, a town well
on the way to Madrid. Here a Council of War decided to retreat
in view of the lack of information either about the fate of Barcelona or about Berwick's movements, and to attack Badajoz or
Ciudad Rodrigo. The official reason given for turning back was a
shortage of supplies. It was true that the Portuguese supplies had
been stored in the Alemtejo for an attack on Badajoz and were not
conveniently placed, but the army was now in Castile, where corn
was plentiful. The enemy had destroyed some of the local
supplies, but Galway complained that the Portuguese themselves

[1] Add. MSS 28057, fos. 9, 13, 33, 42, 55, 67, 71, 77, 79, 83, 108–9, 119, 125; S.P. 89/19,
Methuen to Hedges, 22 March, 18 Apr. 1706. Minas was almost captured at Alcántara
but was rescued by the count of Atalaya, who was himself killed.

had looted and wasted food which could have been kept for their advance, and that the Portuguese generals could have made do, if they had been better disposed. As soon as they had begun their retreat they met the news of the relief of Barcelona, and a messenger from King Pedro with orders to continue their advance. In Lisbon Methuen was in despair, and wrote to Godolphin: 'I must own that all the suspicions, all the belief I had of ye tricking of ye Ministers here and of ye open villany of our Generals there has not so far prepared me for this great blow.' The duke of Cadaval absented himself from the council on the plea of gout and the king was ill again and no more to be seen. It was at this moment that Methuen received a Whitehall letter which will evoke the sympathy of any government servant to this day, rebuking him for making advances without sanction to pay for essential stores for Gibraltar.[1]

Methuen now conceived the idea that all the Portuguese troops paid by the allies should be put under Galway's command. But Schonenberg violently opposed this plan and even Galway thought it neither advisable nor practicable. But now the good news came from Barcelona and also information that the Portuguese generals had resolved to advance towards Ciudad Rodrigo. This was not incompatible with a march to Madrid and Galway had agreed.

Methuen was now past trusting even the king and had lost all confidence. Nevertheless, the news was good. The Brazil fleet entered the Tagus on 29 May and the army took Ciudad Rodrigo without difficulty and advanced to Salamanca, where the Allies were greeted by the city and university authorities with an address of welcome. But a long letter came from Minas arguing against any further advance and Galway believed that he meant to

---

[1] António de Castelo Branco, *Comentarios*, ed. Gastão de Mel(l)ode Mat(t)os (Coimbra, 1931), p. 58; Add. MSS 28057, fos. 115, 166, 170. According to C.O. 91/1 Methuen advanced £42,427 3s. 6d. for Gibraltar between Sept. 1704 and March 1706. Padre Cienfuegos, King Charles's representative, proposed that the allied troops were useless in Portugal and should all be sent to Catalonia.

go no further. Methuen thought the same and it was agreed with Godolphin that, if Minas retreated, Galway would return and leave Portugal. Methuen's threats were very ill taken, but he insisted on himself seeing the orders which the king alleged he had given for a further advance, and he sent money and equipment and shoes for the army directly to Galway. On 27 June the good news came of Ramillies, and Methuen in a conciliatory mood paid a call, his last one as it transpired, on the king. On the same day Galway reached Madrid and wrote from there:

The young Marquis of Minas goes with Montagu with this to Lisbon; you cannot caress him too much. I hope I shall receive by the next courier your letter for his father the Marquis de Minas; tho I have not always had reason to be satisfied with him, he is the only man of them all I could have got hither, so I would have all things set fair with him and forget all that is past. I write to my Lord Treasurer that I believe it would become the grandeur of the Queen to make him a present of some jewel.[1]

It was an hour of triumph for Portugal when their army entered the capital of their late masters. At first there was an appearance of welcome, and, according to a description by the Portuguese colonel Castelo Branco, the nobility and their ladies flocked to see the victors and to admire the order of their appearance, for in Madrid they had never seen an army. 'When the loud thunder of their cannon saluted King Charles, Madrid was overawed; his portraits were exhibited in all the public places and amid scenes of jubilation the Portuguese threw money to the crowd from the windows.'[2] Even an English officer wrote quite optimistically to his father, though he showed a greater appreciation of the dangers to come.

After the fatigue of 41 days march we are arrived at our desired port and I think on this side it may more properly be called a conquest than

[1] Add. MSS 28057, fos. 127, 131, 160–2, 194, 196, 200, 204, 210, 216, 237, 262, 266. Minas had his jewel in 1708. Cunha Brochado, 'Cartas ao Conde de Viana, 1705–10', *O Instituto*, vols. 9 and 10 (Coimbra, 1930), letter 60.
[2] Castelo Branco, *op. cit.* pp. 72–4.

a revolution, since in the whole campaign there has not been above three Spaniards joined us (and those of no note) unless the towns and villages by which we passed, who tendered themselves to the obedience of King Charles rather out of fear than inclination. The Grandees have all left Madrid, some to their country houses and others to follow the Duke of Anjou, who has taken with him all the plate, jewels and rich furniture belonging to the palace. The Magistracy of the Town seem very well pleased with this change and the People are generally passive and wish that either one or other of the Kings had power enough to protect them and put an end to the war. The Duke of Berwick is on the march with the few forces he has left towards Navarre, tho some of his Parties are so near us that they have this day killed and taken three or four of the foragers of my Regiment. But as soon as the King joynes us, either with or without the assistance of the Portuguese, we hope to clear Spain of the French. Our Noble Allies have been very humoursome ever since the taking of Rodrigo and have been for going back several times. The last time they proposed it was two or three days ago, when we were within three leagues of Madrid, and their only quarrel was that King Charles had written a letter to my Lord Galway, and none to the Marquis of Minas, and in the superscription with him commanding the army, which they urged was not only a slight but a reflection of the Portuguese Generals. However My Lord has at last brought them hither, which no Body believed he would be able to effect.

The Town is much finer and the Inhabitants more numerous than I expected, and I believe we have had twice the number to visit our Camp than the Army consists of, with four or five hundred coaches filled with Ladyes as well as Dons; and the news they tell us this evening is that Seville has certainly declared for us and that the garrison of Pamplona has murdered a great many of the French and turned the rest out of the Gates. We hope to have the King with us in eight days.[1]

In Lisbon Soares da Silva related that Madrid surrendered with demonstrations of joy and acclamations of King Pedro with the title of Restorer. There was a service of thanksgiving in the

[1] Add. MSS 7077, fo. 148. This letter has been wrongly attributed to James Stanhope, who was in attendance on King Charles and was no stranger to Madrid. The writer was clearly on Galway's staff.

cathedral, which the king and all the Court attended in gala dress. He added that the contentment of the land was beyond description and understandably so, for the Portuguese were not made for such things and could not hope for so much, and all that could be before and could be afterwards, seemed apocryphal and legendary.[1] Da Silva spoke only too truly, for the dream of Portuguese victory was soon to have a rude awakening.

As soon as Barcelona was relieved, Peterborough was impatient to hustle King Charles on the way to Madrid by Valencia, which indeed was the best route. The King's Council twice approved the plan and Peterborough left to prepare the way. But Peterborough could give no assurance that he could arrange for a royal progress in the style expected by the German councillors. The suggestion of the historian Klopp that he positively dissuaded the king from coming to Valencia, because he hoped to have the glory of entering Madrid himself, before even Galway did, appears exaggerated, but he made no secret of his contempt for the German ministers and for their fondness for protocol. They in their turn were attracted by the idea of taking the alternative route through Aragon. This way had some merit, as it would enable King Charles to establish his rule in Sarragossa and perhaps to receive by way of contribution much needed funds and supplies. The king set out for Valencia, but when he reached Tarragona he turned aside towards Sarragossa and nothing that Stanhope or the Portuguese ambassador or messages from Galway or Peterborough could do, dissuaded him. He wrote to Queen Anne to explain that he had been obliged by the lack of subsistence to give up the idea of going to Valencia and no doubt Prince Lichtenstein felt that he had a good case for blaming Peterborough for his failure to give any assurance that there would be money or troops enough in Valencia to conduct the king.[2]

[1] Soares da Silva, *op. cit.* p. 73.
[2] Klopp, *op. cit.* XII, 133, 142–4, 543–9; Woodruff, *op. cit.* pp. 297–308; Add. MSS 31134, fos. 341–3: Col. St Pierre to Lord Raby.

The delay was fatal. It was an insult to the Castilians and the mood of Madrid soon hardened into a cold antipathy. Galway and Minas kept Madrid open for six weeks, but when King Charles reached Guadalajara at the beginning of August his cause was already lost. The duke of Berwick had mustered enough reinforcements to resume control of the situation and King Philip re-entered his capital. Galway at last joined King Charles, but they were obliged to retire towards Toledo in the hope of keeping communications with Portugal open. Peterborough tardily arrived too, but with only a small force. He would not be content with anything less than the supreme command of the allied armies, and, though Galway offered to serve under him, he soon left to pursue his pleasures and new grandiose schemes in Italy. For this even his greatest admirers found it hard to excuse him.[1]

Methuen heard of the occupation of Madrid in the first days of July, but he was not well enough to attend the celebrations or to receive the young marquis of Minas. He wrote again to Hedges and Godolphin to ask leave to retire and gave them details of his expenses in Lisbon, which were consuming his private fortune. He also discussed with Alegrete plans for a revision of the Quadruple Treaty to suit the changed circumstances, but he found Alegrete uncompromising and reluctant to allow Portuguese troops to serve under the king of Spain or a Spanish captain general, even in Spain. Also, to the astonishment of Methuen, he was anxious even in this hour of victory for the safety of the Portuguese army. Methuen did not live the few weeks required to show how right Alegrete's fears had been.[2]

On 25 June Methuen was trying to persuade the Portuguese to march into Andalusia to take Cadiz, but he met with no response; they were not interested in English ambitions and feared a French counter-attack from Navarre. On 2 July he received his last letter from Hedges, and it was unusually kind. Hedges wrote:

[1] Add. MSS 31134, fos. 350, 365. [2] Add. MSS 28057, fos. 254, 266.

You cannot receive a more convincing proof of Her Majesty's entire satisfaction in your conduct than in what I wrote to you by Her Command last Wednesday, of which I enclose a copy, but since Your Excellency seems to be concerned at some reflections you have heard have been made here in relation to the Fort of St Julian's firing upon Sir John Leake, I am to assure you that Her Majesty is well satisfied of your good Intentions in all your behaviour and is so well persuaded of your zeal and application in Her service, as is likewise everybody here for whom you need to have any regard, that you can suffer no prejudice in Her Majesty's good opinion of their esteem from any aspersions of that kind.

On 8 July Methuen wrote to Galway at Madrid to excuse himself for having been too ill to see the young Minas and ended with the postscript: 'For God's sake, My Lord, make my excuses for not writing to the King of Spain and to Lichtenstein.' The next day he wrote for the last time to Hedges to tell him he would have the news of Madrid from Galway's aide-de-camp Montagu, and to complain about the bad condition of all four packet-boats.[1]

For some weeks Methuen had been in bed with an illness described as a mixture of rheumatism and gout. On the morning of 11 July he felt better and ate a good dinner, but after his siesta he awoke speechless and continued so until the next morning at 6 o'clock, when he died. His household was taken by surprise and had no time to summon Consul Milner or Chaplain Willcocks. According to Milner's private letter to Paul, only Methuen's friend and 'cousin' William Browne, another merchant named Garnier, his secretary Plumpton, and an English Catholic from Cadiz named Stevens were present.[2] However, the two ladies of the house were with him, as Da Silva noted with relish. After describing the victory celebrations he continued:

...nothing but prodigies and miracles. Only John Methuen, whom the devil keep, did not want (and how wrong he was) to wait the end of

---

[1] S.P. 104/109, Hedges to Methuen, 4 June 1706; S.P. 89/18, Methuen to Hedges, 9 July, and Hedges to Methuen; Add. MSS 28057, fo. 290.
[2] MS at Corsham Court, Milner to Paul Methuen.

them, for missing too much his colleague Roque Monteiro he betook himself to the other world, for the gout rose to his head, and he died gallantly between two girl friends, and with an apothecary by his head, or two perhaps if two claim it, and his venerable bones, which were the devil's own, were sent to England in a small sailing vessel to be buried in the holy sanctuaries there.

Indeed his body was embalmed and in 1708 Paul took him home to rest in Westminster Abbey close to his fellow workers for the Grand Alliance, George Stepney and Alexander Stanhope. Several of the principal players were near to escorting him. Roque Monteiro preceded him by two weeks and Queen Catherine by six months; King Pedro followed six months after. Alegrete soon had a stroke but he survived two or three years. Only the septuagenarian duke of Cadaval was as well as ever and lived to the age of ninety.

Methuen was a man who kept everything under his own hat, and his staff did not even know whether he had made a will, though he had done so before leaving England and had made provision for Sarah Earle. Hedges, however, had been informed about it. Milner made an inventory of his possessions and of government property, but did not dare to open any official mail before he received orders from London. These came after a month or two and the news that Paul Methuen had been reappointed to Lisbon.[1]

[1] Soares da Silva, *op. cit.* p. 73; Cunha Brochado, Cartas, *op. cit.* letter 48. Methuen's will is at Somerset House and there is a copy also at Corsham Court.

CHAPTER 13

ASSESSMENT OF
THE METHUENS AND OF THE
METHUEN TREATIES

THERE were general expressions of regret at Methuen's death. Marlborough wrote to Godolphin and Hedges that it was very unlucky at this conjuncture, when there was most need of him, and John Milner said it was a great disappointment to the service. However, Marlborough in a private letter to the duchess said, 'You know what my opinion has always been of him. I believe his son, by what I've heard of him is an ingenious young man.'[1] It must be admitted that, although Methuen was missed as a useful ambassador, expressions of personal regret for his loss as a man were rather few.

It is not hard to understand why this should have been so. Methuen was already passing his prime when he emerged from the world of lawyers and merchants, to which he belonged, into the upper circles of diplomacy and politics. He was a plausible man and made many political friends, but he lost many of these by his very devotion to the service of King William's interests. Unlike his son Paul, who made a good showing as a great social success, John Methuen remained essentially a man of the middle class, whose personal friends were of the stamp of William Browne, the Lisbon merchant. Although as long as his health permitted he did his best, he did not care for society and was uncomfortable and pompous in the role of lord ambassador. He was also a secretive man, and even before overwork and ill health cloistered him he was rather proud to be considered an enigma.

[1] *Marlborough's Letters and Despatches*, III, 78-9; Marlborough, *Correspondence with the Duchess of Marlborough* (1838), I, 110; Add. MSS 5441, fo. 197.

Methuen left a voluminous correspondence from the time of his first going to Lisbon until his death, but very little of it throws light on his personal doings, and the records for the first forty years of his life are almost blank. Only his letters to the marquis of Halifax among the archives of Earl Spencer at Althorp lift the curtain a little. In them he liked to depict himself as a man of quiet and studious tastes, devoted to his house and garden, and to reading. He was a little more earthy than this, but the description was applicable when he first went to Lisbon. He did not then aspire to play a part in great events or to become a famous ambassador. However, in 1694 he was already tempted by the thought that Lisbon might become the scene of a great negotiation for the settlement of Europe, in which he could play a part.[1] Ambition grew upon him, and as he was an industrious person he became an acknowledged expert on Portugal and on trade matters. It was natural that with his family background and City connections he should become a commercial expert, but it was rather surprising that he made himself so much at home in Portugal. He was lucky to have the opportunity to help Queen Catherine of Bragança in her affairs and to become a personal friend of the royal family, but he also developed an affinity with the Portuguese. Even his appearance, which was dark and foreign-looking, prepared him for this, though as far as is known he had no foreign blood, and there is no definite evidence that he had ever travelled abroad, though it is likely that he had done so. Through his family influence and property in Wiltshire he had been able to secure a seat in Parliament and this earned him the consideration of the Whigs in power, who found his vote useful. King William liked to employ dependable men of modest standing with no strings attached to them and selected him for promotion. Methuen became commissioner of trade, lord chancellor of Ireland, and then the ambassador for an important negotiation. So far from leading a quiet life and restoring his health, he was

[1] MS at Althorp, Methuen to Halifax, 21 Sept. 1694.

323

destined to ruin it and to kill himself in the performance of duties which were increasingly burdensome and obsessive.

Methuen's office of Master in Chancery was acquired by purchase, and the legal work was distributed to each of the twelve masters in rotation. It was a profitable office and no doubt enabled him to save money, but the tenure of it throws little light on his capacity as a lawyer. Lord Somers did not think very highly of it and one source described Methuen in Ireland as a 'bad and dilatory equity judge, very desirous to do right, but doubtful how to do it, and afraid of committing grave mistakes, prone to put off any but the plainest causes'.[1] However, according to other accounts he did a good deal to reform the judicial machinery and bring it up to date and in one instance at least, that of the case of the bishop of Londonderry, he was not afraid to take controversial decisions which resulted in an appeal reaching the House of Lords at Westminster. The criticism of his alleged hesitations does not take into account the fact that his appointment as lord chancellor was more political than judicial. Methuen's task was to persuade the Irish Parliament to carry through the programme planned for it in London. The more important cases, which came before him as lord chancellor, had political implications which could not be ignored; he had to go carefully in order not to stir up too much political animosity. So the question of his capacity must remain open.

Methuen's enemies in Ireland called him a schemer and a conjurer. He was often referred to as dark and obscure; in later years John Macky summed him up 'as a man of intrigue, very muddy in his conceptions, not easily understood in anything'.[2] Some of the obscurity was due in his later years to overwork and ill health but he undoubtedly enjoyed secrecy. His first recorded letter was addressed to Dr John Wallis, the famous cryptographer.[3] Possibly he had been employed on some confidential

[1] J. R. O'Flanagan, Lord Chancellors of Ireland (1870), I, 3.
[2] John Macky, Memoirs of the Secret Service, p. 143; Cal. of S.P. (1698), pp. 259, 419 ff.
[3] Add. MSS 32499, fo. 251, Methuen to John Wallis.

work by King William. Certainly he applied himself to intelligence work in Portugal with zest and employed a network of agents in Cadiz and elsewhere.

In the years following Methuen's death both Portugal and the Allies were disillusioned with the Peninsular venture and very critical of the treaty which had committed them to it. As the Tories were enjoying an increasing influence and Methuen had not been on good terms with several of the leading Whigs, it was not surprising that his reputation suffered an eclipse and that the somewhat sinister character which he had earned rendered it an easy target for his enemies. Swift expressed an extreme Tory view of him: 'a profligate rogue without religion or morals, but cunning enough, yet without abilities of any kind'. Lord Rivers accepted readily enough all the Lisbon gossip against Methuen and even the imputation that he had been guilty of disloyalty to his country. It had been generally acknowledged that he had done well in cajoling the Portuguese to bring their army to Madrid, but Schonenberg took the credit and persuaded John Milner without too much difficulty that Methuen had been vacillating even in this. Now that Methuen's whole policy was discredited, few ventured to defend him save only his old patron Godolphin.[1] A few years later the wheel turned full circle. When the Whigs came into power, the good effects of Methuen's commercial treaty were making themselves felt and the name of Methuen was idolised. While the Tories thought Methuen should have been hanged, the Whigs said that a statue should be erected in his honour in every market-town in England. Boyer, in his annals of the reign of Queen Anne, described Methuen 'as a man of great parts, much improved by study, travel and conversation with the best, whose manly eloquence showed in the House of Commons upon many important and nice occasions'. But although a Methuen legend was now established, no one was interested in

[1] Jonathan Swift, *Collected Works* (1814), x, 313, *HMC Bath*, I, 145–50, 155, 160–1; S.P. 89/19, Milner to Hedges, 30 Aug. 1706.

vindicating the record of John Methuen personally; the legend applied to Paul as much as to his father and the two men were often confused.[1]

Rivers went so far as to suggest that Methuen had been disloyal and in correspondence with the enemy. He was not apparently aware that these charges had been dismissed as absurd by the Cabinet a year earlier. However, he included Galway in his charge of treason and this was more than the government could swallow. After Rivers met Galway in Spain he changed his tone, and he also specifically acquitted Paul Methuen of any complicity with the offences alleged to have been committed by his father. Paul generally escaped criticism and was on speaking or even friendly terms with many of his father's enemies, including Swift.

John Methuen was no debauchee, though his morals were average and he could not be described as a religious man. In his younger days he liked to pose as an advanced thinker and in his will made in 1702 he used none of the pious phrases customary in such documents. But he conformed, communicating regularly and serving at one time as churchwarden in Bradford-on-Avon.

Methuen was also accused of being venal. This was not unlikely in the circumstances of the time. The line between corruption and the justifiable acceptance of perquisites was hard to draw. Marlborough and Robert Walpole were accused of drawing it too much in their own favour; on the other hand Robert Bridges founded the dukedom of Chandos and a princely fortune on the profits of his office as paymaster general, but not a whisper was heard against him. A great deal of public money passed through Methuen's hands, but he complained that his lord-chancellorship had made inroads on his private fortune and that his Embassy had been ruinous. Such facts as are known confirm the truth of his statements. He was £3,000 in debt at the end of his lord-chancellorship and sold property at Beckington in Somerset to be able to

[1] Abel Boyer, *History of the Reign of Queen Anne, 1703-13*, V, p. 495. Possibly Boyer was referring to Paul; and in Tindal's *Continuation of Rapin's History of England* (1745), the Methuen Treaties are indexed under Paul Methuen.

meet his creditors. At Lisbon he expected to break even, for he drew an ambassadorial salary, while Paul continued to be paid as minister. However, the cost of living rose enormously in Lisbon during the war and although Methuen was economically inclined he entertained freely in Lisbon, as to the surprise of James Vernon he had also done in Dublin. Paul Methuen was also put to great expense in attending on the two kings and in his various journeys and missions; in the autumn campaign of 1704 he had to provide accommodation for Galway. Yet, although Joseph Addison expected there would be difficulty over Methuen's accounts, they passed the keen scrutiny of Parliament at a time when the Tories were in the ascendant and the Methuen stock low. In 1709 Paul Methuen obtained a discharge for £202,071 1s. 8d. advanced for subsidies and for the expenses of Gibraltar.[1] He also received a final discharge for the Old Merchants' Debts and, in view of his father's services, for the gold and silver plate issued to his Embassy valued at £1,272 15s. 0d. and £5,583 5s. 0d. Perhaps Paul Methuen took some of this plate home and it was this which gave rise to the story that he left Lisbon with a shipload of ill-gotten gains.[2]

In later years Paul Methuen became a very wealthy man, but on his return to England in 1708 he was in comparatively straitened circumstances and retired to a thatched cottage at Bishops Cannings. He inherited a considerable property there, but during his father's absence abroad the rents had fallen into arrears and it was some time before Paul could bring the estate into order again. It appears that he acquired his riches later, partly by inheritance from various relatives but principally by careful administration and prudent speculation. The legacies of £1,500 to his daughter Isabella and of £500 to Sarah Earle left by John Methuen do not

---

[1] Harleian MS 226412, 9 Jan. 1709; Bodleian MS D 23, fos. 69–70; Paul Methuen to Bishop Burnet; Addison, *Letters*, ed. W. Graham (Oxford, 1941), 15, 19 Nov. and 10 Dec. 1706. *Cal. of S.P.* 2, 28 Jan. 1701; S.P. 89/19, Paul Methuen to Hedges, 14 Sept. 1706.

[2] José Brochado de Cunha, 'Cartas ao Conde de Viana', *O Instituto*, no. 48, p. 338.

suggest that he had very greatly enlarged the inheritance left to him by his father forty years before or that he disposed of any large sum in cash, though he may have owned considerable landed property.

John Methuen's personal character emerges reasonably well from investigation. The graver charges against him seem to have been inspired by political animosity. His talents are harder to assess and may have been to a greater or less degree mediocre. But he made up for any lack of them by his industry and zeal, and, although his inability to take a narrow departmental view landed him in a great deal of trouble, it also meant that his persistence achieved in the end what was required of him. Fortunately for him his scope was doubled by the constant co-operation of his son Paul, whose qualities made up for his father's failings.

The father-and-son partnership of John and Paul was unusual. In a sense it outlasted the life of John Methuen, for Paul completed his father's career by filling the posts of ambassador at Madrid and secretary of state, before retiring to lead a life of his own as a connoisseur of the arts and a man about town. In his old age Paul Methuen grumbled at the misfortunes which in the prime of life excluded him from ever returning to high office. He fell out with Walpole and belonged to a splinter party of the Whigs, which never returned to favour; so Paul Methuen after a period as an official in the royal household became no more than a well-known Opposition member of Parliament. But in fact he was happy to be this as he never cared for the burden of high office or for piling up work in the manner of his father, though he disposed of the problems which he found on his desk with great competence and speed. His help to his father was invaluable. He took charge with success towards the end of his father's first mission, and as minister in Portugal from 1697 to 1702 established a reputation for himself. During those five years John Methuen was able to keep in touch with Portugal, so that on his return in 1702 it was easy for him to pick up the threads. In 1702 and 1703 he was able to return again to England and Paul Methuen held the fort for him during the crucial moments of the Portuguese abrogation of the Franco-Spanish Alliance and the conclusion of the Quadruple and Triple Methuen treaties. During the war Paul Methuen discharged all the active roles which his father could no longer perform. He acted as liaison with the fleet at Cadiz, and went through both the Portuguese campaigns. He visited Gibraltar and Morocco, attended on King Charles when the war moved to the Mediterranean, and returned to London to speak up for his father. John Milner suggested that towards the end Paul was tired of playing a subordinate part, but John Methuen worked hard to secure for him an independent post and there is no other indication that Paul ever gave his father anything less than unreserved loyalty. Indeed in his last letter he offered to go to Madrid to help his father's installation, in the event of his being appointed ambassador there. As Paul Methuen was very socially inclined and made many friends this co-operation over a period of fourteen years was a great source of strength to Methuen, who was a less popular character and during his last years was unable to go about. Furthermore, in a small oligarchic society a knowledge of personalities was invaluable, and a team of two men who had some years of experience and absolute confidence in each other could achieve a position of strength in circles where few men worked together and even members of the same group or party were often at loggerheads. For the historian the unbroken series of Methuen dispatches from 1692 to 1708 constitute an unrivalled source. They are particularly valuable because so many contemporary Portuguese archives have disappeared. Private Portuguese memoirs, etc., of the time are very rare and there are not many secondary sources, and such as these are have tended to concentrate upon descriptions of Marlborough's wars to the exclusion of events in the Peninsula.

When John Methuen was called on to go to Lisbon in 1702 he and Paul had had ten years' preparation for this great negotiation.

For John Methuen his experiences in Portugal in 1694 and 1695 had been a rehearsal, which had given him a very definite idea of the part he proposed to play. His many talks with King Pedro had convinced him that nothing could be done without offers of subsidies and of concessions of Spanish territory. He was also sure that Portugal could not remain neutral. Paul Methuen had recently been converted to the idea but he had only resigned himself to accepting the neutrality of Portugal because the larger aim of a belligerent alliance seemed for the time being out of the question.

John Methuen rejected any suggestion of Portuguese neutrality, because he believed that France would never agree to any compromise that would be acceptable to the Allies and would allow them to use Portuguese ports. He was also strongly influenced by his recollection that during the last war Portugal's neutrality had enabled her to acquire an increased share of international trade at the expense of the maritime powers. He looked at this trade largely from the point of view of a Lisbon merchant dealing with Anglo-Portuguese trade and Portuguese-American trade, but he was not disinterested in direct Anglo-American trade. Writing to Lord Rivers after Methuen's death, Charles Montagu said that Methuen had been the ruin of allied affairs in Spain and the minister of Portugal rather than of England, for he had diverted the war 'from the West Indies, where it would have enriched England, and injured Spain, to carry it into a place where England had no assistance, for Portugal had our money, and France the silver of the Indies'.[1]

To make Methuen responsible for the abandonment of the policy of a maritime and colonial war was to impute to him powers which he did not possess. The diversion of allied forces from the West Indies was due to circumstances outside his control. The principal reason was the insistence of the emperor on the presence of the allied fleet to help him in Italy. When Marl-

[1] *HMC Bath*, I, 155.

borough conceived of the design of an attack from the Mediterranean to support his march on the Rhine, and the Toulon plan
was given priority in England's secret plans, England embraced
the Mediterranean scheme with fervour. But it was the emperor
who was responsible in the first instance. The United Provinces
were less interested in Marlborough's Grand Design, which in any
case was largely a secret kept by himself and Heinsius, but King
William before his death had been influenced by the necessity to
placate the emperor. The maritime powers could not allow him
to concentrate entirely on Italy and run the risk that after an
arrangement with Bavaria he would withdraw his armies from
the Rhineland, where they were some help to the defence of the
Dutch Barrier. The only remedy was to help him in Italy in
return for Imperial help in the north.

Nevertheless, the allies dropped their West Indian schemes with
reluctance. Marlborough included them in the treaty of Grand
Alliance, but the emperor would not agree to the allies' proposals
for a joint expedition to America or guarantee the trade privileges
in the Spanish colonies, which the allies desired. Furthermore, the
allies found that the logistics of a large-scale expedition were much
more baffling than they had anticipated and that they had not the
resources to send fleets to the Mediterranean or the Peninsula and
to the West Indies simultaneously.

The defection of Portugal had barred the use of Portuguese
ports, and the Allies decided that they must control the Straits
before they could safely enter the Mediterranean in force. They
decided to attack Cadiz and this was a project in which Methuen
took a lasting interest. However, the failure there in 1702 made an
operation based on Portugal indispensable either as a substitute for
a second attack on Cadiz or as a supporting operation, and underlined the opinion already held by Methuen that Portugal must be
brought in as an active belligerent. There were many besides
Charles Montagu who concluded that Methuen gave away too
much to bring this about. From time to time such different

personages as the Almirante de Castile and Lord Peterborough testified that this impression of Methuen was wrong, and naturally the Portuguese insisted that the supplies, subsidies, and troops accorded to them by the Methuen treaties were no more than were indispensable to enable them to enter the war. Whether this was the case or not, King Pedro and his ministers were adamant on the subject and Methuen gave the Cabinet at home a clear indication of their requirements before he even left London. Therefore whatever Methuen's faults were in detail it does not seem that he could have made a better bargain for the allies and this was shown to some extent by the fact that Schonenberg and Waldstein, his keenest detractors, had little success with the Portuguese when they negotiated with them according to their own lights. Waldstein made no progress at all and Schonenberg met with a rebuff when he claimed Methuen Commercial Treaty privileges without any corresponding concession.[1]

Ideally one can surmise that Portugal would have fared better with a smaller and more efficient army and a few ships to guard her coast. The allies would have done well to resign themselves to leave twelve ships under Portuguese command, and to have avoided the difficulties of co-operation with the Portuguese army and the quarrels about the command by landing their troops in Spain and leaving the Portuguese the task only of defending their frontier and capturing such Spanish forts as they could take. It was no fault of Methuen that this could not be brought about, and the failure to send the officers and technicians promised made the deficiencies of the Portuguese forces greater than they need have been, but Methuen undoubtedly underestimated the difficulties. No one foresaw how inadequate the Portuguese cavalry would be to meet the French, but Methuen failed to realise that although the Portuguese forces had fought well enough a generation before in their war of independence, they were not fit to face trained French

---

[1] S.P. 80/20, Stepney to Hedges, 7 Apr. 1703; *HMC H. of L. Reports*, VII, n.s., 500–6; Add. MSS 20818, fo. 7.

troops and in spite of their religion and similar language would be no more welcome in Castile than the English or Dutch.

The enlargement of the Portuguese army, impractical as it was, suited King Pedro, who aspired to lead his own army into Spain. A larger Allied element would have been better and this was recommended by Schonenberg and Waldstein, but, as events turned out, it would not have been possible. The emperor's contingent, which would have been Catholic and lessened at least one difficulty, could not be provided and England eventually had to assume the obligation to provide the emperor's third in both money and men. She furnished the money but the double quota of men proved too much. The great preponderance of Portuguese troops made it all the easier for the Portuguese to insist on retaining the command in their own hands, and the many deficiencies of the treaties, and the troubles which resulted from them, aroused severe criticism. Colonel Richards, who had a better opportunity than most of evaluating the situation, blamed Methuen for not having taken advice of any military experts and at the outset was very critical. But he gradually realised that the fault did not lie with Methuen or indeed with any particular person or even nation. The Portuguese went 'councilling, from junta to junta and from conference to conference' and settled nothing; but similar delays arose also in London. As Richards put it, he thought there must be Portuguese in the English Councils also. The Portuguese were the most inexperienced of the Allies and had the greatest difficulties to combat, but this was no reason for all the foreign ministers and generals to blame Portuguese incompetence to cover their own failings or to get greater powers for themselves.[1]

The Quadruple and Triple Treaties of Alliance became known as the Methuen Treaties rather than as the Treaties of Lisbon. This was right, for they had the stamp of Methuen upon them. What he had proposed in London and put into the mind of King

[1] Stowe MS 467, fos. 44–5, 70, 78; Add. MSS 20817, fos. 390–1.

Pedro, eventually emerged, though of course with many variations in detail. Their terms were regarded as onerous in the allied
capitals but they were accepted as being advantageous. It was only
when the Peninsular War turned out badly that they were
generally condemned. The Portuguese had from the beginning
feared that they were only being used as a diversion to weaken
French power and the allies thought that the results did not justify
the cost. However, the cost in men, though heavy, had been
small in proportion, and much of the money spent on supplies had
gone into the pockets of allied merchants. Portugal had been an
inadequate ally but she could claim to have borne the brunt, and
at the signing of the peace to be receiving very little for it.

Methuen had done well to succeed in concluding the Quadruple
and Triple Treaties. He perhaps fulfilled his orders imperfectly,
but owing to his knowledge and experience of Portugal, had
done as well as, and probably better than, an outwardly more bril-
liant ambassador.

John Methuen was, however, essentially a trade expert and
it was for his commercial treaty that he was best remembered.
This was his distinctive achievement, for which as a member
of a family of clothiers and as an amateur in wines he had long
hoped. Trade was often uppermost in English and Dutch minds.
Ministers had to think in terms of armies and political issues, and
the commercial rivalry of English and Dutch was such that it was
wiser not to discuss trade issues with third parties when both
English and Dutch were present. Except in moments of great
crisis, as when there was imminent danger of an invasion, the
maritime nations put trade first. So a great deal has been said
about the influence of the occupation of the Barrier Forts in
February 1701 and of the recognition of the Pretender in September 1701 in bringing about the striking change in English public
opinion in the course of the year, but the damage done to trade
by the defection of Portugal and by the embargo placed by King
Louis on English trade with France and his stoppage of Anglo-

Dutch trade, particularly in slaves, with the West Indies, played perhaps an equally important part.[1]

John Methuen was lucky to have his work to do in Lisbon at a time when there was still a little movement in Portuguese society. Government was in the hands of an oligarchy, and although power centred in the king there was still some discussion of political matters at least in inner circles. During the Partition Treaties Paul Methuen laughed at the French ambassador for supposing that his secret talks with the king could possibly remain unknown to Paul in Lisbon and during the Methuen negotiations the reverse process functioned, for leaks regarding Methuen's secret talks were constantly occurring. But there was some give-and-take and it was possible to have useful contacts. In the following reign everything was frozen up. The king scarcely consulted his Council of State and only spoke to one or two cardinals. An English minister complained that the secretary of state had become a mere clerk and that it was impossible to extract an opinion on any political matter out of any Portuguese.[2] In Methuen's day this was not yet the case and as, after their long years in Lisbon, John and Paul Methuen between them knew everybody, John Methuen was ready to take advantage of the favourable moment to make his commercial treaty. The treaty could not have been made if the Quadruple Treaty, and even more the Triple Treaty with its guarantees of Portuguese integrity and of reciprocity in matters of trade privilege, had not prepared the way, but Methuen saw his chance. He achieved the removal of the restrictions on the cloth trade which the merchants had desired for so long, and he gave the Portuguese a concession for their wine trade without the British tax collector losing a penny or himself risking much parliamentary objection. The treaty was of minor importance for the moment and indeed its most obvious result was to exacerbate relations with the Dutch minister in Lisbon, but when the

---

[1] *Hardwicke Papers*, II, 450.

[2] S.P. 89/44, Castres to Stone, 20 Jan. 1744; S.P. 89/35, Tirawley to Newcastle, 20 Aug. 1729.

Quadruple Treaty became obsolete it proved to be the sheet anchor for the continuation of the Anglo-Portuguese alliance, which guaranteed the integrity of Portugal and Brazil and the prosperity of the Portuguese wine trade in return for freedom to trade with and through Portugal. Methuen failed to fulfil the second aspiration of the Portugal merchants in London, which was to secure the privilege of trading direct with Brazil, but through Lisbon English merchants nevertheless had their share and received Brazilian bullion back. The Lisbon Factory was indeed content to accept the restrictions on the direct trade with Brazil, as, if they had been removed, other nations would have claimed similar privileges and the English share in the trade might well have diminished.[1]

The verdict therefore on the work of John Methuen must on the whole be favourable. It was easy to find fault with him, but through his co-operation with his son and his experience of Portugal he had a substantial influence on the events of his time. The Quadruple Treaty helped to weaken France and the efforts of Methuen kept Portugal in the war and assisted in the defence and maintenance of Gibraltar. The war could conceivably have been won by other means, but the form it took contributed to the establishment of England as a Mediterranean power and enabled him to leave as a monument his commercial treaty, which continued to be useful for the better part of a century.

[1] C.O. 388/18, II, 20 Oct. 1716. Report of British Factors.

CHAPTER 14

PAUL METHUEN, AMBASSADOR AT LISBON, AND PORTUGAL'S RECESSION FROM THE WAR, DECEMBER 1706–JULY 1708

PAUL METHUEN had an adventurous time in Savoy. He landed at Oneglia and travelled with a convoy of mules and loads of much needed gunpowder across the mountains to join the duke of Savoy on his retreat from Turin. He was on active service in close attendance on the duke until his triumphant return to his capital on 7 September. The duke appreciated his company and wrote cordially about him to Queen Anne. This was the great adventure of Paul's life and won him the praise of Voltaire, who in his history of the campaign described him as the bravest, frankest and most generous Englishman that ever represented his country abroad. He matched his physical courage by diplomatic prudence. He refused to be inveigled into various grandiose schemes suggested to him in Barcelona by Peterborough or to be implicated in the representations on behalf of the Savoyard Protestants with which his predecessor Chetwynd had annoyed the duke. It is tempting to link Paul's name with a contract made in 1707 to supply the Savoyard army with English cloth, but it was his predecessor, Richard Hill, who made this possible by obtaining in January 1705 a reduction of the duty in Savoy on cloth.[1]

Paul received the news of his father's death and the orders to

---

[1] R. Hill, *Diplomatic Correspondence*, II, 482. An account of the Savoy campaign is given by Paul in his diary in S.P. 89/19 and in an MS letter to the duke of Shrewsbury dated 12 Oct. 1710 at Corsham. Voltaire, *Œuvres complètes* (Paris, 1785), XII, 13–14; *Le Campagne de Guerra in Piemonte* (pub. fratelli Bocca, Torino, 1943), V, 492, 414, 519, 524; S.P. 100/29, merchants' memorial of Jan. 1711.

return to Lisbon in Turin. At first he excused himself from accepting the Lisbon post. He alleged the great difficulties of negotiation with the Portuguese. In spite of his great experience and knowledge of that Court his father had sunk under the burden and it was unlikely he would succeed better. Schonenberg, under pretence of greater zeal for the service of his masters, had opposed whatever John Methuen and Galway thought most for the public good and interest of England, and no English minister could hope to prevail without at least having the character and authority of ambassador. Furthermore, the expense was great and his private affairs would be ruined if he could not now devote time to them.[1]

Most people thought that Paul was only angling for promotion to the rank of ambassador, but time showed that his reluctance was genuine and that he meant what he said. He agreed nevertheless to go for the time being to Lisbon; after some weeks' delay, owing to the difficulty of finding a ship, he reached Lisbon at the end of the year, a few days before the death of King Pedro. In due course credentials to the new king, John V, were sent to him in the capacity of ambassador, but it is interesting that the younger Lord Sunderland, now secretary of state, thought it diplomatic to convey the queen's official congratulations to the king on his accession through Lord Rivers. Although an ambassador and a personal friend of King Pedro, King Charles and the duke of Savoy, he had not the status of a peer of the realm.[2]

Rivers had arrived in Lisbon in October with much needed supplies for Portugal. He was in a cantankerous mood for he had had many crosses to bear. His original orders to land near Bordeaux and to instigate a rising of French Protestants with the help of the Cevennois leader Cavalier had been countermanded after many frustrating delays. His next instruction was to carry out a plan to land at San Lucar with a view to the capture of Cadiz and

[1] S.P. 89/19, Paul Methuen to Hedges, 14 Sept. 1706.
[2] S.P. 104/208, fo. 10.

Seville.[1] This plan, which was intended to be secret, was delayed by the storms which damaged the fleet. Rivers himself had to change to another ship and when he reached Lisbon after a month at sea required at least a month to refit. Meanwhile an appeal for help from King Charles caused further orders to come from London to proceed to Catalonia, but these were again countermanded and he was told to remain in Lisbon.[2]

The Portuguese were pressing for this and for the reinforcements which Lord Rivers carried with him to be left in Lisbon. They were anxious to rescue Minas, whose army was stranded at Valencia, and even offered to take part in a new march on Madrid. Galway had asked Marlborough to have the reinforcements left in Lisbon and, although the new king declared that he would abide by the Alliance, there were fears that he might not do so. These justified the keeping of a sufficient allied force in Portugal. Rivers was plagued by the stream of orders and counter-orders and embarrassed by precise instructions to persuade the Portuguese to relinquish the supreme command and to agree to the direct payment of Minas's army by the allies. He had no orders regarding the course he was to take if the Portuguese refused, and he was determined in no circumstances to serve under Minas or Galway or any other general. Finally in January he made up his mind to do what pleased him best, regardless of orders, and he left for Alicante. Da Cunha protested vehemently in London against this further desertion of Portugal.[3]

There was great confusion of allied plans. Rivers did not know that Galway had asked for his troops to be left in Lisbon, and was indignant when he heard of it. News of the worsening situation of King Charles only gradually reached London and ministers there did not know whether they should relieve Galway on

[1] Klopp, *Der Fall des Hauses Stuart*, XII, 151–3; *HMC Bath*, I, 92. Col. Richards suggested the San Lucar plan (see Stowe MS 471, fo. 48).
[2] *HMC Bath*, I, 112, 115, 125–7, 146.
[3] S.P. 104/208, Sunderland to Paul Methuen, 14 Jan. 1707; Add. MSS 20817, fo. 727; *HMC Bath*, I, 138–9, 159; *HMC Portland*, 2nd ser., IV, 648.

22-2

account of rumours that King Charles was no longer satisfied with him or leave him in command on account of his influence with the Portuguese. Eventually they asked Rivers to report on the situation and told him he could have the command, but only if Galway insisted on relinquishing it. However, when they received complaints from Rivers about Galway they decided to support Galway and ordered Rivers to leave him in command. When Rivers reached Alicante he received a cordial personal letter from the duke of Berwick but only a formal note from Galway by the hand of James Stanhope. Nevertheless, Stanhope arranged a meeting between the two men, and when Rivers found that there had been a misunderstanding about the Lisbon reinforcements and Galway was only too anxious to relinquish his command, he obeyed his latest orders to leave Galway in charge and sailed for home.[1]

At a time when the Spaniards were retaking their forts from the Portuguese, Godolphin still supposed that Galway was triumphing in Madrid and proposed a withdrawal from the Mediterranean in order to concentrate on other projects. But Marlborough was still talking of his Grand Design and even thought of going to Savoy himself. However, the Toulon plan was again given priority, and Admiral Shovell was ordered to return to Lisbon to prepare for an attack on Toulon as soon as he had taken Rivers to Spain. Now the question of Peterborough came up. He had not been consulted about the Toulon plan, but he heard of it and desired to be put in charge. Peterborough was now back in Spain and in favour again with King Charles. But the ministers in London were still considering King Charles's earlier request for his recall, and they ordered him out of Spain in January 1707.

Peterborough, before leaving Spain, had advised the allies to remain on the defensive until the duke of Savoy could invade France, but Galway was eager to advance and Stanhope supported

[1] *HMC Bath*, I, 81, 128, 142, 165; Corbett, *England in the Mediterranean*, pp. 287–91, 296; Owen, *War at Sea in the Reign of Queen Anne*, p. 39; *Le Campagne de Guerra en Piemonte*, p. 514.

him and Minas also. Stanhope may well have been influenced by the expectation of peace feelers from France. Berwick's cordial note to Rivers could be interpreted as an overture. There were rumours that he was preparing to retreat and Stanhope himself later engaged in a mysterious negotiation with the duke of Orleans. Although Berwick gave some support to these stories by evacuating the town of Tecla with valuable stores, he was in point of fact expecting a strong reinforcement of 12,000 men which, in order to have a free hand in Naples, the Emperor Joseph had agreed to allow to leave Italy. Galway only heard that French reinforcements were on the way a day or two before the battle of Almanza and his own forces had been depleted by the withdrawal of a substantial part of his army upon the orders of King Charles to protect Catalonia. The reinforcements brought by Rivers were under-officered and inexperienced. Those brought by Admiral Byng were of no better quality and in any case did not reach him in time. Nevertheless, although Galway was painfully aware of his weakness, he decided that the lesser evil was to risk an advance and at a Council of War held on 24 April his colleagues agreed with him.[1]

The upshot was the disaster of Almanza, in which the allied cavalry were driven from the field and the infantry after some hard fighting were decimated. Galway and Minas escaped with some 3,000 men, but the remainder of the army of about 11,000 infantry and 4,500 cavalry were killed, wounded or taken prisoners. It was a disaster of the first magnitude, for which the English and Dutch roundly blamed the Portuguese. This was not altogether just. Their cavalry were outflanked and routed, but they suffered some casualties, and the infantry took their part at the outset, though they were no match for trained and well-equipped troops in an open field. The magnitude of the defeat was so stunning that there were no objective accounts. Colonel

[1] Tindal, *Continuation of Rapin's History of England* (1745), IV, ii, 7; Stowe MS 474, fos. 10, 14, 18; Add. MSS 20818, fo. 72.

Richards, who might have written one, was at Alicante and could only confirm to Godolphin the undiluted badness of the news. Even in Lisbon few details were received.

King Charles in his first mortification accused both Galway and Minas of running away, but the Whigs were strong enough to defend Galway, who later in 1711 weathered a full parliamentary inquiry. He was retained in Spain until February, when he left to take up the appointment of ambassador in Lisbon, embarking with him the marquis of Minas and 1,200 Portuguese survivors of Almanza. A body of cavalry under the younger count of Atalaya remained to serve under Stanhope and in one or two actions to vindicate the credit of Portuguese arms.[1]

Paul Methuen in the meanwhile was trying to make the Portuguese cede the supreme command and agree to direct payment of their subsidised troops by the Allies. He made no headway and reported that the Portuguese situation was hopeless without a complete reorganisation. The fortresses taken from Spain were all recaptured, and in December 1707 Paul thought that Portugal was exhausted and would be conquered or forced to submit unless the war was won for them in Catalonia. He continued, however, to believe that the use of Lisbon harbour was indispensable, though after the capture of Gibraltar, and in 1708 of Port Mahon, this was disputable. Sunderland thought that Portugal was out of the war and the offensive alliance might well be turned into a defensive one.[2]

Nevertheless, in November 1707 the Portuguese made a serious effort to reform their army. A royal decree abolished the feudal organisation by provinces, and increased the establishment

---

[1] For contemporary accounts see A. de C. de Castelo Branco, Comentarios, pp. 110 ff.; Add. MSS 20818, fos. 73–7; Agostino Umicalia, Memorie Istoriche de la Guerra, 1701–13 (Venezia, 1736), 446–50; Soares da Silva, 'Memorias, 1701–15', Gaçeta em Forma de Carta, p. 106; Coimbra MS 3008, fos. 244, 248; Stowe MS 474, fo. 29; Berwick, Memoirs, I, 486; Agnew, Henri Massue de Ruvigny, Earl of Galway, 113–18, 152–80.

[2] Klopp, op. cit., XII, 287. Voltes Bou, El Archiduque Carlos de Austria, pp. 135, 206, 219, 235; Bodleian Add. MS D 23, fo. 69, Paul Methuen to Bishop of Salisbury; S.P. 104/208, Sunderland to Paul Methuen, 22 July 1707.

of officers and the pay of officers and men. It also laid down scales of rations and equipment. But in 1709 an allied report stated that the Portuguese would starve if the allies did not give them corn, and had no clothes but what the allies bought them. The marquis of Fronteira, the commander of the Portuguese forces, was quoted as saying that captains of horse sold their shirts to buy bread, and the soldiers died of hunger, while the horses, if they were not sent away to Lisbon, would die too for want of forage. As Rivers said of him in Spain, the Portuguese soldier had often little choice between desertion, starvation or living on plunder. As for the reforms, they sounded good on paper, but they had little effect.[1]

Paul Methuen remained as ambassador in Lisbon throughout the disastrous year of 1707 and for some months after Galway's arrival. He did not leave until August 1708. The records for the period are scanty and Paul's activities can only be gleaned from Sunderland's despatches to him and from a few letters. No one except Galway or Paul Methuen was considered capable of taking on the awkward mission to Portugal or showed any inclination to do so. Ministers insisted on Paul accepting the Lisbon Embassy, but showed no disposition to offer him any of the more congenial posts which fell vacant, such as the Legation at The Hague or a commissionership of trade.[2] Sunderland, however, treated him with consideration and commended warmly all he did. The tale of disasters continued and when in August 1707 the long-desired attack on Toulon took place, even the magic of Prince Eugène failed to work. In spite of the exceptionally good co-operation given by Admiral Shovell the siege ended in mutual recriminations and withdrawal, though not entirely without result, for the French had sunk fifty of their own ships in the harbour. Shovell sailed homewards to be drowned in a shipwreck in the Scillies; the Dutch were tired of the war, and thwarted Marlborough in

[1] Soares da Silva, *op. cit.* pp. 127–33; S.P. 89/88, fo. 55: discourses of affairs of Portugal, c. 1709.
[2] Bodleian Add. MS D 23, fos. 69–70.

Flanders and diminished their contribution in the Peninsula; the war was still to bring some victories to the allies, but the interest in England for it was waning, and the position of Marlborough, the great artificer of its strategy, was being sapped.

It was now that Paul Methuen left Lisbon and ended the sixteen-year Methuen tenure of the Lisbon mission. As an obscure young man he had stepped into his father's shoes in 1696, and again in 1703, when he concluded the treaties. He did so again in 1707, and then in a reluctant way, for poor health and other interests exceeded his ambition. He proceeded to the top, after which he receded gradually into private life, except for his membership of Parliament. In Lisbon his embassy was a disappointing time, and though he mixed well with the Portuguese he did not share the uncommon sympathy for and understanding of Portugal of his father. But he achieved a reputation and had talents which perhaps surpassed those of his father. Soares da Silva described Paul's departure in the following curious passage:

'Queen Anne has been graciously pleased to make the great Paul Archbishop of Canterbury. What do you say to that? After all, his learning and his virtues thoroughly deserve it and will be the great and august glory of the Anglican Religion. His place as ambassador to this Court will be taken by Galway, who will be a very suitable successor to the old rogue Don John Methuen.' This irony was the equivalent of a cartoon in a modern newspaper and should be taken in the same way. It reflects the disgust felt about the war and towards the men who had conducted it. Da Silva may have been thinking of the efforts which English representatives in Portugal and Spain were making to obtain recognition for the chaplains of the English Factories and for freedom of Anglican worship. The subject aroused great public interest and was worked up for propaganda purposes by the French. Da Silva quoted in January a manifesto of King Charles denying that he had made over some churches for their heretical devotions.[1] To understand, however, the reference to the arch-bishop of Canterbury one must realise that he was not a solemn and venerable character to the Portuguese, but a figure of fun; they could not get over the fact that he had a wife or believe that he stopped at one; he was a symbol of the lubricity which all men love to attribute to foreigners. A few years later Lord Tirawley, another ambassador to Lisbon, earned a similar sobriquet and great popularity by keeping a harem and falling easily into the role that was expected of him.

[1] Soares da Silva, *op. cit.* pp. 96, 147.

CHAPTER 15

EPILOGUE

AFTER the departure of the Methuens Portugal's share in the war diminished. Paul on reaching England took his father's seat as member for Devizes. There was keen competition for it. A letter in 1705 remarked that it would be very hard to oust Methuen, as the Low Church party was supported by Wharton and Sunderland and many justices of the peace. The writer spoke of an expenditure of £5,000 since the last election and said that if an offer of £500 were made for the vote of a Common Councilman, Methuen's agent Diston would cap it with £1,000.[1] Nevertheless, Paul was accused of corruption in 1711 and disqualified. He was disgusted by this treatment and stayed out of Parliament until 1714, when he was elected the member for Brackley. He held this seat until 1747 and never sat again for Devizes, though his agent Diston did so. He was not therefore in the House of Commons in 1713, when the fate of the Methuen treaty was decided, and it was left to his old friend James Stanhope to speak up for it. Most of the time he lived in semi-retirement at Bishops Cannings, but his poverty must have been relative, for as a hobby he kept a stable of fine Spanish horses. He also renewed the lease of the estate and at some stage acquired the freehold. He punctually discharged the obligations of his father's will and had already written in 1707 from Lisbon to ask James Milner to pay Sarah Earle and Ann Browne their legacies, as he thought they might need the money. Their signed receipts survive and must serve as their monument, for no more is heard of them.[2]

It is a tribute to Paul Methuen's reputation that, while his father's name was under something of a cloud, he continued to be offered

[1] *HMC Portland*, 2nd ser., IV, 178.   [2] The receipts are at Corsham Court.

posts of importance, though never those which he fancied. Although he had been abroad so long, he took his place in the inner circles of society and, from references in the duchess of Marlborough's correspondence, was clearly regarded as a man of note. He reluctantly served as a lord of the Admiralty from November 1709 to December 1710, but he refused a request from Robert Harley to accept a mission to Holland to arrange the Dutch naval quota for the year, and also a special request from the queen to go to Milan to arbitrate between his old friends the duke of Savoy and the new Emperor Charles. But he continued to rank as a leading Whig and was included with Sunderland and Wharton in Steele's dedication of the bound volume of the *Spectator*. After the queen's death and the Whig return to power he was made a lord of the Treasury and given in 1715 the appointment of ambassador to Spain, to which his father had aspired.[1]

In spite of a vein of pessimism and many complaints of ill health Paul Methuen took his public duties in his stride. His letters give the impression of a businesslike and methodical man with a sincere love of his country, courage and tenacity in refusing to be put upon, and a good deal of humanity. But there was another side to his personality, of which his letters give little indication. He was a great poseur, dilettante and lady's man. His adventures abroad were not allowed to lose anything in the telling and he liked to be thought a past master in gallantry. He had charm and ability and this did him no harm. Lord Rivers thought the better of him for it and it was no bad thing to be thought a gay dog by the duchess of Marlborough, and perhaps even by Queen Anne. All the same, some of the great ladies of society spotted that his demeanour was a little exaggerated and un-English and did not spare him the acid of their tongues. Lady Mary Wortley Montagu laughed at his flirtation with Madame Kilmansegg, the blonde fat

[1] Marlborough, *Correspondence with the Duchess of Marlborough* (1838), pp 258, 390; MS letters from Shrewsbury and Harley at Corsham Court; Peter Smithers, *Life of Joseph Addison* (Oxford, 1954), p. 247.

347

favourite of King George I.[1] 'Lord Halifax [Charles Montagu] wished to secure Madame Kilmansegg's favour and thought himself in a fine road to the Lord Treasurer's staff by furnishing her with money and a lover. Mr Methuen was the man he picked for the purpose. He was one of the Lords of the Treasury. He was handsome and well-made; he had wit enough to affect any part he pleased and a romantic turn in his conversation that could entertain a lady with as many adventures as Othello, and it was no ill way of gaining Desdemona. Women are very apt to take their lovers' characters from their own mouths; and if you will believe Mr Methuen's own account of himself, neither Artamenes nor Orondates ever had more valour, honour, constancy and discretion. Half of these bright qualities were enough to charm Madame Kilmansegg; and they were soon in the strictest familiarity, which continued for different reasons to the pleasure of both parties till the arrival of Madame Schulemberg, which was hastened by the German ministers, who envied the money accumulated by Madame Kilmansegg.'[1]

Paul Methuen was sent by the new secretary of state, James Stanhope, on a special mission to conclude a new treaty with Spain. Stanhope had himself concluded an advantageous treaty in 1708 but this of course had lapsed. Paul was instructed that the preservation of commerce with Spain was one of the chief motives for entering into the late long and expensive war and one of the principal benefits expected from the conclusion of peace. It was of the greatest importance to the interests of Britain and to the riches of her dominions.[2]

Paul stayed four months in Madrid, but although he was received politely he made no progress, and the reply to his memorandum, when eventually it came, was unsatisfactory. Meanwhile he had fallen seriously ill, so he was glad of an excuse to return home, which he did by way of Lisbon. He was received

[1] Lady Mary Wortley Montagu, *Letters* (1861), I, 132.
[2] Egerton MS 2170, fos. 11, 31, 45.

with great honours there and took part in a curious incident, in which he helped in the search for the king's schoolboy brother, Prince Manoel, who had run away to sea on an English ship. He arrived home again in the first days of December 1715.[1]

Stanhope had already in October sent an ultimatum to Cardinal del Giudice, but this was rendered unnecessary by a complete change which took place in the government at Madrid. The news of the death of King Louis XIV reached Madrid on the day of Paul Methuen's departure; the duke of Orleans, now regent, was inclined to discourage the Jacobites, and Alberoni, who at the same moment came to power in Madrid, decided to conciliate England and Holland. It happened also that Alberoni was an old crony of Stanhope, who made no difficulty about assisting good relations by the remittance of a handsome present. Bubb Dodding-ton, whom Paul had left in charge, found himself on 14 December the signatory of a commercial treaty which gave almost all that Paul Methuen had asked. This was followed by another satisfactory agreement about the Asiento or Slave Trade. The treaties seemed a triumph and although Paul Methuen had little to do with them, except in so far as he had taken the trouble to cultivate Alberoni, he was connected with them in the public estimation and received a good deal of credit. Unfortunately the great expectations aroused by the treaties were disappointed: they were poorly observed and relations with Spain improved for only a short time; and after a promising beginning Stanhope's hopes of achieving a general settlement of Europe were frustrated.[2]

Although his mission had been a failure and his health jeopardised Paul Methuen was at the zenith of his personal prestige. Lord Orford was in great concern about his health and the duchess of Marlborough thought he had not been so fond of his journey to

---

[1] *Ibid.* fos. 273, 328, 331, 334; S.P. 94/84, 27 Sept., 16 Nov. 1715.

[2] Add. MSS 15936, fos. 26, 28; Egerton MS 2170, fos. 171, 185–212, 273, 328, 331, 334; S.P. 94/84, 29 July, 1, 6 Sept., 11 Dec. 1715; McLachlan, *Trade and Peace with Old Spain* (Cambridge, 1940), pp. 67–77; S. Harcourt-Smith, *Alberoni* (1943), p. 117; Davenport, *European Treaties*, III, 254.

Spain as to deprive her of the hope of seeing him soon at Blenheim. In July 1716, when Stanhope went abroad, he made Paul
acting secretary of state in charge of the Southern department instead of leaving the Northern secretary, Townshend, in charge, as
was the usual practice. Stanhope, upon returning in December,
took over the Northern department from Townshend, and Paul
became Southern secretary. He found the work too taxing for his
health and was soon asking to be relieved, but he carried on until
April 1717, when he left the government with Robert Walpole.
For a few months he was corresponding with Lisbon about the
old familiar subjects. Children had been kidnapped, the Portuguese forts had fired on a British ship by mistake, and the Brazil
fleet urgently required a convoy.[1]

While Paul was in office, it was rumoured that the king might
retire to Hanover, leaving the Prince of Wales as regent and Paul
Methuen as secretary of state. Nothing came of this and after
resigning his lordship of the Treasury Paul held no further post
until 1720, when Walpole returned to office and appointed him
comptroller of the Royal Household. In 1725 he exchanged this
office for that of treasurer of the Royal Household and was made
a Knight of the revived Order of the Bath. He resigned his office
of Treasurer in 1730 and held no further post though he continued
to be a well known figure in the House of Commons, and as late
as 1741 scored a notable success when he secured the election of
his friend Lee as chairman of Committees by a majority of three
over Walpole's candidate. This was regarded as the beginning of
Walpole's fall. Two hundred and forty-two members voted for
Lee and 238 against, which Horace Walpole described as the
greatest number which ever lost a question.[2]

Paul Methuen had lost two of his oldest friends with the deaths
of Stanhope and Sunderland, and he fell out with Walpole. His

[1] S.P. 94/84, 27 Sept., 16 Nov. 1715; Egerton MS 2170, fo. 23; Mark A. Thomson,
Secretaries of State (Oxford, 1932), p. 122, fo. 23; Add. MSS 15836, fos. 81, 96, 99, 104.
[2] *HMC Polwarth*, I, 367. Basil Williams, *James Stanhope, 1st Earl Stanhope*, p. 237;
Horace Walpole, *Letters*, I, 100.

association with the Prince of Wales, and afterwards with the princess dowager, kept him permanently in Opposition, but there is no reason to believe that he ever had Jacobite sympathies. In Parliament in the reign of George I he was regarded as the first of their enemies.[1]

In his old age Paul Methuen grumbled about the shortness of his public career but in reality he set much store by his social success, which began on his return to England and was kept up well into old age. He was a member of the Hanover Club, an exclusive offshoot of the Kit Cat, which numbered Addison and Steele among its members. The animadversions of Swift and of Charles Montagu, Lord Halifax, on his father were no bar to his friendship with them and Voltaire accorded him a flattering reference in his description of the siege of Turin. Gay, in an epistle to Pope, spoke of 'Methuen of sincerest mind, as Arthur grave, as soft as womankind'. Steele dedicated the seventh volume of the *Spectator* to him and praised his part as an ambassador in promoting commerce and his military renown in Savoy. He also referred to his graceful address in horsemanship, the use of the sword and dancing, and his genial hospitality. Only Horace Walpole, who never forgave anyone who opposed his father, lost no chance to sneer. He admitted that Paul had won a reputation as the first gentleman of his age, but argued that this was false, and that he was a *poseur*, a braggart and sordidly penurious. Paul had been rude to Lord Chesterfield over a game of billiards and told many tall stories about his hunting lions in Africa and his gallantries. Walpole's best story was of his behaviour with Queen Caroline. When the king was in Hanover, the Walpoles often had the queen to dinner in Chelsea and invited Paul to come in afterwards for a game of cards. The queen enjoyed his company and used to tease him about his passion for reading romances, the whodunits of the day. One evening he told her that he was sick and tired of romances and was now reading a silly thing. When the queen

[1] *HMC Stuart*, VII, 567.

pressed him to know what it was, he replied, 'A history of the Kings and Queens of England.' Walpole gave this as an instance of his coarseness of nature, but it seems more likely that he had become politically obnoxious and Walpole found it a good excuse for taking offence.[1]

Paul always liked to pose as a great beau and Horace Walpole could still make a jocular reference to it in 1743, when he had passed his seventieth year. In spite of his sociable habits Paul was something of a dark horse like his father but he seems to have been kind-hearted. He was on affectionate terms with his mother, who seems to have been rather a difficult woman, though it is only through him that we get any indication of what she was like. When she died at Chelsea in 1723 she left a number of small legacies to her dependants and friends. Paul doubled the amounts, saying he had often tried to persuade her to be more generous without success. He showed his generosity by making provision for the Woodcock girls, the five orphaned granddaughters of his sister Mary, and in his will gave legacies to a number of old friends. He died in 1757 at the age of eighty-five, and nearly fifty years had passed since he left Portugal, but the Lisbon memories were still strong. Several beneficiaries dated from those days or were descendants of his father's friends.

Sir Paul was said to have left over a quarter of a million pounds and the story persisted that his fortune included bags of Portuguese gold and that £50,000 in specie was found in his house. This may have been an invention or an exaggeration, and there is no mention of such treasure in the careful inventory which Paul made of his property before his death. He did, however, leave a balance of £60,000 or £70,000 in the Bank of England, and his London house in Grosvenor Square contained many valuable pictures and much furniture. As Sir Paul never married, his heir was his cousin

[1] Swift, *Journal to Stella*, 2 Oct. 1710; Voltaire, *Œuvres complètes*, XXI, 13–14; Horace Walpole's 'Notes on Dr Maty's Memoirs of Chesterfield', *Philobiblon Society*, II, 7, and Horace Walpole, *Letters*, I, 284.

Paul Methuen of Bradford-on-Avon, for whom he bought Corsham Court, in which to place his collection of pictures.[1]

Whatever the precise value or nature of his fortune, Sir Paul Methuen died rich and famous. The commercial treaty and the work for trade of John Methuen, which at the time had been regarded by the government as secondary to political work and the co-ordination of the war effort, were now all that was remembered. Moreover, it was almost forgotten that it was John, and not Sir Paul, who was responsible. The name of Methuen was indissolubly linked with port-wine, which from being the drink of the Whigs had become a national symbol, and as early as the 1730s could be described by a Portuguese geographer as the generous wine of the Douro, the ambrosia of the north.[2] Port was already rising in social status, though it was still principally a favourite of the clergy and of the rising middle class; the best people drank champagne and burgundy, and if they took Portuguese wine, preferred Lisbon at the high table. John Methuen himself is not known to have drunk port-wine, and the wine named Methuen after him was a Lisbon red. Sir Benjamin Keane, who was proud of his taste in wines, ordered a cellarful of port for his brother, the head of a Cambridge college and a budding bishop; as a native of King's Lynn, which had a flourishing trade in port-wines, he must have been familiar with port, but for his Embassy in Madrid he always ordered his favourite Lisbon Carcavelos, though the Upper Douro was nearer to Madrid than Lisbon. But the decade 1720–30 had been boom years for the export of wine from Oporto, and by 1720 the addition of brandy to the wine during fermentation had become a general practice. This was the principal characteristic which distinguished port-wine, so the wine of Sir Paul's mature and later years can be regarded as true port, though the development of the choicest vintage wines was yet to be discovered. In the 1750s indeed much

---

[1] This information is derived from papers at Corsham Court.
[2] António de Oliveira Freire, *Descripção de Portugal* (1739), p. 22.

port was the heavy turbid liquor with a strong bitter taste which Dr Johnson could stomach, but Boswell could not; there is no doubt that the suppression of French wines from common use and the enormous increase in the consumption of spirits debased for several generations the people's taste. But good port was slowly being developed, and at the banquets of the lord mayor and of the livery companies it was served in royal quantities. Some of the wine followed the example of Madeira and made the voyage to America and returned improved. The name of Methuen crossed the seas, too, and the governor of Massachusetts, George Dummer, chose the name of Methuen for a new town on the borders of his state and of New Hampshire. Methuen is now a city of 25,000 inhabitants.

In conclusion it is fitting to quote the honourable amends which Charles Montagu, Lord Halifax, made to the name of John Methuen in the debate on trade with Portugal in the House of Lords in 1713. The version quoted of his remarks was included in the preface to the collected edition of the *British Merchant* dedicated to Sir Paul and reads:

Your father, often Ambassador Extraordinary to the King of Portugal procured for Great Britain the glorious Treaty of Commerce, by which she gains a Million a Year.

By this Treaty we paid our Armies in Spain and Portugal, and drew from there in the late War considerable sums for our Troops in other Parts, without remitting one farthing from England, and at the same time coined in the Tower above a million of Portugal gold in three years.

By this Treaty we gain a greater balance from Portugal only than from any other Country whatsoever; and at this time it is the only Country, from which we have any bullion worth the naming.

By this Treaty we have increased our Exports thither about £300,000 a Year to near a Million and a half.

And such was the address of this great Man, at that critical Time, when the Ministry of Portugal were extremely in the interest of France, and great projects were forming in favour of the French Trade to the disadvantage of ours, that he carried this Treaty by his personal interest with the King, with whom alone he transacted it, whose chief Minister knew nothing of it until he had orders to sign it; or if he did, he durst neither own it nor oppose it. And what is yet more surprising we did not so much as give any Equivalent (but what Portugal was possessed of before) for all these advantages, as is evident from the following volumes.

The *British Merchant* declares that he deserves to have his Statue erected in every Trading Town in Great Britain, and it is with but common justice he does so; for while his great Abilities did not only enrich his Country, whilst he lived, but left us a most valuable inheritance behind him, and we reap the Fruits of his Wisdom and Love to his Country at this Hour.[1]

[1] *British Merchant*, ed. Charles King (1721), vol. 3, Dedication.

BALLAD AGAINST METHUEN TO THE TUNE OF 'LILLIBULLERO'[1]

Two opposite Parties divided the House,
What the one would have done, the other would spoil,
There is likewise a third not worth a louse,
Shadow and substance, Molesworth and Moyle,
Methwin, Methwin, Chancellor Methwin,
Shadow and substance, Molesworth and Moyle.

With his reason as clear as his countenance is,
Chancellor Methwin, Molesworth and Moyle,
With the mouth of an ass and a conjurer's fiz,
Shadow and substance, Molesworth and Moyle,
Methwin, Methwin, Conjurer Methwin,
Shadow and substance, Molesworth and Moyle.

From selling of Ireland and playing of tricks,
Shadow and substance, Molesworth and Moyle,
The Doctor's reduced to mending of pricks,
Mountebank Methwin, Molesworth and Moyle,
Methwin, Methwin, Culpepper Methwin,
Shadow and substance, Molesworth and Moyle.

He committed his son to the Jesuits' care,
Protestant Methwin, Molesworth and Moyle,
For fear he should want a Protestant heir,
Protestant Methwin, Molesworth and Moyle,
Methwin, Methwin, Protestant Methwin,
Shadow and substance, Molesworth and Moyle.

[1] In S.P. 32/11, fos. 76–77.

There is no man can say, but he speaks as a friend,
Pollitick Methwin, Molesworth and Moyle,
When he gave us the grants to begin at each end,
Pollitick Methwin, Molesworth and Moyle,
Methwin, Methwin, Chancellor Methwin,
Shadow and substance, Molesworth and Moyle.

The doctors by opening his fundament,
Chancellor Methwin, Molesworth and Moyle,
Made him write for a Portugal resident,
To show it was not done in a heat,
He has left him at Lisbon to make him compleat,
Methwin, Methwin, Chancellor Methwin,
Shadow and substance, Molesworth and Moyle.

To secure the church to be of his side,
He has made Toland his spiritual guide,
So in England as Ireland there are Parties three,
The spiritual, temporal, Toland and he,
Spiritual Methuen, Molesworth and Moyle,
Methwin, Methwin, Chancellor Methwin,
Shadow and substance, Molesworth and Moyle.

EXPLANATION ATTACHED TO BALLAD

When the Act for the resumption of grants was first proposed in the
House, Chancellor Methwin was much for it, but would begin with
the grants of Charles II. Sir William Culpepper meeting him at the
Blew Posts and being a stranger to him asked of a Gentleman, who was
in the company, who he was, and the Gentleman whispered that he
was a great Doctor lately come from Portugal and had learned to speak
English pretty well and had great skill of a Clapp, upon which Sir
William being much indisposed that way, the first opportunity took
him aside in a corner of the room and offered to retain him. The
Chancellor said he had given up all his practice, nor would he be
retained in any case; then he pressed him, that tho' he did not generally
practise, he might in this case give his opinion and then the Chancellor
asking to know his case, he told him that he had lately been fluxed for

the clapp and was still very ill and wanted his assistance, at which His Lordship was very angry and the company hearing the jest was very well pleased. Thirdly Toland is the person who has lately set up a new sect of religion beyond the Socinians and was a great favourite of the Chancellor and was carried with him into Ireland to be His Lordship's Secretary but then by order of the House of Commons was committed and had his books burned by the Hangman and is now in great disgrace but still in favour with his Lordship.

PORTUGUESE CURRENCY

In the time of the Methuens Portugal was only beginning to get her own gold from Brazil and was still dependent on Spanish sources for gold and silver bullion. The principal gold coin was the moeda or moidore, which was minted in Portugal and in Brazil and was worth 4,800 reis, on the average about 28s. The term moeda was not, however, often used for reckoning; the denominations most customary were milreis, cruzados, patacas, and Spanish pesos or dollars or douros, and these were indiscriminately employed. The cruzado or crown of 400 reis (2s. 6d.) was a silver coin minted both in Brazil and Portugal, but cannot have been common about 1700, as John Colbatch did not know of it as a coin. The commonest silver coin was the pataca or Portuguese dollar, minted in Brazil, which was worth 320 reis or 2s. and, as it happened, was almost equal to the Dutch guilder. It is not to be confused with the pattacoon, a much larger denomination used in Amsterdam and worth in 1705 £2. 8s. 0d. in bank drafts or £2. 16s. 0d. in specie. Commoner still was the Spanish peso or dollar or piece of eight worth 750 reis or about 4s. 9d. For cash payments it was necessary to reckon in denominations for which coins were available, but large sums were usually calculated in milreis (1,000 reis), for which there was no corresponding coin. The milreis was normally worth 5s. 9d., though it occasionally rose to 6s. or more and in 1696 during the English currency crisis John Methuen once had to pay as much as 7s. 6d. The average fluctuated between 5s. 2d. in 1708 and 6s. 1d. in 1700. The exchange was subject to seasonal variations occasioned by the vintage and the arrival or non-arrival of the Brazil fleet and moved in favour of Portugal before and during the first years of the War of the Spanish Succession and against her in the later years of the war. Methuen dealt mostly in pieces of eight and cruzados, but the subsidies payable under his treaties were payable in patacas except for the cost of the horses to be provided by King Pedro at Allied expense, which were reckoned in milreis.

The rates of exchange in Methuen's time can best be gleaned from casual references to actual transactions in his despatches and in the Calendars of Treasury Books. Professor C. R. Boxer gives a good table of Portuguese money, weights and measures in his *Golden Age of Brazil* (University of California, 1962), appendix VII, and much information is to be found in H. E. W. Fisher's thesis (London, 1962), 'Anglo–Portuguese Trade, 1700–70'.

APPENDIX 3

SOME STATISTICS OF THE ENGLISH CLOTH AND WINE TRADE WITH PORTUGAL AT THE TIME OF THE METHUEN TREATY[1]

EXPORTS OF WOOLLENS

	1701	1702	1703	1704	1705	1706	1707
		(In pieces)					
Double bays	8,401	15,937	12,812	8,650	8,292	412	9,155
Single bays	80	147	578	421	329	468	176
Minikin bays	5,728	8,117	10,764	10,247	11,676	94	9,513
Broad cloth	4	20	29	70	163	327	399
Long cloth	129	153	274	2,292	5,129	2,935	1,658
Short cloth	207	244	661	5,658	3,476	1,981	657
Spanish cloth	107	113	486	3,005	3,647	2,386	876
Kerseys	31	24	224	555	833	599	216
Double northern	—	6	34	285	2,090	1,591	479
Single northern	—	15	—	—	180	28	2
		(In pounds)					
Woollen cloths	—	—	2,220	—	—	—	—
Cloth remnants	1,289	280	2,769	2,082	5,047	520	2,966
		(In goads of 4½ ft length, and pieces)					
Cottons, plains and Welsh plains	953g	2,140g	2,964g	1p	30p	1,218g	966g
Northern cottons	1,550g	—	2,940g	4,200g and 70p	1,907g and 175p	10,146g	4,918g
		(In yards)					
Flannel	538	320	5,706	1,426	217	808	350
Frieze	300	159	380	6,280	1,706	2,608	600

[1] As compiled by Charles Davenant in 1707–8: P.R.O., M.A.F. 7/1, fos. 29–31 and 74–8.

EXPORTS OF WOOLLENS (*cont.*)

	1701	1702	1703	1704	1705	1706	1707
(In pounds)							
Perpetuanas	352,245	592,604	754,503	749,825	790,849	840,248	582,900
Says	26,920	76,889	61,598	66,701	60,477	69,910	49,816
Stuffs	147,496	244,707	278,037	93,656	283,257	273,235	207,304
Stuffs with silk	476	—	366	10	226	433	20
(By number)							
Rugs and Irish rugs	12	22	21	6	—	—	329
(In dozens)							
Woollen stockings							
Men's	4,434	5,043	14,728	23,144	21,082	6,968	6,051
Women's	93	84	2,534	2,562	330	937	232
Children's	1,309	1,511	4,534	3,366	3,528	1,929	1,969
Worsted stockings							
Men's	7,554	12,329	19,072	20,834	26,377	20,489	15,617
Women's	15	48	237	20	20	264	118
Children's	318	485	1,238	481	236	185	231

EXPORTS OF OTHER PRODUCTS SUBJECT TO THE PRAGMATICAL DECREES

	1701	1702	1703	1704	1705	1706	1707
(In dozens)							
Carolina hats	—	9	4	7	3	18	—
Felt hats	53	61	164	237	62	72	1,198
Beaver and castor hats	746	921	2,130	1,624	1,620	2,148	2,003
(In pounds)							
Gold and silver lace	69	46	151	53	195	129	79
Thrown silk	32	50	110	82	20	34	61
Wrought silk	5,298	3,151	4,780	4,671	4,719	5,843	4,563

EXPORTS OF FOODSTUFFS

	1701	1702	1703	1704	1705	1706	1707
(By number or in tons)							
Biscuits (tons)	1,940	1,050	19,466	7,237	5,904	6,902	—
Bread (tons)	10	55	1,243	214	—	—	11,029
Cod, ling and hake	—	18t	6,581	2½t	146t	296t	—
Sizable cod, ling and hake	104,660	14,860	57,050	43,661	73t	49t	53,832
Undersize cod, ling and hake	4,300	12,620	14,700	4,640	—	35t	5,000
Newfoundland cod, ling and hake							
Wet	—	—	5,000t	—	—	—	—
Dry	—	—	1,814t	—	—	—	208t

EXPORTS OF FOODSTUFFS (*cont.*)

	1701	1702	1703	1704	1705	1706	1707
		(*In barrels*)					
Red herrings	20	173	649	242	212	121	176
White herrings	62	145	30	101	63	9	45
		(*In hogsheads*)					
Pilchards	410	157	1,162	697	27t	5	2,486
		(*In firkins*)					
Butter	186	359	1,339	570	111	464	142
		(*In quarters*)					
Barley	1,500	5,596	30,399	29,678	9,199	186	1,720
Beans	115	—	1,210	24	—	—	—
Flour	37	422	1,988	1,871	2,109	3,579	2,547
Oats	—	—	1,141	29	—	—	—
Pease	68	17	828	1,509	53	23	540
Rye	1,021	2,753	27,821	19,871	3,572	1,146	3,928
Wheat	7,056	27,843	80,618	85,342	61,779	80,343	132,068

The export of grain from England ceased in the latter part of the war but was renewed from 1715 onwards. In 1731 the value was estimated to be 160,000 milreis but the import from Africa, the Levant and Italy was very much greater, 1,800,000 milreis. Butter and grain were, however, exported in considerable quantities from Ireland. The figures for butter in 1701, 1702 and 1703 were in firkins 14,729, 21,940 and 35,224 respectively (M.A.F. 7/1 and for Ireland 15/5, 6, etc.). The imports of fish from England and from the Newfoundland fisheries continued to be important and were estimated to be 50,000 tons in 1729 and as much as 80,000 tons in or about 1731 (Azevedo, *Épocas de Portugal Económico*, p. 468).

In 1731, when Anglo-Portuguese trade was at its highest, the value of woollen products exported from England according to figures quoted by Azevedo was 2,400,000 milreis. The corresponding value of imports from Holland and from France was 300,000 and 600,000 milreis respectively.

In the list of exports it is difficult to pin down any items which clearly benefited from the abrogation of the pragmatical decrees. In theory most of the new draperies and worsted fabrics including some of the bays might have come under the sumptuary laws, but much depended on the colour and appearance of the cloth and scarcely a single item seems to have been entirely prohibited before the treaty. Many articles were imported to meet the needs of the war but the increase in Spanish cloths and in perpetuanas and serges can perhaps be directly related to the Methuen treaty. The effect was to produce a general increase, which persisted after the war and was facilitated by the continuation on an enlarged base of the wine trade. The figures for the import of wine to England before and after the treaty were as follows.

	Total in Pipes	Of which from Oporto
1701	15,917	6,154
1702	12,732	3,930
1703	18,806	7,567
1704	21,326	10,078
1705	18,143	6,188
1706	9,954	5,732
1707	19,348	10,706
1708	20,689	7,419

After 1708 the average was about 15,000 pipes, rising in 1715 to 23,000–24,000 and never sinking below that level. The proportion of wine shipped at Oporto, which had not greatly exceeded the wine from Lisbon and other parts of Portugal, rose to two-thirds in 1715 and in 1725 to three-quarters. Wine accounted for five-sixths of the Portuguese export trade and was supplemented by a considerable export from Madeira and a little from the Azores. Southern fruits, dye-stuffs and a few Brazil products such as logwood and hides accounted for the rest. The trade in Brazil sugar had lapsed, though some of the best quality was still sent to England and there was an appreciable trade with the Mediterranean countries.

ADMIRAL ROOKE'S INSTRUCTIONS TO LEAVE LISBON AND SAIL TO THE MEDITERRANEAN IN MAY 1704[1]

Fo. 56. Paragraph from Rooke's open instructions. This instruction is crossed out in the original and was not observed:

You are to sail with the Fleet under your command as soon as you think it proper towards Cadiz, leaving at Lisbon and on the coast of Portugal such and such a number of ships as upon advice with the King of Portugal and his Ministers the circumstance of affaires and the Treaty of Allyance between Us and them shall require.

Fo. 57. List of agenda drawn up on the basis of Rooke's instructions.

(1) Whenever any attempt shall be made on Cadiz or Gibraltar or any port of Spain in ye Mediterranean to be assistant with your Fleet.
(2) Till there be fresh occasion, to endeavour to destroy enemy salt works at [?] Pequais and to convey arms etc to the Cevennois, if it is possible. Signals as last year. [Note: This passage is scarcely legible.]
(3) If the Duke of Savoy should send to him or he should otherwise have notice of ye French attempting Nizza, that without loss of time he immediately proceed to relief of it.
(4) To go to Palermo or Naples and assist Emperor's army and our friends there. To correspond with the commander of the imperial armies and with our Ministers at Turin and Florence.
(5) Reparation for Plowman. [Note: Plowman was a merchant who had a claim arising from losses at Florence.]
(6) To destroy the French in the Adriatic and to view Buccari, and leave ships there, if judged needful and proper.

[1] S.P. 46/67, fos. 56-8.

(7) To encourage the Algerines to break with France.

(8) To destroy the French in any ports of Venice.

(9) To take all Italians and treat as Prisoners of War, which are on board any French vessel of war, and require of their Masters a prohibition of such service.

(10) To prevent the French from joyning their Fleet and if the Toulon Fleet endeavours to come out of the Straits, to follow it and to destroy Toulon.

Fo. 58. Admiral Rooke's secret instructions:

Whereas there are some Services of the greatest importance which we have thought fit to commit to your care and conduct and wherein We cannot hope for any success without all possibly secrecy, We do therefore signify to you Our Intentions therein by these private Instructions and would have you, notwithstanding what is contained in Our other Instructions apply yourself in the first place to the execution of these Services.

You are already acquainted by the Earl of Nottingham, pursuant to Our command, with the resolution We have taken to attempt Toulon, with the Duke of Savoy's readiness to concurre therein, and with the Orders we have sent to Our Envoys Extraordinary in that Court to concert the proper methods of executing this designe. We need therefore only add that you will receive upon your arrival in the Mediterranean an account from Our said Envoy, of what shall have been concerted and resolved by him with the said Duke, or otherwise you may send to Nizza or Villafranca some light frigate for advice from him, and upon notice from him of the resolutions taken you are to cooperate with the Fleet under your command in the execution of them.

In order hereunto you will receive from our own office a Plan and Description of that Port and if you should have any opportunity to get any further or later description of it, you must be sure to do it in such a manner as may not give the least Ombrage or Jealousy of this designe, whereof you must not take the least notice to the Ministers of Portugal or any other person whatsoever till you shall think it altogether safe and necessary to consult about the execution of it at a Council of War.

You must therefore spend no more time in alarming the coast of Spain pursuant to Our other Instructions, than what may be necessary to cover the designe without losing the opportunity of effecting it, or meeting the Duke of Savoy's Forces at the time and place appointed, if they should march by land.

This being the first and principal thing We leave it to you to execute what follows in these Instructions in such manner and at such time as you shall judge consistent with it, giving still this attempt on Toulon the preference, excepting ye relief of Nizza, if that should be attempted by the French, as you were directed by our Instructions dated March 14th, and excepting the following of the Toulon squadron, in case they pass the straits, which in respect of Our own safety and the safety of Our Dominions must be your principal care pursuant to the last article of our other instructions.

BIBLIOGRAPHY

MANUSCRIPT SOURCES

State Papers (Foreign)   *Public Record Office*

Portugal
S.P. 89/16 to 20. Lisbon correspondence between 1684 and 1710.
S.P. 89/88. Miscellaneous Lisbon letters, 1703–12.

Holland
S.P. 84/222. Lord Dursley's letters from The Hague.
S.P. 84/224/8. Letters of Alexander Stanhope and James Dayrolles from The Hague, 1701–6.

Empire
S.P. 80/17 to 21. Letters of George Stepney from Vienna, 1702–3.
S.P. 105/66 to 70. Vienna archives, 1702–3.

Spain
S.P. 94/74 and 75. Madrid letters, 1696–1707.
S.P. 94/84. Letters of Paul Methuen and Bubb Doddington, 1715–16.

Foreign Ministers in England
Portugal
S.P. 100/37, 1684–1710.

Germany
S.P. 100/10, 1690–1723.

Royal Letters
S.P. 102/44, 1690–1745.

Secretary of State's Letter Books
Portugal
S.P. 104/108 and 9. Sir Charles Hedges, 1704–6.
S.P. 104/195/198. Miscellaneous letters to Portugal and Spain, 1695–1701.
S.P. 104/208. Earl of Sunderland, 1707–8.

Holland
S.P. 104/69 to 72. Letters to The Hague, 1689–1706.

BIBLIOGRAPHY

State Papers (Domestic)

Naval

S.P. 42/6 and 7. Secretary of Admiralty's letters, etc.

S.P. 42/67. Admiralty Orders, 1703–6.
Memorandum of Oporto merchants, 1706, etc.

Admiralty Papers

Adm 1/4088/9. Letters from secretaries of state to the council.
Adm 3/17 to 20. Naval papers, board minutes, etc., 1702–5.
Adm 1/376. Naval papers, admirals' letters, etc., 1705–16.
Adm 1/48, 5/4011, 5/4184. Log books of the *Antelope, Gloucester, Expedition*.

Colonial Office Papers

C.O. 388 series. Board of Trade correspondence.
C.O. 389 series. Entry book, petitions of merchants, etc.
C.O. 390 series. Miscellaneous commercial papers.
C.O. 91/1. Gibraltar. Mostly later papers but contains a few earlier papers from 1705 onwards.

English Port Statistics

Statistics of commodities entering London and the outports or exported from them are to be found in the E 190 series. The London statistics are excellent until 1697, when they cease. The outport statistics are sporadic but continue into the eighteenth century.

Customs and Commercial Statistics

A summary of the woollen cloth exports is given in M.A.F. 7/1.
For the Inspector General of Customs figures see Customs 2/8, 2/9, 2/10, etc., and 3/6, 3/7, 3/8, etc.
For Irish Customs see 15/2, 15/3, etc.

State Papers (Domestic)

S.P. 32/11 contains a copy of the burlesque of *Lillibullero* about John Methuen.

Treaty Papers and Treaties

S.P. 103/66 Copy of Portuguese *asiento* agreement with Spain.
S.P. 108/341. Anglo-Dutch renewal of former treaties, 1703.
S.P. 108/389. Full powers to the Marquis de Alegrete to negotiate the Methuen commercial treaty.
S.P 108/391. Treaty of 16 May 1703 between England, Portugal and Holland.
S.P. 108/392. Treaty of 16 May 1703 between England, Portugal, Holland and the Empire and ratifications.
S.P. 108/393. Methuen commercial treaty and ratification.

Supplementary

S.P. 110/89. Lisbon Factory Report, 1715.

Private Papers loaned to P.R.O.

P.R.O. 30/15/6. Manchester papers. These contain John Methuen's draft instructions of April 1702 with emendations in his handwriting.

Sloane British Museum

2294   Account of Court of Portugal. Written in French about 1698. A large part of it has been published by Professor Prestage in a separate of Arquivo Histórico de Portugal, Lisbon, 1935.

Harleian

2264   Paul Methuen's discharge for the Lisbon accounts.

Egerton

2170   Letters of Bubb Doddington from Madrid, 1715–16.

Lansdowne

1152 A   Account of King Pedro II in 1682.

Stowe

466/7 and 8   Diaries and letters etc. of Colonel John Richards, an English Catholic Engineer officer attached to the armies of King Pedro and King Charles in Portugal and Spain, 1704–10.

Additional Manuscripts

5437/41   Naval papers 1701–6. Correspondence of the admirals with the Methuens, earl of Galway, etc.

7077   Extract from letter of an English officer to his father after capture of Madrid in 1706.

9721   Correspondence of William Blathwayt and George Stepney.

9744   Political papers and correspondence relative to Portugal, 1690–1706.

15572   Correspondence, 1692–4, of Hugh Greg, His Majesty's minister at Copenhagen.

15936   Letters from Paul Methuen as secretary of state to Henry Worsley at Lisbon.

17677 series   Copies of correspondence in French or Dutch between the Dutch Ambassadors in London and The Hague transcribed from the archives of the United Provinces: 17677, YY, 1702 and ZZ, 1703; 17677 secret, WWW, 1703–4, and XXX, 1705.

18827   Three letters from John Methuen in 1696 and other correspondence.

20817/18   Memoirs in Portuguese of Don Luis da Cunha, Portuguese Minister and then Ambassador in London, 1697–1716. They are said to have been begun in 1706 and completed in 1715.

21489   Letters from Alexander Stanhope, mostly from Madrid in 1693. Also letter from John Methuen, 1693.

21491   Letters from Paul Methuen to Blathwayt, etc., in 1701.

22908   Correspondence of Rev. John Colbatch, chaplain at Lisbon. His letter of complaint in 1696 to the bishop of Salisbury and reply has been published by the Historical Association, Lisbon Branch, *Annual Report*, II (1938), 99–140.

23726   Diary of Thomas Cox, a young English merchant staying in Lisbon, c. 1701.

28056/7   Godolphin Osborne Papers. Letters from John Methuen, etc., in 1705–6 to Godolphin.

28103   Miscellaneous letters from Methuen, Peterborough, etc., in 1704.

28905   Ellis Papers (miscellaneous foreign correspondence of John Ellis). Include letters from Alexander Stanhope at Madrid to James Vernon.

28925   Original correspondence regarding Vigo, 1702.

28946   Southwell Papers. Miscellaneous. Rooke at Cadiz. Paul Methuen's instructions in 1702. Drafts and copies, etc.

29568   Hatton Papers. Original letter describing reception of Archduke Charles in England, etc.

29588   Hatton Finch papers. Letters addressed to Nottingham in 1720.

29590   Hatton Finch Papers. John and Paul Methuen's letters and Lisbon correspondence, 1702–3.

29591   Hatton Finch Papers. Instructions, minutes, etc., 1702. Queen's orders to Admirals Rooke and Shovell.

31134   Raby Papers. Letters from Col. St Pierre to Lord Raby about the Royal Dragoons and other correspondence.

32499   Letter book of Dr John Wallis.

34335   Southwell Papers. Paul Methuen/Blathwayt correspondence, 1696/1720.

35101   Southwell Papers. Lisbon letter book of Francis Parry, 1668/80.

37991   Blathwayt/Nottingham letters, 1692–3.

37992   Register of Blathwayt correspondence, 1693–1701.

38152/3   Southwell Papers. Letters of Sir Richard Cox from Ireland, 1687 onwards.

38159   Duke of Ormonde's journal at Cadiz, 1702.

40774   Vernon Papers containing Paul Methuen/Blathwayt correspondence of 1700 and copies of a few earlier papers.

24-2

Other repositories

Bodleian Library

Rawlinson MS 423. Diary of a French merchant at Lisbon 1695–6.

Add. MSS D 23, fos. 69–70. Letter of Paul Methuen to bishop of Salisbury, 29 December 1707.

Earl of Nottingham's Letter Book, 1693. Letters from William Blathwayt. (MS at present in custody of Historical Manuscripts Commission.)

At Corsham Court

The Methuen archives are indexed alphabetically. There are not many papers from John and Paul Methuen's early days, but there are copies of the wills of John Methuen, and of his parents, Paul Methuen and Grace Andrews, and some other letters, papers and accounts.

Earl Spencer's archives at Althorp

John Methuen's letters to the Marquis of Halifax, 1693–5, as indicated in HMC Appendix to 2nd report, p. 16.

Somerset House

Last wills of John Methuen, 1706, Paul Methuen, senior, 1667, and Grace Andrews, 1700.

Bank of England

Bank account of Paul Methuen from 1720.

Hoare's Bank

Bank account of John Methuen in 1697.

Somers Papers

At Reigate Town Hall. Letters to Lord Somers of John Methuen, Sir John Rushout, etc.

Rijksarchief, The Hague

Correspondence of Johannes Woolfsen, Minister Resident of the States General at Lisbon, 1693–4, nos. 7024 and 7369.

Letters from John Methuen to Franciscus Schonenberg, Minister of the States General at Lisbon, no. 7024.

Archives of Dutch Legation at Lisbon and Schonenberg correspondence, 1702–8, nos. 7369, 7370, and 7025/6.

BIBLIOGRAPHY

University Library, Coimbra

MS 2974. Twenty-seven letters of José da Cunha Brochado, Portuguese Envoy in London, to Diogo de Mendonça Corte Real in Lisbon, 19 June to 20 August 1710.

MS 3008. 176 letters from José da Cunha Brochado, Portuguese Envoy in Paris, afterwards in Lisbon, to Luis da Cunha in London and others, 7 September 1703 to 15 March 1718.

MS 510. Copy of propaganda pamphlet distributed by Methuen.

Note on Portuguese MSS

Most of the early Portuguese archives were lost in the Lisbon earthquake and not many documents for the period 1690–1710 survive either in the ministry of Foreign Affairs, the Torre del Tumbo, or the National Library at Lisbon. Luis Teixeira de Sampayo describes the documents at the ministry of Foreign Affairs in *O Arquivo Histórico do Ministerio dos Negocios Estrangeiros* (Coimbra, 1926) and states that there are few papers there of earlier date than 1710. There are some letters from Luis da Cunha from London, but they deal almost entirely with the question of the payment of the subsidies. MS 1444 'Santo oficio at the Torre del Tumbo' is entitled 'Conferencias com os Embaixadores de Inglaterra', but is interrupted from February 1703 to October 1704, that is, during the crucial period of the negotiation of the Methuen Treaties. In an article in *O Instituto*, a periodical published at Coimbra, vol. 76, Sampayo deals carefully with the antecedents of the Methuen commercial treaty, in so far as they are touched on in the MS sources.

The unpublished memoirs of Luis da Cunha, Portuguese minister in London from 1697 onwards and afterwards one of the plenipotentiaries at Utrecht, throw a useful light on the Portuguese point of view. There is a copy in the British Museum, Add. MSS 20817 and 20818 (see p. 371).

The letters of José da Cunha Brochado, lately acquired by the library of Coimbra University, do something to fill the gap in Portuguese sources. MS 2974 contains twenty-seven letters from Da Cunha, when he was Portuguese envoy in London. They were addressed to the Portuguese foreign secretary, Diogo de Mendonça de Corte Real, between 19 June and 26 August 1710. The longer series of 176 letters in MS 3008 were written by Da Cunha between 7 January 1703 and 15 March 1718. The few earlier ones were written by him from Paris, where he was ambassador, and on his slow journey home to Lisbon by way of Holland and England. The majority are written from Lisbon and the letters are mostly addressed to Luis da Cunha, Portuguese minister in London.

MS 510 at Coimbra is an early transcript of the manifesto issued by John Methuen for distribution in Portugal at the end of 1702.

PRINTED SOURCES

Addison, Joseph. *Letters*, ed. Walter Graham. Oxford, 1941.

Ailesbury, Marquis of. *Memoirs*. Roxburghe Club, 1890.

Berwick, Duke of. *Memoirs*. 1779.

Bolingbroke, *Letters and Correspondence*, ed. Gilbert Parke. 1798.

Burchett, Josiah. *Naval Transactions*. 1720.

Cadaval. *Os manuscritos da Casa de Cadaval respeitantes ao Brasil*, ed. Virginia Rau. Lisboa, 1958.

Calendar of State Papers (Domestic Series); *Calendar of Treasury Books*.

Campagne de Guerra in Piemonte, Anon. Fratelli Bocca, Torino, 1943.

Carleton, Captain George. *Memoirs*. Oxford, 1840.

Castelo Branco, António de Couto de. *Comentarios*, ed. Gastão Mel(l)o de Mat(t)os. Coimbra, 1930.

Castro, Ferreira Borges de. *Collecção de Tratados*, vol. 2, Lisboa, 1856; and *Supplemento*, vol. 10, ed. J. Biker, Lisboa, 1873.

Chaby, General Claudio Bernardino Ferreira de. *Synopse dos decretos remetidos ao Extincto Conselho de Guerra*, vol. 3. Lisboa, 1872.

Clarendon and Rochester Correspondence, 2 vols., ed. S. W. Singer. 1828.

Cobb, Samuel. *The Portugal Expedition, 1704*. Pamphlet and poem.

Cole, Christian. *Memoirs of Affairs of State*. 1733.

Collecção de Leis Extravagantes. Coimbra, 1819.

Coxe, Archdeacon William. *Memoirs of Marlborough*. 1818.

——*Life and Administration of Sir Robert Walpole*. 1798.

——*Correspondence of the Duke of Shrewsbury*. 1821.

Cunha, José Brochado da. 'Cartas ao Conde de Viana, 1705–10', *O Instituto*, Revista Scientífica e Literaria, vols. 9 and 10. Coimbra, 1930.

Cunha, Luis da. *Instrucções a Marco Antonio de Azevedo Coutinho*. Coimbra, 1929.

Dalrymple, Sir John *Memoirs of Great Britain*. 1790.

Davenport, F. G. *European Treaties*. Washington, 1934.

Duguay-Trouin, R. *Mémoires*. Ed. Henri Malo. Paris, 1929.

Dumont. *Corps universel diplomatique*. Hague, 1731.

García Mercadal, ed. *Viajes de Extranjeros por España e Portugal*. Madrid, 1952.

Grimblot, P., ed. *Lettres de Guillaume III et Louis XIV*. 1848.

Harrach, Graf F. B. von. *Tagebuch*, ed. A. Gaedeke, *Arch. für Öst. gesch.* 48. Wien, 1872.

Hardwicke Papers. Miscellaneous State Papers from 1501 to 1706, ed. P. Yorke, Earl of Hardwicke, 2 vols. 1778.

Hatton Correspondence, n.s. 22/3. Camden Society, 1878.

Heinsius Correspondence, *see* Marlborough.

Hill, Richard. *Diplomatic Correspondence*, ed.　R. W. Blackley. 1845.

Historical Manuscripts Commission. Reports and Bath, Buccleuch and Portland Papers, also scattered references in Dartmouth, Downshire, Finch Hatton, Polwarth and Stuart Papers. House of Lords.

House of Commons Journals.

Howell, T. B. *State Trials.* 1812.

Lexington papers, ed. Hon. H. Manners Sutton. 1851.

Louville, Marquis de. *Mémoires.* Paris, 1818.

Marlborough, Duke of, *Correspondence with Heinsius*, ed. B. v. t'Hoff. The Hague, 1951.

——*Letters and despatches*, ed. Sir G. Murray. 1845.

——*Correspondence with Sarah, Duchess of Marlborough.* 1838.

——*Conduct of the Duchess of Marlborough*, ed. N. Hooke. 1742.

Melo de Matos, *see* Castelo Branco.

Montagu, Lady Mary Wortley. *Letters.* 1777.

—— *Works*, ed. Lord Wharncliffe, 2 vols. 1861.

Navy Records Society. *Journal of Sir G. Rooke*, ed. Oscar Browning. 1897.

——*Life of Captain S. Martin*, ed. Clements R. Markham. 1895.

——*Life of Admiral Sir John Leake*, ed. Geoffrey Callender. 1920.

Pepys, Samuel. *Private Correspondence, 1679–1703*, ed. J. R. Tanner. 1926.

Prestage, Edgar. *Memórias sobre Portugal no reinado de D. Pedro II.* Separate of *Arquivo Histórico de Portugal.* Lisboa, 1935. Contains excerpts from BM Add. MSS Sloane 2294.

Recueil des Instructions aux Ambassadeurs de France, 18 vols. Paris, 1885; Portugal, vol. 3; Spain, vol. 12. ed. Vicompte de Caix de St-Aymour.

Rijksgeschiedkundige Publicatien, kleine serie, XXIII, ed. N. M. Japikse. 's-Gravenhage, 1927.

Saint-Simon, Duc de. *Mémoires*, suppl. ed. Boislisle. Paris, 1890.

Soares da Silva. 'Memorias, 1701–15', *Gaçeta em Forma de Carta.* Oeiras, 1931.

Swift, Jonathan. *Journal to Stella.* Everyman Edition.

——Collected Works (1814).

Tessé, Maréchal de. *Mémoires et Lettres*, vol. 2. Paris, 1806.

——*Lettres*, ed. Comte de Rabuteau. 1886.

Vernon Letters: 'Letters illustrative of the reign of William III', by James Vernon, ed. G. P. R. James. 1841.

Walpole, Horace. *Letters*, ed. Mrs. Paget Toynbee. 1903.

Walpole, Robert, *see* Coxe.

Weensche Gezantschap's Berichten, ed. C. van Antal and J. C. H. de Pater. 's-Gravenhage 1934.

CONTEMPORARY WORKS

Arbuthnot, John, see *Later Stuart Tracts.*

Aubrey, John. *Natural History of Wilts.*, ed. J. Britton. 1847.

——*Wiltshire*, published by Wilts. Arch. Soc. 1862.

Boyer, Abel. *History of the Reign of Queen Anne, 1703–13.*

British Merchant. Collected edition, ed. Charles King. 1721.

Brockwell, Charles. *History of Portugal.* 1726.

Bromley, William. *Travels through Portugal, Spain, etc.* 1702.

Burnet, Gilbert, Bishop of Salisbury. *History of his own Time.* Oxford, 1823.

Burney Collection (newspapers). British Museum.

Colbatch, Rev. John. *Court of Portugal.* 1700. (For his MS letters *see* BM Add. MSS 22908.)

Collection of Parliamentary Debates.

Compleat History. London, 1702.

Corpus Institutionum Soc. Jesus. 1702.

Cunha, Luis da. *Testamento Político.* Lisboa, 1820.

——*Obras*, vol. I. 1820.

Defoe, Daniel, *Plan of English Commerce.* 1728 or 1743 edition.

——*Reasons against the War with France.* 1701.

——*The Trueborn Englishman*, see *Later Stuart Tracts.*

Fagel, Baron Nicolas François de. *Account of the Campaign in Portugal, 1705.* (Trans. from Dutch.) London, 1708.

Freire, António de Oliveira. *Descripcão de Portugal.* Corografica, 1739.

History of the Expedition into Spain, 1702. Anon. London, 1702.

Kennet. *History of England.* 1706.

Lamberty, G. de. *Mémoires pour servir à l'histoire du XVIII*ᵉ*siècle.* Amsterdam, 1735.

Later Stuart Tracts, ed. E. Arber. 1903. (For Defoe, *Trueborn Englishman*, and J. Arbuthnot, John Bull, etc.)

Luttrell, Narcissus. *Brief Relation of State Affairs.* 1857.

Macky, John. *Memoirs of the Secret Service.* 1733.

Memorie Istoriche de la Guerra, 1701–13, ed. Agostino Umicalia. Venezia, 1736.

North, Roger, *Examen*, 1740.

——*Lives of the Judges*, ed. Augustus Jessopp. 1890.

Salmon, W. *The Compleat Physician.* 1693.

Smith, John. *Wool.* 1747.

Somers Tracts, 13 vols. 1748.

Theatrum Europaeum, vol. 16. 1715.

Tindal, *Continuation of Rapin's History.* London, 1745.

Umicalia, see *Memorie Istoriche.*

Walpole, Horace. 'Notes on Dr Maty's Memoirs of Lord Chesterfield', *Philobiblon Society*, vol. XI.

BIBLIOGRAPHY

LATER WORKS

Agnew, Rev. D. C. A. *Henri Massue de Ruvigny, Earl of Galway*. Edinburgh, 1864.

Albrecht, J. *Englands Bemühungen um den Eintritt Portugals in die Grosse Allianz*. Bremen, 1933.

Almeida, Fortunato de. *História de Portugal*, vol. 4. Coimbra, 1922–6.

Ameal. *História de Portugal*. Porto, 1942.

Anderson, A. *History of Commerce*. 1801.

Anderson, M. S. *Europe in the 18th century*. 1961.

Ashton, J. *Social Life in the Reign of Queen Anne*. 1882.

Ashton, T. S. *Economic History of England in the 18th Century*. 1955.

Atkinson, W. J. *History of Spain*. Penguin edition.

Azevedo, J. L. de. *Épocas de Portugal Económico*. Lisboa, 1947.

Azevedo, Pedro A. de. *Doença e Morte de Dom Pedro II*. Porto, 1911. Separate of *Arquivos de História de Medicina Portuguesa*.

Baretti, Joseph. *Journey from London to Genoa*. London, 1770.

Baudrillart, A. *Philippe V et la Cour de France*. 1890.

Bou, *see* Voltes Bou.

Bowden, Peter J. *The Wool Trade in Tudor and Stuart England*, 1962.

——'Wool Supply and the Woollen Industry', *Economic History Journal*, ser. 2, IX, 44.

——*The Wiltshire Woollen Industry*. 1943.

Boxer, C. R. *Vicissitudes of the Anglo-Portuguese Alliance*. Lisbon, 1958.

——*Carreira da India*. Separate. *Centro de Estudos Históricos Ultramarinos. Os Commemoracões Henriquinas*, pp. 38–85. 1961.

——*The Golden Age of Brazil, 1695–1750*. University of California Press, 1962.

British Diplomatic Representatives, 1689–1789, ed. D. B. Horn, Camden Society, vol. 46. 1932.

Bromley, John. 'The French Privateers, 1702–13'. In *Historical Essays 1600–1750*, presented to David Ogg, ed. H. F. Bell and R. E. Ollard. London, 1963.

Bryant, Arthur. *Samuel Pepys*, vol. 3. Cambridge, 1938.

Burke, O. J. *Lord Chancellors of Ireland*. 1879.

Burton, J. H. *History of Reign of Queen Anne*. 1880.

Campbell. J. C. *Lives of the Lord Chancellors*. 1845.

Carreras y Bulbena, Joseph Raphael. *Carlos d'Austria*. Barcelona, 1902.

Carvalho, Alfredo. 'Os Portugueses em Bordeaux, en Siglo 17', *O Instituto*, ser. 4, vol. 20, p. 52, and vol. 22, pp. 59 and 114.

Chapman, Hester W. *Mary II*. 1953.

Churchill, Sir Winston. *Marlborough*. 1933.

Clark, Sir G. N. 'War Trade and Trade War', *Economic History Review*, ser. 1, I, 262.

Clark, Sir G. N. *The Seventeenth Century*. Oxford Paperback, 1960.

Cobbett, W. *Parliamentary History, 1806–20*.

Coombs, Douglas. *Conduct of the Dutch*. The Hague, 1958.

Cooper, C. P. *Brief Account of the Proceedings of Chancery*. 1828.

Corbett, Julian S. *England in the Mediterranean*. 1904.

Corrêa, Francisco Antonio. *Tratado de Methuen*. Lisboa, 1930.

Coxe, Archdeacon William. *History of House of Austria*. 1807.

——*Life and Administration of Sir R. Walpole*. 1798.

Cunningham, Alexander. *History of Great Britain*. 1797. (English translation of the Latin original.)

Cunningham, William. *Growth of English Industry and Commerce*. 1882.

Devizes, History of. 1859.

Drinkwater, John. *Siege of Gibraltar*. 1785.

Dumouriez, C. F. *Etat présent de Portugal*. Hambourg, 1797.

Edwards, F. L. *James, 1st Earl Stanhope, 1673–1721*, 1925.

——*British Foreign Policy*. London, 1925.

Ehrman, John. *The Navy in the War of William III*. Cambridge, 1953.

Elliott, J. H. *Imperial Spain*. London, 1963.

Ferreira Martins, General. 'O Poder Militar de Gran Bretanha e a Aliança Anglo-Lusa', *O Instituto*, vol. 94(ii). Coimbra, 1939.

Figanière, F. D. de. *Católogo dos MS Portugueses no Museo Británico*. Lisboa, 1853.

Fisher, H. E. W. 'Anglo-Portuguese Trade, 1700–70'. Unpub. thesis, London, 1961.

Fortescue, Hon. J. W. *History of the British Army*, vol. I. 1899.

Foxcroft, Miss H. C. *George Savile, Marquis of Halifax*, 2 vols. 1898.

Francis, A. D. 'John Methuen and the Anglo-Portuguese Treaties of 1703'. *The Historical Journal*, III, 2, 1960, 103–24. Cambridge.

——*Some reflections on the Methuen Treaties*. V colóquio internacional de estudos luso-brazileiros. Coimbra, 1965.

——'Portugal and the Grand Alliance', *Bulletin of the Institute of Historical Research*, XXXVIII, May 1965, 71–93.

Freitas, Bernardino José de. *Memórias de Braga*.

Gaedeke, Arnold. *Die Politik Österreichs in dem Spanischen Erbfolgekrieg*, Leipzig, 1877.

Girard, A. *Le Commerce français à Séville et Cadiz aux temps des Habsbourgs*. Paris, 1932.

Guedes, *see* Marques Guedes.

Guerra Tenreiro, A. *O Douro, Esboços para a sua História Económica*, vols. 1 and 2, Oporto, 1942; *Conclusões*, 1944.

——*Ainda o Tratado de Methuen*, Oporto, 1943.

Harcourt-Smith, Simon. *Alberoni*. 1943.

Harkness, D. A. B. 'Eighth and ninth articles of Commercial Treaty with France of 1713', *Scottish Historical Review*, vol. 21, p. 219, 1923–4

Hill, Christopher. *Century of Revolution*, 1961.

Holdsworth, Sir William. *History of English Law*. 1956.

Horn, D. B. *The British Diplomatic Service*. 1961.

Instituto. Revista Scientífica e Literaria. Published in Coimbra. Series 4. For articles see Ferreira Martins; Sampayo, Luiz T.; Carvalho, Alfredo; Cunha Brochado.

Jones, Rev. W. J. *Bradford on Avon*, 1907.

Jonge, J. C. de. *Geschiedenis van het Nederlandsche Zeewezen*, vol. 4, part 2. Amsterdam, 1841.

Kearney, H. F. 'Political Background to English Mercantilism', *Economic History Review*, ser. 2, II, 484.

Kenyon, J. P. *Robert Spencer, Earl of Sunderland*. 1958.

Klopp, Onno. *Der Fall des Hauses Stuart*, 14 vols. Wien, 1875–88.

Künzel, Heinrich. *Das Leben und der Briefwechsel des Landgraven Georg von Hessen-Darmstadt*. Friedberg und London, 1859.

Landau, Marcus. *Geschichte Kaiser Karl VI als König von Spanien*. Stuttgart, 1889.

Lane, Margery. 'The lighter side of Diplomacy under William III', *Nineteenth Century Magazine*, vol. 102, pp. 558–65.

——'Diplomatic Service under William III', *Royal Historical Society Transactions*, 4th ser., vol. 10.

Lecky, *History of England*, vol. 1. 1902.

Lees, R. M. 'Council of Trade', *English Historical Review*, no. 54, p. 39.

Legg, L. G. Wickham. *Matthew Prior*. Cambridge, 1921.

Legrelle, A. *La Diplomatie Française et la Succession d'Espagne*, 4 vols. Gand, 1888–92.

Lipson, E. *Economic History of England*. 1931.

Livermore, H. V. *History of Portugal*. Cambridge, 1947.

Lodge, Sir Richard. 'The Methuen Treaties' in *Chapters in Anglo-Portuguese Relations*, ed. E. Prestage. 1934.

——'The Lisbon Factory', *Historical Society Journal*, 4th ser., no. 16.

——*History of England*. 1910.

——*History of Modern Europe*. 1903.

Macaulay, Lord. *History of England*. 1914 edition.

McLachlan, J. O. *Trade and Peace with Old Spain*. Cambridge, 1940.

Mackay, Janet. *Catherine of Bragança*. 1937.

Mahon, Lord (5th Earl Stanhope). *History of the War of Succession in Spain*. 1832.

Marcus, G. J. *A Naval History of England*. 1962.

Marques Guedes, A. *A Aliança Inglesa*. Lisboa, 1938.

Mayer, F. M. 'Die Allianz Portugals', *Zeitschrift für die Österreichischen Gymnasien*, 35. Jahrgang. Wien, 1884.

Michel, R. F. *Les Portugais en France*, 1882.

Morland, W. H., *Akbar to Aurangzebe*, 1923.

Nada, John. *Carlos the Bewitched*. 1962.

Nicholson, T. C. and Tuberville, A. S. *Charles Talbot, Duke of Shrewsbury*. Cambridge, 1930.

Noorden, Carl van. *Europäische Geschichte. Der Spanische Erbfolgekrieg*, 3 vol. Düsseldorf, 1870-82.

Oakley, S. P. 'William III and the Northern Crowns'. Unpublished thesis, London, 1961.

O'Flanagan, J. R. *Lord Chancellors of Ireland*. Dublin, 1870.

Ogg, David. *England in the Reigns of James II and William III*. Oxford, 1963 edition.

Oman, Carola. *Mary of Modena*. 1962.

Ortiz, Antonio Dominguez. *La Sociedade Española en el Siglo 18*. Madrid, 1955.

Otruba, Gustav. *Prinz Eugen und Marlborough*, Weltsgeschichte im Spiegel eines Briefswechsels. Wien, 1961.

Owen, J. H. *War at Sea under Queen Anne*. Cambridge, 1938.

Parnell, Hon. Arthur. *War of Spanish Succession*, 1905.

Peres, Damião. *A Diplomacia Portuguesa e a Sucessão de Espanha*. Barcelos, 1931.

——*História de Portugal*, vol. 6, ed. D. Peres. Barcelos, 1934.

Plumb, J. H. *Sir R. Walpole*. 1956.

Ponting, K. G. *History of West England Cloth Industry*. 1957.

Prestage, Edgar. *Portugal and the War of the Spanish Succession*. Cambridge, 1938.

—— *The Royal Power and the Cortes in Portugal*. Watford, 1927.

——*Chapters in Anglo-Portuguese Relations*. 1934.

——ed. 'The Anglo-Portuguese Alliance', *Royal Historical Society Transactions*, 4th ser., xii, 34, also printed in *Revue Historique Diplomatique*, Jan./Mars 1936, and at Coimbra in 1936 under title *A Aliança Portuguesa*.

Quadro Elementar, Manoel Francisco Barrose Sousa de Mesquita de Macedo Leitão e Carvalhosa, Visconde de Santarem, ed. Luis Augusto Rebelo de Silva. Lisboa, 1860.

Ramsay, G. D. *The Wilts Woollen Industry*. 1943.

Rau, Virginia. *A Exploracão e o Comercio de Sal de Setubal*. Lisboa, 1951. *See also* on p. 374 under Cadaval.

Rowse, A. L. *The Early Churchills*. 1956.

Russell, Col. Frank. *The Earl of Peterborough*. 1887.

Sampayo, Luiz T. *Arquivo Histórico do Ministerio dos Negocios Estrangeiros*. Coimbra, 1926.

——'Para o Tratado de Methuen', *O Instituto*, vol. 76.

Santarem, Visconde de, see *Quadro Elementar.*
Schomberg, Capt. Isaac. *Naval Chronology.* 1802.
Sellars, Charles. *Oporto Old and New.* 1899.
Sergio, António (ed.). *Antologia dos Economistas Portuguesas.* Lisboa, 1924.
Shillington and Chapman. *Commercial Relations of England and Portugal.* 1907.
Simon, André. *History of the Wine Trade in England during the 17th century.*
—— *Port,* 1934.
Smithers, Peter. *Life of Joseph Addison.* Oxford, 1954.
Somerville, Dorothy. 'Dates in the Vernon correspondence', *English Historical Review,* vol. 48, Oct. 1933, p. 624.
Sousa, Carlos Hermangildo de. *O Tratado de Methuen.* Aveiro, 1938.
Stanhope, Hon. A. *Spain under Charles II.* 1840.
Stebbing, William. *The Earl of Peterborough.* 1906.
Tenreiro, *see* Guerra Tenreiro.
Thomson, Mark, *Secretaries of State.* Oxford, 1932.
—— 'Louis XIV and William III', *English Historical Review.* April 1961.
—— 'Louis XIV and the Grand Alliance, 1705–10', *Bulletin of Institute of Historical Research.* May 1961.
Trend, J. B. *Portugal.* 1957.
Trevelyan, G. M. *England under Queen Anne,* 3 vols. London, 1930–4.
—— 'Peterborough and Barcelona', *Cambridge Historical Journal,* vol. 3, 1931, pp. 253–9.
Turner, Mary. 'Anglo-Portuguese Relations in the War of Spanish Succession'. Unpublished thesis, Oxford, 1952.
Van den Haute, Gabrielle. *Relations Anglo-Hollandaises.* Louvain, 1932.
Victoria County History of Wiltshire.
Voltaire. *Œuvres complètes,* vol. XXI. Paris, 1785.
Voltes Bou, Pedro. *El Archiduque Carlos de Austria.* Barcelona, 1953.
Welch, P. S. 'The Maritime Powers and the Evolution of the War Aims of the Grand Alliance, 1701–4'. Unpublished thesis, London, 1940.
Williams, Basil. *James Stanhope, 1st Earl Stanhope.* Oxford, 1932.
Wilson, Charles. 'Cloth Production and International Competition in the 17th Century', *Economic History Review,* December 1960.
Wiltshire Archaeological Magazine.
Wolf, J. B. *The Emergence of the Great Powers.* Rise of Modern Europe Series, ed. W. B. Langer. New York, 1951.
Woodruff, Philip. *Colonel of Dragoons.* 1951.

INDEX

INDEX

INDEX

Hedges, Sir Charles, secretary of state, 167,
226, 251, 272, 279, 297, 322
and Methuen treaties, 136-8, 175-6, 199
Heinsius, Anthony, Grand Pensionary of
Holland, 50, 331
and Partition treaties, 84, 90, 95
and Portugal, 46, 123, 165, 179, 182, 210,
287, 292
and Spain, 140, 160.
Hesse-Darmstadt, Prince George, Land-
grave of, 220-3, 234, 246, 251, 266,
287, 294
and Cadiz, 131-2, 142-3, 147
and Catalonia, 63, 102, 129, 157, 236,
238-9, 278, 296-9
and Gibraltar, 275-86
personality, 129-30, 244, 249, 281-2, 300
Hill, Richard, Minister to Savoy, 231, 239,
279, 296, 311, 337, 365-6
Hobbes, Thomas, 43
Hogue, La, battle of, 50
Holland, see Dutch, international relations,
States General, trade, etc.
Hooper, Captain, 303
Hop, Jacob, Dutch minister, Vienna, 90.
Hopson, Vice-admiral, 145
horses, see army
Houblon family, 3, 60
Huguenots, 52, 69-70, 189, 258
Hungary, 70, 80
Hyères, 238

indigo, dyestuff, 19
Inquisition, see Portugal
intelligence
naval, 54, 143, 291, 296, 325
see also Methuen, John, newspapers, etc.
international relations
Anglo-Dutch relations, 98, 102, 139,
158-9, 165, 264-6, 286-9, 293, 331;
commercial, 84, 147-8, 165, 195-6,
199-200, 226-7; maritime, 271, 273,
305-9; see also diplomatic service,
Fagel, Methuen and Schonenberg, etc.
Anglo-Spanish, 48-52, 57, 60-4, 88, 91,
97, 103
Portuguese-Spanish, 6-10, 48-51, 57, 62,
64, 99-100, 115-19, 225, 234
see Louis XIV, Pedro II, treaties, etc.
Ireland, 67-71, 88, 324, 327
trade, see trade

troops, 142, 255, 288
Italy, 125, 146, 155, 158, 176, 229, 270, 275,
297

Jacobites, 21, 29, 31, 56, 64, 80, 104, 119,
123, 214, 349, 351
James II, King, 103, 107
Jason, John, 245-6
Jason, French privateer, 309
Jeffreys, 64
Jersey, Edward Villiers, earl of, 86, 93
Jesuits, 4, 16, 21, 35-6, 206, 285
Jews and New Christians, 10-11, 37, 88,
162-3, 188, 200, 229, 259
John IV, king of Portugal, 34
John, prince of Brazil, then King John V,
29, 35, 38, 74, 263, 335, 338-9
Johnson, Dr Samuel, 354
Jones, Israel or Jezrael, 284
Joseph, archduke of Austria, king of Rome,
then Emperor Joseph I, 36, 103, 123,
153, 171, 180, 341
judge conservators, 20
Jumper, Sir William, 304

Kainitz, Dominic Andreas, Count, Austrian
statesman, 132, 167
Keane, Sir Benjamin, ambassador at
Madrid, 353
kidnapping, 21, 81, 350
Killigrew, Admiral, 52, 56
Kilmansegg, Madame, 347-8
Kit Cat Club, 351
Klopp, Onno, historian, 318
Künzel, Heinrich, historian, 300

Lagos, 52, 54, 56
Landau, 153
Laurenço, count of, 156
Lavenham, 16
Leake, Admiral Sir John, 164, 271-3, 278-
84, 305-9, 320
Lecky, W. E. H., historian, 216
Lee, Sir George, 350
Leganez, marquis of, 140
Legge, Captain, 280-1
León, kingdom of, 7
Leopold II, Emperor, 135, 139-40, 154,
157-8, 160, 165-7, 172,
and the Archduke Charles, 103-4, 124-5,
169, 181, 219

388

Methuen, Grace, *née* Ashe, Mrs Paul, mother of John Methuen, later Mrs Peach finally Mrs Andrews, 2–3
Methuen, Henry, son of John, 60
Methuen, Isabella, daughter of John, 327
Methuen, John, minister at Lisbon, lord chancellor of Ireland, ambassador at Lisbon
antecedents and early career, 1–5
and Almirante of Castile, 157, 207–8, 226–8, 332
and army, 257–8, 262, 288, 290, 300–1, 307, 313–16, 319
and ballad *Lillibullero*, 69, 356
and Catherine of Bragança, 25, 30–1, 210, 288
as commissioner of trade, 65–7
and communications, 23, 53, 55–6, 145, 149–50, 238
in England, 70, 73, 90
and public finances, subsidies, etc., 74, 183, 227, 229, 231, 258, 267, 280
and Galway, 67–71, 263, 326
and Gibraltar, 56, 266, 277–80, 283–4, 286, 303, 315, 336
and Godolphin, 112, 138, 204, 226–7, 238, 263, 292–3, 315, 319, 322, 325
and Hedges, 291, 303–5, 319–20
instructions, 113
and intelligence, 56, 249, 291, 325
as lord chancellor of Ireland, 67–71, 128, 174, 182, 324
as Master of Chancery, 4, 251, 324
as member of Parliament, 5, 57, 63, 67–8, 203, 205, 325
and navy: convoys, 23, 159, 164, 235, 258, 303–10; disputes with, 236–8, 241, 271–8, 303–4, 306–8; and fleet, 64, 113, 125, 133, 144–5, 234–8, 268; and Admiral Leake, 271–3, 284; and Admiral Rooke, 55–6, 128–30, 145, 149–50, 152, 235–9, 258, 275, 279–80, 290
and Paul, 4, 111, 120, 173, 177, 326–9, 351, 353
and King Pedro, 25, 28, 31, 66, 124–6, 146–7, 149, 163, 225, 233, 235, 238, 307, 310, 333–5; audiences with, 42, 47–8, 124–6, 148, 159–60, 164, 170, 172, 196, 257, 316

personal: ambition for Madrid embassy, 285, 329; character and tastes, 4, 5, 15, 22, 42–4, 60, 68, 71, 115, 149, 183, 226–7, 229, 289–93, 322–36; criticisms of, 68–9, 137, 147, 167, 174–7, 251, 271, 290–3, 304, 310–11, 322–7, 344; difficulties in 1698–1700, 68–9, 86–7; health, 4, 42, 68, 183, 224, 234, 238, 319–21; movements, 41, 63–6, 111, 126–7, 172–3, 182; praise of, 67, 69, 114, 170, 181, 185, 202–3, 205, 295, 324–5, 327–8, 332, 334
Portuguese sympathies, 1, 42, 66, 114, 137, 323, 330, 332–3, 355; appreciation of Portuguese troops, 155, 158, 259, 332
and propaganda, 135
and Schonenberg, 115–17, 124, 127–8, 137–40, 173, 226–7, 233, 271, 286, 292–3, 310, 332, 338; co-operation with, 115, 146–7, 149, 151, 158, 160–1, 170–3, 263, 266–7, 305; differences with, 117, 127, 135, 137, 208, 226, 265–6, 278
and secrecy, 32, 93, 115, 149, 159–60
and treaties; commercial treaty, 184–218, 335, 353–5, negotiations of 1693–4, 47–9, 56–8; Grand Alliance, 47, 70; Quadruple and Triple treaties of 1702–3, 154–77
and Waldstein, 114, 140, 149, 167, 170, 332
and Whigs, 5, 67–9, 289, 323, 325
and William III, 5, 49, 55, 66, 69, 87, 322–4
and wines, 1, 42, 204–5, 353–4
Methuen, Mary, daughter of John, Mrs Simpson, later Lady Anderson, 352
Methuen, Mary, *née* Chivers, wife of John, 3–4, 352
Methuen, Massachusetts, 354
Methuen, Paul, father of John, 1–2, 186
Methuen, (Sir) Paul, eldest son of John, Minister at Lisbon, Morocco, Barcelona, Turin, lord of the Treasury, secretary of state, ambassador at Lisbon and Madrid, Comptroller of the Royal Household, etc., 63, 70, 221, 236, 263, 313–14
complaint against, 86–7, 99–100
at Cadiz, 131, 144–5, 147

INDEX

116, 123–4, 138, 210, 220, 289, 292, 296, 321

Stanhope, James, son of above, brigadier, minister at Barcelona and subsequently 1st Earl Stanhope and prime minister, 142, 208, 214, 217, 226, 243, 245, 253, 257, 274, 299–300, 317–18, 340–2, 346, 348–50

States General, 44, 98, 116, 120, 171, 173, 176–7, 81–3, 209–10, 230, 237, 265, 301

Steele, Sir Richard, 347, 351

Stepney, George, Minister at Vienna, 102, 129, 132, 136–9, 154, 156, 160, 172, 181, 219, 321

personality, 124, 166–7, 175–6

Stevens, from Cadiz, 320

Subsidies

Dutch Portuguese, 170–1, 178, 209–10, 229–30, 295, 302, 305, 311

Anglo-Portuguese, 169, 171–3, 183, 199–200, 202, 229, 280, 305, 342

Savoy, 230

sugar, 17–18, 188, 195

sumach, 19

sumptuary laws, *see under* Portugal government, pragmatical decrees

Sunderland, Charles Spencer, 3rd earl, 287, 289, 338, 342–3, 346–7, 350.

Sunderland, Robert Spencer, 2nd earl of, 5, 67–8

Sutton, Robert, *see* Lexington

Sweden, 44–6, 55, 62, 84

Swift, Rev. Jonathan, 325, 351

Tagus, river, 7, 61, 105, 127, 131, 133, 178, 180, 201, 223, 238, 253–4, 260, 270, 306, 308–9

Tallard, count of, French ambassador, 83–4

Tangier, 143, 280, 284

Tarragona, 299, 318

Tatler, 213

Tecla, 341

Tessé, Marshal, 262–3, 282, 296, 301–2, 312–13

Tetuan, 376–7

tobacco and snuff, 17–18, 32, 75, 122, 142, 147, 150, 188, 195, 227

Toland, 358

Toledo, 319

Tomar, 262

Tor Bay, 53, 130

Torcy, Count, French ambassador, London, 97, 99

Tories, 60, 68–9, 103–4, 128, 213–15, 258, 270, 325

Torre del Tumbo, 36, 372

Toulon, 60, 62–3, 225, 239–40, 270, 296–7, 331, 340, 343, 366–7

Tourville, Admiral, 52, 54, 56, 58

Townshend, Charles, 2nd Viscount, 350

trade

Anglo-Spanish, 102, 207, 211; Spanish colonial, 217

Anglo-Italian, 212

French, 19, 44–5, 186, 212–16

Irish, 70, 88, 363

linen trade, 70

war trade and contraband, 44–9, 51, 59, 76, 148, 165, 334

see Brazil, corn trade, fish, Dutch, Portugal, woollen cloth, wine

Trade, Council of, 74–6

Tras os Montes, Portuguese province, 6

treasure, *see* Spain treasure fleet

treaties

Anglo-French commercial of 1713, 211–15

Dutch commercial with Portugal, 206–11

Dutch-Bavarian of 1698, 91–2

French-Spanish-Portuguese of 1701, 73, 99–101, 125–6, 133, 135, 329

Grand Alliance, 48, 101–3, 110, 113, 128–9, 132, 144, 145, 165–7, 211, 268, 331

Methuen commercial treaty, 184–218, 289, 335

Methuen Quadruple Treaty, 112, 146, 148, 160–1, 168, 171–2, 179–80, 182–4, 229, 234, 310, 319, 329, 332–6

Methuen Triple Treaty, 112, 146, 168, 172, 177, 179, 182, 184, 207, 211–12, 272, 329, 333–5

Methuen negotiations of 1693–4, 47–9, 55–8, 330

naval convention, England, United Provinces, Spain, 50–1, 58, 64

Partition Treaties, 82–6, 88–95, 98, 335

proposal to Portugal in 1701, 98

Spain-England, commercial, 226, 348–9

Utrecht, 206

Trenchard, Sir John, secretary of state, 204